Theodore Roosevelt in his study at Sagamore Hill in 1905.
Reprinted by permission of the Theodore Roosevelt Collection, Harvard College Library.

THE FRANKLIN AND ELEANOR ROOSEVELT INSTITUTE SERIES ON DIPLOMATIC AND ECONOMIC HISTORY

General Editors:
Arthur M. Schlesinger, Jr., William vanden Heuvel, and Douglas Brinkley

---

FDR AND HIS CONTEMPORARIES
Foreign Perceptions of an American President
EDITED BY CORNELIS A. VAN MINNEN AND JOHN F. SEARS

NATO: THE FOUNDING OF THE ATLANTIC ALLIANCE
AND THE INTEGRATION OF EUROPE
EDITED BY FRANCIS H. HELLER AND JOHN R. GILLINGHAM

AMERICA UNBOUND
World War II and the Making of a Superpower
EDITED BY WARREN F. KIMBALL

THE ORIGINS OF U.S. NUCLEAR STRATEGY, 1945-1953
SAMUEL R. WILLIAMSON, JR. AND STEVEN L. REARDEN

AMERICAN DIPLOMATS IN THE NETHERLANDS, 1815-50
CORNELIS A. VAN MINNEN

EISENHOWER, KENNEDY, AND THE UNITED STATES OF EUROPE
PASCALINE WINAND

ALLIES AT WAR
The Soviet, American, and British Experience, 1939-1945
EDITED BY DAVID REYNOLDS, WARREN F. KIMBALL, AND A. O. CHUBARIAN

THE ATLANTIC CHARTER
EDITED BY DOUGLAS BRINKLEY AND DAVID R. FACEY-CROWTHER

PEARL HARBOR REVISITED
EDITED BY ROBERT W. LOVE, JR.

FDR AND THE HOLOCAUST
EDITED BY VERNE W. NEWTON

THE UNITED STATES AND THE INTEGRATION OF EUROPE
Legacies of the Postwar Era
EDITED BY FRANCIS H. HELLER AND JOHN R. GILLINGHAM

ADENAUER AND KENNEDY
A Study in German-American Relations
FRANK A. MAYER

THEODORE ROOSEVELT AND THE BRITISH EMPIRE
A Study in Presidential Statecraft
WILLIAM N. TILCHIN

TARIFFS, TRADE AND EUROPEAN INTEGRATION, 1947-1957
From Study Group to Common Market
WENDY ASBEEK BRUSSE

SUMNER WELLES
FDR's Global Strategist . . . A Biography
BENJAMIN WELLES

THEODORE ROOSEVELT
—AND THE—
BRITISH EMPIRE

A STUDY IN PRESIDENTIAL STATECRAFT

William N. Tilchin

St. Martin's Press
New York

ISBN 0–312–12091–5

Library of Congress Cataloging-in-Publication Data

Tilchin, William N., 1950–
    Theodore Roosevelt and the British Empire / by William N. Tilchin.
        p. cm.
    Includes bibliographical references and index.
    ISBN 0–312–12091–5
    1. United States — Foreign relations — 1901–1909. 2. United States — Foreign relations — Great Britain. 3. Great Britain — Foreign Relations — United States. 4. Roosevelt, Theodore, 1858–1919.
    I. Title.
    E756.T55   1997
    327.7304'09'041 — dc21   96–48922
                                           CIP

Interior book design by Harry Katz

First edition: September 1997
10 9 8 7 6 5 4 3 2 1

— Contents —

List of Illustrations vii

Preface ix

PART I

Theodore Roosevelt and the British Empire through 1903: Securing the Special Relationship

1. The British Empire and Theodore Roosevelt: Setting the Stage 3

2. Roosevelt and the British Empire, 1901–1903:
   Forging a Friendship 21
   Statecraft Rooseveltian Style 21
   South Africa, Canada, and Other Imperial Matters 23
   England, Germany, and the Caribbean Region 25
   The Special Relationship: Overcoming the Last Major Hurdle 36
   Roosevelt, Britain, and the Asian Balance of Power 49

PART II

Theodore Roosevelt and the British Empire, 1904–1906: Solidifying the Special Relationship

3. Roosevelt, Britain, and the Great International Crises, 1904–1905 55

4. Roosevelt, Britain, and Rival Powers, October 1905–December 1906 81

5. The English-Speaking Peoples and Their Tightening Bond 95
   Theodore Roosevelt and British North America 95
   The English-Speaking Peoples and Their Empires 99
   Roosevelt and the Tightening Anglo-American Bond 104

PART III

The Special Relationship Triumphant:
Jamaica, 1907

6. The Earthquake and the Swettenham Incident 117

7. Anglo-American Damage-Control Diplomacy:
The Incident Contained 135

8. The Friendship Undiminished: Theodore Roosevelt,
the British Government, and the Closing of the Incident 153

PART IV

Theodore Roosevelt and the British Empire, 1907–1909:
A Seasoned Friendship

9. Roosevelt and the British Empire: Two Remaining Issues 171
The Final Years: An Introductory Overview 171
Roosevelt, Britain, and the Japanese Immigration Problem 172
Roosevelt, Britain, and the Persisting Challenge of the
Newfoundland Fisheries 182

10. Roosevelt and the Troublesome Olympic
Games Controversy of 1908 187

11. Roosevelt and the British Empire: Intimate Last Years 209
England, Germany, and the Episode of the Two Interviews 209
Roosevelt and Imperial Matters: Focus on British India 215
Expressions of Anglo-American Unity 225

Epilogue and Conclusion 239

Notes 245

Bibliography 283

Index 289

— List of Illustrations —

Frontispiece   Theodore Roosevelt in his study at Sagamore Hill in 1905.

Page 22   Theodore Roosevelt at the helm of the ship of state.

Page 37   Map of southeastern Alaska and the Alaskan boundary dispute.

Page 233   Portrait of President Theodore Roosevelt. Painted by Philip László in March 1908.

for Carol, Ben, and Lizzie

— Preface —

● ○ ●

This volume is the product of a long-standing interest in Theodore Roosevelt, particularly in his thinking and actions in the field of foreign policy. Its broad subject is Roosevelt's presidential diplomacy. More precisely, this is a book focusing on the way President Roosevelt thought about and managed U.S. relations with Great Britain and its worldwide empire and on his contribution to the emergence of a "special relationship" between Britain and the United States during the opening decade of the twentieth century. And because (or so it will be argued) Roosevelt's conceptions concerning the pivotal Anglo-American relationship were so sound, and his handling of this relationship was so skillful and effective, this book is also offered as a study in high-quality presidential statecraft.

Theodore Roosevelt's historical reputation has risen markedly in the second half of the twentieth century.[1] Because historians have long hailed Roosevelt's conservation and other progressive domestic policies and his accomplishments in these areas, their increased admiration for the twenty-sixth president must be primarily attributable to a heightened appreciation of his approach to and record in foreign policy. In the preface to *An Uncertain Friendship: Theodore Roosevelt and Japan, 1906-1909*, published in 1967, Charles E. Neu cited Howard K. Beale, *Theodore Roosevelt and the Rise of America to World Power* (1956) and William H. Harbaugh, *The Life and Times of Theodore Roosevelt* (1961) as he expressed the following concern: Especially "in the study of Roosevelt's foreign policy . . . the pendulum of historical revision has swung so far in the direction of praise that there is a danger Roosevelt will become a figure almost larger than life, always wise and farsighted, gravely balancing power and responsibility."[2] It is revealing of Roosevelt's enhanced stature today that Beale's portrayal of his presidential statecraft, upon which Harbaugh drew heavily, was significantly *less* laudatory than those offered in most major studies of the subject published since the appearance of Beale's watershed book.[3] Indeed, the author of this volume has been sufficiently impressed to make the following assertion in an essay published in 1993: "It is difficult to escape the conclusion that in the foreign policy arena Roosevelt was probably the greatest of all U.S. presidents."[4]

There would seem to be a number of reasons for Roosevelt's belated recognition as one of the foremost diplomatists in American history. The nature of the accessible historical record is such that eventual movement in this direction was practically inevitable. The powerful legacy of Henry F. Pringle's *Theodore Roosevelt: A Biography* (1931), however, posed a formidable impediment. Pringle's one-dimensional caricature of TR cast an enormous shadow over historians' efforts to imprint a more accurate picture of Roosevelt on the public mind.[5] Added to the challenge faced by those seeking to put Pringle's book in its place was the sheer bulk of Roosevelt's correspondence and other pertinent sources of evidence.[6] It took the publication of the eight volumes of *The Letters of Theodore Roosevelt* (1951-1954), masterfully selected and annotated by Elting E. Morison and his associates, to render the task of revision more manageable.[7] To borrow a term from Frederick W. Marks III, the "righting"[8] of the history of Roosevelt's foreign policy has since proceeded reasonably rapidly—but also gradually in the sense that the Pringle caricature began to be set aside in the 1950s, was further dismissed in the 1960s, and has been almost totally discredited in the 1970s, 1980s, and 1990s.

Contemporary developments as well have undoubtedly abetted the growing appreciation of TR's diplomacy. The time-tested soundness of the American doctrine of nuclear and conventional deterrence—which functioned well for many years and eventually set the stage for the Gorbachev era and the end of the Cold War—has reminded historians of Roosevelt's emphasis on preparedness and of the relative stability and peace among the powers that marked his presidency. The imprudent and ultimately disastrous American venture in Vietnam has caused some historians to think more highly of a president who perceptively distinguished vital interests from secondary ones, who would undertake foreign policy initiatives only after thoughtfully considering their likely ramifications, and who, once he had decided to act, would do so decisively. Big Stick diplomacy's architect has acquired increased respect in the wake of episodes such as the American withdrawal under fire from Lebanon in 1984, where a president spoke loudly and then retreated in embarrassing disarray. The historian-president in firm administrative and intellectual control of the ship of state (admittedly in a less complicated time) has assuredly gained in esteem during a period in which several chief executives have been handicapped by their ignorance of history and by their inability to conduct a well-managed or coherent foreign policy. Most recently, the bold and well-orchestrated assault by George Bush—who claimed TR as his model and hero—on the war-making capacity of Saddam Hussein's Iraq has evoked recollections of Roosevelt's agility as a statesman and his readiness to employ military

force to resist aggression (although there was little else about Bush's presidency—
certainly not his policy toward Iraq before August 1990 or following the cease-fire
of March 1991—that suggested much connection with TR).

The unmistakable tendency among historians of Roosevelt's diplomacy to present their subject in an increasingly favorable light does not suggest the onset of
an all-encompassing new consensus. The extensive array of source materials
pertaining to TR's foreign policy, including Roosevelt's own voluminous correspondence and his imposing output of published articles and books, gives historians ample room for varying interpretations and differing emphases. So do
Roosevelt's penchant for secret diplomacy and his obvious desire for an illus-
trious place in history. The very complexity of TR's intellect and of his character also contributes to his elusiveness as a historical figure. Certain aspects of
Roosevelt's diplomacy, most notably his conduct as the United States acquired
the Panama Canal Zone, are and seem likely to remain highly controversial.
Moreover, many facets of Roosevelt's foreign policy, among them the main
topic of this book, are still in need of closer examination.

In many regards, nonetheless, there is substantial agreement among historians of Roosevelt's diplomacy. It is generally accepted that Roosevelt possessed a keen understanding of the intricate network of international
relationships and of the fragile power equilibriums upon which peace during his
era largely depended. Most researchers concur that Roosevelt was a strong,
activist president in the foreign policy realm, that he yielded only insofar as was
politically necessary to the constraining force of American isolationism, and that
he was a highly capable, sometimes brilliant, and very successful statesman. His
settlement in 1905 of the Russo-Japanese War and his fruitful efforts to resolve
the Moroccan dispute during 1905 and 1906 are usually singled out for particular praise. Roosevelt, historians tend to agree, viewed imperialism—at least its
upstanding (as he saw it) American version—primarily as a force for the
advancement of Western civilization and the betterment of mankind, and not as
a vehicle for economic aggrandizement. Few if any dispute that he pursued and
established American hegemony in the Caribbean. Most acknowledge that TR
perceived Japan and Germany as potential enemies of the United States (along
with Russia, which he viewed more as a future than as a current menace), and
that he labored assiduously for friendship with Japan (caring much less about
the Open Door in China) while seeking to maintain at least a surface harmony
with Germany, succeeding in both endeavors.

Where Great Britain and its empire are concerned, additional areas of
agreement are apparent. Historians generally realize that Roosevelt believed

absolutely in the doctrine of peace through strength: The "righteous" nations should always be well-armed and should take particular care to build up and preserve a preponderance of naval power in order to be able to deter aggression and to defend their interests. There is broad acceptance of the notion that TR saw the United States and Great Britain as the two most righteous nations. Correspondingly, it is usually recognized that Roosevelt considered Britain an essential friend for America, and that he cultivated and solidified the Anglo-American special relationship. Yet some students of Roosevelt's diplomacy would raise questions about these perspectives,[9] and even among the majority of historians who share them there is debate over the president's primary motives. A number emphasize an identity of strategic interests, while others stress imperial solidarity and a common civilizing mission.[10]

⊠   ⊠

Considering the centrality of Great Britain and its holdings both in Theodore Roosevelt's major diplomatic endeavors and in his worldview, it is a little surprising that no historian heretofore has delved systematically and deeply into Roosevelt's diplomacy toward Britain or into the place of the British Empire in TR's foreign policy thinking. The important subject of Roosevelt and Japan has been amply treated,[11] but no book—neither the major studies of Roosevelt's diplomacy,[12] nor the specialized works on Anglo-American relations such as Bradford Perkins, *The Great Rapprochement: England and the United States, 1895-1914* (1968),[13] nor any of the more narrowly focused studies of Roosevelt's foreign policy—has accorded to Roosevelt and the British Empire the attention the topic deserves.

A thorough investigation of Roosevelt's dealings with and ideas about Great Britain and its empire can shed new light on many of the president's pronouncements, decisions, and actions in the arena of diplomacy. It can also illuminate a critical formative stage of the twentieth-century Anglo-American partnership that has been at the forefront of the largely successful international struggle against the forces of despotism, aggression, and terror. It is time, therefore, for such a study to be undertaken.[14]

A close analysis of Theodore Roosevelt and the British Empire can be expected to provide answers to a series of distinct (if sometimes overlapping) and significant questions. How did the president view and respond to British positions and actions during the many important diplomatic episodes in which the United States and England were involved as primary or secondary players? How did Roosevelt's perspectives on the Anglo-American connection evolve as his presidency unfolded? To what extent and in what manner did TR see Britain and its empire contributing to the maintenance of a secure balance of power and thus to international peace and stability? What did Roosevelt perceive as the role of the British Empire in promoting the progress of civilization and, thereupon, the improvement of the human condition? How effective was the president in his efforts to manage and to shape the Anglo-American relationship? Finally, what insights, if any, does a study of Roosevelt and the British Empire offer regarding the practice of statecraft?

⊰   ⊱

Chronologically this volume is principally concerned with the presidency of Theodore Roosevelt, which lasted from September 1901 until March 1909. There is no denying that Roosevelt said, wrote, and thought a great deal about the British Empire and Anglo-American diplomacy before and after his White House years, or that prior to September 1901 and after March 1909 he was on numerous occasions able to have an impact on American foreign policy. A plausible case can be made that he accelerated both the onset of war with Spain in 1898 and the intervention of the United States in World War I. (Moreover, any study of any facet of TR's presidency is strengthened by the provision of appropriate pre-presidential background material, a task that chapter 1 seeks to perform.) But Roosevelt's ideas and actions as president were naturally of immensely greater historical moment. Had TR never become president, Lewis L. Gould correctly observes, he would be no more than "a fascinating minor figure in American history."[15]

There is an additional reason why limiting analysis to the presidential years is particularly well advised in the case of Theodore Roosevelt. The rise in President Roosevelt's historical reputation has not been accompanied by a broader reevaluation of his career. It continues to be true that most historians who also look at the pre-presidential and post-presidential TR are less positive about his foreign policy outlook and statements during those phases of his life than about his diplomacy as president. Marks is essentially correct when he admiringly identifies the following elements as the foundation stones of President Roosevelt's statecraft: caution, patience, informality, discretion, courtesy, empathy, firmness, unassailable credibility, intellectual brilliance, a cosmopolitan spirit, a sound moral undergirding, and a clear-headed grasp of the role played by power in determining the course of international affairs.[16] But apparently this formidable combination of qualities consistently guided Roosevelt's behavior only when the awesome responsibility of presidential power was resting on his shoulders. When he was not in the White House, an unenviable belligerent streak, exacerbated by frustration with the perceived shortcomings of the current decision makers, sometimes took over. Beale portrays the TR of the 1890s as a rather unharnessed jingo.[17] In *Théodore Roosevelt:*

principes et pratique d'une politique étrangère [Theodore Roosevelt: Principles and Practice of a Foreign Policy] (1991), Serge Ricard remarks along the same lines: "At the close of the Spanish-American War, he appears to have been seized by a sort of imperialist hysteria, which contrasts astonishingly with his prudence and restraint when he becomes president and takes control of the diplomacy of the United States."[18] The president himself acknowledged in a private letter of December 1, 1904, an earlier tendency to be excessive in his rhetoric: "Some of the expressions" found in his pre-presidential historical writing, he admitted, "were overdrawn, overcolored, and made in a way which would naturally provoke bitterness on the part of believers in the men whom I attacked."[19] John Milton Cooper, Jr., whose *The Warrior and the Priest: Woodrow Wilson and Theodore Roosevelt* (1983) offers a laudatory assessment of Roosevelt's presidential statesmanship, declares insightfully that the post-presidential TR "could hardly help missing the only job that ever satisfied him: . . . Just as exercising power had restrained and fulfilled him, so relinquishing power unleashed and diminished him."[20] And David H. Burton observes with reason that aspects of Roosevelt's conduct during his later years "seemed to twist the old adage that power corrupts."[21] One might say in summary that Roosevelt was at his best—by far—when it mattered most.

⊰   ⊱

This book seeks to provide a balanced presentation of the subject of Theodore Roosevelt and the British Empire. However, a caveat is necessary. The Jamaica incident of 1907, the focus of part III, and the Anglo-American Olympic Games controversy of 1908, the subject of chapter 10, are accorded extensive attention—more extensive than their relative importance might appear to merit.

There are a few reasons for the thorough treatment of these two matters. First, because no other author has closely investigated either episode, a full accounting of each seems worthwhile. Second, each of these episodes is of genuine significance to this study. The Jamaica incident in particular offers a highly illuminating window on the depth of Roosevelt's attachment to the Anglo-American special relationship during the closing years of his presidency. And third, it is hoped that readers will find the narratives not only revealing but interesting and entertaining as well.

⊰   ⊱

A brief note on sources is in order. Much of the evidence for chapters 2-5 and 9-11, along with some of the evidence for chapters 1 and 6-8, is drawn from private letters written by President Roosevelt.

Undoubtedly Roosevelt's letters are most useful when read by a trained eye. They frequently sport embellishment, overabundant verbiage, partially insincere flattery, largely insincere self-effacement, and an overemphasis on the high-minded aspects of their author's motivation. Important information and opinions are prone to be withheld from many recipients.

Nevertheless, TR's letters are extremely valuable as primary sources. Verbose or not, they are invariably clear.[22] In contrast to the president's public speeches, in which he generally exercised politically astute circumspection, his letters tend to be very candid. Especially when the addressee is a close friend or trusted associate (such as Henry Cabot Lodge, Whitelaw Reid, William Allen White, Joseph Bucklin Bishop, Leonard Wood, William Howard Taft, Elihu Root, Gifford Pinchot, Lyman Abbott, George von Lengerke Meyer, Cecil Spring Rice, Arthur Lee, George Otto Trevelyan, and John St. Loe Strachey) or family member, the researcher is likely to discover a reasonably comprehensive snapshot of Roosevelt's perspectives at a particular time on the issues about which he is writing.[23]

Most important, Roosevelt's letters, despite the aforementioned excesses, are nearly always fundamentally honest. Edmund Morris, author of the Pulitzer Prize–winning *The Rise of Theodore Roosevelt* (1979),[24] asserts in an article published in 1989 that TR "was almost boringly decent, well-meaning, and truthful. In the course of thirteen years of research I have yet to find an example of him telling a deliberate lie." Morris goes on to refer to Roosevelt as "one of the most veracious leaders in our history."[25]

The published collection of *The Letters of Theodore Roosevelt* is, as previously noted, an invaluable tool for Roosevelt scholars. Morison and his colleagues so skillfully selected the letters included in their eight volumes that Roosevelt's thinking on every major and most minor issues of his presidency is brightly illuminated therein. Richard H. Collin acclaims the results of Morison's massive enterprise: "Going through the files of rejected letters from the Morison manuscripts" at Harvard, "I expected to find a substantial number of omitted letters of value. I found almost none. In each instance the editors had carefully annotated the rejected letter, giving the reasons for rejection, generally because it closely duplicated another printed letter or it was of a routine bureaucratic nature."[26] Still, it will invariably be necessary for researchers, as it has been for this one, to supplement their use of the Morison collection by utilizing the Theodore Roosevelt Papers stored at the Library of Congress and Harvard University. It is here where letters sent *to* Roosevelt can be found; moreover, when one is digging deeply into a specific question, one encounters in the Roosevelt Papers numerous useful letters written by TR that were excluded from Morison's compilation.

✄　✄

Many people have contributed to this project in a large variety of ways. Although this is not an exclusive list, I would like to recognize Howard Chudacoff, Perry Curtis, Joe Decker, Bob Drayer, Joe Fulginiti, Linda Greer, Dane Hartgrove, William Hixson, Mike Hochberg, George Kellner, Peter Levine, John MacLennan, Anthony Molho, Karen Mota, Cathal Nolan, Keith Rowson, David Tapalian, Arlene Tilchin, Marcia Tilchin, Mike Tilchin, David Underdown, Paul Varg, John Watkins, Ann Werner, Vic Werner, and Evan West. The Brown University Department of History covered my travel expenses during 1989-1990, and the Sigma Alpha Mu Foundation awarded me Samuel Miller Award grants for 1990-1991 and 1991-1992.

My dear mother, Jeannette Katz Tilchin, and my very special parents-in-law, John and Yvonne Giliberto, have been continuous well-wishers and timely visitors whose support has really meant a lot to me. My father and great friend, Asher Tilchin, has been an especially active and attentive booster and supporter.

I would like to thank my colleagues in the College of General Studies at Boston University for their advice and reinforcement. In particular, I would like to mention Brendan Gilbane, dean of CGS; Jay Corrin, chair of the Division of Social Science; Jay Zawacki, Michael Kort, and June Grasso, fellow students and teachers of American diplomatic history; Ted Davis of the Division of Science, who shares my interest in Theodore Roosevelt; and my "teammates" Robert Wexelblatt (for whose feedback on my scholarship and overall encouragement and support I offer my heartfelt gratitude), Jim Wilcox, Sam Hammer, Andrea Kozol, and Beverly Yu.

Those playing important roles in the later stages of the writing and production of this book include Wallace Dailey, curator of the Theodore Roosevelt Collection at Harvard, and Simon Winder, Michael Flamini, Alan Bradshaw, Debra Manette, Karin Cholak, Jessica Stretton, and Ariana Grabec at St. Martin's Press. I am greatly appreciative of Douglas Brinkley, Arthur Schlesinger, Jr., and William vanden Heuvel for selecting this book for the distinguished series of which they are the editors.

As is apparent in the text and notes, I have benefited enormously from the work of numerous other students of Roosevelt's diplomacy. Here I will name only a small number. My correspondence with David Burton and my correspondence and discussions with Fred Marks (as well, of course, as their writings) have been of both practical and inspirational value to me. The excellent bibliographical essay in Dick Collin's 1985 book proved to be extremely timely and useful. Serge Ricard's wide-ranging and highly impressive *Théodore Roosevelt: principes et pratique d'une politique étrangère* has been a particularly valuable resource, and my several interactions with Serge have been both enjoyable on a personal level and stimulating on an intellectual one.

There are three scholars to whom I owe special thanks. Jim Patterson, eminent historian of modern America, has displayed genuine interest in my work and my career over an extended period and took very seriously his role as second reader of my doctoral thesis in History at Brown University. This book is undoubtedly better for his input, and I am truly grateful. Both in our extensive personal correspondence and through the quarterly *Theodore Roosevelt Association Journal*, John Gable has nourished my interest in Roosevelt for more than fifteen years. Moreover, John's support has been an invaluable asset to my progress as a Roosevelt scholar, for which I offer him my sincerest appreciation. And my thesis director, Charles Neu—the author of *An Uncertain Friendship: Theodore Roosevelt and Japan, 1906-1909*, and a leading authority on TR's diplomacy—first suggested a study of Roosevelt and the British Empire and was an extremely encouraging and helpful adviser as I carried the project through the dissertation stage. And since the completion of my work at Brown in 1992, Charles has remained a highly supportive friend and colleague.

My greatest source of strength in this endeavor, as in all else, has been my family. First I will acknowledge (eccentric though it may be) the steady (and steadying) companionship of the canine members of the family, Winston J. and the late Jolie. My wife of twenty years, Carol T. Giliberto, has contributed to this enterprise in so many tangible and intangible ways that I would not know where to begin to enumerate them. Our son, Ben Tilchin, has been a keenly interested party for many years. A very thoughtful young person, Ben read in its entirety Roosevelt's *Through the Brazilian Wilderness*, from which he shared with me his insights, and he has advised me perceptively on matters of illustration and design. Since she arrived in 1991, nine years after Ben, our curious and cheerful daughter, Lizzie Tilchin, has brightened every day of every year—certainly not an insignificant contribution to the author's work.

PART I

Theodore Roosevelt and the
British Empire through 1903:

SECURING THE
SPECIAL RELATIONSHIP

The British Empire and Theodore Roosevelt: Setting the Stage

● ○ ●

No master plan drove the growth and development of the mammoth British Empire. Rather, the empire grew and evolved in a somewhat haphazard fashion as the governments of Great Britain responded over the centuries to the perceived exigencies of the day. One historian, writing from the vantage point of 1870, aptly refers to the empire as "the untidy legacy of three centuries of maritime endeavor and the by-product of two great trade route systems—in the Atlantic and in the East."[1] By the early twentieth century this empire would be significantly larger still and even more "untidy."

The history of the British Empire can be broken down into several eras. The years from its early seventeenth century beginnings until 1783 featured Britain's entry into intense competition for colonies, aggressive colonial expansion both for trade and for settlement, relatively benign rule with the notable exception of Ireland, a high point with the defeat of France in the Seven Years' War of 1756-1763, and the dramatic loss of thirteen North American colonies. The half-century from 1783 to 1833 saw the extension and elaboration of British rule in India, the launching of new colonial enterprises in portions of Australia and New Zealand, initial steps toward the institution of "responsible government" in colonies of settlement, a turning away from mercantilism in favor of freer trade within the empire, the union of Great Britain and Ireland in 1800, a long and ultimately successful war against Napoleonic France resulting in numerous colonial acquisitions, the abolition of slavery in the empire in 1833, and, over-all, a remarkable recovery from the aforementioned North American debacle. Great Britain's pinnacle as an imperial power may have been reached during the period 1833-1874, an era marked by a financial and industrial eminence combined with an uncontested naval supremacy, the widespread granting of responsible government accompanied by the decline of trusteeship for native populations, and the further extension and consolidation of British power in India, where gains on the periphery served to buttress Britain's position.

The next three decades can be looked at as a somewhat paradoxical era in the history of the British Empire—with regard both to the attitudes of British imperialists and to the actual effects of the great enlargement of the empire that occurred. When the avid imperialist Benjamin Disraeli took over the premiership from the more ambivalent William Gladstone in 1874, a period of expansion in Africa, Asia, and the Pacific ensued. But—and this is one paradox—it was insecurity more than confidence that inspired and sustained this expansion. The time of England's industrial primacy was passing, and extending the territory under British control was one way of fighting off the effects of this decline. More important, rivals were challenging British supremacy in the Mediterranean and elsewhere more vigorously than at any time since the demise of Napoleon, and the bold strategist Disraeli and his successors (including Gladstone himself) endeavored to fend off these challenges and to reassert Britain's leading role on the world stage.

The actual effects of late nineteenth and early twentieth century expansion also were paradoxical. Between 1874 and 1902 Britain annexed nearly five million square miles of territory containing close to one hundred million people. Extending its worldwide network of ports and naval bases while in possession of a fleet superior in all respects to those of its rivals, the British Empire appeared to be growing stronger as well as larger. As noted, however, the expansion of these years took place in an atmosphere of doubt—justified doubt—about the durability of the Pax Britannica. And in a certain sense this expansion resulted in a *weakening* of the empire, for in the process Britain overextended itself. Needing to deploy its formidable but not unlimited power over a rapidly growing area, Britain found itself on the defensive starting in the 1880s. In the opening years of the new century, the country would be compelled to abandon the "splendid isolation" of its most glorious days and to seek allies both formal (Japan, France, and even Russia) and informal (the United States) in order to defend its burgeoning interests and increasingly vulnerable position. The substantial participation in the defense of the empire by the self-governing colonies—which in turn insisted on a meaningful voice in the conduct of British foreign policy—would also come to be required. In reality the empire peaked well before it attained its greatest size.

The scramble for Africa was a particularly intense aspect of the history of late nineteenth-century imperialism. While periodic conferences among the powers served to relieve much of the tension that accompanied this scramble, England went to the very brink of war to push French forces out of the Sudan in 1898 and did actually go to war in 1899 (the Boer War) to win control of the two Afrikaner republics sitting astride Cape Colony, no routine matter as it turned out. Africans themselves frequently revolted against foreign domination, and the British, like their rivals, used force to put down these revolts.

Coinciding with the commencement of the presidency of Theodore Roosevelt, 1901-1902 was an especially eventful time in the history of the British Empire. In 1901 the Australian colonies finally came together in a federated commonwealth. The Committee of Imperial Defence, a high-level coordinating body dealing with the military needs of the entire empire, was established in 1902, evidencing the genuinely cooperative approach toward security issues that had taken hold. That same year, on the other hand, the cause of a centralized federation of the empire, which had enjoyed considerable support since the 1880s and whose leading advocate was Colonial Secretary Joseph Chamberlain, failed decisively at the Coronation Conference. Also in 1902 the bitterly fought, internally divisive, and internationally unpopular Boer War was brought to a successful conclusion, putting the Transvaal and the Orange Free State firmly into British hands and marking the onset of a lengthy respite in British expansion in Africa. Finally, 1902 witnessed the signing of the Anglo-Japanese Alliance, an agreement that British leaders hoped would ease the pressure on their overextended navy in the Pacific. Here was Britain's first unambiguous admission that the good old days of splendid isolation had forever passed.

The British Empire as it stood in 1902 was massive and sprawling. Quite literally the sun never set on it. The United Kingdom of Great Britain and Ireland was the anchor. In the Mediterranean were Gibraltar and the islands of Malta and Cyprus. On the continent of Africa, there were self-governing Cape Colony, self-governing Natal, the Transvaal, the Orange Free State, the protectorates of Bechuanaland and Swaziland and Basutoland,[2] Southern and Northern Rhodesia, and Nyasaland in the south; Zanzibar, Uganda, the British East African protectorate (later Kenya), the British Somaliland protectorate, and the Sudan in the east; Egypt in the north; and Gambia, Sierra Leone, the Gold Coast (modern Ghana), and Nigeria in the west. In the Atlantic's African waters were Saint Helena, Ascension, and Tristan de Cunha. The Indian Ocean, Arabian Sea, and Bay of Bengal contained many island holdings of the empire, of which the most important were Socotra, Mauritius, the Seychelles, the Kuria Maria Islands, the Cocos Islands, and especially Ceylon. In Asia, India, the empire's "crown jewel," was joined by Burma, the Straits Settlements (including Singapore), the Federated Malay States, Johore (these last three being parts of Malaya), Sarawak, British North Borneo, Brunei (these last three being protectorates on the island of Borneo), Hong Kong, Wei-hai-wei, Shanghai (these last three in China), and Bahrain and Kuwait on the Persian Gulf. The Pacific held self-governing Australia (including the island of Tasmania), self-governing

New Zealand (with the island of Niue and the Cook Islands), Pitcairn Island, the Fiji Islands, Papua, the Gilbert and Ellice Islands, most of the Solomon Islands, the protectorate of Tonga, Tokelau, and the New Hebrides (shared with France). Britain's North American empire consisted of the huge, self-governing Dominion of Canada and self-governing Newfoundland. Farther south in the Western Hemisphere were the Bahamas, Barbados, Bermuda, Jamaica, the Leeward Islands, the Windward Islands, Trinidad, and Tobago in the Caribbean; British Honduras and British Guiana in Central and South America, respectively; and the Falkland Islands off the Atlantic coast of Argentina.

So the British Empire of 1902 was truly a global phenomenon. It encompassed people of many races and an immense assortment of cultures. It was governed, broadly speaking, in four different ways: (1) "responsibly" by the local inhabitants of the self-governing colonies; (2) with ultimate British control tempered by various degrees of representative institutions; (3) with total (or nearly total) British control exercised by the British government under the crown colony system (or in a few cases still by chartered companies); and (4) indirectly, through the agency of traditional rulers, with widely varying levels of interference by Britain. Within each of these broad categories, specific arrangements were practically as numerous as the colonies themselves. Needless to say, this empire was a major force to be reckoned with by a new American president seeking a peaceful, stable world in which his nation's interests could be protected and his concept of civilization could be successfully promoted.

⋊   ⋉

Anglo-American relations during the first twelve decades of U.S. independence can hardly be described as friendly. A great deal of mutual antipathy between the two nations endured long after the American Revolution. Potentially dangerous disputes over territorial and neutrality issues were common. In retrospect—in light of the near hostilities of the 1790s, the tensions of the late 1830s surrounding Canadian insurrectionary activities, the Oregon dispute of the 1840s, the *Trent* and warship supply crises of the Civil War years, the postwar bitterness over the "*Alabama* claims," and the persistence of American dislike for Britain, particularly intense among Irish Americans—it is somewhat surprising that only once, in 1812, did the two countries actually go to war against one another. Almost until the end of the nineteenth century, Britain was still the bête noire of the American people, and "twisting the lion's tail" was still good politics, as the Sackville-West affair of 1888 amply demonstrated.[5]

However, the relative quiet of the years following the resolution of the *Alabama* claims (in combination with an as yet dimly perceived growing mutuality of sympathies and interests) paved the way for what Bradford Perkins aptly calls "the great rapprochement" of 1895-1914,[4] launched rather inauspiciously by the Venezuelan boundary crisis of 1895-1896. When the disagreement over the Venezuela–British Guiana boundary first arose as an issue in Anglo-American relations, both governments reacted in the familiar historical pattern: American leaders evinced bellicosity, and British officials responded with condescending indifference. Secretary of State Richard Olney's strongly worded note of July 1895—featuring his altogether audacious declaration that "the United States is practically sovereign on this continent"[5]—was not taken seriously, and it required President Grover Cleveland's threatening message in December to shock the British out of their complacency. They quickly decided to yield to the American demand for arbitration, and toned-down U.S. rhetoric enabled them to do so gracefully. The precise terms were settled in September 1896; as it happened, the arbitral award three years later was largely favorable to Britain.

The negotiation in 1897 of a broad Anglo-American arbitration treaty, although the Senate eventually defeated it, was an indication that a more amicable relationship was beginning to take hold in the aftermath of the Venezuela quarrel. Olney, however, was certainly premature in asserting that "the American people . . . feel themselves . . . part of one great English-speaking family."[6]

The most critical years of the great rapprochement were 1898 to 1903.[7] And the most critical event of these years was the Spanish-American War of 1898. As Britain's problems with Germany, France, Russia, and the Boer republics were growing, and as the untenable nature of the revered old policy of splendid isolation was fast becoming apparent, British leaders demonstrated during this war their great determination to cultivate American goodwill. Correspondingly, Britain's conduct opened American eyes to some of the benefits the United States could derive from a friendship with its old foe.

While joining the continental powers in encouraging peace, England was uniquely solicitous of U.S. feelings in its prewar diplomacy; and during the war British neutrality policy was decidedly favorable to America. The United States was permitted to use facilities in British ports and colonies that were closed to Spain. A strong Spanish naval unit sailing for the Philippines by way of the Suez Canal was denied refueling rights in Egypt and was forced to turn back. Americans were allowed to gather military intelligence in Gibraltar and to send it to the United States, while Admiral George Dewey had permission to maintain communications with Washington via the Hong Kong cable. British officials encouraged the United States to annex both Hawaii and the Philippines. Moreover, in stark contrast to the hostility prevailing on the continent, British public opinion from the outset was heavily partial to the United States. Charles S. Campbell, Jr., describes a "substantial unanimity" of support for America and for Anglo-American friendship among leading Britons and also among the general populace.[8] And grateful Americans reciprocated, all the more so because of a widely believed legend that a British squadron had blocked hostile action by German ships against Dewey's fleet in Manila Bay, and another that only British opposition had prevented intervention by a concert of European powers. Suspicions of a secret Anglo-American alliance, although entirely unfounded, were rampant in both countries and in Europe. Clearly a new era had commenced.

Key figures in both nations' governments were promoting the new friendship with commitment and vigor. John Hay, a person of undisguised affection for Britain who served as American ambassador to the Court of St. James and then was elevated to the position of secretary of state by President William McKinley in the immediate aftermath of the Spanish-American War, proved to be a very able diplomatist and was perhaps the single most influential individual. Since Hay was appointed with his attitude toward England in mind and permitted to shape American foreign policy for the three remaining years of McKinley's presidency, the president too would have to be considered a major player. So would Joseph Choate, Hay's successor at the American embassy in London, and so would the remarkably effective Henry White, second-in-command there under both men. Senator Henry Cabot Lodge of Massachusetts, although sometimes sidetracked by parochial political concerns, was another leading advocate of closer ties. On the British side, Sir Julian Pauncefote, ambassador in Washington from 1889 until his death in 1902, played a crucial role. From London essential support for Pauncefote's diplomatic undertakings came from Lord Salisbury, prime minister from 1895 until 1902 and also foreign secretary until 1901, and two staunch friends of the United States who served in his cabinet, Arthur Balfour and Joseph Chamberlain.

Certain notions were rapidly gaining currency among these men and other leading thinkers in England and America. The perception of a mutuality of strategic interests was taking root, as Britain and the United States sought to uphold the status quo in Asia and, at the outset of the new century, to adjust the situation in the Caribbean in the direction of greater U.S. control. Bolstering this perception was growing concern in both countries about the designs of Russia and the upstart powers, Germany and Japan. American theorists were ceasing to view Britain as a potential enemy, and their British counterparts were adopting a similar outlook on America. Reinforcing strategic considerations were philosophical and cultural ones. Most prominent among these were the bond of a shared language; the increasing sense of a common political, racial, and cultural heritage and destiny; and the growing belief, particularly following the American takeover of the Philippines, in a joint obligation to spread the benefits of civilization (the "white man's burden").

The year 1899 saw a number of manifestations of the new spirit, despite the fact that it began with the collapse of a Joint High Commission seeking to resolve a series of Canadian-American disagreements, foremost among which was the location of the boundary line between Alaska and British Columbia. In March America and Britain collaborated against Germany during a struggle for control of Samoa. At the Hague peace conference of May through July, they cooperated in the establishment of an arbitral court. In October a modus vivendi defusing for the time being the Alaskan border question was worked out. Particularly important was Hay's issuance in September of the first Open Door notes (calling for equality of commercial opportunity in China, to be followed the next July in the midst of the anti-foreign Boxer Rebellion by his second notes requesting respect for Chinese territorial integrity), which clearly displayed the commonality of Anglo-American interests in the most dangerous international hot spot of the time.

Both countries became engaged in combat in 1899, the United States endeavoring to suppress the Filipino independence fighters and the British seeking to take over the Boer republics. Considering England's enthusiastic approval of U.S. annexation of the Philippines, its support for America's war there was to be expected. America's pro-British neutrality during the Boer War, however, was politically a more complicated proposition, at least until after the election of 1900, for McKinley and Hay. Throughout the world the Boers were viewed as heroic underdogs resisting a domineering bully. Even in the United States that perception was widespread. But Americans were also pulled in the opposite direction by the legacy (and the parallel) of the Spanish-American War, enough so that Hay was able to disregard the opponents of his policy; Democratic efforts to make political hay (pun intended) out of it in 1900 failed. Hay's consistent stance against the Boer proposals for international involvement, toward which Britain's continental rivals were far more sympathetic, assured that the British would be able to carry on until victory.

Until the Boer War, Canada had been upheld by England in the former's insistence that any British agreement to revise the isthmian canal treaty of 1850 in accord with American wishes be linked to American concessions on the Alaskan boundary. The United States, however, was becoming impatient about the canal issue, and America's friendly policy during the Boer War impelled the internationally assailed British to consent to dissociate the two matters. When the treaty drafted by Pauncefote and signed by Hay in February 1900—requiring that any American-built canal be unfortified and open on equal terms to the ships of all nations during war as well as peace—proved unacceptable to the Senate, the British acceded in March 1901 to renegotiate the terms, and Hay and Pauncefote resumed their work.

The genuine sorrow in America with which the news of Queen Victoria's death in January 1901 was greeted, and the correspondingly genuine grief in Britain brought on by the assassination of McKinley that September, provide good evidence that the people in both countries had developed considerable fondness for one another. Such an attachment would have been hard to imagine even a decade before. The masses, having been affected by recent solidarity during difficult times, were absorbing some of the strategic, philosophical, and cultural ideas of the politicians and theorizers who were forging the new relationship.

Challenges to the rapprochement undoubtedly loomed, foremost among them the seemingly intractable Alaskan boundary dispute. But the state of Anglo-American relations was unprecedentedly friendly and promising as Theodore Roosevelt assumed the presidency in September 1901.

⚔ ⚔

Theodore Roosevelt, the second of four children and the older of two sons, was born into wealth and comfort in New York City on October 27, 1858. His gentle and loving father, Theodore, Sr., was a businessman and a philanthropist whose family's Dutch roots in the area were over two centuries deep, while his equally gentle and loving mother, the former Martha Bulloch, had grown up in a prosperous plantation family in antebellum Georgia. The father's public-spiritedness and humanitarianism markedly impressed Theodore from an early age. The Civil War was an awkward time for young Theodore's parents, his mother quietly sympathetic to the Confederacy (in whose service her brothers and other family members were fighting), his father, a wholehearted and active supporter of the Union, choosing not to fight with real regret but out of deference to Martha's feelings.[9] Yet the family unit remained and would always remain extremely close-knit.

Like his siblings, the highly intelligent and curious Theodore never attended an elementary or secondary school but was instead educated at home by private tutors. Frequent visits to the countryside, including long summers in Oyster Bay, New York, from 1874 on, and extended sojourns abroad in 1869-1870 (to Great Britain and eight continental European countries) and 1872-1873 (to England, Egypt and the Nile, the Holy Land, Turkey, Greece, Austria, Germany, and Switzerland) were among the many benefits of his family's high station. The development of a passionate and, as it turned out, lifelong interest in nature preceded Theodore's enrollment at Harvard in 1876.

But life had not been without difficulty for the older son. A frail physique and especially a severe asthmatic condition had posed a real challenge to the boy's (and in the second case his family's) mettle. Determined efforts had been made to conquer both these handicaps. At Harvard, at last, Theodore was largely able to defeat them.

Roosevelt flourished at Harvard. He came into his own socially, enjoyed a range of physical activities, and was academically very successful (if not particularly stimulated), qualifying for Phi Beta Kappa. During his senior year he began work on his first book, *The Naval War of 1812*, published in 1882. He was intense in everything he did, never more so than in his pursuit of Alice Lee, to whom he was married in 1880. Only the tragic death from stomach cancer in February 1878 of his beloved forty-six-year-old father, which stunned the family and tormented Theodore for months, scarred his otherwise happy Harvard years.

Roosevelt's extraordinary political career began in 1881. Finding his encounter with Columbia Law School disillusioning, TR turned to politics, seeking and gaining election as a Republican to the New York State Assembly, where he served with distinction for three one-year terms. His investigation of the wretched cigar-making tenements of New York City in 1882 sparked what would become an enduring commitment to reform. And he won national attention for a courageous attack on the corruption of the state's most powerful monied interests in the Judge Westbrook affair.

In 1883 Roosevelt became involved in a cattle-ranching venture in the Dakota territory (an ultimately unremunerative enterprise that would absorb many thousands of his inherited dollars) and also started planning the permanent home he would soon begin building on prime land he had purchased in Oyster Bay. He was finding politics rewarding and his marriage to Alice, who was now pregnant, fulfilling. He was happy and, despite uncertainties about the direction of his professional life, had no reason to doubt that he would continue to be.

Then an incredible personal tragedy struck. On February 14, 1884, two days after the birth of a daughter, Roosevelt's mother and his wife both died, the former from typhoid fever, the latter from Bright's disease (chronic inflammation of the kidneys).

Roosevelt attempted to cope with this horrible twist of fate by working at his assemblyman job like a man possessed. He tried to ignore his misfortune after entering in his diary: "The light has gone out of my life."[10] That June he was in Chicago as the youngest delegate at the Republican National Convention, tirelessly leading the Republican reformers' fight to deny the nomination to frontrunner James G. Blaine. Although unsuccessful, his earnest struggle won him a great deal of favorable publicity, and his post-convention endorsement of Blaine—an act condemned by many of the reformers who bolted—established a reputation for loyalty to the party that was to serve him well. It was also in Chicago that the most important and most intimate male friendship of his life, with Henry Cabot Lodge, started to take root.

TR's Badlands saga then began. Between that summer and the fall of 1886, he spent a total of more than a year, a few months at a stretch, living the life of a rancher and hunter in this rugged Dakota country. His intense experiences there built his confidence and were extremely exciting for him. He wrote about them with great passion and color in *Hunting Trips of a Ranchman, Ranch Life and the Hunting Trail,* and *The Wilderness Hunter.* His health improved dramatically. And he formed an emotional bond with the West during this period that was to prove everlasting. Five return visits to the Badlands over the next decade suggested the depth of his attachment.

The years 1886-1897 were eventful ones for TR in terms of family, literature, and, to a lesser extent, politics. In December 1886 he married Edith Carow, a close childhood friend, and following a leisurely honeymoon in England and on the continent, they took up residence at Sagamore Hill, the spacious and very comfortable new Oyster Bay house that would have been called Leeholm had Alice not died. The daughter of Theodore and Alice, also named Alice (who until then was being cared for by Anna, Theodore's older sister, a lifelong confidante whom he trusted absolutely), soon had plenty of company. Another Theodore was born in 1887, followed by Kermit in 1889, Ethel in 1891, Archibald in 1894, and Quentin in 1897.

Sagamore Hill was a sometimes chaotic but fundamentally contented household. Theodore and Edith had a happy, romantic, mutually supportive marriage, and they raised and guided their offspring with firmness on the one hand and patience and understanding on the other. The father, himself always a boy in many ways, loved to play with the children and to read and tell them stories, while they, in turn, both respected him greatly and adored him.

Meanwhile, books poured forth from TR's pen, with works of history predominating. To his *Thomas Hart Benton,* written during his Badlands period, were added a second biography, *Gouverneur Morris,* and, most notably by far, *The Winning of the West,* a classic four-volume history of the frontier from 1769 to 1807 that was highly regarded in its day and still continues to impress professional historians.[11] There were also a short history of New York City and *Hero Tales from American History,* a book of historical sketches for children that Roosevelt and Lodge coauthored.

Outside of the political arena following his disappointing third-place finish in the 1886 race for mayor of New York, Roosevelt was soon itching to return to it. He did so in 1889 by accepting an appointment by the new Republican administration of Benjamin Harrison to serve on the U.S. Civil Service Commission. Not surprisingly, he proved to be a zealous reformer and upholder of the civil service laws. In 1893 Democratic President Grover Cleveland reappointed TR, who continued his determined crusade to improve the quality of the nation's civil service until resigning in 1895 and becoming president of New York City's Board of Police Commissioners. Roosevelt characteristically refused to play the game in this new post, running into the greatest resistance when he insisted on enforcing the widely ignored law against Sunday sales of alcoholic beverages. In 1897 an embattled and frustrated but unbowed TR left the board with his reputation as a man of strength, courage, and conviction not only intact but enhanced.

The combination of entreaties from New York State's Republican leadership (which was eager to see Roosevelt leave) and the solicitations on his behalf by the influential Senator Lodge was too much for William McKinley to withstand, so in the spring of 1897 the new president named Roosevelt assistant secretary of the navy. A longtime believer in a strong American navy and an expansionist foreign policy who was delighted to be close to the centers of power, TR took full advantage of opportunities to express his views and to affect naval and diplomatic decisions. He continually outmaneuvered his unenergetic superior, John D. Long, most memorably in February 1898 when he sent off (as acting secretary during a one-day absence by Long) his famous telegram to Admiral Dewey concerning operations in the Philippines in the event of a war with Spain. TR was in fact eager for such a war. Indeed, his private letters and public statements during the latter half of the 1880s and the 1890s contain enough evidence to justify labeling him a militarist during this pre-presidential phase of his adult life.[12]

When war came in April 1898, Roosevelt was not going to read about it in an office in Washington. He resigned his Navy Department post forthwith in order to organize and lead a volunteer cavalry regiment in Cuba, and he did so despite Edith's poor health at the time and the urgings of family members and friends, including Lodge, to stay put. TR then pulled strings to ensure that he and his Rough Riders saw action at the front. In what he later called his "crowded hour,"[13] he led his men up fortified Kettle Hill in defiance of a hail of Spanish bullets that inflicted heavy casualties on his regiment, and one of which nicked his elbow. After taking the hill, Roosevelt gloried in his own heroism and that of his troops, which not accidentally (as TR had arranged for reporters and photographers to accompany his regiment) were heavily publicized back home.

New York's scandal-ridden Republican party then nominated the nationally popular Colonel Roosevelt for governor in 1898. When he narrowly defeated his Democratic opponent, the presidency of the United States for the first time became less a distant and unlikely objective and more an attainable goal. And his stature was elevated by the excellent reform record he achieved as governor. He used his veto power liberally, and he bucked Senator and state party boss Thomas Platt whenever he believed it necessary, advancing thereby the cause of economic justice at the expense of corporate privilege and corruption. Roosevelt's changes in the state civil service system also upset Platt. For the second time, Platt could not wait to be rid of him.

Although Roosevelt accepted the 1900 Republican vice presidential nomination with ambivalent feelings, he campaigned with extraordinary vigor once nominated, with advocacy of the new imperialist foreign policy a central theme. When McKinley, aided by his running mate's efforts, swept to a second and even more decisive victory over William Jennings Bryan, a sort of enforced vacation seemed to loom for the driven TR. And for several months he did indeed enjoy his family and pursue his many intellectual and recreational interests to a degree that had not been possible in recent years.

This pleasant, unpressured interlude was to be short-lived. On September 14, 1901, President McKinley died from an assassin's bullet. As prescribed by the Constitution of the United States, forty-two-year-old Theodore Roosevelt, "that damned cowboy" in the eyes of intimate McKinley associate Mark Hanna and the youngest man ever to assume the presidency then or since, took the oath of office.[14]

⊰   ⊱

Well before assuming the presidency, Theodore Roosevelt had become a prominent figure within the coterie of leading American expansionist thinkers. These influential men were big-navy advocates who shared many ideas about strategy, American power, American political and cultural superiority, and American beneficence. They interacted frequently, in informal gatherings and by mail. During the 1880s and 1890s, this circle came to include Roosevelt, Henry Cabot Lodge, Henry and Brooks Adams, William W. Rockhill, William E. Chandler (who as Chester Arthur's secretary of the navy launched the new navy in 1883), Benjamin F. Tracy (who as secretary of the navy under Benjamin Harrison carried forward Chandler's work), William P. Frye, William Sheffield Cowles, James Russell Soley, Charles H. Davis, Henry H. Gorringe, Stephen B. Luce, Henry White, Richard Olney, and Alfred Thayer Mahan, among others. On the whole they were far more concerned with extending American power and enhancing the United States' security and prestige than they were with promoting the nation's economic interests. Brooks Adams, whose pessimistic prophecies in *The Law of Civilization and Decay* disturbed but were ultimately rejected by Roosevelt, was somewhat out of step with most of this generally optimistic group.

Theodore Roosevelt possessed a more independent and original intellect than is sometimes attributed to him. One widespread belief is that the naval historian and philosopher Alfred Thayer Mahan profoundly influenced TR's thinking on naval and related matters.[15] In a 1971 essay, however, Peter Karsten convincingly argues that Roosevelt's naval ideas—as first spelled out in detail in 1882 in his *The Naval War of 1812*, a well-researched study acclaimed by naval enthusiasts both for the history that it presented and for the "lessons" that it offered—were highly developed well before he became acquainted with Mahan. (More truly influential, in fact, were TR's encounters as a youth with his ex-Confederate naval officer uncles, Jimmy and Irvine Bulloch, living in exile in England.) Moreover, whereas TR's views on preparedness and the need for a modern, efficient navy had taken shape by his early twenties, Mahan, eighteen years older than Roosevelt, "was a latecomer to the philosophy of sea power," publishing nothing on the subject prior to 1888.[16] As Mahan's stature grew during the 1890s and beyond, the politically astute TR often cited Mahan's *The Influence of Sea Power Upon History, 1660-1760* and other writings in an effort to advance their common objectives. Thus, asserts Karsten, "traditional views . . . fail to consider Roosevelt's own, pre-Mahanite consciousness of the significance of sea power. . . . Mahan's ideas were integrated by the Bull Moose into an already-existing, vigorous mental framework. . . . Rather than continuing to argue that Mahan 'influenced' Roosevelt, it would be more meaningful and accurate to say that Roosevelt 'used' Mahan."[17]

The well-traveled Roosevelt came into the presidency, notes Howard K. Beale, with "a direct knowledge of the world and its people that no previous president save the Adamses, Jefferson, and Monroe had possessed."[18] This avid American nationalist and navalist had long been attentive to important developments affecting the foreign policy of the nation. And having come to know personally many British intellectuals and members of the ruling elite, it is not at all surprising that the pre-presidential Roosevelt had thought at great length about Anglo-American relations.

The friendships he had established with a number of prominent Britons had served to accentuate Roosevelt's interest. He developed a tight bond with the foreign service officer Cecil Spring Rice, who also was a favorite and a regular correspondent of Edith. TR and Spring Rice hit it off grandly when they met by chance in 1886 (a few weeks after which Spring Rice stood as best man at the wedding in England of Theodore and Edith), and the mutual affection endured. Edith "felt as if one of the family had gone when you left," Roosevelt wrote his friend in 1896; while TR was in Cuba, Spring Rice described him to Edith "as a pure, high, noble and devoted character" unsurpassed "in our present world."[19] Upon learning in Cairo of Roosevelt's sudden accession to the presidency, Spring Rice confided to his brother: "The U.S. is awfully lucky to get the best man possible by a fluke."[20]

Arthur Lee, the British military attaché who was with Roosevelt in Cuba in 1898, proved to be another close friend for the duration. The complete trust and temperate candor that characterized their relationship took hold right away, as was clear when Member of Parliament Lee wrote to Vice President Roosevelt that while England was "always willing to go further in the way of concession and friendly service to the United States than to all other nations of the earth combined, . . . it can not be all give and no take, and your people should remember that we are also very proud and very powerful."[21] Lee would function as a sort of unofficial ambassador to the United States and a valuable back channel to the British government while TR was president; indeed, he would be President Roosevelt's most important English correspondent.

Among the other influential Britons with whom Roosevelt began to correspond prior to his presidency were George Otto Trevelyan, the distinguished historian and politician who would be the recipient of some of Roosevelt's most introspective, revealing, and literary presidential letters; John St. Loe Strachey, the determinedly pro-American editor of *The Spectator* whose ideas on a wide range of political and military subjects were remarkably similar to TR's; historian of the United States James Bryce, author of the acclaimed 1888 study *The American Commonwealth* (for which he sought and received from TR a limited amount of assistance) and Britain's ambassador to the United States during the final two years of Roosevelt's presidency and beyond; and Rudyard Kipling, the renowned romantic imperialist writer. David H. Burton's definition of the broad philosophical foundation of the Roosevelt-Lee friendship could be extended as well to TR and his other leading British correspondents: "the need to maintain the political supremacy of the English-speaking peoples, which in turn they saw as essential to progress."[22] Roosevelt and his English friends, Burton claims, "saw Anglo-American hegemony in the world as the working out of a historical process." As *The Winning of the West* shows, TR in particular viewed American frontier expansion as "an extension of the larger movement of 'men speaking English' across the world begun centuries ago."[23] It was only natural that both the perception of a mutuality of strategic interests arising from concerns about the designs of rival powers and the close personal ties between Roosevelt and Spring Rice, Lee, Bryce, and others would reinforce TR's philosophical disposition toward Anglo-American amity.

On the six biggest issues affecting British-American relations in the decade that preceded his presidency—the Venezuelan boundary dispute, the Spanish-American War, the question of China, the Alaskan border, the control of a future trans-isthmian canal, and the Boer War (the last four still unresolved in September 1901)—Roosevelt held strong opinions and expressed them in his letters with conviction. The same holds true for Anglo-American relations in general and for the British Empire and its future.

When the Venezuelan boundary matter approached crisis stage with Cleveland's belligerent message of December 1895, Roosevelt displayed little sympathy or patience with the British position. To Lodge he wrote that he was "very much pleased" with Cleveland's statement, condemned "anglomaniacs," and declared: "Let the fight come if it must; I don't care whether our sea coast cities are bombarded or not; we would take Canada."[24] (Acquiring Canada would, in fact, remain a serious desire of the jingoistic young TR for at least a couple of more years.) Roosevelt was certain that the Monroe Doctrine was at issue: It would be "preposterous," he claimed in an essay written early in 1896, "to lay down the rule that no European power should seize American territory which was not its own, and yet to permit the power itself to decide the question of the ownership of such territory." He then hopefully expressed the view that "the lesson taught Lord Salisbury is one which will not soon be forgotten by English statesmen."[25]

Never again was Roosevelt to entertain such bellicose feelings toward Britain. That country's conduct during the Spanish-American War solidified TR's earlier belief in the desirability of a strong Anglo-American connection. To Spring Rice he wrote in November 1898: "Isn't it nice to think how closely our two nations have come together this year?"[26] In 1899 he confessed in a letter to William Archer: "I should not republish my Venezuela article now. . . . Fundamentally I feel that all the English speaking peoples come much nearer to one another in political and social ideals, in their systems of government and of civic and domestic morality, than any of them do to any other peoples."[27] To Lee in 1900 he offered this revealing, if overstated, comment: "The attitude of England in 1898 worked a complete revolution in my feelings and the attitude of the continent at that time opened my eyes to the other side of the question."[28]

Even before the Spanish-American War, Roosevelt told Bryce that "I cordially sympathize with England's attitude in China."[29] Later, while vice president, TR wrote to Mahan, concurring with the author of *Problem of Asia* that Anglo-American "cooperation and the effective use of sea power on behalf of civilization and progress . . . is of the utmost importance for the future of Asia, and therefore of the world."[30]

The hard line Roosevelt would take on the Alaskan boundary as president was foreshadowed in two letters he sent to Lee shortly after assuming the vice presidency. In March 1901 he stated flatly: "I have studied that question pretty thoroughly and I do not think the Canadians have a leg to stand on."[31] He reaffirmed this view in April as he rejected Lee's call for arbitration: "This Canadian claim to the disputed territory in Alaska is entirely modern."[32]

Roosevelt was a leading opponent of the Hay-Pauncefote canal treaty of February 1900, which, in the opinion of Charles Campbell, nobody criticized "more cogently" than TR.[33] While he "regretted" opposing an agreement drawn up "on our initiative" and "was well aware" that refusal to ratify "would be peculiarly irritating" to the British, he believed that "in the event of our having trouble with Germany or France it would be far better not to have the canal at all than to have it unfortified."[34] In such a situation, conversely, a fortified canal in American hands "would add to our strength."[35]

Despite an ancestry that might have inclined him to support the Transvaal and Orange Free State or at least to assume a more equivocal position, Roosevelt was fully in agreement with the McKinley administration's pro-British neutrality during the Boer War. In a long letter to Strachey of January 27, 1900, the governor of New York spelled out his perspective: "I feel very strongly, in the first place, that it is the interest of the English-speaking peoples, and therefore of civilization, that English should be the tongue South of the Zambesi, and that the peaceful fusion of the races and the development of South African civilization can best go on under the British flag; and in the second place, I feel a keen remembrance of England's friendly attitude during the Spanish-American war."[36] TR's respect for the spirited Boers did grow as the war dragged on; he wrote to Lee in March 1901 that "the eighteen months' warfare has given many people a strong feeling that the Boers must possess altogether exceptional qualities."[37] However, the vice president told Spring Rice in July, his own views were fundamentally unchanged: "A good many of the Boer leaders have called upon me, most of them with a certain dignified sorrow that though I was of Dutch blood, I seemed to have no sympathy with them. . . . As a matter of fact, I had and have the warmest personal sympathy with them, and yet I have always felt that by far the best possible result would be to have South Africa all united, with English as its common speech."[38]

Roosevelt, moreover, saw the international balance of power and vital U.S. interests at stake in the Boer War. Should Britain somehow be defeated, "I believe in five years it will mean a war between us and some one of the great continental European military nations, unless we are content to abandon our Monroe Doctrine for South America."[39] The "one" he was referring to was Germany: "The only power which may be a menace to us in anything like the immediate future is Germany."[40] By 1900, asserts Serge Ricard, a leading student of TR's pre-presidential thinking on foreign policy, Britain had become in Roosevelt's eyes "an objective ally" against Germany.[41]

Many of Roosevelt's comments suggest that he could be counted among the committed backers of Anglo-American friendship prior to assuming the presidency. On the eve of the Spanish-American War, he wrote to Bryce: "There seems to be a gradual coming together of the two peoples. They certainly ought to come together."[42] The war, as noted, significantly strengthened TR's enthusiasm. To Lee he declared in its aftermath: "I feel very strongly that the English-speaking peoples are now closer together than for a century and a quarter, and that every effort should be made to keep them together; for their interests are really fundamentally the same, and they are far more closely akin, not merely in blood, but in feeling and in principles, than either is akin to any other people in the world."[43] In an 1899 letter to Elihu Root, TR identified Britain as "the country to which we are most closely bound."[44] Following the election of 1900, Roosevelt contentedly told Strachey: "No republican of any prominence made any allusion to England . . . save in an entirely friendly spirit. Bryan sought to arouse . . . hostility to England, but I do not think he accomplished very much."[45] Then, in an oft-quoted remark to Spring Rice, the new vice president said: "I think the twentieth century will still be the century of the men who speak English."[46] And a few months before McKinley's assassination, TR outlined his attitude in a letter to Lodge: "On the whole I am friendly to England. I do not at all believe in being overeffusive or in forgetting that fundamentally we are two different nations; but yet the fact remains, in the first place, that we are closer in feeling to her than to any other nation; and in the second place, that probably her interest and ours will run on rather parallel lines in the future."[47]

Before his presidency Roosevelt was both hopeful and concerned about the future of the British Empire. Australia was a central focus of his hopes. To Spring Rice in 1896 he expressed the view that "even if in the dim future Russia should take India and become the preponderant power in Asia, England would merely be injured in one great dependency."[48] He elaborated revealingly in 1899: "To you India seems larger than Australia. In the life history of the English speaking people I think it will show very much smaller. The Australians are building up a great commonwealth, the very existence of which, like the existence of the United States, means an alteration in the balance of power of the world and goes a long way towards insuring the supremacy of men who speak our tongue and have our ideas of social, political, and religious freedom and morality."[49] Once again to Spring Rice, Roosevelt wrote approvingly in March 1901 of the "abounding vigor . . . in Australia."[50]

On the other hand, TR wrote in July 1901, "it certainly does seem to me that England is on the downgrade." He thought that the British Empire was too "spread out." He expected that Britain would "lose ground relatively to Russia in Asia."[51] Such a state of affairs was very disturbing to Roosevelt. "The downfall of the British Empire," Roosevelt, upset by Britain's "evident lack of fighting edge," told his sister Anna soon after the Boer War commenced, "I should regard as a calamity."[52]

The various foregoing references to "the English-speaking peoples" suggest the importance of the concept of "race" in Theodore Roosevelt's worldview. In *Theodore Roosevelt and the Idea of Race*, Thomas G. Dyer notes that TR (and his contemporaries) "broadly construed" the term, permitting "a significant variety of human groups to be recognized as races."[53] In Roosevelt's mind, racial qualities were both inherited and acquired, and traits acquired in one generation could be inherited by later generations. Races he considered inferior therefore could advance through assimilating the more desirable qualities of superior races, a notion that fit in nicely with his view of American and (with exceptions) British imperialism as altruistic and uplifting. "The idea that a race must maintain a very high fertility rate to avoid losing its identity to a people of superior breeding powers" was "a principal cornerstone of his racial theories."[54] It is important to add that for Roosevelt, as Ricard points out, the concept of "the English-speaking peoples" was an *inclusive* one, emphasizing a "community of language and values" rather than common ethnic origins.[55] Dyer perceives a "dynamic quality" to Roosevelt's racial theories; nonetheless, "his celebration of the heritage, exploits, and destiny of the 'English-speaking race' continued largely unabated throughout his life."[56]

All of Roosevelt's ideas about the British Empire and Anglo-American relations, although serious and interesting, were in actuality of limited consequence prior to September 1901. Other than on the first Hay-Pauncefote Treaty, almost certainly ill-fated in any case, he did not make much of an impact on decisions affecting the American-British relationship.

Then, suddenly and dramatically, everything changed. If, as Campbell contends, the incoming president "was pretty much an unknown quantity as far as his attitude to Britain was concerned," he would not be so for long.[57] The future of the developing special relationship was now largely in Roosevelt's hands. His responses to specific situations involving American and British interests and the evolution of his thinking on a number of broader issues would henceforward be matters of great import for the United States, the British Empire, and the world.

Roosevelt and the British Empire, 1901–1903: Forging a Friendship

● ○ ●

STATECRAFT ROOSEVELTIAN STYLE

As is true of most successful leaders, President Theodore Roosevelt was skillful both in selecting capable subordinates and in managing them. In many areas of domestic policy, he gave his top appointees substantial leeway in making decisions and in setting administration policy. In the arena of diplomacy, however, the self-confident and historically knowledgeable president for the most part held strong, well-defined views and was less willing to share authority. Especially when dealing with the foreign policy matters he saw as most important—including nearly all issues centered on Anglo-American relations—Roosevelt charted the broad course of American policy *and* attended personally to the significant details of its execution. In these cases, as Charles E. Neu puts it, TR "held in his own supple hands all the strands of American policy."[1]

Actually, two excellent secretaries of state, John Hay and Elihu Root, worked under Roosevelt, and time and again the president availed himself of their services. He did so because he had confidence in their abilities and because their ideas about foreign policy largely coincided with his own. With Root in particular Roosevelt enjoyed collaborating closely. The president sometimes sought and received advice not only from Hay and Root but also from other trusted friends and associates, such as William Howard Taft, Henry Cabot Lodge, and George von Lengerke Meyer. Operating in the informal, personal style he preferred, with no set inner circle of advisers, TR would solicit the counsel of different individuals at different times, as it suited his needs.

But fundamentally, as Lewis L. Gould describes it, Roosevelt liked to "move with secrecy and quiet to shape events, letting only a few close friends know even a portion of the larger picture."[2] Even with the small number of overseas

1902 FINDS THE HELM IN SAFE HANDS.

Theodore Roosevelt at the helm of the ship of state.
From the edition of *Puck* of January 1, 1902.
Reprinted by permission of the Theodore Roosevelt Collection, Harvard College Library.

American diplomats whom the president liked and trusted—Whitelaw Reid and Henry White prominent among them—important communications tended to be in the form of private letters dispatched outside the established channels. Often when TR appeared to be seeking advice, moreover, he was really looking for a stamp of approval for decisions he had already made. In effect, he frequently functioned as his own secretary of state and as his own secretary of the navy. Thus, throughout his presidency, Roosevelt maintained a tight grip on the reins of diplomacy. *His* foreign policy was just that.

SOUTH AFRICA, CANADA, AND OTHER IMPERIAL MATTERS

Although believing, in the words of Howard K. Beale, that "Britain's preeminence would last out the twentieth century,"[3] Theodore Roosevelt was aware at the outset of his presidency of evidence portending a much earlier British decline. A letter of October 1901 from his German friend, Hermann Speck von Sternburg, commenting on "the gloomy news from South Afrika [*sic*]" brought this response from Roosevelt: "What you tell me about England's decay makes me feel rather sad, but is in exact accord with my own observations and with what I hear from other sources."[4] Not wishing to encourage this decay, President Roosevelt steadfastly upheld the McKinley administration's pro-British neutrality until the end of the Boer War in 1902. But he remained disturbed by Britain's lackluster military performance, which he attributed largely to increasing materialism and frivolity in British society. As he wrote to his son Theodore, Jr., in 1903, "I have not a doubt that the British officers in the Boer War had their efficiency gravely reduced because they had sacrificed their legitimate duties to an inordinate and ridiculous love of sports."[5]

Still, on the whole, President Roosevelt viewed the outcome of the Boer War with optimism and satisfaction. In two letters written right after the Treaty of Vereeniging, TR urged upon John St. Loe Strachey "a universal amnesty" and proclaimed: "I am certain that the Boer farmer can become part of an English-speaking, homogeneous population of mixed origins, which will not only make South Africa an important country but a very valuable addition to the English-speaking stock throughout the world."[6]

⋠   ⋡

Having years ago abandoned the idea of "taking Canada" from the British Empire, and having come to perceive British Canada as a wholly acceptable political entity, Roosevelt showed in 1903 that he may not yet have completely lost interest in gaining control, under the right circumstances, of portions of the

United States' vast northern neighbor. Abbott Lawrence Lowell, seeing a weakening Anglo-Canadian bond as the inevitable effect of the absence of preferential British duties for the empire's self-governing colonies, offered this analysis to TR in June 1903: "It is not impossible that the time may come when the western part of Canada will be so situated that it might fall in to us [*sic*] by a sort of attraction of gravitation, if the feeling on the two sides of the border were sufficiently friendly." Lowell urged that Roosevelt be "conciliatory" toward Canadian officials and on "tariff and trade policy so far as is possible."[7]

Roosevelt's reply, given here in full, was certainly suggestive: "I agree with you absolutely. I have always tried to speak in as friendly a manner as possible of Canada. As far as I can influence affairs we shall adopt an entirely friendly position towards Canada in every way."[8]

Paradoxically, however, one can simultaneously view TR's comments as indicative of support for and solidarity with the British Empire. While not wanting to rule out western Canada's voluntarily joining the American union at some point in the distant future, it was in the meantime toward *British* Canada that TR was intending to be "entirely friendly."

≪   ≫

In Roosevelt's eyes, the most important qualities shared by the most "civilized" nations and peoples included "social efficiency"; a desire and capacity for order; a willingness selflessly to undertake noble tasks; and the "manly virtues," success at breeding and fighting being prominent among such virtues. British imperialism reflected the high state of British civilization. In a speech delivered two years prior to his presidency, Roosevelt observed: "England's rule in India and Egypt has been of great benefit to England, for it has trained up generations of men accustomed to look at the larger and loftier side of public life. It has been of even greater benefit to India and Egypt. And finally, and most of all, it has advanced the cause of civilization."[9] TR carried this perspective into his presidency. In April 1902, for example, he declared in a letter to Albert Henry George Grey, a British colonial administrator, that the work of the late Cecil Rhodes "in Matabeleland represented a great and striking conquest for civilization."[10]

The American position in the Philippines provided a similar test and a similar validation of America's own civilization. In the pre-presidential speech just quoted from, Roosevelt followed his praise for Britain's accomplishments in Egypt and India with these words: "If we do our duty aright in the Philippines, we will add to that national renown which is the highest and finest part of national life, will greatly benefit the people of the Philippine Islands, and, above all, we will play our part well in the great work of uplifting mankind."[11] In 1901, in his first annual message to Congress, Roosevelt more precisely defined the

United States' purpose: "We hope to do for them what has never been done for any people of the tropics — to make them fit for self-government after the fashion of the really free nations."[12] Indeed, the Philippines and all questions connected with the American role there — ending the insurrection, addressing charges of brutality on the part of U.S. troops and punishing perpetrators, monitoring the operation of the civil government, resisting demands for what he considered a premature promise of Filipino independence, trying to resolve religious complications, seeking a preferential tariff bill — were central concerns of President Roosevelt during 1901-1903. Pleased that U.S. labors appeared to be paying off — the United States had so far been "marvelously successful" with its mission in the Philippines, he claimed in a speech delivered in August 1902, asserting soon afterward in a letter to a leading anti-imperialist that "the bulk of the [Filipino] people are entirely satisfied"[13] — TR was vigilant against any relaxation of America's effort. For, as he wrote to James Francis Tracey, who would later serve the administration as an associate justice of the Supreme Court of the Philippines, "no more important work can be done at this time for our country than that done by the men connected either with the civil or the military work in the Philippines."[14]

Other "civilized" nations also had a role to play "in the great work of uplifting mankind." President Roosevelt viewed Japan as the most suitable mentor for China. Toward Germany and Russia he was more ambivalent, due to suspicions about their designs and doubts about how fully civilized they really had become. Serge Ricard correctly notes that Roosevelt "encouraged" France in its "'civilizing mission' in regions of the world that it considered to be its legitimate spheres of influence."[15] Even a small country such as Belgium might lend a hand; in a letter of December 1902 to Maria Longworth Storer, TR commented: "What an extraordinary thing it has been, the way Belgium has played her part in the international development of Africa and to a certain extent of Asia."[16]

As David H. Burton remarks, however, "in any comparison of the accomplishments of the non-English and the English [-speaking] peoples, . . . Roosevelt held that those of the latter were of a different and higher quality. The triumphs of the English . . . stood in instructive contrast to the political occupations resting on force that typified European domination in Asia and Africa. Under English inspiration the ideas of western man were better able to take root and to reproduce, at times on an even grander scale, superior institutions."[17]

ENGLAND, GERMANY, AND THE CARIBBEAN REGION

"After the Venezuelan episode of 1895," argues Beale, "Britain and America gradually and almost unconsciously worked out a mutual understanding that

America was to dominate the Western Hemisphere."[18] But British acceptance of this "mutual understanding" was not yet assured at the time Theodore Roosevelt assumed the presidency. Hence, American control of the Caribbean was at the top of the new president's foreign policy agenda.

⋉   ⋊

Agreement on the isthmian canal question was crucial. Roosevelt's well-reasoned and vocal opposition to the first Hay-Pauncefote Treaty of 1900 has been noted. Britain's efforts to link canal negotiations with the Alaskan boundary question had met with stubborn American resistance and had had to be abandoned. With the Boer War and troubles with Russia in East Asia adding urgency to Britain's quest for a strengthened friendship with America, Ambassador Pauncefote and Secretary of State Hay had resumed canal negotiations in March 1901, and within a month Hay had drafted a new treaty—ultimately accepted after only limited adjustments—permitting American control and fortification.

On the day before Hay presented his draft treaty to Pauncefote, Vice President Roosevelt had emphasized the fortification issue in a letter to Arthur Lee. America's insistence on fortification, TR explained to Lee, was tied to its concern about possible war with some other power, not with England. Roosevelt reasoned that the canal "would immediately fall" into Britain's hands in the event of an Anglo-American war. Indeed, "if the possibility of war between England and the United States were all there was to consider," it would actually be "to the advantage of the United States to have outside powers guarantee the neutrality of the canal in time of war."[19]

The second Hay-Pauncefote Treaty was essentially completed by the time TR assumed the presidency. Roosevelt promptly assured Hay of his support for the secretary of state and the canal treaty and immediately took an active role in the ratification effort. Joseph Choate, the American ambassador to Great Britain, informed TR that he "was very much rejoiced to hear from the Secretary of State that you are in perfect accord with him in regard to the Isthmian Canal Treaty."[20] On September 30 the new president wrote to Hay that the treaty would "cover any possible canal across the Isthmus" and passed along Senator Lodge's "hearty support."[21] In another letter to Hay written five days later, Roosevelt observed: "The treaty does seem to be in fine shape; . . . I think we can get it through. In my judgment we should get it in as soon as the session begins; delay will give time for quarrels which will lessen our chances."[22] Then TR replied to Choate's letter. "I am delighted with the Isthmian Canal Treaty," he declared.[23] To Lodge he optimistically predicted "that the opposition to it will now completely break down."[24]

The formal signing of the revised canal treaty occurred on November 18, 1901, and Senate ratification was achieved on December 16 by a vote of seventy-two to six. Roosevelt's optimism had been well-founded.

Arthur Lee was exuberant: "I hardly need tell you how delighted I was to see this morning that the much debated Canal Treaty had weathered all opposition, and had been ratified by the Senate by such an overwhelming majority. The smooth success of the Treaty has been very near my heart, and it has been my earnest desire all along to do any little thing that I could to remove any of the earlier difficulties that existed upon this side of the water." Lee's contribution had included meeting with Lord Lansdowne, Arthur Balfour, and other government officials to offer "some new lights on the American side of the case."[25]

Ambassador Pauncefote noted with evident satisfaction the unhappiness of Britain's rivals with his hard-earned achievement: "The success of the Canal Treaty has been a great blow to my 'chers collegues' here. Not one of them has offered congratulations, & throughout they have maintained a lugubrious silence. It was hoped no doubt that the Treaty would again be mangled in the Senate & that the entente cordiale would perish with it. If we now settle the Alaska trouble they will be in despair."[26]

Roosevelt did his best to downplay the British capitulation. His response to Lee's letter typified his gracious demeanor: "I must say how pleased I was by the ratification of the treaty. Really I think it is as much to your interest as to ours."[27] Now the president could look ahead to "one of the greatest bits of work that the twentieth century will see"—truly to be among the most time-consuming and challenging undertakings of his years in the White House—"the Isthmian Canal."[28]

⫷   ⫸

"I most earnestly desire to have Germany and the United States work hand in hand," President Roosevelt told Speck von Sternburg a couple of weeks after assuming the presidency.[29] While meaning what he said, Roosevelt knew well that this "desire" would not be easily realized.

Germany—like Japan and Russia—aroused concern in Roosevelt because it was, as Beale asserts, "an economically powerful, militarily effective rival power."[30] The president saw Germany as the one power that might threaten America's position in the Western Hemisphere. TR's barely unsuccessful attempt—thwarted, the U.S. ambassador to Germany believed, by German pressure on Denmark's government—to buy the Danish Virgin Islands in 1902 was tied to his wariness of Germany. More generally, moreover, Roosevelt considered what Raymond A. Esthus terms "the Bismarckian attitude toward war" as "something civilized nations should outgrow."[31] And, not least, the "mercurial temperament" of the highly aggressive and ambitious Kaiser William II made German policy, as Richard H. Collin claims, "unpredictable."[32]

Thus Roosevelt tread carefully when relations with Germany were at issue, approaching even matters of protocol with great prudence. In anticipation of the visit to the United States in February 1902 of Prince Henry of Prussia, for example, the president told Hay that "I want to be just as courteous as possible with these people."[33] Closer to Prince Henry's arrival, TR worried: "When we come to go into the state dinner how in the name of heaven will we avoid hurting various Teutonic susceptibilities?"[34] His description to the journalist-politician Whitelaw Reid of "the Secretary of the German Navy, von Tirpitz," as "an exceedingly able man" probably reflected concern as much as it did admiration.[35]

Roosevelt believed that the presence in America of his friend Speck von Sternburg, formerly first secretary of the German embassy in Washington, would eliminate some of the awkwardness in U.S.-German relations, so he actively lobbied for Sternburg to be assigned here. To Hay he wrote on November 7, 1901: "Do you think there would be any way . . . of finding out whether the German Government would be willing to put Baron Speck von Sternberg [sic] back here in some capacity?"[36] The following month TR posed a similar question to Andrew Dickson White, the American ambassador to Germany: "Do you suppose that you could sometime say a word to the Kaiser to the effect that if it suited him it would be very agreeable to me to have Speck sent back to Washington?"[37] The president then offered more explicit directions in response to a letter from White: "I think that the best thing to do would be sometime to sound whomever you deem wisest, whether the Kaiser or von Bulow, as to Speck's being sent here; of course it being understood that if there is the slightest objection to it I would not dream of making the request."[38]

On March 6, 1902, Roosevelt drafted a lengthy and forthcoming, but rather indiscreet and misleading, letter to Sternburg himself. "I do not think you can build with any confidence upon being sent here," declared the president. "My impression is that they do not want to have anyone over here whom they would regard as being too close to me." Roosevelt was "convinced that the United States and Germany can work in the closest intimacy . . . for the benefit of both, not only in China, but in South America as well"; however, he was doubtful that the German government shared his outlook.[39] But TR thought better of sending this letter and in its place penned a much briefer and more circumspect one: "I should like to write you at length, but I simply don't dare to in my present position, for any accident that would put into other hands a confidential letter of mine might have very serious consequences. I have as yet received no encouragement whatever in reference to my desire to have you here."[40] Sternburg, as it turned out, would be named Germany's ambassador to the United States less than a year later—when the Venezuelan intervention crisis of 1902-1903 awoke the German government to the unhealthy state of German-American relations.

⫷   ⫸

President Roosevelt worried a great deal less where England was concerned. Various historians have succinctly captured the reasons. William C. Widenor contends that TR "foresaw an Anglo-American combination dominating the world in the interest of civilization."[41] Beale comments similarly on Roosevelt's "belief . . . in the oneness of the American and British interest and his conviction that in combination the Americans and the British could dominate the world—to the advantage of civilization."[42] Ricard points to a "community of interests," an "affinity of cultures," and an "ethnocentric" imperial vision that elevated the role of the "English-speaking peoples."[43] Collin emphasizes "powerful and mutually compelling interests," including the opposition of Roosevelt and British officials to "German expansion in the Western hemisphere."[44] Esthus stresses TR's "fundamental . . . conviction that Britain was a friend and Germany was a potential enemy."[45]

Such an outlook was apparent right from the start of Roosevelt's presidency. To Ambassador Choate he pledged: "I shall do all that I can to preserve unbroken the friendly relations between the two countries."[46] When John St. Loe Strachey—whom TR would not meet in person for another year—told Roosevelt soon after McKinley's death that he and most other Britons believed "the executive office would fall into worthy hands" and were finding some consolation in this belief, Roosevelt replied with sincerity: "You are one of the men to whom I am willing to write with the most absolute confidence."[47] In his aforementioned letter to Arthur Lee following the ratification of the second Hay-Pauncefote Treaty, Roosevelt declared with satisfaction: "The tone of the speeches with reference to England was admirable."[48] Germany's attempt early in 1902 to discredit Britain's prewar policy toward the United States and Spain in 1898 through the publication of documents was alleged by the journalist George Washburn Smalley to have provoked this response from Roosevelt: "Not only do I not believe this Berlin story, but I know it is false."[49]

⫷   ⫸

The Venezuelan crisis of 1902-1903 provides an excellent opportunity to juxtapose Roosevelt's contrasting perspectives on Germany and England. The ire this episode stirred in the president was far from evenly distributed.

As historians have pointed out, both Germany and Great Britain badly miscalculated the American reaction to their joint military expedition against Venezuela. Regarding the former, Beale observes: "Germany was trying

desperately to go 'hand in hand' with America, to win and keep her friendship.
. . . Had she foreseen what the American reaction was going to be, she would
almost certainly have refrained from the venture entirely."[50] As to the latter,
Charles S. Campbell, Jr., comments: "Most probably Britain's apparent care-
lessness about America was attributable to errors of judgment. . . . Deprived of
mature counsel from America during the interregnum after the great ambassador's [Pauncefote's] death, just when intervention was being planned, the government seems simply to have underestimated the dangers."[51]

Based on what they saw as sufficient evidence, both England and Germany
were confident that the United States would not object to their heavy-handed
attempt at debt collection. In October 1901 Roosevelt informed Sternburg of the
acceptability of "transitory intervention on the part of any State outside of
South America, when there was a row with some State in South America."[52] In
his annual message that December, TR announced that the United States did
"not guarantee any state against punishment if it misconducts itself, provided
that punishment does not take the form of the acquisition of territory by any
non-American power."[53] Later that same month, when the German embassy
informed the State Department that Germany "might be forced to blockade
Venezuela or even temporarily occupy the customs houses," Hay, offering no
objections, "merely quoted from Roosevelt's message."[54] Warren G. Kneer comments that when the British government decided definitively in October 1902
on joint action with Germany, "the Cabinet seems to have spent little time worrying about the attitude of the United States. Lansdowne assured the Cabinet
that Britain could 'assume the acquiescence of the United States and I do not
think we need do more than inform them when the time comes of our intention
to act with Germany.'" Kneer goes on: "The Foreign Office was convinced that
neither the President nor Hay was unduly alarmed over the prospect of
European intervention."[55] And on November 13, 1902, Michael Herbert, the
new British ambassador to the United States, reported to Foreign Secretary
Lansdowne a renewed assurance from Hay. The secretary of state was sorry
"that European Powers should use force against Central and South American
countries," but the United States "could not object to their taking steps to
obtain redress for injuries suffered by their subjects, provided that no acquisition of territory was contemplated."[56]

In London apprehension was not altogether absent. Back in February the
Colonial Office indicated to Lansdowne "that it does not appear to Mr.
Chamberlain that joint action with Germany" would "be likely to lead to useful
results."[57] Herbert expressed his own doubts in a November letter sent to
Lansdowne soon after the ambassador had heard from Hay: "I wish we were
going to punish Venezuela without the aid of Germany, for I am not sure that joint

action will be very palatable here."[58] But Lansdowne was undeterred, terming the partnership with Germany "perhaps unlucky . . . but . . . quite inevitable."[59]

The plans for joint intervention were carried out. As expected, ultimatums were ignored by Venezuelan president Cipriano Castro. Britain and Germany therefore seized (and partially destroyed) the Venezuelan navy beginning December 9; they bombarded the forts of Puerto Cabello on December 13; and a British-German-Italian blockade of Venezuela was formally promulgated December 20. Venezuela's attempts to fight back were of little avail.

The reaction of the American public was decidedly unfavorable, and criticism within Great Britain was widespread as well. Henry White, the American chargé d'affaires in London, wrote to Hay on December 15 and 17: "I am expressing privately to my friends in the Government grave fears" that England "will, if hostilities continue, be involved . . . in some action which will estrange if not antagonize [sic] American public feeling." Prime Minister Balfour had been told directly of White's "earnest hope that he would not allow his government to be led by Germany into doing something to exacerbate our public opinion."[60] Herbert confirmed these concerns in a message sent to Lansdowne on December 16: "The impression prevails in Washington that Germany is using us, and our friends here regret, from the point of view of American good feeling towards us, that we are acting with her."[61] Other, more urgent communications from Herbert pertaining to the crisis appear to have been intentionally destroyed.[62] In England, meanwhile, a parliamentary debate occurred on December 15, in which, as Kneer relates, "the government's critics denied the necessity of the intervention, . . . deplored the agreement with Germany, and questioned the effects of the affair on relations with the United States."[63]

The British government, finding itself on the defensive, proclaimed its sensitivity to American feelings. Lord Cranborne, representing the Foreign Office, responded before Parliament. The United States, he said, takes a "very reasonable and sensible view of the situation." Americans understand "that the insistence of England that the Venezuelan Government should meet its engagements and respect the rights of British subjects is in no way an infraction of the Monroe Doctrine, and . . . that no nation in the world has been more anxious than England to assist them in maintaining that doctrine."[64] The following day, December 16, Prime Minister Balfour declared in the House of Commons: "We have no intention, and have never had any intention, of landing troops in Venezuela or of occupying territory, even though that occupation might only be of a temporary nature."[65]

Perhaps the greatest historiographical controversy of Theodore Roosevelt's presidency has concerned whether he issued a private ultimatum to Germany demanding that its government either agree to submit its claims against

Venezuela to arbitration or face the U.S. Navy. By any reasonable standard, this controversy should now be considered resolved. Indeed, a near consensus among historians has come to exist; as Serge Ricard puts it, "the reality of the 'ultimatum' is no longer seriously disputed."[66]

But there does remain some real uncertainty about the date, context, and form of the president's ultimatum. The controversy initially focused on an ultimatum of December 1902. In support of numerous historians who wrote before them, Frederick W. Marks III in 1979 and Edmund Morris in 1989 put forward strong cases—somewhat different from one another but both built on extensive and carefully assimilated circumstantial evidence—that Dexter Perkins was in error and that TR did indeed present Ambassador Theodor von Holleben with a December ultimatum and prepare to carry it out.[67]

Then, in 1991, Ricard injected an important new theory into the debate. What Ricard argues, quite persuasively, is that the ultimatum actually was issued in the early part of February 1903 (or perhaps on January 31) during the "second phase" of the crisis. Ricard understandably wonders whether Roosevelt, having supposedly given Germany an ultimatum in December, could then possibly have been so quiescent about continuing German military aggression against Venezuela in January. In contrast, Ricard sees "the Rooseveltian method" clearly in evidence with the sudden softening of Germany's position during the second week of February. In presenting his argument, Ricard astutely utilizes telegrams dated February 3 and 19, 1903, from the newly appointed Ambassador Sternburg to his government, and journalist Alexander Powell's 1932 account of a conversation he had had with Roosevelt in March 1909. Roosevelt had specifically identified 1903 as the year and Sternburg as the ambassador as he recounted the episode to Powell. While appropriately acknowledging the great likelihood that "no hypothesis will ever perfectly integrate" all the key pieces of evidence, Ricard has carried out an impressive investigation and just may have unraveled this complex and long-standing mystery.[68]

December ultimatum or no, President Castro had publicly proposed arbitration on December 9, and the U.S. government strongly supported his proposal, with Roosevelt sending a fleet of warships to the waters near Venezuela to emphasize that support to Germany. First the British and then the Germans accepted the principle of arbitration, and by December 18 a very dangerous stage of the crisis had passed.

By this point, powerful anti-German feelings were prevalent in both Britain and America. "Ironically," Kneer contends, "Lansdowne's own Venezuelan policy had greatly intensified the new British Germanophobia which he himself deplored."[69] From Washington, Herbert noted "with malevolent satisfaction" the "somewhat remarkable . . . explosion of feeling against Germany here."[70]

On December 26, 1902, Roosevelt wrote four letters reflecting on the events of recent days. "We have had a little flurry over the Venezuelan business here," said the one that went to William Howard Taft, "but it bids fair now to be settled on an entirely satisfactory basis."[71] A few days later a letter to Chicago journalist George Wheeler Hinman indicated that Germany, not Britain, was TR's chief worry. "There should be no territorial aggrandizement by any European power under the cover of the collection of . . . a debt." Roosevelt had sent a "note to Germany in the matter last spring," he informed Hinman, in which he had "put our position as strongly as it has ever been put to a foreign power."[72]

Anticipating, like Roosevelt, a quick end to the intervention, Ambassador Herbert was relieved and optimistic. He expressed his outlook in a letter to Lansdowne: "The Administration has been most friendly throughout, and, if the dispute be referred without delay to arbitration, which at the moment of writing seems probable, it will be almost safe to affirm that the friendly relations between Great Britain and the United States, instead of being impaired, have, if anything, been strengthened by the Venezuelan incident."[73]

However, efforts to reach some preliminary understandings and to agree on the terms of arbitration were not immediately successful, owing partly to the presence of Herbert Bowen, an abrasive and untrustworthy American diplomat, at the center of the negotiations as *Venezuela's* representative. Then, on January 21, in a disproportionate response to the firing upon of one of its warships, Germany bombarded and destroyed Venezuela's Fort San Carlos. "Are the people in Berlin crazy?" was Roosevelt's private reaction.[74] A couple of weeks afterward, with the talks remaining stalled, with an American fleet under the command of Admiral George Dewey positioned to intervene, and with a private presidential ultimatum to Germany having lately been issued (if, as seems probable, Ricard is correct), the president stated in a letter to his oldest son: "My chief difficulty at the moment is the Venezuela matter in which Germany takes an impossible stand."[75]

Henry White's diplomacy, agitated domestic opinion, the political opposition, and disturbing reports from America together were pushing the British government to arrive at a settlement. The disturbing reports were a particular cause for alarm; on February 7 Herbert warned Lansdowne that Britain's standing in America was declining and that "our good relations with this country will be seriously impaired if this Alliance with Germany continues much longer. . . . The time has almost come, in American opinion, for us to make the choice between the friendship of the United States and that of Germany."[76]

Lansdowne remained reluctant to lean heavily on Germany, but when Bowen modified the Venezuelan position and Germany still resisted settling, the foreign secretary informed his German partners that Britain might have to go it alone. An additional Venezuelan concession to Ambassador Sternburg eliminated the possibility of an Anglo-German showdown over Lansdowne's threat.[77] On February 13, 1903, the protocols were signed, and the blockade was then lifted.

A week or so later, President Roosevelt met with Herbert, to whom he spoke pointedly. According to the ambassador's report, Roosevelt was very critical of Germany's actions but also "stated, . . . with some asperity, 'she would never have dared to behave as she has if England had not been acting with her.'" Herbert went on to assert that "from the point of view of continued friendly relations between Great Britain and the United States, the Venezuelan negotiations were not brought to a close a day too soon." The ambassador declared as well that he was struck by the harsh language used with regard to Germany "by men in the highest positions at Washington." He found this reality rather promising, assuming that England had learned the right lesson: "The anti-German spirit cannot fail in the long run to be of benefit to Anglo-American relations. . . . Germany is now gradually taking Great Britain's place in the American mind as the 'natural foe,' and the more general this feeling becomes, the more will the American people be instinctively drawn towards the people of Great Britain with whom they have so much in common." Herbert cautioned, however, "that this theory will not hold good if Great Britain is in any way associated with Germany in the future."[78]

As he looked back on the Venezuela incident later in his presidency, Roosevelt would on occasion charge the British government with misconduct and "stupidity" but would never suggest hostility to the Monroe Doctrine or other serious transgressions. "The English behaved badly in Venezuela," he wrote to Lodge in June 1903; to Ambassador Whitelaw Reid in June 1906, TR stated disparagingly that "the English" had "permitted themselves to be roped in as an appendage to Germany in the blockade of Venezuela."[79]

The country that had "roped in" Britain was far and away the primary focus of Roosevelt's displeasure and concern. In a letter of 1905 to Cecil Spring Rice, TR declared: "I think I succeeded in impressing on the Kaiser, quietly and unofficially, and with equal courtesy and emphasis, that the violation of the Monroe Doctrine by territorial aggrandizement on his part around the Caribbean meant war, not ultimately, but immediately."[80] In a letter of 1906 to Henry White, TR again displayed the suspicions he had entertained about Germany's designs: "At the time of the Venezuela business I saw the German Ambassador privately myself; told him to tell the Kaiser that I had put Dewey in charge of our fleet to maneuver in West Indian waters; that the world at large should know this merely as a maneuver, and we should strive in every way to appear simply as co-operating with the Germans; but that I regretted to say that the popular feeling was such that I should be obliged to interfere, by force if necessary," should Germany look to have any territorial designs in the hemisphere.[81]

⫷   ⫸

While the Roosevelt Corollary to the Monroe Doctrine—according to which the United States undertook to employ its power at its own discretion to counteract "wrongdoing" by its hemispheric neighbors to the south—was not proclaimed by the president until 1904, its roots are located in the Venezuelan affair. The government of Great Britain was an early advocate. In a speech in Liverpool on February 14, 1903, the day after the protocols were signed, Prime Minister Balfour told an approving audience that "the Monroe Doctrine has no enemies in this country that I know of. We welcome any increase in the great influence of the United States of America upon the great Western Hemisphere. . . . It would be a great gain to civilization if the United States . . . were more actively to interest themselves in making arrangements by which these constantly recurring difficulties between European Powers and certain States in South America could be avoided."[82]

Continued apprehension about Germany's intentions—despite the recent realization of his desire to have Sternburg assigned as the German ambassador to the United States—also began to move TR toward his corollary. On March 13, 1903, he described to Hay a meeting in which Sternburg had proposed that a great power syndicate take charge of Venezuela's finances, and that the United States take the initiative to organize it. Roosevelt had rejected this idea, telling Sternburg that the American people interpreted the Monroe Doctrine to mean "that no European power should gain *control* of any American republic." In a forthcoming speech, he intended to explain "that the American people will never consent to allowing one of the American Republics to come under the control of a European power by any such subterfuge" as pretending to be "guaranteeing or collecting a debt."[83]

That German designs on the Western Hemisphere remained a worry for TR in the wake of the Venezuelan episode is nowhere clearer than in a letter he wrote to Hay on April 22, 1903: "Both the Dutch and the Danish possessions in America will be constant temptations to Germany unless, or until, we take them. The way to deliver Germany from the temptation is to keep on with the upbuilding of our navy."[84] Roosevelt saw himself, as he put it in a letter to Hay that August, "steadily engaged in the business of teaching the Kaiser to 'shinny on his own side of the line.'"[85] Responding in September to a letter from Admiral Henry Clay Taylor, the president made this suggestive inquiry: "You say that with the big guns we stand abreast of the English. Taking all the guns together, can you say how we do as compared with the Germans?"[86]

THE SPECIAL RELATIONSHIP:
OVERCOMING THE LAST MAJOR HURDLE

"Viewed in large outline," argues David Burton, President Roosevelt's foreign policy "looked forward to a time when, *appropriate adjustments having been made*, the United States and Britain would live together peacefully while acting in concert to oversee much of the world."[87] Following the completion of the canal treaty at the end of 1901, by far the biggest such "appropriate adjustment" yet to be arrived at related to the disputed border between Alaska and British Columbia. Indeed, "demarcation of the boundary" quickly became, as Campbell contends, "a *sine qua non* of stable Anglo-American relations."[88]

The Alaskan border controversy revolved around the meaning of the Anglo-Russian Treaty of 1825, upon which the Russian-American Treaty of 1867 was largely based. Although there existed legitimate points of disagreement, the British position was weakened by the fact that Canada and Britain had acquiesced in the American interpretation of these treaties until the gold rush in the region of Canada's Klondike River in the late 1890s dramatically increased the economic significance of the location of the boundary line. The boundary matter was highly complex and had many elements, but the only really crucial question throughout the on-and-off negotiations of 1898-1903 was the American stranglehold on the economically vital Lynn Canal, to which Canada claimed access.

Britain's abandonment in 1901 of linkage between the Alaska and canal issues, explained previously, upset Canada and undercut its position. Linkage or no linkage, however, President Roosevelt's mind on the essential question was made up early on, and it seems unlikely that he could have been persuaded to abandon his stance under any imaginable circumstances.

With the Hay-Pauncefote Treaty having resolved the canal problem, Arthur Lee attempted to sensitize Roosevelt to the awkwardness of the British situation concerning Alaska: "I feel sure that you will recognize the extreme difficulty of our position as regards Canadian wishes. During the last decade Canada has set an example to the rest of the Empire in matters of practical patriotism, and even at this moment is making fresh sacrifices to show her complete loyalty to our cause in South Africa." The British people were feeling "gratitude towards the Colonies" and "would vigorously resent any action which could be construed into a neglect of Colonial interests."[89]

While Secretary of State Hay had overseen the American side of the Alaska negotiations since their onset in 1898, and had himself devised the modus vivendi that had been in effect since 1899, President Roosevelt took charge in 1902. Although at one point rendered "disconsolate" by TR's "intransigence,"[90] Hay continued to provide effective assistance as the negotiations proceeded; but

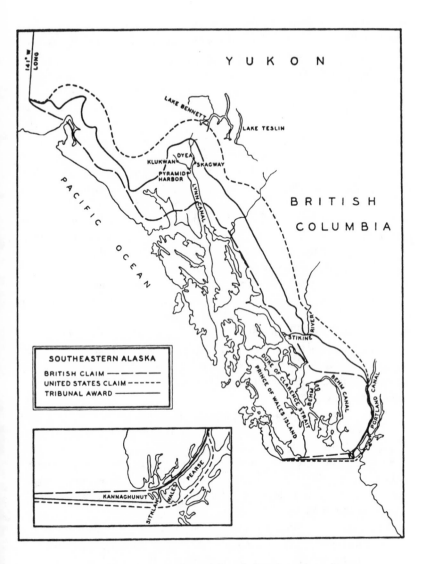

Map of southeastern Alaska and the Alaskan boundary dispute.
From Charles S. Campbell, Jr., *Anglo-American Understanding, 1898-1903*
(Copyright 1957). Reprinted by permission of the Johns Hopkins University Press.

Roosevelt was now running the show. His belief, shared with Lodge years later, "that Hay could not be trusted where England was concerned" may have been a factor.[91] Of greater consequence, however, was TR's hands-on foreign policy style. The Alaskan boundary dispute was a major diplomatic episode, and during such episodes, as noted, the president generally assumed the lead.

With the threat of violent outbreaks between Canadian and American miners increasing in the frontier region, Roosevelt ordered troops to the area in late March of 1902. Secretary of War Elihu Root was told to dispatch "additional troops as quietly and unostentatiously as possible so as to be able promptly to prevent any possible disturbance along the disputed boundary line."[92] In 1909 the president would tell Lodge that he had "moved troops up into Alaska so as to be able immediately to take possession of the important disputed points and hold them against small bodies of Canadians in the event that the effort to come to an agreement resulted in nothing,"[93] a significant secondary motive to which he seems retrospectively to have accorded disproportionate weight.

In a long letter to Hay of July 10, 1902, the president let his secretary of state know exactly where he stood: "In the cabinet room there stands a globe made in London by the map makers for the Admiralty. On this the boundary in question is given as it is on the British admiralty charts of the same period, this boundary being precisely that now claimed by us, which was also the boundary claimed or conceded by both the British and Canadian authorities until the last few years." Only the less significant "southernmost portion" of the boundary was open to disagreement on the basis of the original Anglo-Russian Treaty, and "even this doubt must necessarily vanish in view of the construction put upon the terms of the treaty for over three-quarters of a century.

"The Canadian contention," Roosevelt continued, "is an outrage pure and simple," and arbitration was out of the question. While he was "willing to appoint three commissioners on our side to meet three commissioners on theirs and try to fix the line, . . . I should definitely instruct our three commissioners that they were not to yield any territory whatsoever, but were as a matter of course to insist upon our entire claim."[94]

Less than a week later, Roosevelt added: "I appreciate . . . the possibility of trouble, although I think if we put a sufficient number of troops up there the miners will be kept in check." Canada he angrily accused of submitting a "wholly false claim . . . in a spirit of bumptious truculence. . . . I feel a good deal like telling them that if trouble comes it will be purely because of their own fault; and although it would not be pleasant for us it would be death for them."[95]

In a letter to Strachey written two days later, however, the nationalistic TR displayed both worry over the possibility of damage to the Anglo-American friendship and some empathy with the awkward British position that Lee had described to him earlier. "Just at the moment in my relations with Great Britain I am suffering from anxiety," he confessed. It was true that, as a matter of principle, he believed he could not compromise on the Alaskan boundary. "Yet I thoroughly understand how the English in the moment of victory [in the Boer War], when the Canadians as well as the citizens of the other colonial commonwealths have stood by them so loyally, feel that they must stand by the Canadians in return."[96]

Strachey, even more worried "about this wretched boundary dispute," sensed a softening and attempted to exploit it: "I see of course your objection to arbitration, but I also see what a terrible position it will put us in here if you refuse and especially people like me who insisted that the American demand for arbitration in the case of Venezuela [in 1895-1896] must be yielded to." Strachey found reassuring his certainty that both TR and Prime Minister Balfour "will count your political lives failures if war should come between the two English-speaking nations."[97]

Roosevelt, sympathetic to England's plight though he may have been, refused to give way. Indeed, when an American army officer discovered an apparent boundary marker well inside territory that everyone had previously considered Canadian, the president's attitude, if possible, stiffened. He gave new instructions to Hay: "It seems to me that there is good reason for believing that the boundary we should have by rights would take in more land even than the boundary as claimed on the Russian and American maps and as admitted on almost all the English and Canadian maps." In subsequent border negotiations, TR ordered "this letter of mine, together with the report of Lieutenant Emmons, the affidavits, etc., to be surely placed before the negotiators."[98]

Still, Roosevelt desired to make it as easy as possible for Britain to back down from what he saw as its unsustainable position on the boundary. On January 24, 1903, England—dragging along a reluctant Canada—and the United States signed the Hay-Herbert Treaty. It called for "six impartial jurists of repute who shall consider judicially the questions submitted to them." Each side would appoint three of the six, with a majority of four required to reach decisions.

Roosevelt, as seen, had made it clear to Hay that he would keep the three Americans on a short leash. The president was very sensitive to charges that he had conceded anything of consequence. Responding to the lawyer George Frederick William Holls, an opponent of the new treaty, TR asserted that "an arbitration is where some outside body decides the question at issue between the two parties. . . . There is no 'proposition for an arbitration,' with an uneven or an even number of judges, or under any name, or upon any condition, which has ever received or will ever receive my sanction."[99]

Senate ratification could not be assumed. Northwestern shipping and trading interests were especially vehement in their opposition. One day before the vote on ratification, Holls predicted in a letter to Strachey that the Hay-Herbert Treaty had "no chance whatever of being ratified."[100]

But Senator Lodge foiled the treaty's detractors. By confidentially revealing, with the president's permission, the identity of the three American commissioners—himself, Secretary of War Elihu Root, and former Democratic Senator George Turner of Washington—and then by executing a clever parliamentary maneuver, Lodge achieved ratification without a roll-call vote on February 11.

Many contemporaries were, and historians have been, critical of Roosevelt's appointment of "jurists" who were hardly "impartial."[101] But these selections— finalized only after two Supreme Court justices had declined—may have been required for Senate ratification and, in any case, should be viewed in the context of TR's purpose in agreeing to a commission. Campbell puts it well: "In his view, . . . the tribunal was not a means of finding the truth—that was known already— but a device to help a friendly country, which had blundered through deference to an obstreperous colony, climb down from an untenable position."[102]

Even with Lodge, Root, and Turner representing the United States, President Roosevelt was leaving nothing to chance. On March 17, 1903, he gave these men precise written instructions, justifying his doing so by referring to a recent speech by Sir Wilfrid Laurier, Canada's prime minister, demanding that the two Canadian commissioners uphold the Canadian claims:

> Inasmuch as . . . I regard these claims as untenable, and inasmuch as . . . the position taken by Mr. Laurier . . . is as far removed as possible from the judicial, I feel that I should briefly call your attention to my view of the question which you have to decide.
>
> You will of course impartially judge the questions that come before you for decision. The claim so roundly asserted by Mr. Laurier . . . to Skagway and Dyea, and therefore of course Pyramid Harbor, is not in my judgment one of those which can properly be considered open to discussion. The treaty of 1825 between Russia and England was undoubtedly intended to cut off England, which owned the Hinterland, from access to the sea. The word lisière . . . means the strip of territory bordering all the navigable water of that portion of the Alaskan coast effected [sic] by the treaty, and this strip of territory is American of course. Equally of course in interpreting the treaty a prime consideration is the way in which all authorities interpreted it for the sixty years immediately succeeding its adoption. There is entire room for discussion and judicial and impartial agreement as to the exact boundary in any given locality—that is as to whether in such locality the boundary is to be pushed back ten marine leagues, or

whether there is in actual fact nearer the coast a mountain chain which can be considered as running parallel to it.

In the principle involved there will of course be no compromise. The question is not in my judgment one in which it is possible for a moment to consider a reconciling of conflicting claims by mutual concessions.[103]

According to the Hay-Herbert Treaty, each side was to have up to six months from the exchange of ratifications to prepare its case (two months), to put together its counter-case (two months, which could, however, be extended in the event of "special difficulties which may arise in the procuring of . . . additional papers and evidence"[104]), and to prepare its written argument. As ratifications were exchanged on March 3, 1903, the tribunal was scheduled to convene on September 3.

A crisis soon arose over the question of extending the time limit. Canada found that it would need additional time to ready its counter-case.[105] Already aware of Lodge's determination to return to America for a special session of Congress in November, the British government nonetheless went to bat for its beleaguered colony. On June 16 Lansdowne sent a message to Herbert. The foreign secretary stated that the Hay-Herbert Treaty "expressly contemplates . . . an application . . . for an extension of time," and that he expected the United States to be reasonable.[106]

An indignant Lodge, believing that Canada was stalling in an effort to force his resignation, urged the president on June 23 to "take a stiff tone" against the Canadian request.[107] Pointing out several days later that England had from the beginning been aware of his and Root's strong objections to any delay, he complained: "The British are trying to crowd us, and I feel very strongly that we ought to say to them plainly that if they cannot dispose of this matter early in October that it had better go over to the following summer. I am sure that would bring them to time."[108]

Not only did the president support his friend; he assumed an even more strident stance than Lodge had recommended. On June 29, having just arrived at Oyster Bay where he annually spent most of the summer, Roosevelt wrote to Hay. "I strongly object," he declared, to either a delay *or* a postponement. "I don't want the thing pending during a presidential campaign, and moreover if the English decline to come to an agreement this fall, under any pretense, I shall feel that it is simply due to bad faith, — that they have no sincere desire to settle the matter equitably."[109]

An important conciliatory message seems to have been hidden in this rather severe letter. At first glance, one might see Roosevelt's "presidential campaign" reference as simply reflecting his desire to strengthen his prospects for

reelection in 1904 by achieving a boundary settlement in 1903. Such a political calculation unquestionably affected his timetable, but it probably was not
the primary consideration. For as developments were to reveal, Roosevelt
was willing to compromise on secondary aspects of the border dispute in
order to facilitate a settlement. He surely sensed that "during a presidential
campaign," an opportunistic opposition party might make it impossible for him
to do so, likely resulting in a failed negotiation and a heavy blow to the Anglo-
American relationship.

Significantly, moreover, on July 8 Roosevelt wrote Lodge a *personal* letter
decidedly less unyielding than his letter to Hay. Here TR told his impatient
friend that a brief delay should be considered acceptable: "While on the one
hand I should peremptorily decline to let the case go over until next summer, on
the other hand I should feel that it would be an act of petulance and folly on our
part to break off the negotiations if the British simply requested ten or fifteen
days extra, or even a month." Such a request "could under no conceivable circumstances be taken as an evidence of bad faith." TR reminded Lodge of the big
picture: "The Alaska boundary . . . is altogether too important a matter . . . to forfeit a single chance of bringing it to a successful conclusion."[110]

Nevertheless, President Roosevelt himself was in reality less patient than this
letter suggested and was in any case entirely unwilling to countenance "a *serious*
delay." So with the irritated British threatening to terminate the proceedings over
the question of a postponement, Roosevelt stepped up the pressure in the form
of another letter to Lodge—this one *not* personal—dated July 16. Lodge carried
this letter to London, where he showed it to Joseph Choate and Henry White
and made sure that leading British officials learned of its thrust. In the absence
of a decision by November, TR declared, "I should ask Congress . . . to make an
appropriation to enable me to run the line on our own theory. . . . When Congress
assembles I must be able to report the success or failure of the negotiation so that
action can be taken accordingly."[111] Clearly Roosevelt was leaning hard on
America's new friend. Britain, not surprisingly, opted to endure Canada's dismay
and agreed to convene the tribunal on September 3.

Because the three American commissioners appeared certain to take one side
and the two Canadian commissioners the other, the tribunal's one Briton, Lord
Chief Justice Alverstone, was in a pivotal position. Roosevelt's efforts began to
focus on this key individual, as the president embarked on the second half of
what Campbell calls his "master plan." In the first he had assured—by appointing Lodge, Root, and Turner to the tribunal—that the United States "at least
would not lose." Now "he wrote a succession of strongly worded letters,
addressed to various American officials but intended for the edification of Lord
Alverstone. . . . Roosevelt confidently expected the British government to become

ware of their uncompromising tone, and he hoped it would then see the advisibility of making clear to the Chief Justice its requirement of a decision."[112]

When U.S. Supreme Court Justice Oliver Wendell Holmes, then in London, nformed TR of Joseph Chamberlain's criticism of his appointments to the tribunal,[113] the president responded on July 25 with perhaps the most important f all the letters he wrote on the Alaskan matter that summer and fall. It reveals a determined and adroit diplomatist in control from a distance both of the details of a very complicated negotiation and of the broader context within which he was operating. It is worth considering at length.

"If you happen to meet Chamberlain again," Roosevelt advised Holmes, "you are entirely at liberty to tell him what I say, although of course it must be privately nd unofficially. Nothing but my very earnest desire to get on well with England and my reluctance to come to a break made me consent to the appointment of a Joint Commission in this case." The Canadian position, "which England has backed," had "the scantest possible warrant in justice," and TR had opted for a commission only "to give a chance for agreement" and to avoid asking Congress for an appropriation which will enable me to run the boundary on my own hook."

Most of Britain's claim, Roosevelt asserted, was entirely baseless. For example, "the claim of the Canadians for access to deep water along any part of he Canadian coast is just exactly as indefensible as if they should now suddenly claim the island of Nantucket."

Fortunately, continued the president, there were "two or three lesser points on which there is doubt," and these "the commission can genuinely consider. There is room for argument about the islands in the mouth of the Portland Channel. I think on this the American case much the stronger of the two. Still, he British have a case." Likewise, "there is a chance for honest difference and honest final agreement" about "whether there actually is a chain of mountains parallel to the coast within the ten-league limit."

TR went on to defend the three American commissioners—who were, after all, his own agents operating under the guidelines of his instructions to them of March 17—as "anxious . . . to do justice to the British claim on all points where here is even a color of right on the British side." With "the objection raised by certain Canadian authorities" that Root, Lodge, and Turner "had committed hemselves on the general proposition," Roosevelt displayed impatience: "No man in public life in any position of prominence could have possibly avoided committing himself on the proposition, any more than Mr. Chamberlain could avoid committing himself on the question of the ownership of the Orkneys if some Scandinavian country suddenly claimed them."

In the concluding paragraph, Roosevelt endeavored to drive home his central point to the British officials for whose edification this letter to Holmes was principally intended: "Let me add that I earnestly hope the English understand my purpose. I wish to make one last effort to bring about an agreement through the commission, which will enable the people of both countries to say that the result represents the feeling of the representatives of both countries." Should such an agreement prove unattainable, "there will be no arbitration," and "I shall take a position which will prevent any possibility of arbitration hereafter." The president insisted that he was acting generously and that he was doing so in order "to exhaust every effort to have the affair settled peacefully and with due regard to England's dignity."[114]

On August 8 Holmes obligingly visited Chamberlain with Roosevelt's long letter in hand. Chamberlain reported to Balfour that same day: "Only his intense desire to remain on good terms with England had induced him to allow such a matter to be the subject of discussion at all. He went on to say that, if the arbitration [*sic*] did not result in a satisfactory agreement, . . . he would then take possession of the line to which the United States was clearly entitled."[115]

Holmes was proving to be a useful surrogate, but the president, believing that counting on any one channel of communication would be too risky, was carrying on a multipronged diplomatic offensive. In a comment undoubtedly meant to be transmitted through the British embassy to the Foreign Office, Roosevelt told Hay in a handwritten letter of July 29: "With England, over the Alaska business, I do hope she will understand that if we can't come to an agreement now nothing will be left the United States but to act in a way which will necessarily wound British pride."[116] To Lodge TR wrote encouragingly on August 6: "I have had as thoroughly satisfactory talks with both Root and Turner as anyone could desire. I think you will find them in absolute harmony with you."[117]

On August 8 Roosevelt followed up these discussions with downright militant letters to both Turner and Root. Should there be, he wrote to the former, "captious objections on the part of the English, I am going to send a brigade of American regulars up to Skagway and take possession of the disputed territory and hold it by all the power and force of the United States."[118] His "present feeling," he advised Root, was "that if on the main issue the British hold out and refuse to agree with us I shall at once establish posts on the islands and sufficiently far up the main streams to reduce at [*sic*] all the essential points of our claim to actual occupancy, and shall then ask Congress to appropriate money for at least a partial survey of the territory between the posts. This will not be pleasant to do and it will be still less pleasant for the English."[119]

Lodge, functioning as a trusted personal emissary, reported from London to Roosevelt, also on August 8, in a letter partially upbeat and partially pessimistic. Ambassador Choate "has the whole matter well in hand, understands the situation thoroughly, and has been putting a [*sic*] strong and effective pressure upon them."

However, Lodge cautioned, "from what Choate said I am not over sanguine that we shall reach any agreement. I doubt very much if Lord Alverstone will part from the Canadians and decide the case on the evidence." Lodge had scheduled meetings for later that same week with Balfour, Chamberlain, and Alverstone.[120]

With the convening of the Alaskan Boundary Tribunal on September 3, President Roosevelt began to focus even more closely than before on the details of the boundary discussions. In a brief note written in reply to a suggestion from Hay, TR declared: "I agree with all you say about those little islands. I should be glad to use them as a makeweight in the Alaska boundary matter. If we can come to an agreement over them, all right; if not, arbitrate — before the Hague Court by preference."[121]

Roosevelt also kept up the pressure. In response to a discouraging communication from former Secretary of State John Foster, who was in charge of the preparation and presentation of the American case, TR on September 21 again wrote to Hay.[122] Irritatedly referring to the British as "the jacks," the president threatened that "if they force the alternative upon us," we will "simply announce that the country is ours and will remain so" and take the necessary military measures.[123] On September 26 he wrote in a similar vein to Henry White.[124] And to Root on October 3, he reworded a warning also issued in the letters to Hay and White: "I do wish they could understand that this is the last chance."[125]

Meanwhile, Lodge and the president exchanged highly significant and highly revealing letters on September 24 and October 5. These letters are significant because they show that a final settlement was clearly within reach and to a large extent define the shape of that settlement. They reveal both that the Alaskan boundary was in reality being dealt with more as a political and diplomatic than as a legal question and that even on the lesser aspects of the dispute TR was heavily involved in the decision-making process.

Lord Alverstone, Lodge reported, was seated between him and Root, and "has opened himself pretty well now to us both." The British jurist seemed inclined to side with the United States on "the main contention," meaning "that the line goes round the heads of the inlets." On all other boundary issues, as Lodge outlined, Alverstone was strongly supporting Canada, "his idea being, I presume, to try to let the Canadians down as easily as possible." While the American delegation was inclined to compromise, its members were reluctant to yield "too much" and, in any case, needed a line that was "tenable" from a legal standpoint. "I have given you all these details," the senator concluded, "because if you do not approve in any respect the course we are taking I wish you would cable to Root or to me on receipt of this anything you feel we ought to do or to know. My own impression is that we shall reach a decision very soon, probably even before the arguments are completed."[126]

Roosevelt was pleased with what his friend had written and, while throwing in new instructions on a couple of very small aspects of the border dispute, on the whole responded very encouragingly: "I was immensely interested in your letter of September 24th. This may be too late to reach you before the decision is made; but I did not cable, because you seem to me to be handling the affair exactly right. Of course, we can yield on the Portland Canal Islands, if Alverstone goes with us on the main contention" — although the rights of an American cannery on one of the islands would have to be protected. Roosevelt was also willing, if there really was a discernible mountain chain, to agree to a narrowing of the territory held by the United States. However, "on the Stikine River [between the Portland Canal and the Lynn Canal] I do not think under any circumstances we should go below the line we have already occupied and which was set by the Canadians themselves thirty-odd years ago." The president emphasized once again "that the British have no case whatever." Alverstone, therefore, "ought to be satisfied with the very minimum — simply enough to save his face and bring an adjustment. Rather than give up any essential we should accept a disagreement. . . . We must not weaken on the points that are of serious importance."[127]

It appeared briefly that a deadlock might result from Alverstone's proposal on October 12 of a narrow American coastal strip unacceptable to the United States. A cable of October 15 sounded out Roosevelt on an eighteen-month adjournment, to which, Hay replied to Choate the next day, TR would consent, "provided announcement could be made that the United States was getting an unbroken coastal strip."[128] Faced with a real possibility of a breakdown, the president, although not altering his stance on the boundary itself, seems to have had some second thoughts about derailing the Anglo-American friendship by following through precipitately on his military threats. After all, only three months before he had privately characterized the border dispute as "altogether too important a matter . . . to forfeit a single chance of bringing it to a successful conclusion."[129]

All along, but particularly in the final days of the controversy, Roosevelt was well served by his main representatives in England. Commissioners Root, Lodge, and Turner and diplomats Choate and White were in frequent direct and indirect contact with Balfour, Lansdowne, and Alverstone. It turned out that Alverstone was a flexible, skillful, hard bargainer who understood that there had to be a decision but who was trying to do the best he could for Canada. In the end he agreed to a compromise line for the unbroken coastal strip and, when Commissioner Turner proved insistent, even accepted a division of the four Portland Canal islands, with Canada getting the two largest. Roosevelt, as noted, had been willing to yield all four. Canada's bitterness was as great as the United States' satisfaction.

President Roosevelt was truly exuberant about the outcome of this delicate diplomatic struggle. On October 20, when the tribunal's four-to-two split decision was formally announced, he telegraphed his three tribunal appointees: "Congratulate you and thank you heartily on behalf of American people."[130] The same day he wrote a note of thanks (and self-praise) to Oliver Wendell Holmes: "If you will turn back to the letter I wrote you in July last, and which you showed to Chamberlain, you will notice how exactly the Alaska boundary decision went along the lines I there indicated. I cannot help having a certain feeling that your showing that letter to Chamberlain and others was not without its indirect effect on the decision."[131] Again on October 20, he stated in a letter to his son Theodore, Jr.: "I am very much pleased over what has just been accomplished in the Alaska Boundary award. . . . I think that the British Commissioner who voted with our men was entitled to great credit, and I also think that the clear understanding the British government had as to what would follow a disagreement was very important and probably decisive."[132]

⇤   ⇥

During the most difficult months of the "Alaska business" in 1903, President Roosevelt had not communicated with his closest British friends.[133] Awkwardness certainly would have been inherent in any effort either to involve them in Roosevelt's Big Stick diplomacy or to ignore the issue altogether. After the settlement, however, it was easy for him to downplay recent Anglo-American tensions by blaming Canada for the Alaska problem. To Cecil Spring Rice TR sent these words on November 9: "If you get here I want to show you the maps submitted . . . in the Alaskan boundary case. These maps, to my mind, show conclusively that there was literally no Canadian case at all on their main points, and that the two Canadian Commissioners are inexcusable in attacking Lord Alverstone as they have done." Relief was evident when he added: "It has been a very fortunate and happy thing to get the question definitely settled and out of the way."[134]

An exchange of correspondence with Arthur Lee also contributed to the healing process. After receiving a congratulatory message from TR on the occasion of his appointment to an admiralty post in the British government, the thirty-five-year-old Lee—of all Roosevelt's English friends generally the most candid in relaying the British perspective on matters of Anglo-American discord—replied in a letter of November 22 "born of good spirits." Because Lee had "always been persuaded that the Canadians had no case," the boundary decision did not displease him. He did lament that the commission had not been "purely judicial," because if it had been there would be "no difficulty about submitting future disputes to a similar tribunal." He lamented too the verbal abuse to which Lord Alverstone, "one of my oldest and dearest friends," was being very unfairly subjected. Above all, though, Lee was "enormously relieved" that "this really ugly question" had finally been resolved.[135]

President Roosevelt's response lauded Alverstone, who "got every inch of territory for the Canadians that could by any possibility be held to be theirs." TR thought that his praising Alverstone publicly would be harmful to the jurist, "but you are very welcome to show him this letter if you see fit."

Roosevelt also offered Lee an emphatic and coherent retrospective defense of his tribunal appointments. The president was glad that the two Supreme Court justices initially offered places on the commission had declined, because "judicially the case did not admit of a compromise." Instead, therefore, "we needed to have jurists who were statesmen." Only the statesmanship of the American commissioners enabled Canada to receive two of the Portland Canal islands and "thus rendered it possible for a decision to be made." A purely judicial decision "would have been technically proper, but in its results most unfortunate."[136]

⫤   ⫥

Roosevelt would never cease to view his assertive Alaskan diplomacy as decisively advancing the Anglo-American special relationship. In a long and wide-ranging letter on international affairs that he wrote to Spring Rice on November 1, 1905, he included these remarks: "I feel that England and the United States, beyond any other two powers, should be friendly with one another, and what I can legitimately do to increase this friendliness will be done. One of the best manifestations of it, by the way, was my insisting upon having the Alaskan boundary settled right, and taking sufficiently active steps to make the British government understand the seriousness of the situation."[137] In February 1909, less than a month before the conclusion of his White House years, Roosevelt included the following words in a lengthy letter offering unsolicited foreign policy advice to Philander Chase Knox, the incoming secretary of state: "As for England, I cannot imagine serious trouble with her. The settlement of the Alaskan boundary removed the one grave danger."[138] And a couple of years after retiring from the presidency, TR made this observation in a letter to Alfred Thayer Mahan: "The settlement of the Alaskan boundary settled the last serious trouble between the British Empire and ourselves as everything else could be arbitrated."[139]

Historians have agreed with Roosevelt's analysis of the significance of the resolution of the Alaskan-British Columbian border. With this "potentially dangerous" issue out of the way, contends Kneer, "Anglo-American relations were unprecedentedly cordial and free from serious controversies."[140] And according to Collin, "by 1903, the United States and Theodore Roosevelt had consolidated with Great Britain the informal alliance that had started so stormily in 1895 [over the Venezuelan boundary]."[141]

ROOSEVELT, BRITAIN, AND THE
ASIAN BALANCE OF POWER

Theodore Roosevelt was, with modifications shaped by his worldview, an adherent of the balance-of-power principle. As Widenor explains it, Roosevelt "understood the uses of power in international relations and sought peace in concerts of power rather than in a legalistic or paper system."[142] The eminent American statesman and student of diplomatic history Henry Kissinger asserts in his highly acclaimed 1994 book, *Diplomacy*, that Roosevelt "approached the global balance of power with a sophistication matched by no other American president" then or since.[143] Roosevelt fought hard to build up the U.S. Navy—not only to acquire the capacity to protect the United States and its interests militarily but also to gain leverage in his diplomacy—and frequently exhorted British leaders to maintain the supremacy of the Royal Navy. Indeed, it should be emphasized that the "balance" of power desired by Roosevelt was more accurately an *im*balance favorable to the two most civilized, righteous, and responsible powers—namely, the United States and Great Britain.

⚔   ⚓

Just prior to and during Roosevelt's early years as president, China held center stage in the international struggle for power. TR entered the White House in broad agreement with Mahan's recently published *The Problem of Asia*. Mahan saw a grave Russian threat looming over China and called for the United States, Britain, Germany, and Japan to cooperate in preventing Russia from expanding beyond Manchuria.

Initially President Roosevelt addressed the Russian challenge indirectly, stressing his support for the Open Door policy of Hay and McKinley. He explained to Sternburg in October 1901 his desire to see "the Chinese . . . forced to behave themselves—not permitted to do anything atrocious, but not partitioned, and with the ports kept open to all comers."[144] In his first annual message to Congress in December 1901, TR called for leaving "no effort untried to work out the great policy of full and fair intercourse . . . on a footing of equal rights and advantages to all. We advocate . . . not merely the procurement of enlarged commercial opportunities on the coasts, but access to the interior by the waterways with which China has been so extraordinarily favored."[145] Underlying these remarks, asserts Beale, was Roosevelt's acceptance of "the main tenet of Mahan's doctrine about China, the necessity of balancing for strategic reasons Russian power in Manchuria through Anglo-American-Japanese control of the Yangtse Valley."[146]

Despite his awareness of China's importance and his sympathy with Mahan's ideas, Roosevelt was not convinced that China was a vital *American* interest. Prior to the Russo-Japanese War of 1904-1905, he gave China relatively little attention. According to Charles Neu, it was one of those "areas he considered of secondary importance," in which "he allowed subordinates considerable autonomy."[147] Beale concurs: "Before 1904 Roosevelt took surprisingly little active part in the handling of Far Eastern affairs."[148] John Hay dominated the shaping of America's China policy during this period.

Roosevelt hoped that powers with a greater stake in China would take the lead in resisting Russian expansion. The Anglo-Japanese alliance of January 1902, therefore, pleased him very much. Britain pledged to assist Japan militarily should the latter become involved in war against more than one enemy in defense of its interests in China and Korea. The following comment in a letter from Choate to Hay embodied the president's thinking: "It seems to me greatly to fortify the policy of the 'open door.'"[149] Henry White too was in tune with Roosevelt when he wrote to Lodge: "I always think it particularly satisfactory when other nations can be got to do our work or to contribute very materially towards it and this is . . . what the Treaty in question is likely to accomplish."[150] It is very doubtful that England would have entered into this alliance without a clear sense of American approval. Indeed, as Campbell contends, there was among British politicians "an assumption that America was in some sense a third party to the treaty."[151] This assumption was valid. Any foreign power, France or Germany in particular, that might ally itself too closely with Russia in opposition to the Anglo-Japanese alliance would risk the displeasure of the Roosevelt administration.

While the United States did not strongly oppose the existence of a Russian sphere of influence in Manchuria, Hay insisted on an open door for commerce and a Russian troop withdrawal. With Russia failing to meet these demands during 1902 and 1903, Hay, Beale writes, "kept in close touch with the British and Japanese ministers" and "stood up to the Russians as effectively as he could when they knew he could not use force."[152] American cooperation with Britain and Japan, of course, would remain informal, as Hay noted in a letter to TR of April 1903: "I am sure you will think it is out of the question that we should adopt any scheme of concerted action with England and Japan. Public opinion in this country would not support such a course, nor do I think it would be to our permanent advantage."[153]

It seemed to Roosevelt that Manchurian matters were under control when, in 1902, Russia consented to evacuate Manchuria gradually. "I congratulate you," he wrote Hay, "on your success with Russia."[154] But it was not to be so easy.

Russia probably would have fared better with President Roosevelt if it had openly rejected American demands instead of agreeing to them with no apparent intention to follow through. Russia's "mendacity" as much as its policies would seem to account for the high degree of hostility toward that country displayed by Roosevelt during 1903. He literally became "fighting mad." On May 22 TR wrote to Hay, who had been carefully monitoring events and keeping the president up to date: "As for China, I do not see that there is anything we can say, even by way of suggestion. The mendacity of the Russians is something appalling. The bad feature of the situation from our standpoint is that *as yet* it seems that we cannot fight to keep Manchuria open."[155]

Murderous pogroms in Russia and the "impertinent" refusal of its government to receive an American citizens' petition forwarded by the State Department served to compound Roosevelt's anger.[156] He told Hay on July 18 that he had "not the slightest objection to the Russians knowing that I feel thoroughly aroused and irritated at their conduct in Manchuria; that I don't intend to give way and that I am year by year growing more confident that the country would back me in going to an extreme in the matter."[157]

The president's most dramatic letter on the subject, again to Hay, was written on July 29: "I wish, in Manchuria, to go to the very limit I think our people will stand. If only we were sure neither France nor Germany would join in, I should not in the least mind going to 'extremes' with Russia."[158]

Roosevelt's high state of agitation soon eased. Russia made some concessions—this time intending at least partially to carry them out—and the president calmed down. Even minus the concessions, domestic political realities combined with his own conception of the nation's vital interests would undoubtedly have stopped TR from actually "going to extremes."

Meanwhile, Roosevelt vigorously defended his and Hay's policy against critics who charged it was serving Britain's and Japan's rather than America's interests. On June 22, 1903, he wrote to one such critic, his good friend Albert Shaw. "We have always recognized the exceptional position of Russia in relation to Manchuria," contended TR. "We have only insisted upon that freedom of access . . . for our commerce which has been guaranteed to us by the agreement of the whole civilized world including Russia." Moreover, Russia was guilty of "well-nigh incredible mendacity" and "seems to be ingeniously endeavoring to force us, not to take sides with Japan and England, but to acquiesce in their taking sides with us."[159]

Roosevelt was "astounded" by the viewpoint of a second critic, George F. W. Holls. "America's interest" and that alone was driving his East Asian policy, the president declared in a letter of July 4.[160]

The year 1903 ended with Anglo-American relations on a very sound footing. Great Britain had accepted American hegemony in the Caribbean, had emerged relatively unscathed (and much wiser) from the Venezuelan debacle of 1902-1903, and was now urging the United States to play an even more active role in the region. England and the United States were informally working together in pursuit of similar objectives in East Asia. American support during the Boer War remained a vivid memory among appreciative Britons. Linguistic and cultural affinity reinforced the bond forged by a recognition of common Anglo-American interests in a volatile world of great power rivalries. Most important, the thorny and dangerous Alaskan boundary dispute had at last been resolved satisfactorily. Theodore Roosevelt and the British leadership had laid a strong foundation for continuing cooperation and friendship. The special relationship had been secured.

PART II

Theodore Roosevelt and the
British Empire, 1904–1906:

SOLIDIFYING THE
SPECIAL RELATIONSHIP

Roosevelt, Britain, and the Great International Crises, 1904–1905

● ○ ●

Only in retrospect would it become apparent that the Anglo-American special relationship was secure by the end of 1903. To many observers at the time, two very serious international developments—the Russo-Japanese War of 1904-1905 and the Moroccan crisis of 1905-1906—seemed to threaten to undermine it. Britons in particular did not firmly grasp the strength of Theodore Roosevelt's friendship for their country until 1906 at the earliest.

Major reasons for this lack of comprehension were the continuation as foreign secretary of Lord Lansdowne until late in 1905 and, especially, the retention as Britain's ambassador to the United States throughout the period 1904-1906 of Sir Mortimer Durand. President Roosevelt had confidence in neither, and neither understood Roosevelt very well. To the degree that an Anglo-American conflict of interest existed during the Russo-Japanese War, therefore, it was difficult for the president to communicate its insignificance relative to the two countries' common interests in East Asia and to the larger framework of their relationship. Concerning the Moroccan matter, where there really was no Anglo-American conflict of interest, the British government was unable to keep abreast of the actual scope and meaning of TR's adroit and subtle diplomatic maneuvers. It took awhile for Roosevelt to end the confusion.

❧   ❧

The Russo-Japanese War grew out of Japan's anxiety over what it perceived as Russian encroachments on its interests in Manchuria and Korea. To Japan—unlike to the United States—Russian aggressiveness in this part of the world threatened *vital* interests. Counting on its alliance with Great Britain to deter France from joining in on Russia's side, Japan opened the war on February 8,

1904, with a sudden, devastating strike against the Russian fleet at Port Arthur in Manchuria.

Theodore Roosevelt keenly understood the complex international context of this war. While far more sympathetic to Japan than to Russia, he believed that it would be destabilizing for either combatant to be pushed entirely out of the East Asian picture. With France allied with Russia, and England allied with Japan, Roosevelt also perceived a danger to the new Anglo-French entente cordiale, which he strongly endorsed. An ambitious Germany, Roosevelt feared, would spare no effort to use the war as a vehicle for undercutting these bilateral arrangements and escaping its own isolation. From the outset TR was determined to do all that he could to bring the war to a satisfactory conclusion—a conclusion that would restore an East Asian balance of power (with as open a door in China as possible) and preserve the existing balance in Europe. The Treaty of Portsmouth of September 1905—a testament to Roosevelt's tenacity and diplomatic agility—essentially accomplished these objectives and stands as one of the foremost achievements of his achievement-filled presidency.

There were many instances of the coordination of German and American diplomacy during the Russo-Japanese War. However, as Raymond A. Esthus points out, "Roosevelt sought the Kaiser's cooperation" largely because "he viewed Germany as the most likely mischief-maker in the Far East." The "courtship" was "born, not of love, but of distrust."[1]

A genuinely common concern of the United States and Germany at the beginning of the war was the preservation of China's neutrality and administrative integrity outside of the war zone (expected to comprise Manchuria and Korea). Roosevelt responded affirmatively to a German proposal that he urge the belligerents and other powers to support this policy. The powers went along, although not before Lansdowne sent to Washington a series of telegrams asking for a delineation of the neutral territory.

Both the president's desire to encourage constructive behavior on the part of Germany and his irritation with Britain were evident in a letter to Secretary of War Elihu Root of February 16. It was true, Roosevelt explained, that the American "note on the neutrality of China" had been sparked by a German recommendation. However, the kaiser's "suggestion originally was in untenable form; that is, he wanted us to guarantee the integrity of China south of the latitude of the Great Wall, which would have left Russia free to gobble up what she really wanted." Thus, the United States had "changed the proposal by striking out the limitation." Still, TR was happy "to give Germany all credit for making the suggestion." As to England, "Lansdowne drove us half crazy with thickheaded inquiries and requests about our making more specific exactly what it was highly inexpedient to make specific at all."[2]

Germany, not unexpectedly, hoped to use the war to sow discord between Britain and the United States. Prior to the outbreak of hostilities, Roosevelt asked Henry White "to inquire confidentially" into charges by Speck von Sternburg that Britain was planning to take advantage of any fighting by seizing the Yangtze Valley and excluding other nations from commercial activity there. "I am informed by the highest authority," White answered from his diplomatic post in England on February 5, "that there is absolutely not a shadow of truth in the story."[3] Roosevelt thanked White on February 17 "for your information about England's attitude toward the Yangtze valley. It is borne out by her recent action." He added these brief observations: "Germany, I am bound to say, has acted very well. Was it not astonishing that the Russians should have shown themselves so utterly slack and unready?"[4]

Some of the most revealing correspondence of the Russo-Japanese War was exchanged between President Roosevelt and his close friend Cecil Spring Rice. During this period Spring Rice was England's first secretary at St. Petersburg. He was intensely suspicious of both Russia and Germany. Early in 1905 he visited TR as a special diplomatic emissary. Roosevelt was able to focus on the forest as well as the trees during the Russo-Japanese War, and the letters that passed between him and Spring Rice often addressed broad issues.

Following the onset of the war, a worried Spring Rice sent Roosevelt a letter marked by sarcasm, bitterness, trepidation, and even a bit of hysteria. Russia, the diplomat averred, blamed Britain and the United States for Japan's "monstrous" attack "against holy and just Russia" and intended to move against India in reprisal. "What is serious from a wider point of view is . . . the sure and steady movement towards common action of the two great military despotisms—Germany and Russia—on the common ground of spoliation." And there was a real possibility of an even larger continental coalition against Britain, for "the temptation for France to play jackal is so great."[5]

Roosevelt's frank and wide-ranging response was largely sympathetic, although less partisan on the war and somewhat skeptical about Spring Rice's predictions. The United States, TR declared, would stay neutral and was hoping that the war would be geographically contained and without heavy casualties. A Japanese victory—more likely in Roosevelt's eyes than a Russian one—would mean that "all of us will have to reckon with a great new force in Eastern Asia." Should the war result in a stalemate with both parties "fairly well exhausted, . . . peace will come on terms which will not mean the creation of either a yellow peril or a Slav peril." In either case, Roosevelt dismissed as highly improbable "such a continental coalition against England as that of which you speak."

This same letter was marked by an underlying tone of Anglo-American solidarity. Roosevelt was worried that the people of both Britain and the United States were too complacent about their security. England was in greater immediate danger, because it was so "spread out" and so much nearer to the European continent. But in both countries—even more so in America—"the spirit of mere materialism and shortsighted vanity and folly" is "at work for mischief." Roosevelt's bottom line on the Russo-Japanese War had a pronounced Anglo-American twist: "If new nations come to power, if old nations grow to greater power, the attitude of we who speak English should be one of ready recognition of the rights of the new comers [*sic*], of desire to avoid giving them just offense, and at the same time of preparedness in body and in mind to hold our own if our interests are menaced."[6]

Despite his skepticism, Roosevelt did transmit Spring Rice's concern about a continental coalition to Sternburg. The German ambassador assured him that there was no substance to the scenario "which is worrying Springy so much."[7] The signing of the Anglo-French entente cordiale in April 1904 made the realization of Spring Rice's dire forecast appear even more unlikely.

It was to Spring Rice that Roosevelt recounted in delicate detail in early June the substance of a recent meeting with Japan's ambassador to the United States, Baron Kogoro Takahira, and Baron Kentaro Kaneko, another prominent Japanese. TR had warned them, he told Spring Rice, about the "danger of Japan's becoming intoxicated" with its military successes. "The Japs interest me and I like them," he continued. "The good will of our people has been with the Japanese, but the government has been scrupulous in its impartiality between the combatants. . . . I see nothing ruinous to civilization in the advent of the Japanese to power among the great nations." Roosevelt also informed the British government, which opposed such interference, that he was not "laying the ground for any kind of interference by this government in the Far East."[8]

After receiving Spring Rice's reply—a long letter that ruminated gloomily on the implications of the Russian victory anticipated by the British diplomat[9]—Roosevelt sent it on to John Hay accompanied by an analysis far different from and more upbeat than Spring Rice's: "The contingency of which he does not take account is, I think, on the whole, the most likely to happen, namely, that the Japs will win out. . . . The Japs have played our game because they have played the game of civilized mankind." He additionally noted, in words that would not have displeased his English friend: "We may be of genuine service, if Japan wins out, in preventing interference to rob her of the fruits of her victory."[10] It would also not have upset Spring Rice that Roosevelt was at this time preparing contingency plans for a military response in the event of a Russian seizure of an American ship.[11]

Meanwhile, Germany continued its campaign to discredit Britain in the president's eyes. Sternburg claimed that the British were seeking a naval base, controlling the entrances to the Yangtze, on the Chu Shan Archipelago. Desiring to keep Germany in a cooperative frame of mind, Roosevelt stated simply: "I believe in the open door for the Yang Ste [*sic*] just as much as for Manchuria."[12]

On the final day of August in 1904, Spring Rice wrote to Hay, once again projecting a Russian triumph. "There never was, . . . since this world began, such a tremendous engine in one man's hand," he asserted in a misguided reference to the Russian army; it "seems very possible now" that Japan will be "badly broken."[13] But Roosevelt, having read this letter, was unconvinced; as he told Hay, "it is curious how they all think that Russia will win. I do not. Port Arthur has proved a harder nut than the Japanese anticipated, and the recent victory over Kuropatkin, though humiliating to Russia, was not decisive; but as yet I see no indication that Russia will win."[14]

The presidential campaign consumed most of Roosevelt's energies during the weeks before November 8. The day after his landslide victory over his Democratic opponent, Alton Parker, he sent Spring Rice a letter indicating unhappiness with Ambassador Durand and a desire to work more closely with Britain on the Russo-Japanese War. "Great Heavens," an exhilarated TR declared uninhibitedly, "how I wish you were Ambassador here! There are fifty matters that come up [*sic*] that I would like to discuss with you, notably about affairs in the Far East, and you could be of great service to your own country as well as to this country."[15]

Spring Rice's next communication continued the pattern of dark prognostications. Its alarmist tone was symptomatic of an escalating Anglo-German war scare. The diplomat expected Russia "to weaken or even crush Japan" and then "to offer her the friendship of Russia the brave and terrible foe, instead of that of England the faithless and the impotent friend." Next, Japan and Russia, in a settlement facilitated by Germany and France, would "dispose of and partition the good things of the East." In the meantime, it was the objective of the German kaiser—who, Spring Rice asserted, wielded "enormous influence" in Russia—"to have the hegemony of Western Europe and leave the East to Russia." The United States and Britain would be shut out of this process entirely and would have no choice but to accept an unpleasant *"fait accompli."* This letter from Russia also urged Roosevelt to send "a really good Ambassador here."[16] The president acted promptly on this last recommendation, appointing the highly regarded George von Lengerke Meyer.

Three very important letters of December 26-27 demonstrate—just as did his handling of the Alaskan boundary dispute—both Roosevelt's hands-on style when dealing with major diplomatic matters and his capacity and determination to master the complexities of multifaceted foreign policy issues. These letters also show that the president was taking Spring Rice's assessments very seriously. And they reveal, once again, an underlying assumption of an Anglo-American community of interests, alongside some doubts about British fortitude and about the quality of Britain's leadership.

First Roosevelt wrote to Meyer. TR asked his new appointee to observe carefully and to report regularly and in detail "everything we ought to know" about the war, about Russian diplomacy, and about Russia's internal turmoil.[17] Roosevelt emphasized that he needed to be informed promptly of "each phase of any new situation." The president noted America's long-standing difficulties with Russia over East Asia, not the least of which was Russia's "literally fathomless mendacity." The Japanese had displayed far greater integrity in their diplomacy, but Roosevelt was uncertain about Japan's "future attitude." In an evident reference to Spring Rice's forebodings, TR remarked: "It is always possible, though I think improbable, that Russia and Japan will agree to make up their differences and assume an attitude of common hostility toward America or toward England, or toward both. Under such circumstances they might have Germany or France or both in with them." And while "England is inclined to be friendly to us and is inclined to support Japan against Russia, . . . she is pretty flabby and I am afraid to trust either the farsightedness or the tenacity of purpose of her statesmen." Ultimately, the United States would have to keep building its navy and be prepared to face any foreign threats on its own.[18]

Henry White, singled out for praise in the letter to Meyer,[19] was a second recipient of a communication from TR. Roosevelt, who had heard that Spring Rice was to be in London, hoped that White could arrange for the Foreign Office to send the British diplomat to Washington for consultations. "There is no one in the British Embassy to whom I can talk freely, and I would like to have . . . the Foreign Office understand just my position in the Far East, and I would like to know what theirs is." Although the East Asian situation was fluid, "it would be an advantage" for both England and the United States to comprehend clearly the present outlook of the other. "Whether it is my fault or Sir Mortimer's, . . . our minds do not meet; and in any event I should be unwilling to speak with such freedom as I desire to anyone in whom I had not such absolute trust as I have in Spring Rice."[20]

A third and extremely long letter went to Spring Rice himself. Roosevelt had "very definitely concluded what I intend to do if circumstances permit" but was unwilling to commit these conclusions to writing. If "you could come over, . . . it would be very important for your Government."

TR then turned to an analysis of East Asian affairs, an analysis that assumed the complete harmony of Anglo-American interests. "Whether Russia or Japan wins," he wrote, "the victor will in the long run only yield to England or the United States substantially the respect which England or the United States [can] exact by power actual or potential." In any future settlement of the war, "we shall have to look sharply lest our interests be sacrificed. *If it were not for the attitude of England and the United States I think that Germany and France would probably have already interfered on Russia's side.*"

While Roosevelt acknowledged "that all four powers may . . . form a friendly agreement . . . against us"—as Spring Rice had been predicting—"I hardly believe this." In the first place, Japan was too "astute and farsighted" to place its trust in any agreement with Russia. In the second place, "so long as Japan takes an interest in Korea, in Manchuria, in China, it is Russia which is her natural enemy. Of course if Japan were content to abandon all hope of influence upon the continent of Asia and to try to become a great maritime power she might ally herself with Russia to menace the American, the Dutch, or perhaps the English possessions in the Pacific." But such a scenario struck Roosevelt as highly unlikely, for the more exposed Japan would "run . . . the entire risk and an altogether disproportionate share of the advantage would come to Russia. I hardly believe that Japan would fail to see this."[21] In any case, it was incumbent upon Britain and America to "keep our powder dry and our eyes open" and to be "ready to adopt whatever course is called for."[22]

After some initial hesitation, Lansdowne agreed that Spring Rice should visit the United States in January 1905. TR's friend was even instructed, on the initiative of Prime Minister Balfour, to sound out the president on the possibility of a formal alliance among Japan, Britain, and the United States to guarantee the integrity of China.

At the same time, Germany—unaware, naturally, of the position Roosevelt had taken—was still battling gamely to outmaneuver Britain and win the president's favor. Without saying so, Germany was also striving to stay on good terms with Russia and to keep England and Russia apart.

A fifteen-page letter from Sternburg of December 29, 1904—which actually arrived shortly after a cable from the kaiser dated January 5, 1905—laid out some (and betrayed others) of Germany's concerns and proposed a course of action. Sternburg informed Roosevelt of the kaiser's suspicion that peace between Japan and Russia would be followed by "the formation of a mighty coalition against the integrity of China and against the open door." To avert "this danger," Britain and France should "be induced to give a solemn declaration that neither of them, after the conclusion of peace where the belligerents will demand some territory or some advantages as recompensation, will likewise ask for such advantages." While on the one hand "Germany stands for the open door in Manchuria . . . just as in the Yangtze Valley and all over China," on the other hand "it would not be wise to attempt to prevent" Russia and Japan "from demanding some . . . territory." Regarding the German proposal for an Anglo-French declaration, "the Emperor is of the opinion that a move coming from you would promise best results."[23]

Roosevelt accepted the kaiser's recommendation, but with one noteworthy distinction. The president's message to the neutral powers called for respect for China's integrity *without* excepting Manchuria and *without* special status for the belligerents. It might thus be argued that he was as interested in pinning down Germany as he was Britain and France. The American circular was drafted just before the arrival of Sternburg's letter and dispatched just afterward. TR also responded directly to Sternburg, stressing German-American cooperation and refraining from acknowledging the variation between the German proposal and the U.S. circular: "I am in absolute and complete harmony with the views expressed by His Majesty as set forth in your letter, and acted on his suggestion even before your letter was received." Not wishing to mislead Germany beyond a certain point, however, Roosevelt also declared: "I shall be astonished if England is really intending to do as His Majesty thinks likely; but we shall soon see."[24] Six days later the president followed up, cabling Sternburg with word of satisfactory replies from the powers.[25]

While Spring Rice was en route to America, Roosevelt held a conference with Durand. The president outlined his views on appropriate peace terms (which included a Japanese protectorate over Korea and which soon were endorsed by the British government), was frank about his distrust of Germany, and, according to a surprised Durand, repeatedly and emphatically proclaimed that "England and America must stand together."[26] During this very same period in late January, meanwhile, the British government on its own initiative acquired "a comprehensive statement of Japan's peace terms," which, as Esthus explains, Durand promptly shared with TR "in strict confidence."[27]

It was only during the many hours when Spring Rice was with him, however, that Roosevelt could discuss these matters in depth and without inhibition. Hay recorded that the confidential British emissary brought word "that we had only to let them know our programme . . . to have them support our position." On the question of a formal arrangement, Roosevelt made clear to Spring Rice that "an alliance was impossible; that the less said about an understanding the better; but that our interests in the Far East being identical, there ought to be no difficulty in parallel action, and in timely exchange of views."[28] The British government—which had just embarked on an effort to renew the Anglo-Japanese alliance of 1902—was delighted by what Spring Rice reported upon his return. In essence, as George Monger observes, "an unofficial Anglo-American-Japanese accord had been established in the Far East."[29]

In a letter to Meyer of February 6, Roosevelt was entirely candid both about the character of his talks with Spring Rice and about his own outlook on the state of affairs in East Asia. Fundamental was the commonality of Anglo-American interests: "England's interest is exactly ours as regards this Oriental complication, and is likely to remain so." Hence, there should quietly be "a thorough understanding between us and the English as to what is happening." TR also expressed satisfaction with Germany's East Asian policy and a desire for continued U.S.-German cooperation.[30]

President Roosevelt, although a strong proponent of the Anglo-French entente cordiale in Europe, was uncertain about France's East Asian stance. "I cannot believe," he wrote to Charlemagne Tower, the American ambassador to Germany, "that England has any intention of taking part in the partition of China, but there certainly do seem to be suspicious indications as to the possible action of France."[31]

During the second half of the winter of 1905, major Japanese military successes, which Roosevelt followed with great interest, were proving the president right and Spring Rice wrong. On March 9 the newly reinaugurated TR wrote at length to George Otto Trevelyan, once again displaying his confidence in the discretion of his closest British friends and his sense of connectedness with England. In one section of this letter, Roosevelt was pointedly critical of what he perceived as Russia's diplomatic and military ineptitude.[32]

The same day the president also wrote to King Edward VII, who had been eagerly wooing him. He commented that the Russians should "have made peace before the Japanese took Moukden" and could expect increasingly worse terms if they waited for further defeats. In what must have been music to the king's ears, Roosevelt offered this sweeping and telling, even if slightly overdrawn, generalization: "In matters outside our own borders, we are chiefly concerned, first with what goes on south of us, second with affairs in the orient; and in both cases our interests are identical with yours."[33]

The British government naturally was pleased by the turn diplomatic and military events were taking. England's ally, Monger explains, "was inflicting a series of crushing defeats on Russia, the foe she had most dreaded; and if France and Germany intervened to aid Russia it was likely that the United States would come to the support of Britain and Japan."[34] Britain—unlike France, which was very worried about the possible impact a Russian defeat would have on the balance of power in Europe—saw imperial advantages in the diminution of Russian power and was entirely willing to allow the fighting to continue, at least for the time being. And when Durand told Roosevelt about the British intention to renew the Anglo-Japanese alliance, the president reaffirmed his views by expressing "great satisfaction."[35]

On the eve of an extended western hunting trip, Roosevelt sent Hay a letter that indicates the stepped-up pace of diplomatic activity regarding the Russo-Japanese war. "During the past week" TR had met privately with the ambassadors of Russia, France, Britain, Germany, and Japan. The United States joined the three last-named countries in opposing the application of multilateral international pressure for a settlement. In this letter Roosevelt also bemoaned the persistence of an Anglo-German war scare, which he attributed to "mutual distrust and fear."[36]

※

It was at this very time, April of 1905, that a second international crisis—this one focused on Morocco and in some ways even graver than the Russo-Japanese War—quickly assumed a share of center stage. It would hold this position until well into July. These months mark the first and more dangerous phase of the Moroccan crisis, during which Roosevelt's statesmanship contributed heavily to defusing tensions. TR managed nevertheless to keep his involvement completely out of the public eye.

The Anglo-French entente cordiale, formalized in April 1904, had as its basis France's backing for Britain's control of Egypt, in exchange for British support for French control of Morocco. (Spain acquiesced in these understandings in return for various concessions.) The entente was aimed at Germany and, indeed, heightened that country's sense of isolation. With Russia's defeats at the hands of Japan precluding meaningful Russian assistance for France, an emboldened German government decided to take a stand in North Africa. On March 31, 1905, the kaiser visited Tangiers and delivered a belligerent speech on behalf of an independent Morocco with an open door for commerce. The Sultan of Morocco, supportive of the German position, then issued a call for an international conference on the Moroccan question. Sternburg had brought the matter to TR's attention earlier that month, seeking American support for such a conference. Roosevelt pleaded political impediments but assured the ambassador that the American minister in Morocco, Samuel Gummeré, would work together with his German counterpart. The president's instructions to Gummeré, however, suggested priorities in conflict with German objectives; Gummeré was "to work with" the German minister, but only "so far as you can do so without causing friction with France."[37]

Secretary of War William Howard Taft served as Roosevelt's agent during the president's hunting trip. After meeting with Sternburg, Taft wrote to TR on April 5 and expressed his view that the American interest in an open door for Morocco is "not so valuable as to call upon us . . . to range ourselves on the side of Germany in this matter."[38] The president answered that "you are acting exactly right about Morocco. . . . There is at present nothing for us to do in Morocco."[39]

One year later, in an extraordinarily long letter (twenty-two pages, including copies of earlier correspondence, in *The Letters of Theodore Roosevelt*) to Ambassador to Britain Whitelaw Reid marked "absolutely private and confidential," President Roosevelt reviewed the entire Moroccan episode.[40] TR recalled and quoted from a letter of April 13, 1905, from Sternburg in which the latter asserted "that France would 'only continue her aggressive policy in Morocco, aimed at all non-French interests, if she feels sure that England will stand by her and eventually [show] herself ready to back her up by force of arms.' To this the Emperor added that he believed that the attitude of England would depend upon the attitude of the United States, and asked us to tell England that we thought there should be a conference."[41]

As Lewis L. Gould claims, Roosevelt "had little intention of allowing himself to be used against Britain in the interest of Germany."[42] Perceiving the escalating gravity of the situation (although not yet to the extent of granting the western bears a reprieve), TR, then in Colorado, replied to the German ambassador on April 20. Roosevelt did not "feel justified in entangling our Government," because "our interests in Morocco are not sufficiently great." Still, he did ask Sternburg to bring this letter "at once" to Taft and to "tell him exactly how far you want us to go in sounding the British Government. Meanwhile I shall write him . . . and shall suggest his finding out from Sir Mortimer what the British Government's views in the matter are."[43]

TR did write to Taft that same day. Here, naturally, the president was less guarded in expressing his outlook. Morocco was "the Kaiser's pipe dream." Roosevelt opposed American involvement, because the United States had other foreign policy priorities and "no real interest in Morocco." TR informed Taft that Sternburg would be calling on him. The president described himself as "sincerely anxious to bring about a better state of feeling between England and Germany," who were irrationally approaching "a condition of desperate hatred of each other." Roosevelt was, therefore, happy to serve as a messenger by endeavoring to ascertain "England's attitude in Morocco," which he then hoped to pass along to Germany. Taft was to be sure to explain to Durand "that we are taking sides neither with France nor Germany, but that we would like to convey Germany's request for information to England . . . simply from a desire to make things as comfortable between England and Germany as possible." However, Roosevelt cautioned, "if we find that . . . the English . . . think we are acting as decoy ducks for Germany—why we shall have to drop the business."[44]

Taft did communicate with the British ambassador, who then passed on to his government Roosevelt's desire for information. The essence of the British response, as Beale summarizes it, was a "determination to leave to France a free hand in Morocco" and "a statement that England did not intend to attack

Germany but was not afraid of Germany."[45] This "cool rebuff" by Lansdowne to Roosevelt, as Esthus argues, was primarily a result of Durand's and Lansdowne's continuing confusion regarding Roosevelt's diplomatic style and his policies. The foreign secretary accepted Durand's frequent charges that Roosevelt was prone to "impetuousness" and that he was an "unreliable" friend of England.[46] Lansdowne declared, quite astonishingly, in a letter to Balfour on April 27: "Roosevelt terrifies me almost as much as the German Emperor."[47]

With an edgy Germany seeing no progress, Sternburg again wrote to Roosevelt on May 13. In his aforementioned retrospective letter to Reid of April 1906 (hereinafter the "Moroccan review letter"), TR discussed Sternburg's memorandum. The ambassador was "insisting that there must be a general conference and complaining of England for opposing this conference, and stating that the latter would only drop her opposition if I would give her a hint to do so." The kaiser, TR quoted Sternburg, would feel obliged to consider the option of war against France if he were to gain "'no support . . . in connection with the open door and the conference.'" The German ambassador also renewed Germany's charge that Britain was involved in a conspiracy "aiming at the partition of China" (a notion that in TR's eyes was "mere lunacy"). This conspiracy, like the British stance against a conference on Morocco, would be dropped only if England "'finds out in time that it would be opposed by America.'"[48]

Meanwhile, even Spring Rice seems to have been worrying that Germany might be using Roosevelt to further its sinister purposes. He revealed his concern indirectly by writing to TR's wife Edith on April 26: "The Germans have taken advantage of [Russia's losses] to fall on the French. . . . I see that they are asking your President to join in a Conference which will bring the French to order. I hope he won't."[49]

Clearly disappointed by Spring Rice's implication, Roosevelt, back in Washington a week ahead of schedule, answered his friend at some length on May 13.[50] "Of course," this letter began, "in a way I suppose it is natural that my English friends generally, from the King down, should think I was under the influence of the Kaiser, but you ought to know better, old man."

Roosevelt proceeded to group Germany, Russia, and Japan in words that were particularly revealing: "I wish the Kaiser well. I should never dream of counting on his friendship for this country. He respects us because he thinks that for a sufficient object and on our own terms we would fight, and that we have a pretty good navy with which to fight. I shall hope that on these terms I can keep the respect not merely of Berlin, but of St. Petersburg and Tokyo both." Only "on these terms," contended TR, can "the respect of any one of the three . . . be kept. But by combining a real friendliness of attitude with ability to hold our own in the event of trouble coming, I shall hope to keep on good terms with all, and to lend some assistance to Japan in the present war in which I think she is right."

Roosevelt then shared with Spring Rice his near certainty that Germany had no "well-thought-out plans of an attack upon England." True, the kaiser was guilty of exasperating "sudden vagaries like this Morocco policy" and of "violent and often wholly irrational zigzags." Great Britain, however, had no cause to fear him. "You have told me that he would like to make a continental coalition against England. He may now and then have dreamed of such a coalition; and only last December your people were fully convinced he intended to make immediate war on them. But," TR reasoned, "it is perfectly obvious that he had no such thought, or he would never have mortally insulted France by his attitude about Morocco."[51]

Anglo-German antagonism, though, was showing no sign of abating. As a discouraged President Roosevelt wrote to Meyer on May 22, "it is probably hopeless to try to bring about a better understanding between England and Germany. I attempted it in vain."[52]

As the end of May approached, Germany stepped up its pressure on Roosevelt to obtain American support for a conference. It tried to threaten TR with a German-French war, realizing the president's strong desire to prevent such a development. And it tried, through Roosevelt, to threaten England—"if England is successful in causing the refusal of France to join in a conference to settle the Morocco question"—with a German "understanding with France with regard to Morocco" which would "form the basis of a new grouping of European powers," in the hope that this threat would break down Britain's opposition.[53]

As May 1905 was passing into June, the president held meetings with the ambassadors of the three key parties. Irritation with Britain was evident in the narrative Roosevelt offered in his Moroccan review letter. His thoughts on the European military balance also came through clearly. He described Sternburg and France's ambassador, Jean Jules Jusserand, as "sincerely anxious to avert" a Franco-German war. Sternburg, Roosevelt sensed, "did not approve of the action his Government was taking," whereas Jusserand shared "the general French indignation with Germany"; but "each thought that his own Government ought to make concessions to avoid the war." Hence Jusserand was willing to countenance an appropriately structured conference. From Durand, though, TR "could get very little. . . . He was bitter about Germany, and so far as he represented the British Government it would appear that they were anxious to see Germany humiliated by France's refusal to enter a conference," even if war resulted. "I did not think this showed much valor on their part," the president remarked, "although from their point of view it was sagacious, as of course in such a war, where the British and French fleets would be united, the German fleet could have done absolutely nothing; while on land, where Germany was so powerful, it would be France alone that would stand . . . the brunt of the battle." While desiring to help France, which he liked and considered "to be in the right, . . . I did not intend to take any position which I would not be willing at all costs to maintain."[54]

England had been resisting a conference and urging France to resist also. Reid—who had just replaced Joseph Choate as ambassador and who would rapidly establish himself in the president's eyes as a skillful, reliable, and insightful diplomat—cabled TR on June 5: "[Lansdowne] said would like indication views President. Regarded proposal joint action powers represented in Morocco unfortunate, and thought might have been planned to embarrass France."[55] Roosevelt cabled back the next day: "The President has informed German Ambassador that he does not see how America could join in any conference regarding Morocco unless France acquiesced. The President has also told Jusserand of this but does not desire publicity given to matter."[56]

Although the resignation from the French cabinet of Foreign Minister Théophile Delcassé on June 6 appeared to improve the chances for an accommodation, a suspicious England still refused to endorse a conference. Esthus comments on the misguidedness of the British stance: "If Lansdowne had perceived even an inkling of the service Roosevelt would render England and France in the Moroccan question, he should have been stumbling over himself in eagerness to bring the American President into the dispute." Fortunately, Esthus continues, Roosevelt's "irritation . . . did not restrain him from becoming involved in the Moroccan muddle. He was soon knee-deep in the controversy."[57]

A memorandum of June 11 from Sternburg was, TR later recalled, the element that convinced him of the need to take action. The German ambassador referred, mistakenly, to an impending "offensive and defensive alliance" between England and France "which would be directed against Germany" and claimed that Britain was motivated by hostility to "Germany's policy in the Far East." The final portion of the memorandum contained a mixture of foreboding and guarded optimism. If Roosevelt were to decide to "give a hint now in London and in Paris" that a conference would be "the most satisfactory means" of resolving the Moroccan issue, "you would render the peace of the world another great service, without encountering any risk. In case you should not feel inclined to take this step the Emperor believes that your influence could prevent England from joining a Franco-German war, started by the aggressive policy of France in Morocco." Sternburg did see "the retirement of Mr. Delcassé," whose "ruthless statesmanship" had "created" the Moroccan crisis, as a hopeful sign.[58]

The President of the United States, a gifted diplomatist and peacemaker, now stepped forward. In his Moroccan review letter, Roosevelt discussed his decision and the activity that followed it. "It really did look as if there might be a war, and I felt in honor bound to try to prevent the war if I could." For a Franco-German war, TR declared, would "be a real calamity to civilization." Moreover, in light of the ongoing Russo-Japanese War, "I felt that a new conflict might result in what would literally be a world conflagration." The president also became involved "for the sake of France." Through Jusserand — "one of the best men I have ever met" — he advised the French government "that British assistance could avail them very, very little" in a war against Germany, and that "it was eminently wise to avoid a war" by finding an honorable way of saving the kaiser's "self-esteem." Roosevelt foresaw a conference at which "practically all the powers" upheld France's position as greatly diminishing the likelihood of a German attack on France. "I explained," Roosevelt recalled, that "if necessary" at a conference "I would . . . take very strong grounds against any attitude of Germany which seemed to me unjust."[59]

On June 18 Sternburg wrote appreciatively to Roosevelt: "Your diplomatic activity with regard to France, the Emperor says, has been the greatest blessing to the peace of the world."[60] The French government — which, owing to Roosevelt's intimacy and forthrightness with Jusserand, was the only one of the three principal transatlantic governments to understand Roosevelt's thinking and his purposes — was also lauding the president, referring at one point to "the exceptional influence that his advice carries."[61] Meanwhile, the British government was being urged by TR not to stand in the way of France's agreeing to a conference, but England was otherwise largely excluded from the intensive diplomatic activity. This situation was primarily a product of unsatisfactory representation: "It was only because both Jusserand and Sternburg were such excellent men, that I was enabled to do anything at all in so difficult and delicate a matter. I could only have acted with men I was sure of. With such a tricky creature as the Russian, Cassini, for instance, I could have done absolutely nothing; and little or nothing with amiable Sir Mortimer."[62]

Still, Roosevelt strove to reassure the British leadership regarding the overall thrust of his Moroccan policy. On June 16 he wrote to Henry Cabot Lodge, his closest friend, then in England. TR asked Lodge to tell King Edward that while Roosevelt did hope "to remain on good terms" with the kaiser, the idea that he was under the kaiser's influence was "preposterous. . . . Neither you nor I are under British influence," he added, "but you need not mention this! *You can say with entire truth that we intend to have the United States and England work together, just as we are now working together in the Far East.*"[63]

Roosevelt was undoubtedly pleased to learn from Reid in a letter of June 17 that "persistent rumors that the Anglo-French entente was disappearing" in the wake of Delcassé's resignation were "entirely without foundation."[64] A second letter from Reid, this one dated June 23, appeared to validate the wisdom of bypassing Britain while arranging a conference. The British, Reid related, "regard the whole European situation at the present moment as critical in the extreme and are exceedingly careful about every new move." They seemed to have "confidence in the good faith of France, . . . are grateful for the assurance from the United States that we should not come into the Morocco conference unless it was satisfactory to France and mean themselves to stand by France . . . to an equal or greater extent."[65]

As for the convening of a conference, a serious obstacle remained. France was insisting on bilateral talks with Germany and German concessions on certain key Moroccan issues—including upholding rights gained by France in recent treaties with other powers—prior to the start of any international conference. Germany was refusing to accept such conditions. In a letter to Sternburg on June 25, President Roosevelt, who agreed with France on this important question, did his best to overcome Germany's concerns by downplaying them, by seeking to arouse guilt, by warning of disaster, and by throwing in criticism of England and flattery of the kaiser. France's acceptance of a conference was "a genuine triumph for the Emperor's diplomacy." Roosevelt had worked around Britain while arranging for the conference "because it seemed to me that it would be useless to speak to England; for I felt that if a war were to break out, whatever might happen to France, England would profit immensely, while Germany would lose her colonies and perhaps her fleet." TR proclaimed himself "a sincere admirer and well-wisher . . . of His Majesty." It was "of the utmost importance" that the kaiser's "power and leadership for good should be unimpaired. I feel that now, having obtained what he asks, it would be most unfortunate even to seem to raise questions about *minor details*, for if under such circumstances the dreadful calamity of war should happen, I fear that his high and honorable fame might be clouded."[66]

The president's plea was unsuccessful. He became so concerned about the possibility of German military aggression, he called in Durand and informed him that the United States would assume control of "Dutch possessions in the Western hemisphere" should Germany move against Holland.[67] Still, he remained determined to break the Franco-German deadlock. He offered a formula to Jusserand and Sternburg in the form of "a pencil memorandum as follows: 'The two governments consent to go to the conference with no program, and to discuss there all questions in regard to Morocco, save of course where either is in honor bound by a previous agreement with another power.'" The French and German governments—the latter also feeling pressure from Britain[68]—both assented to Roosevelt's implicitly pro-French proposal. He then indicated to these governments that he wanted "no publicity whatever" given to his involvement—and as it turned out, none was.[69]

In a dispatch to his government, the trusted Jusserand—with whom Roosevelt shared much of his Moroccan correspondence and who in turn allowed TR to preview much of his—praised the president for coming up with a "formula able to be accepted by the two countries, and which would at the same time pay heed to the pride of William II and our rights."[70] Through a Sternburg letter of June 28, Germany also "expresses highest satisfaction and gratitude with regard to the latest step you undertook in the interest of the Morocco conference."

By far the most consequential aspect of Sternburg's letter was an unsolicited pledge—in line with but exceeding the ambassador's instructions—that would be of great service to Roosevelt the following year: "The Emperor has requested me to tell you that in case during the coming conference differences of opinion should arise between France and Germany, he, in every case, will be ready to back up the decision which you should consider to be the most fair and the most practical."[71] TR, Esthus explains, "confided to Jusserand for transmission to Paris the exact words of Sternburg's statement."[72] Actually, as Serge Ricard carefully demonstrates, France had definitively undertaken to attend a conference even before learning of Sternburg's amazing pledge.[73] The true significance of Sternburg's assurance of June 1905 would be its impact on the course of the Algeciras conference of January-April 1906.

In a letter to Lodge of July 11, 1905, in which he discussed his secret mediation, Roosevelt basked a bit in his achievement: "I consider it rather extraordinary that my suggestions should apparently have gratefully been received by both sides as well as acted on." TR also outlined Sternburg's pledge, which he termed "a still more extraordinary thing," of which he intended to be "very wary of availing myself."[74]

There were some final hitches over the location of the conference and the identity of the French representative. Roosevelt, by now deeply engaged in bringing to an end the Russo-Japanese War, nonetheless found the time to help resolve these disagreements. And he viewed it as a hopeful sign that Germany had accepted the legitimacy of special French interests in Morocco so long as these did not conflict with the integrity of Morocco and the open door. By August 1905 the Moroccan dispute—in which Theodore Roosevelt had aligned himself solidly with Britain's interests despite sometimes unhelpful British behavior—seemed to be under control.

At the same time as the Moroccan crisis was starting to unfold in April 1905, Roosevelt was beginning to set the stage for his decisive diplomatic intervention in the Russo-Japanese War. Ambassador Takahira had recently informed him of Japan's requirements. In the April 20 letter to Taft in which the vacationing president instructed his agent with regard to Morocco, he also began to stake out his position on the shape of a Japanese-Russian peace: "I heartily agree with the Japanese terms of peace, in so far as they include Japan having the control over Korea, retaining possession of Port Arthur and Dalny, and operating the Harbin, Mukden, Port Arthur Railway. As to the proposed indemnity and the cession of Russian territory I am not yet prepared to express myself definitely."[75]

May of 1905 was a rather quiet month for TR's Russo-Japanese diplomacy, as the two combatants geared up for another major naval battle. Roosevelt was unhappy but resigned. "For the moment," he told Trevelyan in a letter of May 13, "I have been unable to do anything in getting Russia and Japan together." The Japanese, who had rejected TR's advice to make peace after their great victory at Mukden in March, "just at present . . . feel rather puffed up over their strength"; while Roosevelt found it "impossible to get . . . from the Russians . . . a straightforward answer at all."[76]

Roosevelt was hopeful that the British government would use its influence with Japan in support of his diplomacy when the time came, but he did entertain doubts. Perhaps he was trying to pave the way for such assistance when he wrote to Lodge in London on May 24: "When you see King Edward, explain my very real pleasure that we are able to work together in the Far East."[77]

The day before the commencement of the brief Battle of the Japan Sea, in which Japan's fleet annihilated Russia's, Roosevelt wrote Spring Rice in response to an accusation by Sternburg. According to the German ambassador, Spring Rice had been quoted by Japan "as authority for the statement that there was a Russian-German alliance against Japan and against England; that the German Emperor had really put Russia up to the war against Japan and was hostile to both England and Japan." Sternburg had flatly denied the allegation and had asked that Roosevelt inquire with Spring Rice as to "from whom you got your information."[78] While this accusation may have been unfounded, and while TR probably did not believe it, it is hardly inconceivable. That Spring Rice ignored instead of denying the charge is suggestive.

Talks about arranging a peace conference mediated by Roosevelt began with a private request from the victorious Japanese—who were feeling the strains of war despite their spectacular successes—on May 31. On June 5 the president wrote a detailed confidential letter to Lodge. First he commented on recent military events: "No one anticipated that it would be a rout and a slaughter rather than a fight; that the Russian fleet would be absolutely destroyed while the Japanese fleet was left practically uninjured." Then Roosevelt turned to developments on the peacemaking front: "At the Japanese Government's request, but to use their own expression 'on my initiative,' . . . I told Cassini to say to the Czar that I believed the war absolutely hopeless for Russia; that I earnestly desired that she and Japan should come together and see if they could not agree upon terms of peace; and that I should like to propose this if I could get the assent of Russia and then of Japan, which latter I thought I would be able to get." Roosevelt went on to tell Lodge that he was seeking to engage the assistance of Germany, France, and Britain. (At the end of his letter, TR looked beyond a Russo-Japanese peace, revealingly identifying the two countries he saw as the most likely adversaries for the United States: "We can hold our own in the future, whether against Japan or Germany, whether on the Atlantic or the Pacific, only if we occupy the position of the just man armed.")[79]

Responses from the combatants were encouraging. Immodestly but not exaggeratedly, Roosevelt summarized his accomplishment in a letter of June 11 to his son Kermit: "With infinite labor and by the exercise of a good deal of tact and judgment . . . I have finally gotten the Japanese and the Russians to agree to meet to discuss the terms of peace."[80] Days later it was decided that peace negotiations would take place in the United States.

Roosevelt's basic plan was to avail himself of all potentially useful diplomatic channels to advance his peacemaking endeavor. He sought to influence the Russian government to face reality not only directly but also through the good offices of Germany and France, both of which he found very supportive and helpful. Likewise, he attempted to encourage Japan to be moderate in its demands by his own direct efforts and by securing the assistance of Britain.

For its part, the British government was not disposed to be very cooperative. England viewed Japan's naval victories over Russia as decisively "altering the world balance of naval power" to England's benefit. More than ever before Lansdowne now saw the Anglo-Japanese alliance, whose renewal was then being negotiated, as the keystone of British foreign policy. He would take no actions that might conceivably jeopardize it. As Monger points out, "when Durand telegraphed on 13 June that the Americans would like Britain to urge Japan to moderate her terms, Lansdowne at once instructed him to do nothing of the sort."[81]

Through a letter of June 16 to Spring Rice, TR sought to overcome Britain's hesitancy to play a supporting role in his peacemaking effort: "I am bound to say that the Kaiser has behaved admirably and has really helped me. I hope that your people are sincerely desirous of peace and will use their influence at the proper time to prevent [Japanese leaders'] asking impossible terms." Roosevelt expected Germany and France to persuade Russia "to yield what she ought to yield; and England should make her influence felt in making the Japanese terms not so severe that Russia, instead of granting them, would prefer to continue the war."[82]

That same day Roosevelt wrote an extremely long letter to Lodge, providing a recent history of his Russo-Japanese peacemaking project. The president noted the balance of power as a factor in the timing of his diplomacy: "While Russia's triumph would have been a blow to civilization, her destruction as an eastern Asiatic power would also in my opinion be unfortunate. It is best that she should be left face to face with Japan so that each may have a moderative [*sic*] action on the other." TR asked Lodge "to let no one know that in this matter of the peace negotiations I have acted at the request of Japan and that each step has been taken . . . not merely with her approval but with her expressed desire. This gives a rather comic turn," Roosevelt added in an indication of displeasure with Britain, "to some of the English criticisms . . . that my move is really in the interest of Russia . . . , and that Japan is behaving rather magnanimously in going into it."[83]

The president asked Reid to try to clarify the British position and received a somewhat discouraging reply dated June 17. "I did not think it expedient to put to him bluntly the question whether they really wanted peace," the ambassador wrote, "but mentioned vaguely rumors from unofficial sources implying that they might at this juncture think something else of more immediate importance." Reid had told Lansdowne "that it would be a pleasure to cable something which would dissipate such ideas." Lansdowne had responded "that nothing could be more abhorrent to the British Government than the thought that any action of theirs could tend to prolong bloodshed. *But* he immediately added it would be quite another thing at this stage to bring any pressure upon Japan — especially when they did not even know what Japan's terms were going to be."[84]

TR at first did not comment on the substance of Reid's remarks, possibly because the Moroccan matter was his principal focus during most of June. On June 30 Roosevelt merely thanked Reid for giving him "the exact information I wanted as to the attitude of the English Government on peace," noting how "difficult" it had been for him "to obtain a very clear idea from Durand."[85]

But dissatisfaction with the British stance was apparent when the president, now more fully informed, wrote to Reid again a week later. Roosevelt felt confirmed in his "belief that the English, as I think rather *shortsightedly*, are entirely willing, and perhaps a trifle more than willing, to have the war go on." The president found it "hard to believe that the British seriously think that the Japanese intend to take Vladivostok and give it back in a spirit of magnanimity and I do not believe the Japanese are serious if they ever told the British so. *My own opinion is that it would be better for England to have peace come with Russia face to face with Japan in east Siberia. Under such circumstances the Japanese alliance would be a guarantee against any Russian move toward India or Persia.*" But should the Japanese "take east Siberia they will have done all the damage they could ever do Russia, and Russia would have little fear of them. Indeed," Japan's own best interest would be served "if she now comes to terms and gets an indemnity. If she goes on with the war . . . she will spend a great deal of money and treasure, and may very possibly reduce Russia so that she simply cannot pay an indemnity."

Unfortunately, TR continued, neither Japan nor Britain could be forced "to follow any course other than that which each thinks for its interest, and this is right and proper enough I suppose—although personally I cannot help thinking that it is possible to combine firm adherence to what is ultimately good for one's own country with a genuine desire to try to act decently toward the rest of the world and to help it so far as may be."

What Roosevelt assumed, he then told Reid unhappily, was "that England has indirectly encouraged Japan to ask for so much that peace will be improbable." In marked contrast, "both the German and the French governments will earnestly endeavor to get Russia to come to terms. The Emperor has behaved very well about this."[86]

The British government was obviously worried that its unwillingness to lean on Japan might be harming its friendship with the United States. It assigned to Spring Rice, then in London, the task of explaining the British viewpoint to President Roosevelt. The explanation took the form of a lengthy memorandum, dated July 10, to the Department of State (whose head, Hay, had just passed away), cast as a response to Roosevelt's letter to Spring Rice of June 16. TR's friend undertook to portray Britain as a strong backer of Roosevelt's diplomacy but also as a selfless ally of Japan with little room to maneuver. "Germany and the United States," Spring Rice declared, "are bound to no one and can offer impartial and friendly advice to both parties in the struggle." Even France "can offer advice to Russia," because theirs was "a limited Treaty which does not comprise the Far East." Great Britain, in contrast, "cannot exercise pressure" on Japan to take any step believed by Japan to be contrary to Japanese interests; for "we are sworn allies." Spring Rice assured Roosevelt "that your action in promoting peace meets with the most cordial appreciation in England." And he left open the possibility of British assistance: "Lord Lansdowne in reading your words repeated the phrase, 'I hope the English people will use their influence *at the proper time* to prevent the Japanese from asking impossible terms.'" That time had not yet arrived, but it "may come. When it does, . . . the American Government . . . can be quite sure that their opinion will receive the fullest and friendliest consideration." Spring Rice went on to claim, somewhat disingenuously, that on the whole the course of the Russo-Japanese War had been disadvantageous to Britain's international position.[87]

Roosevelt wrote back on July 24, making clear in a long letter that he was *not* convinced by Spring Rice's arguments. "I wholly fail to understand," the president admonished, "the difference . . . which makes it proper for France, the ally of Russia, to urge Russia in her own interest . . . to make peace, and which yet makes it improper for England, the ally of Japan, to urge Japan in her own interest . . . to make peace."

Yet this same letter also offered revelations that demonstrated Roosevelt's continuing confidence in British trustworthiness and in the solidity of the Anglo-American friendship. "As soon as this war broke out," he confided to his friend, "I notified Germany and France in the most polite and discreet fashion that in the event of a combination against Japan to try to do what Russia, Germany and France did to her in 1894,[88] I should promptly side with Japan and proceed to whatever length was necessary on her behalf. I of course knew that your Government would act in the same way, and thought it best that I should have no consultation with your people before announcing my own purpose." The president additionally revealed what "Lansdowne and Balfour . . . ought to know" but "must keep absolutely secret, namely, that I undertook this move to bring about peace negotiations only at the request in writing of Japan, made immediately after Togo's victory." And the Japanese had given Roosevelt "explicit assurances that they did not want east Siberia" or any other "Russian territory aside from Sakhalin."

Perhaps most important, Roosevelt—who seems to have concluded that British policy would be of limited significance to the peace negotiations, and who realized that this disagreement over the proper British role was interfering with Anglo-American harmony—sent out a reassuring signal that the dispute was, after all, not really a big deal. He described "most of this talk as to what England ought to do" as "academic, because I think the Japanese have probably made up their minds just about what they will accept and what they won't."[89]

Several days later the president corresponded with Reid along these same lines. Overly cautious Britain should make an "effort to get Japan to do what is best both for herself and for England, and that is to make peace instead of insisting upon terms which may prolong the war for an indefinite period." But "I do not think it is very important, for I am not at all sure that the Japs will be influenced by anyone."[90]

By openly doubting the necessity of a British contribution, Roosevelt succeeded in quieting some of the fears entertained by British policy makers, who despite their own reticence about approaching Japan genuinely wished him well in his peacemaking venture. Feeling confident that he could achieve peace without British help, as early as late July Roosevelt began to turn his attention in East Asia, insofar as Britain was concerned, back to the two English-speaking nations' fundamental unity of interests.

Actually, a letter sent that spring to the Japanophile writer George Kennan had previewed the stance the president would assume in the summer. Writing from Japan on March 30, Kennan had argued for "an alliance with Great Britain and Japan, in order to maintain peace, order and justice in this part of the world." He had gone on to contend that "it is a political mistake to cling to a maxim or principle formulated more than a hundred years ago, regardless of the complete change which has since taken place in world conditions."[91] TR answered that Kennan was "talking academically," because the political obstacles would be insurmountable. "Mind you," Roosevelt then revealingly added, "*I personally entirely agree with you.*"[92]

Soon afterward, in June, TR had been pleased to learn from Lodge in England that a "new treaty with Japan was proceeding well."[93] In July the president sent Secretary of War Taft to Japan, where the secret Taft-Katsura understanding was arranged on July 27. In addition to the agreement on mutual respect for Japanese hegemony in Korea and American control of the Philippines, Taft more generally informed the Japanese that "wherever occasion arose appropriate action of the Government of the United States, in conjunction with Japan and Great Britain for such purposes, could be counted on by them quite as confidently as if the United States were under treaty obligations."[94] On July 31 Roosevelt approvingly cabled Taft as follows: "Your conversation with Count Katsura absolutely correct in every respect. Wish you would state to Katsura that I confirm every word you have said."[95] Ricard is certainly correct to characterize the Taft-Katsura agreement as "new evidence of the Anglo-American rapprochement and of a community of interests between the two nations, a new sign of 'Anglo-Saxon' cooperation."[96]

Still, it would be misleading to say that the president was now ready to let England completely off the hook. From Oyster Bay on August 3, he again criticized British timidity in a letter to Reid: "Yesterday Durand was here to say that the British wished peace between Russia and Japan, but did not feel they could bring pressure on Japan. I told him just what I wrote you in my last letter—that if they really wished peace, they would advise the Japs, in their own interest, to make it, and not to insist on too heavy terms." Then Roosevelt continued in a more positive vein: "He showed me the draft copies of the Anglo-Japanese Treaty, which I think a good thing."[97]

Lansdowne had been hoping, and was relieved, to receive Roosevelt's endorsement of Britain's arrangement with Japan. The revised and strengthened Anglo-Japanese treaty of alliance was signed on August 12. Britain and Japan not only recognized, but promised to help defend against rival powers, Japan's special position in Korea and England's in India.

But August was the decisive month in Roosevelt's peacemaking enterprise—the Portsmouth conference having convened in New Hampshire on August 9—so he had little to say about the Anglo-Japanese pact until after the conclusion of Russo-Japanese peace. Especially during the second half of the month, Roosevelt was constantly engaged in an uphill struggle to bring the warring parties to terms. He was closely involved with every detail of the negotiations. He met frequently with the Russian and Japanese delegates. To influence Russia he also worked through Sternburg and Jusserand to secure the assistance of Germany and France, and communicated regularly with the able Ambassador Meyer in Russia. Pressure on Japan, however, came almost entirely from Roosevelt himself.

By August 23 an impasse loomed, and a worried Roosevelt renewed his previously futile effort to persuade Britain to join him in coaxing Japan. "In my judgment," he wrote to Durand, "every true friend of Japan should tell it as I have already told it, that the opinion of the civilized world will not support it in continuing the war merely for the purpose of extorting money from Russia." Japan had every right to insist on holding Sakhalin Island but was unreasonable to demand in addition "a heavy indemnity." As TR saw it, "the greatest act of friendship which the friends of Japan can at this time show her is to do as I have already done, and urge her in her own interest not to follow a course which might do her great damage, and can do her no real benefit. . . . I wish your people could get my views."[98]

The final sentence of this letter to Durand certainly appears to betray irritation and frustration. That Roosevelt was not optimistic about obtaining Britain's support—or, for that matter, about obtaining a peace settlement—is further indicated by a letter he wrote to Henry White the same day: "I am in the last throes of trying to get the Russians and Japanese to make peace. . . . The English government has been foolishly reluctant to advise Japan to be reasonable, and in this respect has not shown well compared to the attitude of the German and French governments in being willing to advise Russia. I have not much hope of a favorable result, but I will do what I can."[99]

A few days later a breakthrough occurred in the peace talks, but little thanks to the British. Roosevelt's appeal to Lansdowne through Durand had extracted from the foreign secretary only a privately recorded, timid excuse for inaction: "Our advice would not be taken and would be resented."[100] Japan, TR informed the kaiser in an August 27 telegram requesting the German ruler to communicate encouragingly to the czar the latest development, had consented to abandon its insistence on an indemnity "reluctantly and only under strong pressure from me."[101] Agreement between the combatants came on August 29.

(That very day Roosevelt summarized his perspectives on Russia and Japan in a letter to scholar-diplomat William W. Rockhill. He had found the Russians extremely "untruthful" and "arrogant." He had been "pro-Japanese before, but after my experience with the peace commissioners I am far stronger pro-Japanese than ever."[102])

⫷   ⫸

The British government, needless to say, was relieved and congratulatory. It also endeavored to grab a little credit and to place its conduct retrospectively in the most favorable possible light. On August 29 President Roosevelt passed along to Durand, for his government, copies of some key pieces of correspondence with Meyer and with Baron Kaneko. In his reply Durand asserted "that you gave [the Japanese] the advice which was best for their interests" and offered "my most hearty congratulations on the wonderful success of your efforts to end the war." Lansdowne, Durand noted, "repeated to Tokyo the telegram I addressed to him on receipt of your letter of the 23rd August, and . . . the Japanese Government . . . referred to it as having been considered in the final council held at the palace."[103]

Any bad feelings toward Britain entertained by President Roosevelt dissipated rapidly after the attainment of Russo-Japanese peace. In a letter to Durand of September 8, Roosevelt asserted that the updated Anglo-Japanese treaty "was a powerful factor in inducing Japan to be wise and reasonable."[104] Along similar lines a magnanimous and forgiving TR wrote to Ambassador Reid three days later: "The Kaiser stood by me like a trump. I did not get much direct assistance from the English government, but I did get indirect assistance for I learned that they forwarded to Japan my note to Durand, and I think that the signing of the Anglo-Japanese treaty made Japan feel comparatively safe as to the future."[105]

On September 16 Roosevelt communicated again with Reid, noting appreciatively that "the English had given me the abstract of the treaty some weeks ago and I received the text of it both from them and from the Japanese just before the signing of the peace."[106] This treaty, TR declared in a letter to Arthur Lee of September 21, "is a very good thing for England and Japan; and I think it is a decidedly good thing for the United States and the rest of the world. . . . I have no patience with the people who clamor about its showing a 'degenerate' condition in England." It would be foolish "to refuse to recognize the growth and the power of Japan, and to make use of it when recognized."[107] Insofar as Japan in particular was concerned, Roosevelt told John St. Loe Strachey, "the Anglo-Japanese alliance really guarantees her against any offensive return by Russia."[108]

In the meantime, congratulations for the president's achievement, which would soon bring him a Nobel Peace Prize, poured in from around the world. In the forefront of those acclaiming Roosevelt were his English friends. Strachey captured their sentiments well: "I simply cannot resist the temptation to tell you how proud and delighted I (like all your friends) was by your great triumph. I know you will value the personal triumph as less than nothing, but your friends have a right to rejoice in that as well as in the fact that you have given peace to the world."[109]

It is telling that the autumn of 1905 began with Theodore Roosevelt pursuing policies both in Asia and in Europe that were fully in accord with British objectives. Britain's unhelpfulness (stemming from conflicting perspectives and priorities, but not interests) during the Russo-Japanese War and its obstructive approach (stemming from severe misapprehensions regarding TR) during the first phase of the Moroccan crisis would seem to have given Roosevelt good reason to begin backing away from the evolving Anglo-American partnership. Yet nothing of the sort occurred; indeed, the partnership weathered these two challenges with flying colors. TR simply did not permit what he saw as irksome and ignorant British behavior to undermine the firm foundation of Anglo-American harmony that he had been instrumental in laying prior to these crises. Friendship with England, Roosevelt emphatically believed, was a valuable asset for the United States in a dangerous world, and he was not about to lose sight of this overridingly important consideration.

CHAPTER

4

Roosevelt, Britain, and Rival Powers,
October 1905–December 1906

● ○ ●

A complex system of great power rivalries remained in place in the aftermath of the Russo-Japanese War. Of the other five major powers, Theodore Roosevelt viewed with the least favor Germany, which he saw as threatening world peace even in the near term, and the vanquished Russia, more a future than a present menace. On the other side, he could imagine no serious conflict between the United States and Great Britain and was becoming increasingly fond of France, which he also considered unthreatening and whose entente with England he approved of unreservedly. Roosevelt's perspective on Japan was the most complicated. While full of admiration for the Japanese and their rapid rise to international prominence, and while informally allied with Britain and Japan in East Asia, he was nevertheless wary of the possibility of trouble between Japan and his own country, a wariness that intensified sharply when anti-Japanese activity on the West Coast began to get out of hand in October 1906. With all these powers, including Germany, the president would continue actively to endeavor to maintain amicable relations.

In such a world there could be no relaxation of America's naval preparations. During the winter of 1905, Roosevelt had written several letters on this issue, outlining a viewpoint that would carry over unchanged into the postwar period. "Our navy is excellent," he asserted in one letter to George von Lengerke Meyer. "We will have no trouble with Japan, or with Germany, or with anyone else if we keep our navy relatively in as good condition as it is now, and if we continue to show that we are honestly and sincerely desirous to deal honorably and fairly by all nations."[1] The United States, TR told George Otto Trevelyan, "is on good terms with other countries, and I believe it wishes to act fairly and justly, and yet to keep a sufficient armament to make it evident that the attitude proceeds not from fear, but from the genuine desire to do justice."[2] In a letter of March 9 to his military friend Leonard Wood, Roosevelt proudly reviewed his accomplishments as a navy-building president and then declared: "This navy puts us a good second to France and about on a par with Germany; and ahead of any other power in point of materiel, except, of course, England."[3] And British naval predominance was something to be encouraged, not feared.

In July of 1906 President Roosevelt was delighted to learn in detail the extremely impressive results of recent naval target practice. Lieutenant Commander William S. Sims illustrated with statistics that "we are now distinctly ahead of the British Navy," particularly with the all-important 12-inch guns.[4] Roosevelt responded with evident satisfaction: "I have not the least fear of our getting into trouble with a foreign power" as long as the United States has the naval equipment it needs and its personnel perform so well. Then he added a revealing inquiry that recalled a letter of September 1903, cited earlier: "I am interested in your comparisons of our work with that of the British Navy. What do you know of the German and Japanese work of the same kind?"[5]

That September TR sharply linked the issues of America's naval strength and its relations with potential enemy powers in a letter to Harvard's president, Charles William Eliot. Roosevelt described the American navy as "an infinitely more potent factor for peace than all the peace societies . . . in the United States," and derided "our professional peace demagogs. . . . Within the last few years," he asserted, "we should have been, and very possibly would be now, within measurable distance of war either with one great European or one great Asiatic power, if it were not for the condition of our navy."[6]

Theodore Roosevelt's growing admiration and enthusiasm for Japan during the Russo-Japanese War, the sense of history that helped shape his perspective, and an important aspect of his thinking on the subject of race are all captured well by a letter he wrote to David Bowman Schneder, an American missionary in Japan, in June 1905. "As for their having a yellow skin," Roosevelt remarked, "if we go back two thousand years we will find that to the Greek and the Roman the most dreaded and yet in a sense the most despised barbarian was the white-skinned, blue-eyed, and red or yellow-haired barbarian of the North—the man from whom you and I in a large part derive our blood." Ancient Greeks and Romans would have responded with incredulity to the notion that "this northern barbarian should ever become part of the civilized world," because "the racial difference seemed too great." The Japanese of today "are a wonderful and civilized people, who . . . can teach this people as well as learning from it, and who are entitled to stand on an absolute equality with all the other peoples of the civilized world."[7]

This enthusiasm for Japan, however, was tempered by uncertainty and concern. Japan "is now a great power and will be a greater power," Roosevelt told Cecil Spring Rice that same June. "I cannot pretend to prophesy what the results, as they affect the United States, Australia, and the European powers with interests in the Pacific, will ultimately be. I believe that Japan will take its place as a great civilized power of a formidable type, and with motives and ways of thought which are not quite those of the powers of our race." TR's policy was to "treat the Japanese in a spirit of all possible courtesy, and with generosity and justice," while "constantly" building the navy and keeping every ship at the ready. "If we follow this course we shall have no trouble with the Japanese or anyone else." On the other hand, if Americans "regard the Japanese as an inferior and alien race, and try to treat them as we have treated the Chinese; and if at the same time we fail to keep our navy at the highest point of efficiency and size—then we shall invite disaster."[8]

It would have been out of character, of course, for Theodore Roosevelt to sit back and await Japan's response to its newly won power and prestige. The balance of power now prevailing in East Asia was clearly to be preferred over the Russian takeover of northern China that had seemed likely before the war. Whereas Russia was, in TR's eyes, brazenly acquisitive and utterly untrustworthy, Japan could be worked with. By supporting Japanese rule in Korea and by upholding Japan's special position in nominally Chinese Manchuria, Roosevelt hoped not only to offset Russian power but also to win Japan's friendship and to steer its energies away from the Pacific, where there was potential for a clash with the United States.[9]

The total approval of the revised Anglo-Japanese treaty expressed by TR during August and September of 1905 has been noted. His enthusiasm did not flag in succeeding months. On October 7 he told Secretary of War William Howard Taft in reference to the Taft-Katsura agreement that "our position could not have been stated with greater accuracy," and went on to assert that the United States shared "the same interests with Japan and Great Britain in preserving the peace of the Orient."[10]

Roosevelt wished to be absolutely sure that Britain, Japan, and France understood his thinking. When a letter from Spring Rice described how the Russian diplomat Sergei Witte "had told the French Ambassador that the United States sympathized with Russia in being hostile to the Anglo-Japanese alliance," TR moved "to set things right." He asked Ambassador Jean Jules Jusserand, as he explained to Spring Rice in a letter of November 1, to inform the French government that Roosevelt "entirely approved of the treaty . . . and believed . . . it was advantageous to the peace of Asia, and therefore, to the peace of the world." The president also contacted Ambassador Kogoro Takahira, and he directed Taft to tell Prime Minister Taro Katsura of the strong U.S. support for "the Japanese position about Korea as set forth in the Anglo-Japanese treaty, and as acknowledged in the treaty of Portsmouth."[11] And Secretary of State Elihu Root spoke to Ambassador Durand, who cabled Lord Lansdowne Roosevelt's assurance "that he was and always had been unreservedly in favor of the Anglo-Japanese treaty."[12]

As a result of both his diplomacy and his reading of Japanese interests, Roosevelt was confident that a Japanese assault on the Philippines in the near future was extremely unlikely. On January 22, 1906, he laid out his view in a letter to a worried Leonard Wood. America's "first-class fighting navy" was a powerful deterrent, and in any case Japan had no intention of attacking. "Her eyes for some time to come," argued TR, "will be directed toward Korea and southern Manchuria." An unsuccessful strike would cost Japan "everything she has gained in the war with Russia," while a successful one "would make this republic her envenomed and resolute foe for all time," would kill the Anglo-Japanese alliance, and would bring together "Russia, the United States, and very possibly Germany and France to destroy her in the Far East." There was, Roosevelt concluded, "not the slightest chance of Japan attacking us in the Philippines for a decade or two, or until the present conditions of international politics change."[13]

Despite his generally favorable outlook on Japan and his relatively benign image of its international designs, Roosevelt persisted in categorizing Japan as more similar to Germany than to Britain. This Japan-Germany identification, grounded in uncertainty and suspicion, was succinctly expressed in one sentence of a letter to Whitelaw Reid of June 27, 1906: "In the same way [as with Germany] my policy with Japan is to be scrupulously polite, to show a genuine good will toward her, but to keep our navy in such shape that the risk will be great for Japan if it undertakes any aggression upon us."[14]

The passage on October 11 by the San Francisco School Board of a resolution segregating Asian schoolchildren marked the beginning of a troubled new phase in U.S.-Japanese relations. It led to a well-conceived and ultimately successful fourfold policy, whereby President Roosevelt sought to make clear to the Japanese government his strong disapproval of Californian behavior (which he characterized as "purely local"[15]), to pressure the Californians to end the blatant discrimination, to work with Japanese officials to find an amicable way to halt the flow of Japanese laborers to the American mainland, and to strengthen the navy. The navy, he hoped, would serve as a deterrent, but he also wanted to be ready in case the situation should spin out of his control.

Throughout the hot-and-cold Japanese-American immigration-racism crisis of 1906-1909, President Roosevelt stayed in close touch with British (and Canadian) officials in an effort to forge a common position and strengthen the American hand. He aimed to build on the part of Japan's ally, Britain, a sense of identification with the problems the United States was confronting. On December 18, 1906, he wrote to British Foreign Secretary Sir Edward Grey—by then in office for a year, and in whom TR found a far more kindred spirit than he had ever found in Lansdowne—a frank and revealing "private" letter focused on Japanese questions. While Russia's "intention to try another throw with Japan for supremacy in easternmost Asia" justified Japan's continuing military preparations, it was possible that these preparations also contained an element of aggressive intent. Regardless, "the labor question, which is itself only one phase of the race question," was "the immediate source of danger" in U.S.-Japanese relations. "People of cultivation and self-restraint" from Japan "can get on perfectly well" with similar people from America, Europe, and Australia. In contrast, however, "most American and Australian . . . and . . . Canadian workingmen will object in the most emphatic way to Japanese laborers coming among them in any number. I think," TR confided, "they are right in so objecting." Roosevelt's plan was to seek an agreement, perhaps informal, on the mutual exclusion of Japanese and American laborers. He hoped thereby to resolve "the only radical cause of friction between the two countries. The Japanese may be reluctant to enter into such an agreement. If so, there is trouble ahead, altho[16] probably not very serious trouble in my time."[17]

Similar themes marked a letter sent to John St. Loe Strachey on December 21. The California problem, Roosevelt observed, presents "a very difficult task. Some day or other it is possible your Government will be brought face to face with the same question. Australia will not have the Japanese, and British Columbia is tending to feel the same way." Roosevelt then referred to his special message to Congress of December 18, in which he had threatened to use "the armed forces of the country to protect the Japanese if they were molested in their persons and property." The dual purpose of this message had been to send a clear signal to Californians and other Americans and "to soothe" the "wounded feelings" of Japan. Achieving this latter objective, TR hoped, would advance the prospects of the U.S.-Japanese reciprocal exclusion agreement he was seeking.[18]

The depth of Anglo-German hostility remained a concern of TR during the four-month interval between the signing of the Treaty of Portsmouth and the commencement of the Algeciras conference. "Each side," Roosevelt said to Reid in a letter of September 19, 1905, "busily accuses the other of every kind of dark and sinister design, and in some cases I know that each side is hopelessly and foolishly wrong." The president urged the ambassador "to try to bring about a better feeling between England and Germany . . . if the chance comes to you in any way."[19] And several weeks later Spring Rice, one of the leading purveyors of accusations of the sort to which Roosevelt was referring, received an indirect admonition. TR called the current Anglo-German hostility "very unfortunate." He was, moreover, "obliged to say that as far as my own experience goes, I have heard just as wild talk, just as inflammatory and provocative talk, among Englishmen as among Germans. Whether anything can ever be done to reduce the feeling I cannot say. If I can do it I certainly will."[20]

The Algeciras conference of January–April 1906, however, was to demonstrate that President Roosevelt had not wavered at all in his determination to constrict the growth of German power and to advance the interests of Great Britain, which in his mind meant advancing those of America as well. What Raymond Esthus accurately terms Roosevelt's "vigorous and decisive" role in bringing the conference to a successful conclusion served not only the cause of peace but also that of the Anglo-French entente cordiale.[21] (As shown in chapter 3, such a characterization would be equally applicable to TR's earlier role in arranging the conference.)

A clear hint of what was to come was given by Roosevelt in a letter of August 23, 1905, to Henry White, later to be appointed chief American delegate: "I want to keep on good terms with Germany, and if possible to prevent a rupture between Germany and France. But my sympathies have at bottom been with France and I suppose will continue so. Still I shall try to hold an even keel."[22]

On November 28 Secretary of State Root sent a letter (accompanying his formal instructions) to White that provided an even fuller preview. "You may find," Root wrote after thorough consultation with the president, "that France has legitimate interests by reason of her proximity to Morocco . . . which ought to be specially safe-guarded. . . . We do not wish to oppose a provision for the protection of those interests." Germany, on the other hand, lacked any "just ground on which she could make" any special claim. "While we are friendly to Germany, and wish to remain so, we regard as a favorable condition for the peace of the world, and, therefore, for the best interests of the United States, the continued entente cordiale between France and England, and we do not wish to contribute towards any estrangement between those two countries."[23]

Thus, as Esthus contends, 1906 began with Roosevelt "firmly aligned" not only with the Anglo-Japanese partnership in East Asia but also with the Anglo-French entente cordiale in Europe.[24] The American role at the Algeciras conference in Spain would provide a clear confirmation that this was, indeed, the U.S. stance.

The Roosevelt administration justified its participation in the conference —
a source of domestic controversy once it was revealed during the fall of 1905 —
on the basis of America's being a signatory to the Treaty of Madrid of 1880 and
consequently a power with treaty rights in Morocco. Certainly TR would have
found another explanation had this one been unavailable.

Still, Roosevelt's initial hope was that the American part could be a relatively
limited one. The president, kept "thoroughly posted" as to developments
through White's "numerous private telegrams" addressed to Root,[25] and also in
frequent direct contact with Ambassadors Jean Jules Jusserand and Speck von
Sternburg, offered this observation in a letter to Meyer of February 1: "I do not
know that I can do anything if the circumstances become strained at Algeciras,
and of course I want to keep out of it if I possibly can."[26]

He could not "keep out of it." On February 19 the president, prompted by
White, proposed to Germany via a letter from Root to Sternburg that the primary responsibility for the police forces of the eight principal Moroccan ports
be entrusted jointly to France and Spain, which would be obligated to maintain
the open door.[27] Germany protested that the American plan "would be tanta-
mount to a Franco-Spanish double mandate and mean a monopoly of these two
countries, which would heavily curtail the political and the economic positions
of the other nations."[28]

Between hearing from the German government and composing his formal
reply, an unhappy Roosevelt wrote a letter to Oscar S. Straus, soon to be
named secretary of commerce and labor, which revealed deep suspicions of and
concerns about Germany. Evidently TR's outlook on Germany was moving
toward that of the British "alarmists" whose "hysteria" he had only recently been
decrying. "Modern Germany," the president asserted, "is alert, aggressive, military and industrial. It thinks it is a match for England and France combined in
war, and would probably be less reluctant to fight both those powers together
than they would be together to fight it. . . . It respects the United States only in
so far as it believes that our navy is efficient and that if sufficiently wronged or
insulted we would fight." Roosevelt wanted "to stay on good terms with
Germany" but was convinced that to "betray weakness" would be counter-
productive to that objective.[29]

On March 1 TR brought Reid up to date regarding his pessimistic reading
of the state of affairs. He lamented that "things do not look as well as they
should in Algeciras." He informed Reid of the German pledge "to follow my
directions" delivered by Sternburg the preceding June; but "as my experience
has always been that a promise needlessly entered into is rarely kept, I never
expected the Kaiser to keep this one, and he has not." Both Germany's "naval
authorities" and its "military authorities" believed "firmly . . . that she can

whip both France and England," rendering it less likely that Germany would come to terms. Roosevelt was hopeful nonetheless—if hardly optimistic—that "we may . . . get an agreement."[30]

Actually, the German government had already decided ultimately to accept a compromise solution favorable to France. But neither Roosevelt nor the delegates at Algeciras seem to have realized it, and on March 5 White telegraphed Root "that a rupture was imminent."[31]

The president, through his secretary of state, proceeded to communicate with the German government, quoting from Sternburg's promise of June 28, 1905, and attempting to portray his proposed solution as a balanced one and even as a sort of victory for German diplomacy. The proposal embodied in Root's letter of February 19 would entail "an abandonment by France of her claim to the right of control in Morocco answerable only" to Britain and Spain, as France "will have accepted jointly with Spain a mandate from all the Powers, under responsibility to all of them for the maintenance of equal rights and opportunities." Such a solution, this proxy letter of March 7 went on to declare, would mark "the triumph of German diplomacy in this matter."[32]

Germany now altered its line of resistance and retreat by backing a new Austrian plan to assign four ports to a French police administration, three to a Spanish one, and Casablanca to Holland or Switzerland. Even Britain found this proposal entirely reasonable and pushed France to accept it. Throughout the Algeciras conference, in fact, England's new Liberal government had been struggling with a somewhat contradictory policy. On the one hand, the government was committed—as its first priority—to standing with France "even to the length of war" against Germany. On the other hand, Britain strongly desired to avoid such a war and believed that France should be flexible up to a point. The Austrian suggestion reflected substantial concessions by Germany, and England encouraged France to look upon it as an honorable solution to the Moroccan crisis.[33] But the French delegation—having learned that Roosevelt had passed on to the French government via Jusserand the invoking of Sternburg's pledge—held out against it.

The same Theodore Roosevelt who had earlier set a goal of moderating Anglo-German hostility now came down forcefully on the side of an insistent France instead of a more accommodating England (although in the end Britain adhered to its priorities and also backed up France's hard line). His opposition to the Austrian proposal was adamant. Root told Sternburg in a letter of March 17 that the United States saw in this proposal the "potential partition of the territory in violation of the principle upon which we have agreed with Germany." To have France or Spain control seven ports and Switzerland—"either in its own interest *or in the interests of any other powers*"—control one meant "the creation of three separate spheres of influence, with inferior right and opportunity on the part of all other powers."[34]

Then TR stepped up the pressure. According to his own recollection, he apprised Sternburg verbally "that if the Emperor persevered in rejecting our proposals and a breakup ensued, I should feel obliged to publish the entire correspondence, and that I believed that our people would feel a grave suspicion of Germany's justice and good faith; but that if the Emperor would yield to what seemed to me our very fair proposals, I should not publish any of the correspondence, and would endeavor in every way to give Germany full credit for what was done."[35] The next day, March 19, Germany capitulated. And Roosevelt, as promised, was generous with encomiums for Germany and its leadership.

In his Moroccan review letter to Reid, Roosevelt described how his anti-German perspective had remained steady during February and the first half of March: "Germany sought to impress us with the fact that all the other powers but England were in her favor," but Russia and Italy also communicated to the United States anxieties about Germany's position. "We became convinced that Austria was a mere cat's paw for Germany, and that Germany was aiming in effect at the partition of Morocco, which was the very reverse of what she was claiming to desire. She first endeavored to secure a port for herself, and then a separate port, nominally for Holland or Switzerland, which we were convinced would, with the adjacent Hinterland, become in effect German." At this maneuver France understandably balked. "Our view," Roosevelt acknowledged, "was that the interests of France and Spain in Morocco were far greater than those of other powers."[36]

Apparently, then, it was not the prospect of the partitioning of Morocco that troubled Roosevelt but rather the prospect of Germany's participation in such a partitioning. Indeed, when the final agreement called for the police of six of the eight ports to be under the administration of only France (four) or only Spain (two) — contrary to the American concept of joint administration for all eight — Roosevelt readily went along.[37]

Toward the end of his Moroccan review letter, the president once again showed his frustration with the continued presence of Sir Mortimer Durand in the British embassy: "I was having very intimate negotiations with Germany and France through Sternburg and Jusserand here; and if Durand had been worth anything I think that England might have helped me a little. But . . . Durand, though a high-minded, honest fellow, is simply entirely incompetent for any work of delicacy and importance." This opinion, Roosevelt claimed, was shared "precisely" by Jusserand and Sternburg and Root.[38]

Another letter to the tactful and trusted Ambassador Reid written a couple of months later made even clearer that TR had considered Britain to be a central player on the Moroccan stage, and that the degree of his contact with the British government had been limited only by the poor quality of its diplomatic representation: "I think you ought to let . . . the King and Sir Edward Grey . . . both know confidentially of the utter worthlessness of Durand. . . . There is no harm in their knowing how strongly I feel; and especially that if he had been such a man as Spring Rice or such a man as Speck or Jusserand, *I would have told him at every turn just what was being done, and the Foreign Office at London would have known every move.*"[39] Once again what is striking, however, is how little Roosevelt allowed this very real and by now long-standing impediment to timely and meaningful communication to affect American policy, which in a sense, as noted earlier, was even more pro-British than British policy itself.

On April 8 Henry White composed a sixteen-page handwritten letter to Roosevelt, providing what TR called "a good bird's-eye view" of the Algeciras conference.[40] In one portion of the letter, White emphasized the importance of American participation, linking it directly to an outcome that he viewed as entirely satisfactory. "Any opinion we expressed (which I did privately very often)" was considered seriously "and often adopted, and there were many occasions during the three months just ended on which my influence, privately exercised, with both French and German Delegates, has brought about pacific terminations to crises which seemed on the point of becoming acute." Additionally, the French government's knowledge "that you were exercising your influence with the German Emperor prevented the French from acceding—as they were advised privately by their friends to do—to . . . the 'Austrian proposal,' . . . and thereby gave time for your opinion as conveyed personally and in Mr. Root's note to Speck of March 17th, to bear fruit and eventually to cause the Germans to give way about the eighth port." The United States, White maintained, could hardly have done better: "All that Germany legitimately claimed in behalf of all the Powers in the way of equality of economic rights etc. has been granted; . . . France's special position has been recognized"; and yet France "has been stopped from taking practical possession of the country which was, I think, her eventual intention as a result of the Anglo-French agreements of 1904."[41]

Roosevelt, greatly impressed with White's diplomatic talents and work habits even before Algeciras, was extremely pleased: "You have done admirable work. You have added to the reputation of our country and you have filled to perfection a difficult and trying position." (To share with White "what has gone on on this side of the water," the president sent him a copy of his Moroccan review letter to Reid, of which Meyer and Root also were recipients.)[42]

No doubt of particular interest to Roosevelt was White's discussion of the Anglo-German (and, related inextricably, the Anglo-French) interplay at the conference. Germany's wildly inaccurate reading—in two opposing directions—of the British position could not have surprised TR, who, however, also had to be encouraged by the somewhat calmer and more rational state of Anglo-German relations prevailing by the close of the gathering.

"Fortunately for France," White narrated, delegate Paul Révoil "was well and most loyally sustained by the British Delegate, Sir Arthur Nicolson, who often by good advice kept him from making tactical mistakes and who backed him up every time . . . and thereby demonstrated the absolute solidity and good faith of the Anglo-French understanding which was a disappointment to the Germans." Germany had believed that its position was "so much more to the interest of the British mercantile and commercial policy" than the position of France, and that therefore "it would not be difficult to detach England from anything but a perfunctory support of the French at the beginning of the Conference. And the contrary was, I think, the greatest of all German disappointments.

"When they found the real state of the case," the chief American delegate continued, "the Germans went to the other extreme and imagined that England intended breaking up the Conference in the hope of driving France into war, the result of which would be the destruction by England of the German fleet, and it took some work to disabuse the Germans of this idea. I strongly combated it every time" it was raised by the German representatives, "and I am glad to say that before the Conference ended they admitted that they were convinced I was right and that the role played by England was a useful one."

Consequently, White was hopeful "that one of the results of the Conference may be an improvement in the relations between Germany and England; and Nicolson seemed rather disposed to agree with me. The Germans would now like this, having ascertained that they have been unable to insert a wedge—much less to make anything like a cleavage—in the Anglo-French understanding which at the conference had all the effect of an alliance." And Germany had an additional reason to seek to "improve her relations with England, as another prospect of the near future is, I have little doubt, and partly as a result of—or rather somewhat accelerated by—the Conference, an Anglo-Russian 'rapprochement'."[43]

However pleased he may have been to see the threat of an Anglo-German war recede, President Roosevelt continued to view Germany warily. "I like the Kaiser and the Germans," Roosevelt declared in his letter to Reid of June 27. "I wish to keep on good terms with them." But he also believed it was "even more important that we should keep on good terms or better terms with the English." He pursued this theme some more later in the letter: "As for the Germans, I really treat them much more cavalierly than I do the English. . . . I am very polite with [the kaiser], but I am ready at an instant's notice to hold my own."[44]

One notable outgrowth of the Moroccan episode was a strengthened fondness for France on the part of TR. Whereas neither the president's alienation from Durand nor his friendship with Sternburg appears materially to have affected his perspectives on the countries they represented, Roosevelt does seem to have upgraded his opinion of France directly as a consequence of his closeness to Jusserand. The intimacy of their relations throughout both stages of the Moroccan crisis was quite extraordinary. "My relationship with you," Roosevelt wrote to Jusserand on April 25, 1906, "has been such as I think has very, very rarely obtained between any ambassador at any time and the head of the government to which that ambassador was accredited." And their bond had been proving extremely "advantageous" to both their countries.[45]

More significant, of course, was that the apparently durable Anglo-French entente meant France more than ever was "playing our game." And the Portsmouth Treaty had earlier ended the possibility of complications developing during the Russo-Japanese War on account of the Franco-Russian alliance.

In retrospect, it is entirely conceivable that the Moroccan crisis, at either stage, could have brought on World War I approximately nine years before it actually began. The peaceful resolution of this crisis—particularly as this resolution occurred on Roosevelt's terms—stands as yet another tribute to his remarkable statecraft.

⤡   ⤢

At no time during his presidency did Theodore Roosevelt view the major powers as equally "civilized," but by 1906 the distinction in his mind between the more civilized and the less civilized seems to have been growing. Several letters written that August display this tendency.

On August 6 TR wrote a cautionary letter to Andrew Carnegie on the subject of the upcoming Hague conference. "It would be a fatal thing," Roosevelt proclaimed, "for the great free peoples to reduce themselves to impotence and leave the despotisms and barbarisms armed." Peace and, even more important, justice are "favored by having those nations which really stand at the head of civilization show, not merely by words but by action, that they ask peace in the name of justice and not from any weakness."[46] "The great free peoples" and "those nations which really stand at the head of civilization" certainly meant the United States and Great Britain and probably meant France too. No others need yet apply.

The next day the president sent Reid a more specific message for the British government on the same subject. Roosevelt supported taking "real steps" to reduce "the chances of war among civilized peoples." It would, however, amount to "idiotic folly . . . if the free peoples that have free governments put themselves at a hopeless disadvantage compared with military despotisms and military barbarisms. I should like to see the British navy kept at its present size, but only on condition that the Continental and Japanese navies are not built up. I do not wish to see it relatively weaker to them than is now the case."[47]

In a letter sent to White a week later, Roosevelt reflected on his relations with the kaiser and on broader questions of international peace and disarmament. The kaiser was "a big man, and on the whole a good man," but carried the burden of "intense egoism." Roosevelt had endeavored to be friendly to the kaiser and his country and had been careful to avoid giving him "legitimate offense." Even "where I have forced him to give way I have been sedulously anxious to build a bridge of gold for him, and to give him the satisfaction of feeling that his dignity and reputation . . . were safe." TR described his influence over the German ruler as "very limited."

This discussion led into a rather contradictory paragraph on disarmament and peace:

> Therefore I have no knowledge whether I could accomplish anything whatever with the Kaiser. I will try, of course. That I can work with France and England I have no doubt; but I would like [War Secretary Richard] Haldane and Grey and would like the French people to understand that in my judgment it is essential that we should have some fair guaranty that a given policy will be carried out in good faith. I should feel it a great misfortune for the free peoples to disarm and leave the various military despotisms and military barbarisms armed. If China became civilized like Japan; if the Turkish Empire were abolished, and all of uncivilized Asia and Africa held by England or France or Russia or Germany, then I believe we should be within sight of a time when a genuine international agreement could be made by which armies and navies could be reduced so as to meet merely the needs of internal and international police work. But at present we are far from any such ideal possibility, and we can only accomplish good at all by not trying to accomplish the impossible good.[48]

The contradictions contained in the foregoing excerpt provide an opportunity to analyze a significant nuance in Roosevelt's thought at the time. On the one hand, he wanted France and Britain to join him in insisting on enforceable guarantees from any other parties to an accord to control armaments, because it would be "a great misfortune for the free peoples to disarm and leave the various military despotisms and military barbarisms armed." Based on many other such references, his obvious implication here is the threesome of Germany, Japan, and Russia. Yet the next sentence announces that these three countries are civilized after all — that the real problem is the weak, "uncivilized" political entities of Asia, Africa, and elsewhere. It simply is not plausible, however, that Roosevelt was reluctant to cut back on armaments because he feared a challenge from China or Turkey. No, it was the Germans, Japanese, and Russians who posed the meaningful threat that the "free peoples" contemplating a reduction of or limit to their armaments had to consider seriously. For Theodore Roosevelt, military strength was a *necessary* but not a *sufficient* condition to enable a major nation to be classified as highly civilized, and perhaps momentarily he himself lost sight of this important aspect of his outlook. Germany, Japan, and Russia occupied a sort of gray area in his thinking on civilized and uncivilized peoples. And they were the major objects of his concerns relating to the advisability of disarmament agreements, because they possessed formidable military power and were deemed capable of misusing it.

George Otto Trevelyan received a less ambiguous letter, dated August 18, from TR. After condemning "the preposterous apostles of peace," Roosevelt offered words that clearly indicated Germany and Japan as the focus of his concern: "If we can come to an agreement to stop the general increase of the navies of the world, I shall be very glad. But I do not feel that England and the United States should impair the efficiency of their navies if it is permitted to other Powers, which may some day be hostile to them, to go on building up and increasing their military strength."[49]

With 1906 drawing to a close, the Anglo-French entente remained in Roosevelt's mind a bulwark against German military adventurism. In a letter to TR of December 4 (in which the reference to Russia gave evidence of Henry White's perspicacity), Foreign Secretary Grey outlined the British view of the entente cordiale. "France," Grey wrote, "is now very peaceful, and neither aggressive nor restless." One welcome by-product of the entente was "good and easy relations for both of us with Italy and Spain. . . . To complete this foundation, we wish to make an arrangement with Russia that will remove the old traditions of enmity." Should the entente somehow fall apart, Germany would "be in a position . . . to make herself predominant upon the Continent. Then, sooner or later, there will be war between us and Germany, in which much else may be involved." Therefore, "to secure peace, we must maintain the Entente with France."[50]

The president was entirely in accord with Grey. "I feel," he declared, "that your good relations with France are an excellent thing from every standpoint."[51]

The English-Speaking Peoples
and Their Tightening Bond

● ○ ●

THEODORE ROOSEVELT AND BRITISH NORTH AMERICA

During the middle years of Theodore Roosevelt's presidency, some additional degrees of awkwardness (on top of those associated with the
Russo-Japanese War, the Moroccan crisis, and the Durand problem)
were injected into Anglo-American relations as a result of complications in U.S.
dealings with Newfoundland and the Dominion of Canada. Attempts to arrange
reciprocity (bilateral tariff reduction) treaties with these two self-governing
colonies and the seemingly permanent issue of the Newfoundland fisheries both
posed difficulties. Roosevelt's handling of these questions sheds further light on
the Anglo-American special relationship as it matured during this period.

⟪ ⟫

Actually, a reciprocity treaty worked out by Secretary of State John Hay and
Newfoundland Premier Sir Robert Bond had been before the Senate since
November of 1902. Senator Henry Cabot Lodge, who earlier had indicated to
Hay that he would go along with the popular treaty, had instead assumed the lead-
ership of the opposition in response to vehement protests from New England,
especially Gloucester, fishing interests. Hay, according to Charles S. Campbell,
Jr., "never forgave him for what he believed to be an unscrupulous betrayal."[1]

Although favorable toward the Newfoundland treaty, President Roosevelt
did not become actively involved in reciprocity matters until 1904. That year the
possibility of reciprocity with Canada came under serious discussion. TR supported the idea but was not optimistic about its chances. He explained in a letter of August 29 to Nicholas Murray Butler: "I hope we can get reciprocity with
Canada. I am doubtful about it," because "the same New Englanders who are

howling for it would violently object to having it if we put in the things that Canada will want."[2]

The following month Hay, sensitive to the president's friendship with Lodge, wrote to TR indicating that the State Department would not provide materials to reciprocity advocates fighting the Massachusetts senator: "I still think Lodge and Moody and Hale were wrong in killing the Newfoundland Treaty—but there are other considerations more important—and of course we all want Lodge reelected."[3] Roosevelt's reply betrayed the beginnings of an irritation with his friend Senator Lodge that would increase in succeeding months: "I have had to say far less than I wished about reciprocity, simply because I cannot get Senators who ought to—(and that means of course the people behind them)—to take a really broad-minded view of the question."[4]

The reelected Roosevelt took up the reciprocity issue in earnest with a series of letters on November 12, 1904. In one he asked Senator and Vice President Elect Charles Warren Fairbanks to explore prospects for a reciprocity treaty with the Canadian government. Acknowledging the slim likelihood of success, TR nonetheless declared: "I am most anxious that a resolute effort should be made."[5]

Also advocating on behalf of the long-dormant Newfoundland pact of 1902, Roosevelt did his best to nudge Lodge into constructive behavior: "Do not make the amendments any more drastic than you are absolutely obliged to, and of course remember that the Gloucester people cannot be trusted to establish the minimum they ought to receive. . . . Where there are good objections to the treaty, amend it; but show a real purpose of trying to get it."[6]

In a third letter, this one to Senator Winthrop Murray Crane, TR discussed reciprocity and then intriguingly—unfortunately without elaboration, although one senses a reasoning based on considerations of strategic naval advantage—compared Canada and Newfoundland. The latter, he contended, was "from the larger standpoint of international politics . . . far more important to have our ally."[7]

Fairbanks's talks with Canadian officials quickly proved fruitless. The Canadians simply were not very interested in reciprocity with the United States. A mildly disappointed Roosevelt, averse to doing any damage to Canadian-American (and Anglo-American) relations, rejected suggestions that the United States publish in righteous indignation the Fairbanks report. "If we publish it," he wrote to Lodge on January 6, 1905, "with a flourish of trumpets as showing that we have put the Canadians in a hole, I believe the impression will be rather that we have tried to play sharp politics than that we have tried to make a treaty." Besides, the president added, "I am much more concerned about the arbitration treaties."[8]

That January saw the Senate amend the Newfoundland treaty, contrary to TR's advice to Lodge, decisively to the disadvantage of Newfoundland, which then naturally rejected it. After his arbitration treaties had been similarly emas-culated, Roosevelt threw up his hands in disgust. "It does seem to me that it would be foolish and undignified to make any attempt to negotiate any further arbitration or reciprocity treaty, with the Senate occupying its present position," he remarked in a letter to Silas McBee, a southern editor. "The individual Senators evidently consider the prerogative of the Senate as far more important than the welfare of the country."[9]

The Roosevelt administration's ill-fated quest for reciprocity agreements with Newfoundland and Canada was played out as a "neighborhood" issue and had no significant impact on the state of Anglo-American relations. Likewise, the British refusal in 1905 to consider revising the regulations governing the killing of fur seals in the Bering Sea (the United States was recommending revisions that would help it preserve the herds) did not lead to recriminations.

⚔   ⚔

An offspring of the failed Newfoundland treaty, however, created a potentially more dangerous problem for the U.S.-British friendship. In retaliation for the Senate's ill treatment of the Hay-Bond Treaty, Newfoundland began in 1905 to place restrictions on American fishing rights in its waters. What Alexander DeConde correctly identifies as "the longest dispute in the history of American for-eign policy"—a problem with eighteenth-century roots—was heating up again.[10]

When Lodge, on behalf of his fishing constituents, urged Roosevelt to take action, he instead got a lecture. "It was a mighty unfortunate thing that we ever undertook" treaty negotiations, lamented the president in a letter of May 15, "and we are all of us to be blamed for having gone into the matter, for as it has turned out, there was not the slightest chance of making any treaty which Newfoundland would be willing even to consider." And on top of questionable American political behavior, Roosevelt implied that "our fisherfolk" were con-ducting themselves rather provocatively.[11]

With tensions rising along the Newfoundland coast, Lodge continued to press Roosevelt. In a letter of August 16, the senator charged Newfoundland with having passed a "very unfriendly" law and Premier Bond with planning to deny Americans fishing rights secured by the 1818 treaty. "They must not inter-fere" with those rights, he insisted. He called for TR to send "a small cruiser" permanently to the area, suggesting that such a move would prevent unpleasant incidents and thereby help "to keep our relations with England on the best pos-sible footing."[12]

Despite being focused at the time on the Russo-Japanese peace talks, President Roosevelt seized this opportunity to admonish Lodge indirectly, to spell out his thinking on the whole reciprocity-fisheries situation, and to make clear that he had no intention of permitting matters to spin out of control. America's course, he argued, "has given deep offense to Newfoundland, and most naturally. If the circumstances had been reversed, this country in its turn would have been deeply angered." The United States should "try to show such patience and forbearance as possible until the exasperation caused by our very unfortunate action has worn off. We have to pay the penalty for our unwisdom and not commit any further act of unwisdom under the irritation caused by the foolishness with which the Newfoundlanders have met our folly." Because the United States had "not been in the habit of having a warship on the Newfoundland coast, to send one now would be a provocative to trouble. . . . The showing made by Gloucester" had been unimpressive, and "we should avoid all appearance of bullying or of inviting trouble. If trouble comes it is far better that it would come under circumstances which prevent any blame for exciting it from attaching to us."[13]

In addition to the temporary discord between the two close friends, TR and Lodge, a couple of points are evident. First, America's conduct had, to his dismay, violated Roosevelt's own standards of good-faith dealing. Second, Newfoundland—and Britain—would have found it difficult to locate a more lucid defender in the United States.

Roosevelt's communications with Lodge on the reciprocity-fisheries issue soon took on the friendly and conciliatory tone that usually characterized their correspondence.[14] On September 6 the president simply and without a trace of bitterness updated the senator: "I have asked Root to take up the Newfoundland matter as soon as possible. If we can tide over this year I think the soreness in Newfoundland will have worn off and we can then come to a decent understanding."[15] Concerning reciprocity with Canada, Roosevelt told Lodge on November 1 that he continued to favor it, even to the point of "complete commercial union between Canada and the United States." However, he believed, the Canadians were far less well disposed toward reciprocity than he was, and besides, "nothing could be done with Canada until we first tried whether [sic] we could get a treaty with Newfoundland."[16]

In May of 1906 Newfoundland placed additional restrictions on American fishermen. This time the president became upset. He was, he informed Ambassador Whitelaw Reid on June 27, "very much afraid that the English are drifting where we shall have to send a warship up to Newfoundland to look after our interests."[17] Reid and Foreign Secretary Grey then proceeded to arrange a compromise modus vivendi, which Bond and most Newfoundlanders believed to be unfair to them. Fishing went forward under the terms of this agreement.

At no time did Roosevelt find the idea of sending an American warship to Newfoundland waters in any way appealing. By the middle of 1906, Anglo-

American relations were as friendly as they had ever been. The letter to Reid of June 27 was undoubtedly designed to spur the British government to act to relieve the building tension in the northwestern Atlantic and eliminate even the remote possibility that a show of force would be required.

Letters to George Otto Trevelyan and Sir Edward Grey demonstrate that TR was actually quite sensitive to and was increasingly identifying with the awkward position in which Newfoundland was placing Britain. "I have far too keen a sense of our own limitations as a national government," he told Trevelyan on September 9, "to fail to recognize similar limitations in Great Britain."[18] Intensifying problems that autumn with West Coast racism and its international repercussions served only to strengthen the president's feeling of a shared dilemma with the other great English-speaking power. "I have the keenest sympathy with your difficulties," he confided to Grey in a private letter of December 18, "when you come to handle matters in which your colonies take a violent and wholly nonimperial interest; for we of course have exactly the same experience when, as in this Japanese matter, the question is one with which a particular State regards itself as peculiarly concerned."

Roosevelt closed his letter to Grey by indicating his determination not to allow the fisheries dispute to disrupt Anglo-American harmony and his confidence that the British shared his view of the question: "I am sure your Government and ours are approaching the Newfoundland and similar matters in exactly the same spirit; and I believe we shall be able, by the exercise of tact and patience and forbearance, to come to an accommodation."[19] And TR reiterated this determination as the new year began when he declared in a letter to Arthur Lee: "I do not intend to permit even our insistence upon the rights as to which we can not very well back down ever to make any serious trouble between you and us."[20]

THE ENGLISH-SPEAKING PEOPLES AND THEIR EMPIRES

Throughout 1904-1906 Theodore Roosevelt maintained his adherence to the belief that imperial rule, properly conducted, over "uncivilized" peoples was a blessing for such peoples and for the world as a whole. And he continued to perceive Great Britain as a foremost civilizing power.

With the issue of Filipino independence under debate during the presidential election year of 1904, Roosevelt penned these general observations in a letter drafted for (but never sent to) Charles Eliot: "Freedom does not mean absence of all restraint. It merely means the substitution of self-restraint for external restraint, and therefore, it can be used only by people capable of self-restraint; and they alone can keep it, or are ethically entitled to it. . . . There are

nationalities and tribes wholly unfit for self-government; there are others sin-
gularly fitted for it; there are many between the two extremes."[21] As an example
of the first group, TR referred in a letter to his son Kermit of November 1906
to "the turning of Haiti into a land of savage negroes, who have reverted to
voodooism and cannibalism."[22]

The British Empire was decidedly a force for civilization. "It was a good
thing for Egypt and the Sudan, and for the world," the president wrote to Cecil
Spring Rice at the beginning of 1904, "when England took Egypt and the
Sudan. It is a good thing for India that England should control it."[23]

Roosevelt's observations on the benefits of imperialism often encompassed
other imperial powers (including those occupying the "gray area in his thinking on civilized and uncivilized peoples" discussed in chapter 4[24]) in addition
to Britain. Responding in September 1905 to a letter from Carl Schurz on the
subject of disarmament, TR offered historical perspective on the linkage
between peace and the military side of imperialism. "Hitherto," he contended,
"peace has often come only because some strong and on the whole just power
has by armed force, or the threat of armed force, put a stop to disorder." (Later
in this letter TR indicated that by "just power" he also meant "civilized
power.") Roosevelt put forward several examples, including France in Algiers,
Russia in Turkestan, and England in the Mediterranean and in Burma.[25] The
following year he reiterated this view in a letter to Andrew Carnegie: "As
things are now it is for the advantage of peace and order that Russia should be
in Turkestan, that France should have Algiers, and that England should have
Egypt and the Sudan."[26]

Japan also merited inclusion. "I think Japan has something within itself
which will be good for civilization in general," Roosevelt stated in a letter to
Trevelyan written just after the signing of the Treaty of Portsmouth. "If she is
treated fairly and yet not cringed to, I believe she will play her part honorably
and well in the world's work of the Twentieth Century."[27]

This "world's work" angle was truly the essence of imperialism for TR.
Economic advantages were incidental and, when necessary, had to be discarded
in the interest of nobler objectives.

In a letter of August 9, 1906, to the British author Frederick Scott Oliver,
Roosevelt made evident both his indifference to economic imperialism and his
desire to see the British Empire — including British North America — kept intact
and even strengthened. "The tariff," the president argued, should "be handled
in whatever way best contributes to solidifying the British Empire and making
it a compact and coherent union."[28]

⊰   ⊱

It is important to emphasize that most of Theodore Roosevelt's imperialist thinking during 1904-1906 concerned the American enterprise in the Philippines either directly or in comparison with other nations' imperial undertakings. Despite his frustrating failure to persuade Congress to abolish or even to reduce the tariff on Filipino products shipped to America, and despite ongoing difficulties relating to Filipino church administration and to American naval capabilities in the western Pacific, overall Roosevelt was very proud of what his nation was accomplishing in the Philippines.

In speeches and in letters, Roosevelt frequently commented at length on the altruistic character of the American effort in the Philippines and on the impressive progress the United States was making there. Excerpts from his public letter to Speaker of the House of Representatives Joseph Gurney Cannon, formally accepting the Republican presidential nomination in 1904, illustrate the pattern well. "During the last five years," Roosevelt averred, "more has been done for the material and moral well-being of the Filipinos than ever before. . . . We have opened before them a vista of orderly development in their own interest. . . . Every effort is being made to fit the islanders for self-government, and they have already in large measure received it." Schools, libraries, roads, health care, and a fair court system were among the American contributions to the improvement of Filipinos' lives. A U.S. withdrawal "would inevitably" spark "bloody conflicts . . . , and just as inevitably the islands would become the prey of the first power which in its own selfish interest took up the task we had cravenly abandoned. . . . Nowhere else in recent years has there been as fine an example of constructive statesmanship and wise and upright administration as has been given by the civil authorities, aided by the army, in the Philippine Islands."[29]

Roosevelt's favorable comparisons between America's work in the Philippines and the effects of British imperialism probably would have remained as inferential as the comparison implied in the preceding sentence *if* the president had not considered himself provoked by a British critic of the United States' Philippines policy, Frank A. Swettenham (whose brother Alexander assumes a central place in part III). Roosevelt decided not to present his defense and counterattack directly to Spring Rice, Lee, Strachey, Trevelyan, or Grey. Why create a new source of tension with his English friends, Roosevelt thought, when the matter was of no immediate import? He was quite angry, however, and he vented this anger in communications with Reid and Lodge.

The president's initial rebuttal was rather mild. Referring to the U.S. struggle under Leonard Wood's leadership to assert control over the Moro country of the Philippines, Roosevelt had these words for Reid in a letter of September 11, 1905: "We have had more difficult work to do than the English have had to do in the Malay Settlements, and it has been done better."[30]

Several months later, after reading a letter from Wood that put forth specific charges of British abuses in various colonies, TR sharpened his response to Swettenham. "From a good deal of inquiry," he declared, "I am convinced that Wood is entirely right. Without question we could find something to copy in some of the British colonies, especially in Cromer's handling of Egypt; but the far eastern British colonies, notably those in the Malay country, can be studied with most benefit by us only with the purpose of learning what to avoid."[31]

As it turned out, it was an article by the American anti-imperialist Charles Francis Adams praising Britain's performance in Egypt that triggered Roosevelt's most comprehensive comparison of British and American imperialism. In a long letter to Lodge of April 30, 1906, the president discussed what he saw as Adams's ignorance and commented at length about Egypt and the Philippines. Lord Cromer, TR believed, was "a big man," but his "task in Egypt has been infinitely easier than our task in the Philippines. He had a large population, orderly, submissive and hard-working"; and, unlike the Philippines, Egypt's "physical configuration is such as to render it a matter of the greatest ease to put down brigandage and insurrection." Moreover, "we are now painfully endeavoring to fit these people for self-government. The English are making no such effort in Egypt."

Roosevelt magnified the contrast between American and British imperialism by turning from Egypt to Malaya. "In the Philippines," he reiterated, "our prime efforts have been to administer the lands in the interest of the natives themselves, whereas in the Malay States the British . . . have raised their revenues chiefly by . . . the encouragement of the sale of opium, and even . . . the traffic in loose women. . . . White capitalists" were "exploiting" Malaya as a deliberate policy of the British government.

The only valuable lessons that Britain's experience in Egypt had to offer the United States, Roosevelt asserted, were already understood except by Adams and other anti-imperialists. First, the United States must not replicate with regard to the Philippines Britain's "wicked" and "foolish" mistake in explicitly promising to leave Egypt. In so doing England had placed itself in a terrible position wherein it was "necessary" for it to break its "plighted faith . . . in the interest of humanity and civilization." Second, such qualities as "courage, efficiency, common sense, and disinterestedness" were essential to the success of any imperial enterprise—although TR was "astonished" that Adams had "to take a trip to Egypt" to learn a lesson readily accessible in lands under American control.[32]

One should not conclude from these letters to Reid and Lodge, of course, that President Roosevelt did not greatly respect and admire the British Empire. He was immensely impressed by the size it had attained, generally approved of the way it was run, and viewed it as a major force for the advancement of civilization and for the maintenance of world peace. He knew that the American empire was minuscule in comparison. But he was at the same time *extremely* proud and sensitive to criticism of the manner in which the United States was handling its little empire. The distant Philippines were a particular source of pride for TR. He considered most criticisms of U.S. administration there totally unfounded, and he took them personally. As great as the British Empire was, it did have some weak spots; moreover, Roosevelt believed that *no* British colony—much less any colony of another power—was being ruled as altruistically and as efficiently as the Philippines. And he wanted his American friends, at least, to know just where he stood.

In November 1906, following his visit to the Panama Canal Zone and Puerto Rico, Roosevelt wrote some words to Trevelyan that suggested the high esteem in which he held the British Empire and the fundamental commonality he perceived between the British and American colonial experiences. "Porto Rico," he observed, "is being admirably governed by a set of as nice young fellows as one could find anywhere; but I suppose in its administration it does not differ materially from many similar dependencies which your people are administering."[33]

Over the middle years of his presidency, Theodore Roosevelt tended to fluctuate between pessimism and optimism in his assessment of the long-range prospects of the British Empire and "the English-speaking peoples." Perceiving disturbing parallels with the English-speaking world of the early twentieth century, Roosevelt claimed in a letter to Florence Lockwood La Farge that "the Roman Empire fell because of 1) decline in population 2) decline in military spirit. All other causes were merely accessory."[34] To Reid he asserted that "the general softening of fibre, the selfishness, the luxury, the relaxation of standards, the growth of a spirit such as that of the anti-imperialists—all these are among the unpleasant symptoms which cannot but give us concern for the future." Discouragement, however, was not the appropriate response. For "there are plenty of good symptoms too; and after all none of us can read the future, and our duty is simple. Let us stand valiantly for what is decent and right; let us strive hard, and take with unshaken front whatever comes, whether it be good or ill. Then the fates must decide what the outcome shall be."[35]

It was in a letter to Trevelyan of March 9, 1905, that TR gave fullest expression to his ambivalent, but on balance more hopeful than despairing, feelings. One major worry was "the diminishing birth rate among our people," termed "an ugly thing" by Roosevelt. "Here the results are not visible owing to the great immigration, but in Australia the effect is alarming, for the population is increasing slowly and moreover at a constantly diminishing rate," even though "the great island continent is very sparsely populated."

There was likewise much uncertainty and uneasiness—but in the end a relatively positive outlook—with regard to the shift of English-speaking populations from rural to urban areas. "In England, in the United States, in Canada, in Australia, and in the English parts of South Africa there is more and more a tendency for the men who speak English to gather into the cities and towns, so that these grow at the expense of the country folk." Such a tendency troubled Roosevelt, because farmers had historically been the group most successful at "governing . . . in times of peace" and at "fighting in times of war."

Nevertheless, TR was endeavoring not to exaggerate the problem: "The most marvelous growth in population and material prosperity, and, I believe, in the average of human happiness, that the world has ever seen in any race, has taken place among the English-speaking peoples since the time when Goldsmith gave poetic expression to the general feeling of gloom which prevailed among educated men at what they were pleased to consider the morbid growth of the cities and the decadence of the men in England." Along with "the evil" of rapid and massive industrialization, there had come "much good." In the final analysis, Roosevelt was "inclined to think that on the whole our people are, spiritually as well as materially, . . . better and not worse off than they were a hundred years ago."

A number of challenges loomed for the English-speaking peoples. "There are plenty of anxious times ahead, and there are many serious evils to face," Roosevelt warned. Still, he predicted, "we shall work through our troubles and ultimately come well out of them."[36]

ROOSEVELT AND THE
TIGHTENING ANGLO-AMERICAN BOND

Theodore Roosevelt's references to "our people" in the excerpts that conclude the preceding section are indicative of a discernible movement on his part toward a closer attachment to Great Britain and its empire during the period 1904-1906. Indeed, these years, 1905 and 1906 especially, are replete with presidential affirmations of Anglo-American closeness.

As has been seen, there were a number of snags in Anglo-American relations in the middle years of Roosevelt's presidency. The British government was less than a wholehearted supporter of TR's diplomacy during the Russo-Japanese War. It was uncooperative as Roosevelt worked in 1905 to arrange for the Algeciras conference. And the Newfoundland fisheries problem once again reared its ugly head. But the first two discordancies failed to prevent Roosevelt from achieving great diplomatic successes, which in a sense took England off the hook, and the third found each side going out of its way to be reasonable in pursuit of a compromise solution. Moreover, unlike the Alaskan boundary dispute, none of these complications was viewed by TR as involving a British challenge to a vital American interest.

Two other factors helped to offset these difficulties. One was the broad commitment to sustaining Anglo-American harmony—in the interests of both countries' security and of civilization and world peace—shared by Roosevelt and many British leaders.

The second was Britain's nearly total acquiescence in American hegemony in the Caribbean region. Leading Britons, as noted, were among the earliest proponents of the Roosevelt Corollary to the Monroe Doctrine, proclaimed by TR in 1904. This corollary asserted an American right to police the Western Hemisphere. Sir John Fisher, who became Britain's First Sea Lord in 1904, moved promptly toward a nearly total withdrawal of British naval power from the region, leaving the protection of British colonial and other interests there in American hands. In a sense the British were fortunate, because, as Warren Kneer observes, "they were able to prove their devotion to Anglo-American amity in an area of relatively small British interests."[37]

⋘   ⋙

His positive feelings about the British Empire did not stop Theodore Roosevelt from expressing a nationalistic distaste for Americans who took up permanent residence in England. To his daughter Alice, then in London with her husband, TR wrote these words on June 24, 1906: "The Americans of either sex who live in London and Paris, and those who marry titled people abroad, are, taking them by and large, a mighty poor lot of shoats, and the less you and Nick see of them the better I am pleased."[38] Moving to England, at least, was a bit less objectionable than moving to another foreign country; as Roosevelt explained to Reid around the same time, "I do not like the Americans who reside abroad; and in the case of an American woman who marries an Englishman (and still more another foreigner) I always feel that the presumption is against her."[39]

Foremost among leading Britons of whom Roosevelt developed a critical opinion during these years were Arthur Balfour and Winston Churchill. When, in 1906, Trevelyan compared former Prime Minister Balfour unfavorably with Robert Peel and William Gladstone—calling Balfour "a man of words, and of no knowledge of solid, bottom, facts"—Roosevelt thanked him "for giving me the first clear idea I have had as to the reason why so many Englishmen whose judgment I respect distrust Balfour."[40]

Toward Churchill, whom he had met in Albany back in 1900, the president was particularly harsh. After reading the young Briton's two-volume biography of his father, Lord Randolph Churchill, Roosevelt shared his reaction with Lodge. "I dislike the father and dislike the son," he admitted, "so I may be prejudiced." True, "the biographer and his subject possess some real farsightedness, especially in their appreciation of the shortcomings of that 'society' which had so long been dominant in English politics." However, their "levity, lack of sobriety, lack of permanent principle, and . . . inordinate thirst for that cheap form of admiration which is given to notoriety . . . make them poor public servants."[41] Roosevelt's judgment of Churchill was so uncharitable and inaccurate, in fact, that in a letter to John St. Loe Strachey he even went so far as to equate Churchill with William Randolph Hearst, "a man whom I so thoroly dislike and despise, . . . a man without any real principle."[42]

Of course many Britons, including friends of TR, also held unflattering views of Balfour and Churchill, controversial public figures that they were. Still, Roosevelt's perspectives on these individuals, as well as on expatriate Americans in England, are significant to this study. In the case of Balfour and Churchill, his remarks reflect more than his negative opinions of these two particular individuals; they also reflect a degree of interest in and awareness of British politics and British public figures that far exceeded his interest and awareness with regard to the politics and public figures of any of the other powers. Concerning the expatriates, TR's criticisms provide a useful counterweight to this proud *American* president's frequent references to "the English-speaking peoples."

Balfour, Churchill, and expatriates notwithstanding, it was a growing *affection* for Great Britain and its people that marked Roosevelt's outlook during 1904-1906. Evidence for this proposition is abundant.

≪　　≫

One indicator of Roosevelt's assumption of an identity of Anglo-American values, perspectives, and interests during this period was the openness with which he discussed America's affairs in his letters to his British correspondents. Soon after the Panamanian revolution, for instance, TR offered Spring Rice a preview of his forthcoming corollary: "The people of the United States and the people of the Isthmus and the rest of mankind will all be the better because we dig the Panama Canal and keep order in its neighborhood."[43] In a letter of November 1904 to Rudyard Kipling, the president derided the American opponents of his Panama policies as "vague individuals of serious mind and limited imagination, who think that a corrupt pithecoid [*sic*] community in which the President" has seized power by force "is entitled to just the treatment that I would give, say, to Denmark or Switzerland."[44] With Spring Rice in 1905, Roosevelt uninhibitedly discussed his corollary, by then in place. The Monroe Doctrine, he asserted, cannot "remain fossilized while the nation grows. . . . We must make it evident on the one hand that we do not intend to use the Monroe Doctrine as a pretense for self-aggrandizement at the expense of the Latin American republics, and on the other hand that we do not intend it to be used as a warrant for letting any of these republics remain as small bandit nests of a wicked and inefficient type."[45] Roosevelt was unquestionably pleased—but no doubt equally unquestionably unsurprised—to learn from Lodge during the busy summer of 1905 that Prime Minister Balfour was "most anxious to have . . . the Panama Canal . . . built for he feels that it will strengthen our position enormously and that with England at Suez and the U.S. at Panama we should hold the world in a pretty strong grip."[46] And it was a Briton, Trevelyan, to whom TR, before reaching American shores in November 1906 following his visit to the Canal Zone, penned a letter extolling the work in progress on the canal: "There the greatest engineering feat of the ages is being attempted. It is the kind of work our people are peculiarly fitted to do."[47]

Although Roosevelt naturally had much in common politically with all his close English friends, probably John St. Loe Strachey was the most in tune with TR across the political board (although a good case could also be made for Arthur Lee). Not only did the two men tend to see eye to eye on Anglo-American relations and on international questions in general, but each could discuss his own and the other's country's internal affairs in anticipation of finding a receptive audience. "I am confident," the "agnostically" protectionist American president agreed with his English correspondent in February 1906, "that protection would be most damaging to Great Britain."[48] Strachey, a leader in the movement for the volunteer military training of local forces in Britain, certainly found Roosevelt in accord when he asserted the following month: "No man is a 'full man' unless he knows how to defend his home and country."[49] Addressing a central philosophical and political issue of their time in a letter written later that year, Strachey had these pleasing words for his presidential friend: Roosevelt was the leader of "all those here as well as in America who are determined on the one hand to fight socialism, and on the other to hold the trusts and the combines in check."[50]

As a voracious reader and prolific author, Roosevelt's thoughts on the Anglo-American connection sometimes found expression in his analyses of literature. A good example is a letter of August 1906 to Frederick Scott Oliver, a biographer of Alexander Hamilton, in which TR affirmed his own American separateness but even more his sense of Anglo-American linkage and superiority. "It is really remarkable," Roosevelt declared, "that you, an English man of letters, and I, an American politician largely of non-English descent, should be in such entire accord as regards the essentials" about Hamilton. "Among free peoples," he added, "and especially among the free peoples who speak English, it is only in very exceptional circumstances that a statesman can be efficient, can be of use to the country, unless he is also (not as a substitute but in addition) a politician."[51]

⚔   ⚔

If the period from 1904 to 1906 is divided into three parts, each comprising one year, a noteworthy pattern emerges. Roosevelt's correspondence during 1904 contains few affirmations of a deep affection for Great Britain and its empire. To be sure, England was seen as a friendly foreign power, but an important theme for TR was that the United States must depend on itself for its security. This theme carried over into 1905 but was increasingly coupled that year with an emphasis on a strong Anglo-American partnership. The year 1906 witnessed the continuation of this trend, as the depth and durability of the Anglo-American friendship became by far the dominant theme.

The president's outlook on the Anglo-American relationship in 1904 is captured well by a letter he wrote that November to the influential political humorist, Finley Peter Dunne, in response to an article by Dunne on England's happiness with Roosevelt's reelection. "In our political life," Roosevelt stated, "unlike . . . in our social life, the temptation is toward Anglophobia, not toward Anglomania. The cheapest thing for any politician to do, the easiest, and too often politically one of the most remunerative, is to make some yell about England." TR insisted, however, that he was no Anglomaniac: "I feel a sincere friendliness for England; but you may notice that I do not slop over about it, and that I do not in the least misunderstand England's attitude, or . . . the attitude of any European nation, as regards us. We shall keep the respect of each of them just so long as we are thoroughly able to hold our own, and no longer." There were no exceptions: "If we got into trouble, there is not one of them upon whose friendship we could count to get us out."[52]

In 1905 Roosevelt wrote in a similar vein to Ambassadors George von Lengerke Meyer and Whitelaw Reid. "I do not believe," TR told Meyer in February, "that any alliance with, or implicit trust in, any foreign power will ever save this country from trouble."[53] To Reid in September the president put it this way: "In international matters I am no great believer in the long-continued effects of gratitude. . . . I think England has a more sincere feeling of friendliness for us than has any other power; but even this English friendliness would be a broken reed if we leaned on it, unless we were entirely able in addition to fight for our own hand."[54]

Roosevelt was just as frank on the subject in several letters to Spring Rice as he was with these Americans. "I would hesitate in counting upon the support of your Government and your people," he commented in a letter of December 27, 1904. "I am not quite sure of their tenacity of purpose, of their fixity of conviction, of their willingness to take necessary risks, and at need to endure heavy losses for a given end." The American and British governments both "must reckon with the possible clamor of the great business interests, who regard anything that will tend to 'unsettle values' . . . as being worse than any possible future national loss or even disgrace; and . . . with a fundamentally sound, but often temporarily unstable or mistaken, public opinion." Roosevelt then put forth his "main point" in general terms: "Each nation . . . must rely for its own safety only upon its own forethought and industrial efficiency and fighting edge. . . . Moreover," he added, "looked at from the standpoint of a long course of years no nation can depend upon the mere friendship of any other, even though that friendship is genuine, unless it has itself such strength as to make its own friendship of value in return."[55] And in letters of May 13 and June 16, 1905, TR again asserted that ultimately the United States stood alone.[56]

But as determined as Roosevelt was not to "slop over" in expressing his friendship for Britain, his affirmations of Anglo-American solidarity did begin to become rather effusive in 1905. Although to Hay in February TR jokingly referred to a letter from King Edward questioning the authenticity of Germany's friendship for America as "a variant on the old song that 'Codlin is our friend and not Short,'" the president's reply could only have delighted its royal recipient. "I absolutely agree with you," declared Roosevelt, "as to the importance, not merely to ourselves but to all the free peoples of the civilized world, of a constantly growing friendship and understanding between the english-speaking [*sic*] peoples." He was determined to do everything he could "to foster" this "feeling of good will"—though he cautioned that "to foster it, we need judgment and moderation no less than the good will itself." He then proclaimed that "the larger interests of the two nations are the same; and the fundamental, underlying traits of their characters are also the same."[57] And Roosevelt followed up by asking Lodge, "when you see King Edward," to "say that I appreciate thoroughly that in the long run the English people are more apt to be friendly to us than any other."[58]

Soon afterward, Trevelyan too received a clear avowal of a special relationship. "We are both living under free governments," TR declared, "and while both of these governments, and the people behind the governments, differ somewhat from one another, they are closer kin than either is to any other folk."[59]

An exchange of correspondence with Arthur Lee during the spring of 1905 provides particularly good evidence of a new readiness on the part of President Roosevelt to write without reservation of his wholehearted commitment to an Anglo-American partnership. Lee, Civil Lord of the Admiralty, was then engaged in planning a visit to America by a British cruiser squadron for later in the year "to emphasize the good feeling and 'fellowship of the sea' which exists between us and the only great Naval Power of which we are not jealous!" Later in his letter Lee enthusiastically attributed "immense significance" to "the new strategic distribution of our Fleets"—especially to "our practical withdrawal from North American and West Indian waters." He applauded "the Admiralty and the Government" for having "the courage of their convictions" in the face of criticisms from "armchair strategists who think that a war with the United States is one of those possibilities against which we should always be prepared." While "nothing is impossible . . .—not even the suicide of the English speaking race"—Lee was "an optimist by profession, and I revel in the thought that within the next few years there will be 75 first class Battleships afloat, all manned by English speaking crews, and constituting the most formidable argument, or guarantee, for universal peace that the world has ever seen."[60]

Roosevelt was eager to receive the British fleet (which visited in November), and his response to Lee was in a similar spirit, lacking even an implied cautionary note: "You need not ever be troubled by the nightmare of a possible contest between the two great English-speaking peoples. I believe that is practically impossible now, and that it will grow entirely so as the years go by. *In keeping ready for possible war I never even take into account a war with England. I treat it as out of the question.*"[61]

A few months later TR repeated this assessment in a letter to Strachey. "I regard all danger of any trouble between the United States and Great Britain," Roosevelt declared, "as over, I think for ever."[62]

The year 1906 was the best one to date for the friendship between England and Theodore Roosevelt's America. The Russo-Japanese War and its attendant awkwardness had ended in 1905. Unlike the first phase of the Moroccan crisis in 1905, the Algeciras conference of 1906 posed no real difficulties for the Anglo-American relationship; and both English-speaking powers viewed the conference's outcome in April as entirely satisfactory. Moreover, the presence of Grey rather than Lansdowne in the Foreign Office eliminated much of the unwarranted uneasiness that had theretofore impeded the development of the bond.[63] TR's optimistic reaction to comments about Grey in a February letter from Strachey—"somehow when you say that he is a Radical Whig you make me feel as if I could get on with him!"[64]—proved to be well-founded. And, not least, it was in 1906 that Roosevelt's long agitation for the removal of Sir Mortimer Durand from the British embassy finally bore fruit.

Henry White, himself a strong backer of the Anglo-American special relationship, obviously knew that the president fully shared his outlook. In one section of his long letter on the Algeciras conference, previously quoted at length, White described the visit of an American naval transport to Gibraltar in February. The American navy men, he wrote, "produced the best impression possible upon the military and naval element at Gibraltar. On Sunday morning I collected a number of them . . . and took them to the military service in the Governor's Chapel where they sat in their uniforms among the British soldiers and joined lustily with the latter in singing 'God Save the King' at the end."[65] Along these lines, while returning from Panama and Puerto Rico aboard the USS *Louisiana* in November, TR related to Trevelyan: "The other day we dined at the chief petty officers' mess, and the men are of the type which make the strength of our navy and of yours."[66]

Naval information passed on to Roosevelt by Lee during the latter's trip to the United States earlier in the fall provides further evidence of the high degree of intimacy the Anglo-American relationship had attained. TR informed Captain William Sims that Lee had shared with the president "the imperative necessity of having twenty-thousand-ton ships, with turbines, making a speed of twenty-five knots and heavily armored, divided into absolutely watertight compartments, and carrying say eight twelve-inch guns and then a battery of light guns for torpedo boats." Lee had also told Roosevelt that "British target practice is now at what they call battle ranges, that is at five to seven thousand yards; and that they do not regard short-range practice as of any real value."[67] It is nearly impossible to imagine this type of information being willingly transmitted to the United States by any other power.

As to Durand, it has been seen that Roosevelt had long been dissatisfied with his performance as ambassador. Ever since the day in May 1904 when, as TR reported to his son Theodore, Jr., "Sir Mortimer proved a bad walker and wholly unable to climb,"[68] there had been disenchantment. During 1905 and much of 1906, Roosevelt quietly campaigned, largely through Ambassador Reid, for Spring Rice to be sent to replace Durand.

At last the Liberal government under Sir Henry Campbell-Bannerman, in contrast to its Conservative predecessor, began to take heed. England's exclusion from the innermost sanctums of TR's Moroccan diplomacy certainly provided a spur. Roosevelt received a signal to this effect from Reid in a letter of June 19, 1906: "The fact that he has not been making a marked success at Washington as compared with Speck von Sternburg and Jusserand seems to be universally understood among the British diplomatists whom I meet and more or less among members of the Liberal party."[69]

Arthur Lee's visit to the United States in October and November was viewed by both the president and his friend as an opportunity for Roosevelt to convey some important information on a variety of issues to the British government and, by inference, to point up the inadvisability of retaining Durand any longer. As a Conservative now in the opposition, Lee asked TR, who readily consented, for a letter that would render it "impossible" for the government "to ignore the story that I have to tell" and assure "that my mission shall not prove futile, or unnecessarily ineffective, through lack of a sufficient credential." Roosevelt, Lee went on, "can trust me to use this 'credential' only when absolutely necessary, and only in the highest quarters, and I should of course never let it out of my possession." Lee also suggested what Roosevelt might say in the desired "credential."[70]

The president's letter conformed closely to Lee's suggestions. Roosevelt thanked Lee "for having come across the ocean at my request to see me and for your kindly consenting to repeat . . . the statements that I have made to you as regards the Hague conference, the Newfoundland fisheries, the seal fisheries, the Chinese Customs, the Russo-Japanese peace negotiations, the Algeciras negotiations and the Venezuela matter." Lee was asked to explain to top officials "why I have adopted this irregular method of communication." Roosevelt praised his British friend's "judgment" and "discretion." Lee stood "for your country's interests first; and I should not respect you if this were not the case. But so far as is compatible with first serving the interests of your country you have a genuine desire to do what is friendly to America."[71] Lee was pleased: "The letter which you have sent me will enormously strengthen my hands."[72]

About a week after this exchange, Roosevelt wrote Grey a letter focusing on the naval limitation question. The president expressed concern about German naval building and then clearly implied that he considered the British and American navies to be players on the same team. "Our building program," Roosevelt stated, "is not only, as is right and proper, far less than yours, but I think far less than that of either Germany or France, or possibly even Japan." He also mentioned his "very nice visit from Arthur Lee, to whom I have told several things which he is to repeat to you."[73]

Encouraging news on the Durand problem soon arrived from Reid. "When the Algeciras matter was mentioned," the U.S. ambassador to Britain had had the occasion to share with Grey information that was "known to Jusserand and . . . Sternburg at the time and, as you told me, would have been known to Sir Mortimer if you had enjoyed the same relations with him. That remark stuck particularly in Sir Edward's memory." Later, Grey had told Reid that Durand would shortly be relieved, although for the time being this decision was "strictly confidential. . . . He then went on to talk about the successor."[74]

Roosevelt was, naturally, "delighted that Gray [*sic*] has waked up about poor Durand. I shall be very sorry to have Durand lose his pension or suffer in any way, but it is a simple farce to have him here as Ambassador." The president, however, was unenthusiastic about the two possible replacements (neither of whom was James Bryce, who actually did take charge of the embassy early in 1907) named by Reid. "I earnestly wish," he told Reid, "they could send either

Spring Rice, or Arthur Lee if Spring Rice can not be spared from Persia [where he had recently been sent as the British minister]. Arthur Lee would be a particularly fine fellow and would be of real help here."[75]

Early in December Grey confirmed Durand's impending termination in a long and important letter to Roosevelt. Although reassigning Durand was "an awkward matter," it was "absolutely necessary" and was "settled." Grey then turned to the question of a successor. He was "really sorry" that it could not be Lee:

> But we cannot take a man from the other side in politics, who has as yet only occupied a subordinate position in his own party, and has always taken a very active, though fair, part in opposition to us. To make him Ambassador at Washington would cause deep resentment in the whole of our Diplomatic Service; would mortally offend our own party; would surprise his party; and would not be understood by public opinion here. . . . I could not explain or justify it unless I could say right out that Lee was being sent because he was your friend and had your confidence, which could hardly be said in public.

Grey did indicate that he might bypass the Diplomatic Service and choose a man of "recognised distinction and position" to be ambassador. In the meantime, he assured Roosevelt, Esmé Howard, the newly appointed councillor of embassy, could be counted on to handle the embassy effectively.

Grey then moved on to issues in Anglo-American relations. He acknowledged and explained the confusion that had existed in England concerning Roosevelt's relations with the kaiser during the Portsmouth negotiations and the president's policy on the Moroccan question. The picture was now much clearer.

Toward the end of this letter, Grey offered his own frank analysis of the Anglo-American special relationship. There existed among the British people, despite "too many sentimentalists, . . . a real friendly feeling towards the United States." It was not a question of "Anglo-Saxon race feeling," because "your continent is making a new race and a new type, drawn from many sources, just as in old times the race in these Islands was evolved from many sources. But common language helps to draw us together." And similar "religious feeling," Grey believed, was another factor. Most important of all in Grey's perspective was "that some generations of freedom on both sides have evolved a type of man and mind that looks at things from a kindred point of view, and a majority that has a hatred for what is not just or free."[76]

Roosevelt, in his reply, was quick to assure Grey that "I quite understand about Lee; and I am sure you will give us a good man." As to the broader question of the special relationship, TR was entirely, almost uncannily, in accord with Grey. Again despite "too many sentimentalists, . . . there is a real friendly feeling among our people toward yours." TR agreed "that it is not Anglo-Saxon race feeling." Rather, "we and you have a common language, essentially a common culture, and . . . much the same kind of religious feeling; and above all, the same kind of way of looking at the great matters that count most in securing just and free government."[77]

The period 1904-1906 ended with the Anglo-American relationship in an excellent condition. Theodore Roosevelt deserves much of the credit for this state of affairs. Neither Britain's unhelpfulness with the president's Russo-Japanese peacemaking effort, nor its obstructive stance toward TR's Morocco diplomacy in 1905, nor the on-again dispute over the Newfoundland fisheries had been permitted to undermine a friendship that Roosevelt's earlier statecraft had been instrumental in securing. Roosevelt never veered off his charted course despite the presence in Washington throughout this time of an inept British ambassador and the continuation in office for two of the three years of a foreign secretary who simply could never understand the president. By the end of 1906, Roosevelt had gone a long way toward establishing with the far more sympathetic Liberal Foreign Secretary Grey the sort of trust and openness that characterized his relationships with Spring Rice, Lee, Strachey, and Trevelyan. TR's friend James Bryce would soon be in charge of the British embassy in Washington. The future of the Anglo-American partnership looked extremely bright. Its solidity would be tested soon enough.

PART III

The Special Relationship Triumphant:

JAMAICA, 1907

The Earthquake and the
Swettenham Incident

● ○ ●

The Swettenham (or Jamaica) incident of 1907 is one of the better-kept secrets of the history of American foreign relations in the early twentieth century. Neither historians studying Anglo-American relations nor those focusing on the diplomacy of Theodore Roosevelt have accorded this incident more than passing attention.[1]

What occurred in Jamaica in January 1907 and the ensuing diplomatic activity admittedly constitute a secondary episode in the history of Roosevelt's foreign policy. Nonetheless, a contemporary issue of *Harper's Weekly* was not inaccurate in labeling the Swettenham incident the century's "first test" of "the tenacity of the bonds ostensibly uniting Englishmen to their transatlantic kinsmen."[2] Indeed, both the nature and the timing of this affair place it in an excellent position to be used as a gauge of the Anglo-American relationship and of TR's perspectives on Great Britain and its empire as the Roosevelt presidency entered its final two years. Less important but not immaterial, the story of the Jamaica incident is entertaining and intriguing in its own right. It is time for this story to be told.[3]

✂   ✄

At around 3:30 P.M. on Monday, January 14, 1907, a terrible earthquake, and then a devastating fire, struck the port of Kingston, the capital city in the British West Indian colony of Jamaica. Later that day the American vice consul in Kingston, William H. Orrett, cabled this message to the Department of State: "Fearful earthquake today city ruined and in flames food wanted consulate destroyed will try to save archives."[4] "Quake and Fire Wreck Kingston," screamed a *New York Times* headline on January 16;[5] and for the next nine days, this natural disaster and its aftermath remained front-page news.

"The first destructive shock," reported the *Kingston Gleaner* when it was able to resume publication on January 18, "lasted about thirty seconds. . . . When the shock subsided, thousands of buildings had fallen with a terrific roar. Not so much fallen, perhaps, as crumbled to dust and debris. Huge walls fell in the commercial part of the city," squashing "all who happened to be on the side-walks or in the streets. Hundreds of people were killed instantly in this way and omnibuses . . . were crushed to atoms." The newspaper praised "a few thoughtful individuals" who, "although injured themselves, started to rescue several of those who were buried. But this humane work was interrupted within five minutes by the approach of fire which had before made its appearance to the west of the city.

"The fire brigade," the *Gleaner* went on, "had been demolished by the earthquake and there were no means of fighting" the fire, which swept over a large area. "Next morning hundreds of bodies were found burned and charred along the principal streets. It is believed that many who had been injured and unable to help themselves were burnt to death by the flames." The newspaper described Kingston's business center as "a mass of ruins" and "conservatively estimated" that the city's "death list will exceed one thousand when all the bodies have been recovered."[6]

Nicholas R. Snyder, the American consul in Port Antonio, Jamaica, a city untouched by the earthquake, offered to the State Department in a dispatch of January 19 a concise description of the tragedy: "The demolition of the city of Kingston is almost complete"; not one "brick or stone building escaped without serious damage," and most "were leveled to the ground. The shock was immediately followed by a fire, which devoured every store and warehouse in the commercial section of the city and all, but two, wharves." Snyder believed "that over one thousand instant deaths have occurred," including "many prominent merchants," while "a conservative estimate of injured persons is five thousand."[7] Three days later Snyder sharply increased his estimates of injured and dead, the latter to 1,800.[8] The previous day, the 21st, Orrett had cabled that "over two thousand" had probably died.[9] Tens of thousands were left homeless.

Among the multitude of expressions of sorrow generated by the catastrophe were a note from Secretary of State Elihu Root to Foreign Secretary Sir Edward Grey and another from President Theodore Roosevelt to King Edward VII.[10] Roosevelt also sent a "personal gift" of food and supplies to Kingston.[11]

Aftershocks of the earthquake continued for many days.[12] Recovery and rebuilding, of course, took years. The largest insurance claims, involving the business portion of Kingston, were settled in January 1909.[13]

⊁   ⊱

The Swettenham incident of January 1907 involved, at least peripherally, many officers and enlisted men of the United States Navy and numerous Jamaicans and British colonial officials. Individuals at the highest levels of both the American and British governments played roles in its diplomatic resolution. But at the center of the incident itself were just two people, Rear Admiral Charles Henry Davis of the U.S. Navy and Sir J. Alexander Swettenham, the British governor of Jamaica.

Davis, a favorite of Henry Cabot Lodge, had been promoted to rear admiral in August 1904. The following year he had been assigned to command the Asiatic Fleet's Second Squadron. At the time of the Swettenham incident, he was serving under Rear Admiral R. D. Evans as division commander, First Squadron, United States Atlantic Fleet.

Alexander Swettenham—whose brother Frank, as seen in the preceding chapter, had incurred Theodore Roosevelt's disfavor by his criticism in 1905 of the American administration of the Philippines—had held the position of governor of Jamaica since September 1904. Alexander too had managed to establish himself prior to 1907 as anti-American in Roosevelt's eyes. Based on reports from Secretary of War William H. Taft and others, Roosevelt had become impatient with what he considered Swettenham's rudeness toward American negotiators and especially his unreasonable obstruction of American efforts to recruit Jamaican laborers to work on the Panama Canal. The president even referred to the matter in his annual message of December 1906: "One of the Governors [in the British West Indies] has shown an unfriendly disposition to our work, and has thrown obstacles in the way of our getting the labor needed."[14] TR's comments on Swettenham in a letter to George Otto Trevelyan that November were more personal and revealing: "The Jamaican Governor, Swettenham, has been extremely offensive in all his dealings with us. . . . Swettenham seems to be what is nowadays a rather rare individual, an old school tory with the old school tory tendency to dislike everything American. It is a quality which is entertaining in *Blackwood*, or the *Saturday Review*, but less entertaining in a government official with whom I am obliged to deal."[15]

⋇   ⋊

With Britain having drastically thinned out its naval presence in the Caribbean in the opening years of the twentieth century, no British warships were in the vicinity of Jamaica at the time of the earthquake. Lord Elgin, secretary of state for the colonies, cabled to Governor Swettenham on January 16: "H.M.S. 'Brilliant' and 'Indefatigable' have been ordered to proceed to Kingston bringing stores from Bermuda and Trinidad."[16] But help was needed immediately, and these ships would not be able to reach Kingston for several days.

The United States government, of course, was well aware of this problem. Esmé Howard, chargé d'affaires ad interim of Great Britain, was at the head of the British embassy in Washington during the period between the departure of Sir Mortimer Durand and the arrival of James Bryce. On January 16 he received a message from Secretary of State Root. After asking Howard to convey to Governor Swettenham "the deep and sincere sympathy which the people of the United States feel for the people of Jamaica in their great misfortune," Root tendered this offer: "If there is anything that we can do to relieve or prevent distress, our Navy Department will be most happy to do it, and Guantanamo is so near to Kingston that perhaps early relief may be afforded from there."[17] And Secretary of the Navy Victor H. Metcalf prepared the way for such relief by wiring to Admiral Evans in Cuba: "Should you find it desirable send vessels Jamaica."[18]

It was Governor Swettenham rather than Root or Metcalf who actually initiated the process leading to an American relief mission. This fact is ironic not only because of the incident that soon took place but also because the governor was so astonishingly unsympathetic to the suffering population of devastated Kingston and so unwilling to acknowledge the scope of the tragedy. These attitudes are apparent in parts of a telegram he sent to Lord Elgin soon after the earthquake: "Burned area being cleared slowly owing to indisposition of population to labour at double usual wages. A few [*sic!*] bodies are still covered with ruins."[19]

On January 15 Swettenham wired the following message to the British minister in Havana, G. W. E. Griffith: "Kindly send immediately bandages lint and wool for those injured by earthquake at cost of colony."[20] Swettenham was therefore technically correct when he insisted later that help from the United States was "unsolicited by this Government."[21] Griffith, however, reacted in the most logical way, turning to the United States. "On the eve of the 15th instant," he explained to Grey in a letter of January 23, "it was rumoured in Havana that an earthquake had occurred at Kingston, Jamaica, and about midnight I received a telegram from the Governor of Jamaica, whereupon I at once repaired to the Palace and found that the Provisional Governor had retired, but he cheerfully responded to my call and, at my request, wrote a telegram to Admiral Evans."[22] The Foreign Office was pleased when it learned that Griffith had acted with such "great promptitude."[23]

At that time the provisional governor of Cuba—which had very recently come under American military occupation—was Charles Magoon. His telegram to Evans, which reached the admiral "shortly after 10:10 a.m." on the 16th, ended in this way: "If possible please respond to call from Governor by sending needed supplies by torpedo-boat to Kingston." Evans, having already attempted on his own to contact the American consul in Kingston regarding possible assistance, moved quickly. "Orders were given," Evans informed the Navy Department,

> for the [battleships] *Missouri* and *Indiana* to get up steam at once. These ships
> have water-tube boilers which would enable them to leave in about two hours.
> Orders were also given to the [destroyer] *Whipple* to start all fires. The *Whipple*
> sailed at 11:30 a.m., with a supply of lint and bandages from the ships of the
> Squadron, and with the Fleet Surgeon and Surgeon McDonnell from the
> [supply ship] *Yankton* on board. The *Missouri*, flying the flag of Rear-Admiral
> Davis, and the *Indiana* sailed at 1:15 p.m., having two additional extra surgeons
> and all that could be spared from the Squadron in the way of lint, bandages,
> and first relief packages.
>
> Admiral Davis was ordered to proceed to Kingston and to offer and give
> any assistance within his power, and to return the *Whipple* to Guantanamo with
> full information as to the disaster unless her services were needed at Kingston.[24]

Following his conversation with Magoon, Griffith had wired Swettenham that
"at my request Governor Cuba telegraphed American Admiral at Guantanamo
to send torpedo boat to Kingston with articles requested."[25] Now, having issued
his orders, Evans replied to Magoon: "Telegram reporting disaster Kingston,
Jamaica, arrived and battleship [*sic*] Missouri and Indiana will sail at noon for
Kingston."[26] Magoon, by the next day more fully informed, in turn informed
Griffith, noting "the Whipple should have arrived at Kingston last night and the
two battleships early this morning."[27]

As the hours passed on January 16, word of the American relief mission was
making its way to American and British officials in Washington. Even before he
formally thanked Secretary Root, Chargé Howard wired to Grey: "United
States Government have already sent ship to Kingston."[28] Then, upon completing a note to Root, Howard learned more and added a handwritten P.S.:
"News has just reached me of the departure of two men of war and a torpedo
boat . . . from Guantanamo for the scene of disaster to render assistance, and I
beg once again to thank you most warmly for this timely aid."[29] And, still on the
16th, he updated Grey, who right away instructed him "to express the high
appreciation of His Majesty's Government at the prompt assistance rendered by
the United States Government in the despatch of their ships to Jamaica to
afford aid to the stricken population of Kingston."[30]

Three brief messages from the Navy Department reached Admiral Evans on
January 17. One read: "Celtic sailed Havana Guantanamo 15th. Upon arrival
send her Kingston but await further instructions regarding issuing stores."[31]
Another, sanctioned by an act of Congress the following day,[32] formally authorized "issuing stores to Kingston earthquake sufferers."[33] A third advised: "Great
caution necessary in approaching Kingston as bottom of sea has changed."[34]

To the *Indiana, Missouri, Whipple,* and supply ship *Celtic,* Evans added one more vessel, the *Yankton.* A primary reason was to enable Evans to keep abreast of the relief effort. From the Atlantic Fleet's flagship *Maine,* Evans contacted Davis, whose mission was now in progress:

1. I am sending the Yankton to Kingston with two associated press agents, and for the purpose of communicating with you, and supplying you with additional bandages, dressings, etc. from the Fleet.
2. She should arrive there about noon tomorrow the 18th instant, and if you have important communications for me, you will direct her to return at once with them, and with such other information as the Department and the public would like to know.
3. In any case, I desire her to return not later than twenty-four hours after her arrival, unless you should have good and sufficient reason to detain her longer. . . .
5. It is desired that you should return with the two battleships when their presence there is no longer necessary, and you will please indicate the probable date of your return.[35]

The *Whipple* landed in Kingston around 11:45 P.M. on Wednesday, January 16. Lieutenant Commander E. A. Anderson located Governor Swettenham a couple of hours later, informing him of the *Whipple's* orders and of the impending arrival of the *Indiana* and the *Missouri.* When told that the United States was ready to help the suffering people of Kingston in a major way, Swettenham, according to Anderson, "expressed himself as being exceedingly grateful." Swettenham led Anderson to the hospital, where the chief medical officer insisted that he had no need for American medical personnel.[36]

Anderson's recall of one aspect of the opening hours of the mission appears to contradict the message with which he soon greeted Admiral Davis. The lieutenant commander told Evans many days later that Colonial Secretary H. C. Bourne had requested of him in writing "that Admiral Davis land a party from the battleships to quell a mutiny at the penitentiary" and also "a working party to clean up the ruins."[37] Previously Anderson had made reference to "the terrible stench" caused by "bodies in the ruins."[38] Yet here is what greeted Davis: "*No landing force necessary.* No medical assistance needed. There is a shortage of food ashore."[39] This contradiction can be reconciled. It is possible that Anderson encountered Bourne before seeing Swettenham, who, as a superior authority, overruled his colonial secretary.

In any case, the two battleships, coming upon a damaged lighthouse at Plum Point, obtained a pilot and anchored around 7:30 A.M. on January 17. Admiral Davis could see right away some of the devastation wrought by the earthquake, although he discovered that "the piers were intact," the "ships in port had held on to their anchors," and the "reports of the sinking of the bottom of Kingston Harbor . . . were pure invention."[40] The British gun emplacements having been "ruined by the earthquake," Davis found "the saluting battery abandoned," and "consequently . . . did not salute the English Flag in entering."[41]

Quickly Davis issued a series of orders. He assigned an officer to inform the American consul that Davis would meet him on shore and to apprise the governor that the admiral would visit him "immediately." He sent ashore the *Missouri's* fleet surgeon, its surgeon, and its chaplain, along with other officers and men, to offer supplies and assistance to injured people and to people in distress. From the Royal Mail Pier, where he had landed, Davis also arranged for the dispatch of a cable reporting his arrival.

Swettenham had retired a few hours before to his residence, King's House, in order to get some sleep, so Davis's messenger returned accompanied by an aide to the governor. This aide drove Davis to Headquarters House, the governor's office, where the admiral found H. C. Bourne, secretary to the governor as well as colonial secretary, in charge. The American vice consul, William Orrett, was there too, and the police inspector, A. D. Wedderburn, arrived soon. "Mr. Bourne assured me," Davis asserted in the highly credible report he prepared over the next several days on his Kingston experience,[42] "that he represented the Governor."[43]

In response to the urgings of Bourne, Wedderburn, and Orrett, Davis took several actions. These included moving the *Indiana* "to a position directly opposite the penitentiary" and landing there "a company under arms . . . to suppress a mutiny among the convicts"; sending "a small armed guard . . . with a working party to secure the archives" of the U.S. consulate; and landing "wrecking parties immediately with orders to operate under the Director of Public Works."[44] Large quantities of provisions were also ordered to be delivered and distributed "as necessary."[45]

Replying three days later to an accusatory inquiry from Governor Swettenham, Bourne and Wedderburn acknowledged that they had authorized Davis to act. Bourne stated: "Admiral Davies [*sic*] acted on my acceptance on behalf of the Governor of his offer. . . . I looked at it as the offer of a friendly neighbour to lend a hand which it would be churlish to refuse, especially when I knew that a landing party though not necessary would be, as it in fact proved itself, very useful." Wedderburn's explanation was similar: "I suggested that a party of American Marines be landed at the general penitentiary, as the prisoners . . . were in a state of insubordination; and . . . the appearance of a party of sailors would have a good effect."[46] Davis himself had taken care to have W. F. Bricker, his flag lieutenant, record in writing Bourne's request for American help.[47]

At the Headquarters House meeting, at which "most of those present were in a highly nervous and excited condition," Admiral Davis found a consensus "that I ought not disturb the Governor." Davis thought otherwise. "I had taken the responsibility," he explained, "of landing armed force on foreign soil, and I felt, notwithstanding the assurances of the Colonial Secretary that he was fully empowered to act in the Governor's absence, that I must see the supreme authority at whatever inconvenience to himself, and I decided to find the Governor."[48] So the admiral accepted an offer by the governor's aide to drive him the three miles to King's House.

At King's House Governor Swettenham and his family were living out of doors, the house having been severely damaged by the earthquake. It was around 10:00 A.M. on Thursday, January 17. "I gave him an account of my proceedings," Davis recalled, "and stated what I had ordered done."[49]

Just what happened next is unclear. According to Swettenham, he expressed opposition to Davis's actions. "The Admiral then said if I disapproved he would be left in the awkward position of having to explain to the American naval authorities how he had landed forces without the Governor's sanction. I then said," Swettenham's report went on,[50] "that as he had generously come with the object of helping us and had acted with the best intentions, I would waive my disapproval of the action already taken and would myself sanction it but I must remain the judge of how long it should continue."[51] Davis reported differently: "The Governor approved of my action, but declined further offers of service. I judged that he thought my presence at Kingston unnecessary. At the same time he seemed indifferent, and in fact he said that I might have a freehand [*sic*] to do what I could."[52] This statement about a "free hand" appears to conflict with Davis's observation later in his report that "every offer of aid had been steadily and consistently declined by the Governor."[53] All that is certain about this interview is that Swettenham expressed serious reservations but did not foreclose the possibility of further American aid.

Swettenham, who "seemed very confident," then drove Davis into town in the governor's own carriage. They stopped en route at the camp of the West India regiment, where the hostile commanding general, J. N. A. Marshall, asked Davis to withdraw his troops from the penitentiary. "I would have given the order to withdraw this company immediately," Davis explained, "but the Governor himself suggested a delay, as he desired to investigate the situation at the penitentiary himself. I drove through the city with the Governor and left him at the penitentiary."[54]

"The situation at the penitentiary" in and of itself constitutes an interesting and ironic dimension of the whole Swettenham incident. This part of the story is revealed in the report of Lieutenant J. L. Sticht of the *Indiana*, the officer in charge of the landing force of seventy-seven men, including four officers, that entered the penitentiary grounds around 11:30 A.M. on the 17th. At that time the convicts, numbering over 600, were "in a state of mutiny." At the request of prison officials, the Americans loaded their rifles "in full view of the convicts" and then proceeded to confine the prisoners. "The general opinion among the prison authorities," Sticht claimed, "was that if the U.S. forces had not landed when they did, serious trouble would have occurred." Then, very curiously, Swettenham himself called upon the Americans for personal protection: "At 1:00 P.M. the Governor of Jamaica arrived to try about twelve leaders of the late mutiny. After paying the customary official call, and tendering the usual services, I went to luncheon. In about fifteen minutes, his orderly requested that I report to him." When Sticht did so, Swettenham asked him to "detail six men under arms" to safeguard the governor and monitor the prisoners undergoing trial. "A guard of six men was immediately detailed and placed outside the door, in view of the convicts, and I remained in the immediate vicinity."[55] Swettenham's own report, predictably, attempted to obscure this development.[56] Shortly after 5:00 P.M. the Americans returned to the *Indiana*.

Meanwhile, Davis had gone back to the *Missouri* "immediately after my interview with the Governor." There he composed a dispatch for Admiral Evans, to be carried by the *Whipple*, which left Kingston at 6:30 P.M. on the 17th and reached Guantanamo at 3:30 P.M. the next day. This dispatch shows a rather confused Admiral Davis trying hard to sort out the many, often conflicting impressions of his first day in Kingston. On the one hand, Swettenham, who "seems to be a man of great power, . . . assures me" that the colonial government is in control of the situation "and in fact has declined every form of relief which I have offered. I feel . . . that an intrusion in the face of such a positive refusal . . . would be unbecoming." On the other hand, "from such information as I can gather from other sources, I am inclined now to the opinion . . . that the Governor overestimates the security of the situation; . . . and that he underestimates the number of dead."

Unsure of the proper course of action, Davis decided to delay a decision until he could investigate further "the conflicting stories, reports, complaints, and rumors." Not wanting to "force my assistance on the Governor," Davis nonetheless considered it his duty "to remain for the present at least."[57] The contents of this dispatch were transmitted by Evans to Washington, where they reached the White House on January 20.[58]

Also on the 17th, the high-strung but conscientious and energetic Vice Consul Orrett passed along his impressions to the State Department. The American naval forces, Orrett wrote, "have rendered great service to the inhabitants of this City. The presence of the Admiral here with his warships has been very much appreciated by the inhabitants."[59]

Davis spent part of the afternoon attending to the needs of about 150 Americans who were stranded in Kingston. At one point he decided to use the *Indiana* to transport these people to Cuba, but it turned out that he was able to arrange for their departure on a German steamer and therefore to keep the battleship in Kingston.

The Davis Report is a little misleading on what happened next. Davis wrote simply: "The Governor returned my call the same afternoon and was received with the usual honors."[60] But the admiral's letter to the governor written the evening of the 17th suggests that here it was Swettenham who reported more fully and accurately. "I requested him as a personal favour," Swettenham wrote, "to omit the usual Governor's salute which he promised to do. . . . I then left, the interview having been entirely friendly. I had not gone 100 yards from the vessel when a salute was fired, which I acknowledged."[61] The matter of this salute, while injecting into the situation an additional element of awkwardness, is not particularly important, as even C. P. Lucas, Swettenham's strongest supporter in the Colonial Office, noted.[62]

Rather more important is Swettenham's contention that he requested Davis "to withdraw his men from shore and I understood from him that he would do so."[63] Davis's report makes no reference to such an exchange aboard the *Missouri* that afternoon. One senses, again from Davis's letter of that evening, that such a conversation did indeed transpire, but that there was somewhat more ambiguity both in the way Swettenham expressed himself and in the way Davis responded.

During the evening Davis received many reports from the medical and other officers who had been on shore during the day. He learned that "the situation was far more grave, the calamity more sweeping, and the sanitary conditions in the city more menacing" than he "had been led to believe" by Swettenham.[64] A very difficult dilemma now confronted him. He could, as one option, obey the governor's wishes and depart from Kingston, leaving the devastated city and its suffering inhabitants to fend for themselves. Or else he could try to find a way to work around and perhaps overcome the governor's resistance and to furnish the aid that was so desperately needed.

Davis chose the latter course. Convincing himself that he had been given a "half sanction" by Swettenham that morning—the "free hand" discussed earlier—the admiral "determined . . . to devote my energies to wrecking the ruins of the burnt district, and as far as possible removing the dead, and to the relief of the wounded who had not been able to obtain relief at the City hospitals. This resolve was based upon the just dictates of common humanity." Having been offered the use of property held by the American Jesuit Fathers, he ordered, on his fleet surgeon's advice, the creation of a makeshift "emergency hospital of our own," on which work was to begin at daylight. Davis also commanded "wrecking parties to land in the morning to cooperate with the Department of Public Works and the Royal Engineers." The admiral, who had already scheduled a meeting with Swettenham for 10:00 A.M. the next day, then proceeded to draft a letter to the governor. It was to be delivered "early in the morning," in advance of their appointment.[65]

⍓   ⍌

At the core of the Swettenham affair—indeed the very factors that made it a significant international incident—are Davis's letter to Swettenham dated January 17 and, especially, Swettenham's reply to Davis of the 18th. These two letters, therefore, merit close attention.

Davis began his four-paragraph letter by apologizing "for the mistake of the salute this afternoon," claiming that his "orders were misunderstood." The admiral asked "that this apparent disregard of your wishes may be overlooked."

Davis informed Swettenham that—"actuated by . . . common humanity—I shall direct the medical officers of my Squadron . . . to aid outlying cases of distress, which would not perhaps come under the observation and treatment of your medical officers." He noted in another paragraph that the men he had detailed to "secure the archives of the United States Consulate" and "to clear away the wreckage" there had also "caught thieves and recovered from them a safe belonging to Milke Bros.' Jewelry store. . . . From this I judge," Davis added, "that the police surveillance of the city is not adequate as to the protection of private property."

The letter's most important sentence follows the admiral's reference to the "working parties from both ships" that had been assisting local authorities "in wrecking and in clearing away the ruins in the streets and buildings. I propose," Davis declared, "to land parties tomorrow morning for the same purpose, *unless you expressly desire me not to do so.*"

Davis realized, of course, that his rather aggressive attempt to outflank Swettenham and win the governor's grudging support for the continuation of American relief might fail. Still, seeking to maximize his chances for success, he ended his letter on a hopeful note: "I shall have the pleasure of meeting you at the hour appointed, namely, ten o'clock, at Headquarters House, and I trust that you will approve my action in these matters."[66]

Davis's letter was delivered to Swettenham by an officer at about 9:40 A.M. on Friday, January 18. At 10:00 A.M. the two protagonists held their scheduled meeting. Swettenham reported that he had told Davis he would "withhold action until I had seen what his men were doing. There was no friction at the interview."[67] Davis described the encounter similarly: "The Governor at this time treated me with great courtesy, . . . and was perfectly frank with me at all times. He promised to give me an answer to my letter later in the day. There was no unpleasantness or misunderstanding between us."[68] Admiral Davis's strategy seemed to be bearing fruit. At a minimum, the American relief effort had gained some time.

"On leaving," Davis continued in his report, "the Governor insisted that I should take his carriage and assigned me one of his Aides as my escort." Although he soon abandoned the carriage, Davis retained the services of the aide—so that "he might be able to give an intelligent report to the Governor of the exact state of affairs"—while conducting "a thorough personal inspection" of the activities of his men and of the general situation in Kingston. This inspection found "the men working assiduously" and "much progress being made."[69]

It appeared as if Davis would have his way when, early in the afternoon, he received a very brief but very encouraging letter from Swettenham. Here is the full text: "I beg to thank your Excellency for the kind assistance which you have rendered to the Government of this colony."[70] Swettenham's report tellingly omitted any mention of this letter. How could he have reconciled it with what happened immediately afterward?

Just why this letter was followed so soon by another of an entirely different character—the second one being delivered to Davis "perhaps an hour later," at about 3:00 P.M.[71]—is open to conjecture. It is possible, but hardly likely, that Swettenham had begun composing his longer letter even before sending off his note of thanks. Far more probable is that his hostility toward the United States—evidently kept largely under control up to that point[72]—combined with a frustrated sense of being outmaneuvered by Admiral Davis to bring forth a rather sudden outburst of sarcasm and indiscretion.

This outburst may have been triggered by the equally anti-American and equally embarrassed Brigadier General J. N. A. Marshall who, according to Swettenham, was waiting for him at Headquarters House when the governor returned from visiting parts of Kingston. A letter from Marshall to Swettenham of January 18 was apparently presented at this time. Marshall, referring to himself as the officer "under whom all military arrangements are bound to be made," sharply condemned the landing in Jamaica of "an armed party of considerable strength" and demanded to know "who is responsible for this extraordinary and totally unnecessary proceeding."[73]

Whatever its precise causes, Swettenham's letter to Davis was extremely undiplomatic. The first paragraph was unobjectionable, and the second, although in substance highly insensitive to the well-being of the population of Kingston, maintained propriety in its form. The rest of the letter, however, was little more than a spate of insults and other offensive remarks, climaxed by the closing paragraph. Here is the body of the letter, in full:

I thank you very much for your kind letter of the 17th (delivered to me this morning), for your kind call, and for all the assistance you have given and have offered to give us.

While I most fully and heartily appreciate your very generous offers of assistance, I feel it my duty to ask you to re-embark your working parties and all parties which your kindness has prompted you to land.

If in consideration of the American Vice Consul's assiduous attention to his family at his country house, the American Consulate may need guarding in your opinion (he was present and it was unguarded an hour ago) I have no objection to your detailing a force for the sole purpose of guarding it, but that party must not have firearms, or anything more offensive than clubs or staves for their functions.

I find your working party this morning helping Mr. Crosswell to clean his store; Mr. Crosswell is delighted to get valuable work done without cost to himself, and if your Excellency were to remain long enough I am sure almost the whole of the private owners would be glad of the services of the Navy to save them expense.

It is no longer any question of humanity: all the dead died days ago, and the work of giving them burial is merely one of convenience.

I should be glad to accept delivery of the safe which the alleged thieves were in possession of from Milke's store. The American Vice Consul has no knowledge of it. The store is close to a sentry post and the officer in charge of the post professes profound ignorance of the incident: but there is still on the premises a large safe which was opened both by fire and by other means.[74]

I believe the police surveillance of no city is adequate for the protection of private property. I may remind Your Excellency that not long ago it was discovered that thieves had lodged in and pillaged the town house of a New York Millionaire during his absence for the summer; but this fact would not have justified a British Admiral in landing an armed party to assist the New York Police.[75]

Several comments contained in Swettenham's report to Lord Elgin do seem to shed some light on his thinking—small-minded and misguided though it was—at the time he wrote his letter. "I thought," he declared, "it was more courteous to the Admiral to deal with his reasons than to ignore them completely." Swettenham also observed, resentfully, that "the officers and men of the American fleet" had "a strong desire to distinguish themselves and to be conspicuous in succouring Kingston." These Americans' "presence reassured the timid," the unappreciative governor went on, their "working parties helped private citizens," and their "expenditure tended to enrich the city."[76]

Faced now with an unambiguous imperative to withdraw his forces from Kingston, Admiral Davis promptly ordered his working parties to cease their activities and to return to their ships. This had become, in his view, "the only course compatible with the dignity of the United States."[77] Because, he explained, coaling arrangements he had made for the *Missouri* precluded the Americans from departing before the following afternoon, the admiral set 4:00 P.M. Saturday, January 19, as his sailing time.[78]

Meanwhile, the new American emergency hospital, put together with great energy and efficiency the morning of the 18th, had been in operation for only a few hours when Swettenham's letter was delivered to Davis. It was "fully equipped," running very smoothly, and providing a high quality of care to patients who were "coming in constantly."[79] Here Davis did *not* call an immediate halt to American relief efforts, but instead directed the surgeons and support staff to continue their work until 1:00 P.M. on the 19th, at which time the Jesuit Fathers would help turn the hospital over to local practitioners. "I felt justified in retaining control of the hospital until the last minute," he rationalized, "as the whole establishment was American property."[80]

As expected, the *Yankton* arrived the afternoon of the 18th, bringing additional medical supplies. These were "not needed," Davis reported, because the Kingston hospitals and the American hospital had been "fully stocked." The admiral ordered the *Yankton* to head back to Guantanamo at 1:00 P.M. the next day.[81] Davis also left with Vice Consul Orrett these orders for the commanding officer of the *Celtic*, which had yet to arrive: "As there is no lack of provisions at Kingston and as the Governor assures me that the stores on board the *Celtic* are not needed, you will, upon receipt of this order, proceed without delay to Guantanamo, Cuba."[82]

⨯⨯   ⨯⨯

On January 18, having sent off his "clever" and "witty" letter, Governor Swettenham seems to have been feeling his oats. He declared indignantly in a letter of that date to Secretary Elgin that he was "astonished and disgusted" when he learned on the morning of January 17 that "two armed parties" had been landed.[83]

By the 19th, however, Swettenham was probably beginning to feel something else—the heat. (Another, less plausible interpretation is that he was still totally oblivious to the personal fiasco that lay ahead for him and saw himself as being magnanimous in victory.) In the morning Davis visited him "to say goodbye."[84] It was an awkward, although outwardly amicable, parting.[85] Later in the day—apparently after the ships' departure since Davis did not receive it for a number of days—the governor wrote the admiral yet another letter. He offered "the profound gratitude" of Jamaica to Davis and his men. Swettenham specifically praised and thanked Davis for "the promptitude with which you despatched the surgical appliances which we needed, the rapidity with which you followed them and devoted [yourselves] to aiding suffering humanity, to guarding your Consular archives and the penitentiary, to assisting in clearing the streets and pulling down walls," all of which "deserve my fullest recognition and gratitude." The governor added an expression of "my most sincere thanks" for Davis's "desire . . . to have done more if my scruples had permitted my acceptance of your Squadron's services so generously rendered."[86]

Over the next couple of days, Swettenham also sent telegrams to Secretary of State Root and Colonial Secretary Elgin. To the former he wired: "Jamaica profoundly grateful to your excellency for expression of sympathy and for the very practical aid so kindly given by Admiral Davis."[87] For the latter he had this message: "Respectfully suggest your telegraphing cordial thanks from His Majesty's Government to United States Government for prompt and powerful assistance rendered by United States Navy under Rear-Admiral Davis to suffering Kingston."[88] And there was an additional telegram to Elgin, briefly summarizing recent events in a manner that implied the absence of any awkward occurrences. It announced the arrival of the *Indefatigable*, "with stores from Trinidad," and encapsulated the American relief mission in these words: "United States steamships 'Missouri' and 'Indiana,' with Admiral Davis, arrived 17th, left 19th, after rendering all possible assistance."[89]

But gracious, laudatory communications with Davis, Root, Elgin, and others could hardly erase Swettenham's recent act of incivility. His letter to Davis of January 18 was a fact. He was going to have to answer for it.[90]

In the perception of the people of Jamaica, there was an "incident" even before they learned about the letter. Most of Kingston's inhabitants viewed Swettenham's demand for an American withdrawal, word of which had spread rapidly through the city, as an extraordinary offense.

C. W. Tait, the mayor of Kingston who had been seriously injured in the earthquake, hastily arranged a meeting with his city councillors at which a letter to Admiral Davis was drafted under Tait's signature. Hoping that Davis would reconsider and remain in Kingston, the local officials gave this letter to a representative of the *Kingston Gleaner*, who was to deliver it to Davis and also publish it in that day's edition. It captures very well a widespread feeling:

> On behalf of the . . . Council as well as all the citizens of this stricken city, I desire to express my deep and sincere regret that any unpleasantness should have arisen to cause you to decide to withdraw the valuable assistance which you have voluntarily and so generously been rendering to this Country and my unfortunate fellow citizens.
>
> Whatever may have been the cause that has induced you to decide to withdraw, we deeply regret it, and we do not approve or take any

part in it; so we ask you not to withdraw your valuable assistance or take offence at the conduct of one man if at a time when overwrought by responsibility and calamity he has acted in a manner that he himself will regret on reflection; and in particular I ask you not to let the sick, wounded, and destitute call in vain for the comforts which until now they have been receiving from your hands, and for which I and they thank and bless you.[91]

Many of the Americans involved in the naval operation testified to the Jamaican people's dismay and anger at Governor Swettenham for ordering the American withdrawal. Those engaged in medical relief work were particularly emphatic on this point. Surgeon O. D. Norton found a "universal sentiment . . . of profound indignation against the Governor" among the patients at the American emergency hospital, "many of whom cried and begged us to stay."[92] Medical Inspector H. E. Ames remarked with regard to a man sent by Swettenham to harass the Americans at the hospital: "As he left me he said 'Unofficially I will say that I agree with you, it is an outrage'."[93] Surgeon W. N. McDonnell commented in a similar vein: "On every hand I heard expressions of disgust and disappointment with the stand taken by the Governor, . . . and I heard several English born subjects express their shame and regret that their government was so poorly represented."[94] And Lieutenant Pitt Scott, who headed a group engaged in removing dead bodies and in other "disagreeable" tasks, noted the downcast spirit permeating Kingston when the citizenry learned of the imminent American departure. Scott quoted "an elderly man of very refined appearance, apparently an Englishman," as exemplifying this spirit: "You know this is a personal matter of *one* person; all the *people* appreciate what you have done for us, and want you to stay."[95]

Once the contents of his letter became known, Swettenham's stock among Jamaicans fell even further. The *Jamaica Daily Telegraph* was able to resume publication on January 22, and in that day's edition it included the full text of the two key letters. The *Daily Telegraph* asserted that the efforts of the American navy had been "magnificent" and "splendid," whereas the behavior of Swettenham had been "inexplicable" and "absolutely reprehensible." Jamaicans, this paper declared, were "indignant at his autocratic, bullying and insulting manner."[96] A Cornell University student then in Jamaica wrote a letter to President Roosevelt containing a similar message: "Everywhere the departure of the American fleet under the unfortunate circumstances attending has aroused a burst of indignation, and along with the shame of this insult the kindliest expressions of friendship for America."[97] Dr. Enos Nuttall, Archbishop of Jamaica, was more saddened than surprised by the incident. "It was merely a result," the *New York Times* quoted Nuttall as saying, "of the dictatorial character of the Governor." Nuttall then criticized Swettenham more generally for "his imperious manner, his frequent abuse of subordinates, and his discourtesy to citizens."[98] Finally, these citizens themselves spoke out in letters to the editors of Jamaica's newspapers. One letter accused Swettenham of treating "with contumely the gallant Admiral Davis of a friendly nation" and of an "exhibition of pride and rank ingratitude . . . which will astonish the world."[99] Another expressed "keen indignation and shame" and urged "public meetings [in] every parish in the island" for the purpose of adopting "resolutions of disapproval" that could then be sent on to Lord Elgin in England.[100]

Just before sailing from Kingston the afternoon of January 19, Admiral Davis replied to the letter from Mayor Tait. Certainly Davis was dissembling to a degree when he declared "that I am not withdrawing my Squadron from Kingston by reason of any unpleasantness, any misunderstanding, or any cause of offense." Why he felt obliged to mislead in this way is unclear. But another passage in this letter did strike at what was, from Davis's perspective, the heart of the matter: "As a foreign Naval Officer, I am bound to respect the wishes and requirements of the supreme authority of this island."[101]

Toward the end of his report, Davis detailed the desperate state of affairs in Kingston and the utter inadequacy of the Swettenham government's response. The city "exists only as a complete ruin." Throughout Kingston "the sanitary conditions are shocking," and "the stench is insufferable." In the face of these conditions, Davis deplored "the want of organization and of organized effort," his own men appearing to him to have been "the only organized and systematized forces in the city." But ultimately there was no getting around the fundamental problem noted just above: "Had I remained longer . . . my position, which had been delicate and embarrassing from the first, would have become wholly untenable and false, derogatory to the dignity of the Flag, and impossible under International Law."[102]

On Sunday, January 20, the Navy Department received a brief message from Guantanamo: "*Missouri, Indiana, Yankton* returned here; services not required Kingston. Davis left orders Kingston for *Celtic* to return here also."[103] An incredible four days of adventure, horror, hard work, exhilaration, gratification, and disappointment had come to an end for the earthquake relief squadron of Rear Admiral C. H. Davis.

⊰   ⊱

Upon learning of the Davis mission's premature termination and the reasons for it, the Navy Department was quick to produce a relevant historical precedent. On March 4, 1895—at a time when Anglo-American relations were still largely unfriendly—three American ships under Rear Admiral R. W. Meade landed over 200 men to fight a massive fire raging in Port of Spain in the British colony of Trinidad. Because the fire had attained "alarming proportions," the men were landed before an invitation could be secured.[104] The next day the governor of Trinidad, F. Napier Broome, wrote a letter to Meade praising the Americans' courage and the "indefatigable exertions" that had "saved . . . much valuable property." Broome's letter concluded on a highly encouraging note: "I beg to assure that this service will not soon be forgotten by the people of Port of Spain and the Colony generally, and that our appreciation of it is much enhanced by the fact that the assistance came from vessels of the United States Navy."[105]

But in 1907—at a time when Anglo-American relations were extremely friendly, as friendly as they had ever been—an American naval landing for disaster relief in a British West Indian colony had, in an ironic contrast, met with a hostile and discourteous reception from the governor. How would people in the United States and in Britain react to this troubling encounter? How would Theodore Roosevelt's government and its British counterpart deal with the issue? The strength of the bond between the United States and Great Britain was suddenly being tested.

Anglo-American Damage-Control Diplomacy:
The Incident Contained

● ○ ●

The story of the Swettenham incident burst forth in many British and American newspapers on Monday, January 21, 1907. "Help Resented, Our Ships Leave," read a headline in the *New York Times*, which published reasonably accurate versions of the two major letters,[1] as did the *London Times* and other journals. It is uncertain whether the letters had come into the possession of journalists inadvertently or, as seems more likely, as the result of a conscious decision by Admiral Davis or one of his officers. Regardless, the Jamaica incident was now in the hands of the British and American governments.

Neither government intended to wait and see how people in the two countries would react. Both governments were concerned that the Swettenham affair might do harm to their rapprochement of recent years. Theodore Roosevelt and Sir Edward Grey were particularly determined to ensure that Anglo-American relations would be unaffected by the Jamaican episode. Thus, the strategy pursued both in London and in Washington was one of aggressive public diplomacy, whose objectives were to downplay the Swettenham incident by isolating the governor of Jamaica, to set the tone for public discussion on the issue, and to bring the incident to a close as rapidly as possible. Of these three objectives, the last would prove to be the most difficult to achieve.

Because the offensive behavior of a British official was responsible for the incident, it was up to England to make the first diplomatic move. As the British had learned during the Alaskan boundary dispute, Theodore Roosevelt was particularly sensitive about questions of "national honor." The United States' honor, indeed, was among the very few political things dearer to Roosevelt than its friendship with Britain. The British government would have to disavow Swettenham's rude act, and then the president would eagerly embrace any such disavowal. TR fully expected England to respond in this way, especially in light of the tightening of the Anglo-American bond that had occurred in 1906. He was not disappointed.

Damage-control diplomacy began immediately in England. The foreign secretary, the colonial secretary, and even the war secretary became involved the very first day. Colonial Secretary Lord Elgin telegraphed Swettenham, request-ing him to "telegraph facts as to alleged friction with American admiral." Concerned that he had been insufficiently explicit, Elgin wired Swettenham again: "If you wrote letter or letters to Admiral of United States Navy, please telegraph exact terms without delay."[2] War Secretary R. B. Haldane cabled Secretary of State Elihu Root—then on a visit to Canada and being represented by Assistant Secretary Robert Bacon—that he had read "what purports to be letter from Governor of Jamaica." Haldane implicitly rebuked Swettenham by expressing his "deep gratitude to American Admiral for generous assistance ten-dered at most critical time."[3] Later in the day Foreign Secretary Grey tele-graphed Chargé d'Affaires Esmé Howard, temporarily in charge of the British embassy in Washington, that Britain was "making official inquiries" regarding the Swettenham letter. Grey asked Howard to "inform the Assistant Secretary . . . that, if the text is correct, I deeply regret that a British official should have addressed such a letter to the gallant admiral who has rendered valuable assis-tance to British subjects in distress, a feeling which is, I am sure, universally shared here."[4] Howard dutifully transmitted Grey's message to Bacon in a for-mal letter that evening.[5]

Grey's telegram and Howard's note appeared in the *New York Times* on January 22 and January 23, respectively. "British Apology at Washington/ No Report from Swettenham, but Minister Acts" was the telling headline on the 22nd.[6]

Bacon had been in contact with President Roosevelt between the arrival of Haldane's and Grey's messages. Right after communicating with TR, Bacon telegraphed Haldane; Roosevelt was seizing his first opportunity to present his position to the British, undoubtedly hoping to encourage further conciliatory pronouncements from London: "The President greatly appreciates your cordial telegram and is glad if the proximity of this country has made it possible to be of the slightest assistance to the stricken people of Jamaica in this crisis." There was an offer of "further aid. . . . We know how cheerfully you would render such aid to us were the circumstances reversed."[7] Bacon verbally conveyed a similar message to Howard when they held their meeting in the evening.[8]

Roosevelt was taking a keen interest in the Swettenham affair and, typi-cally, was managing the details of American diplomacy. Because Grey's telegram had gone beyond Haldane's by explicitly repudiating Swettenham, Roosevelt's response also went farther. Moreover, he saw to its prompt publiation so that the American and British people would become aware of and, he hoped, be influenced by his attitude. TR's reply to Grey took the form of a letter from Bacon to Howard, dated January 22. In part it read: "*I hasten to assure you, on behalf of the President, that this Government will pay no heed whatever to the matter,* and very much appreciates the frank and ready courtesy and consideration shown in this despatch by Sir Edward Grey." Roosevelt, Bacon's letter added, found it "especially gratifying . . . that it has been possible for this country to show in a practical way, however small, its friendship to a community of your people in a time of such suffering and need."[9] "President Ends the Incident" was the way the *New York Times* introduced the article in which the full text of this letter was published.[10]

In Britain as well damage-control diplomacy was in high gear on the 22nd. John R. Carter, first secretary of the American embassy, cabled to the State Department that the Foreign Office had informed him of the Colonial Office inquiry launched the preceding day and had promised to apprise him of its results. Carter described "the universal sentiment of officials, press and the public" as "one of amazement and regret at the alleged action on the part of the Governor." And he related that Roosevelt's response to Haldane's telegram "has created a most excellent impression everywhere."[11] Bacon's reply to Carter carried on the Anglo-American love-fest. "There is little to add to the Department's reply on behalf of the President to Sir Edward Grey's cordial despatch," Bacon declared after expressing satisfaction with Carter's report, "except that *you cannot emphasize too strongly* the high appreciation of its contents by everyone here, officials, press and public, and *the desire of this Government to minimize and disregard the incident.*"[12]

Another major part of Britain's energetic diplomacy on the 22nd was a late-afternoon telegram from Elgin to Swettenham. Unwilling to wait for Swettenham's reply to his cables of the day before, Elgin quoted a newspaper text of the governor's letter to Admiral Davis of January 18 and commented: "If such a letter is correctly attributed to you I must observe that both in tone and expression it is highly improper, and especially unbecoming to His Majesty's representative in addressing the officer of a friendly Power engaged upon an errand of mercy." Then came an order: "I must further require you to withdraw forthwith and unreservedly any such letter, and to express your regret for having written it. Your withdrawal should be telegraphed to me at once, when it will be transmitted to the Government of the United States through the proper channels."[13]

Before receiving this dispatch, Swettenham cabled his replies to Elgin's two telegrams of the 21st, and these arrived at the Colonial Office the morning of January 23. One provided the contents of the two principal letters and also implied that Admiral Davis might have landed armed parties without prior authorization.[14] The other, very brief, disingenuously stated: "Am not conscious of any friction."[15] Winston Churchill, under secretary of state for the colonies, observed in his minute that this latter claim was "palpably untrue."[16] With regard to the letter to Davis, Sydney Olivier, the Colonial Office official who would replace Swettenham as governor of Jamaica several months later, lamented revealingly: "Swettenham has been in the habit of addressing letters more silly and provocative than this to public bodies and humble persons in Jamaica. . . . On more than one occasion I have urged that their impropriety should be pointed out to him. I wish more than ever now that this check had been put on him."[17] There was a consensus within the Colonial Office that the circumstances of Davis's landing should be investigated, but not before "the letter is disposed of."[18]

Disposed of it soon was. Two more telegrams from Swettenham reached the Colonial Office the morning of January 24. True, they betrayed dismay and anger on the part of the governor—who sought to emphasize the involuntary nature of his withdrawal of his letter—and, it was to become clear later, marked the opening salvos of a troublesome new phase of the Swettenham incident. Still, Elgin's order was obeyed. "I respectfully request," one of the cables read, "that following telegram may be sent on to American Admiral, Davis, Cuba, from me through the proper channel: 'At the instance of the Secretary of State for the Colonies I desire to fully and unreservedly withdraw my letter of 18th January, and express regret that I wrote it.'"[19] The other cable was even shorter: "Respectfully apply for permission for retirement on account of age, forthwith to be relieved."[20]

Elgin telegraphed back to Swettenham that same day. He was "glad to receive" word of the withdrawal of the letter to Davis. To the governor's "second telegram" there would be "a separate reply." In addition, the secretary requested that the governor send "a full report . . . by telegraph" of "the circumstances in which armed parties were landed in Jamaica."[21]

Meanwhile, the British government lost no time in advising the United States of the retraction of Swettenham's letter. In the morning on the 24th, the Foreign Office telegraphed Howard in Washington: "You should inform the American Government that the Governor of Jamaica withdraws his letter of the 18th instant to Admiral Davis with an expression of his regret."[22] Howard readily complied.[23] Charles Hardinge, drafter of the Foreign Office's telegram, also wrote a note to Grey. Hardinge asserted that "the incident of the letter is now happily closed" and told Grey about the Colonial Office inquiry into Davis's landing and about Swettenham's request to resign.[24]

That same busy morning, Thursday, the 24th, Howard spoke personally with President Roosevelt. As usual, TR was determined not to allow his position to be in the least misunderstood. After his talk with Roosevelt, Howard wrote

Grey an informative and insightful letter focusing primarily on the outlook of Roosevelt and the American people on the Swettenham incident. The affair, Howard observed, had been "treated . . . by the President . . . from the beginning . . . as of no great importance . . . and as in no way tending to alter the cordial relations now fortunately existing between the two Governments." Howard perceptively contrasted the "remarkably moderate" reaction of the press with the "general outburst of anti-English feeling" that "would probably have occurred some years ago in consequence of an incident of this nature." Still, he predicted too apprehensively, Swettenham's letter "will leave a good deal of soreness behind it, even though it is generally recognised that it has been condemned by His Majesty's Government and the people of Great Britain." Toward the end of his letter, the British diplomat refocused his attention on Roosevelt: "The President . . . said he did not believe, after the correspondence between the two Governments had been published and read, that there would be any general feeling of annoyance. . . . As regards himself, he hoped" the British government realized "that he considered the matter a purely personal one of no real consequence." Howard had "replied that I felt sure that His Majesty's Government had cordially appreciated his messages, as to the meaning of which there could be no doubt whatever."[25]

Robert Bacon did have a concern, which he expressed in a cable to John Carter of January 24, that British government officials might share in the criticism of Admiral Davis's landing of armed men rumored to be in the British press.[26] Davis's dispatch to Admiral Evans of January 17, which included a reference to the authorization Davis had received before sending his bluejackets (enlisted men) ashore, had by now been published. Carter, following an exchange of notes with Charles Hardinge,[27] attempted to reassure Secretary Root, who had returned to the United States from Canada the evening of the 24th, in cables of January 25 and 27. "Criticism rather insignificant, all previous to publication of report [Davis's dispatch to Evans], and confined to a few opposition journals," the first one read.[28] The second noted that while the government was still awaiting Swettenham's report, "neither Colonial Office nor Foreign Office has any reason whatever to think that any irregularity has taken place."[29]

An intriguing aspect of the diplomacy of the Swettenham incident is that Bacon had apparently telegraphed Carter on the 24th without first consulting Roosevelt. The "incident" in Roosevelt's mind was Swettenham's letter—period—and it had already been brought to a satisfactory diplomatic conclusion. The extensive Davis Report had not yet reached the president, who at this time probably worried that if the landing—as opposed to the letter—was allowed to become an issue, it could prove to be a complicated one. He wanted it left alone. There exists in the State Department archives a scribbled, unsigned note stamped January 28, 1907, which almost certainly was written by TR, initiated by him, or (least likely because of Root's absence during the initial days of diplomacy) initiated by Secretary Root with Roosevelt's knowledge and approval. An easily imaginable scenario is that Carter's telegrams came to Roosevelt's attention sometime before late afternoon on the 28th, and that the displeased president either shot off a note and a draft letter to be delivered immediately to Root or telephoned the secretary of state with instructions to act at once. In the mystery note the name of the addressee is illegible. These are the contents in their entirety: "Cable to Carter that we have received the letter of withdrawal and the incident is closed and he had better drop it—see draft of letter to Howard just sent up."[30] This note obviously led to the brief cable from Root to the American embassy in London of the same date, January 28. It read: "Carter's telegram twenty-seventh. Incident is closed by Governor's withdrawal of letter and expression of regret."[31]

The "draft letter" referred to in the unsigned note went to Howard under Root's signature the following day. Its underlying assumption was that the Swettenham letter was and always had been the whole issue. This letter to Howard constituted, in essence, Roosevelt's attempt at an official decree of the harmonious closure of the affair. The U.S. government, Root wrote, "is very appreciative . . . that your Government has in every step of *this little incident* acted in the spirit of the most considerate and cordial friendship for the United States." Moreover, the United States "fully understood the distressing circumstances under which [Governor Swettenham's] letter was written, and *the voluntary withdrawal of the letter closes the incident, not merely in form but in reality.*"[32]

Reports emanating from London suggested that Root's letter had achieved its intended effect. "It is learned," the *Jamaica Daily Telegraph* informed its readers, "that the International phase of the Swettenham incident has been finally closed by the Governor formally withdrawing his letter to Admiral Davis and expressing regret for what he had written."[33]

Even before this flurry of diplomatic activity on the part of Roosevelt and Root, additional encouraging reports were issuing from England. On the day he sent his first telegram, Carter also wrote a longer letter to Root. "The publication of Admiral Davis's report [letter to Evans] and the President's reply through Bacon [on the 24th] to Sir Edward Grey's telegram [of the 21st] which was communicated by the Foreign Office to the press here to-day has had a most excellent effect," Carter told the secretary of state. There was "universal condemnation of Swettenham in every quarter." Carter ended with a revelation indicative of the trust and friendship prevailing in Anglo-American relations at the beginning of 1907: "I heard last night from a member of the Foreign Office, most confidentially, that Swettenham's resignation would be accepted."[34]

Equally indicative of the solidity of the Anglo-American bond was a speech delivered in Manchester on January 25 by James Bryce, soon to sail for Washington to assume his new post as ambassador. Anglo-American relations "never have been better," Bryce declared enthusiastically. Then he elaborated: "The incident fresh in your memory need be referred to only for the sake of saying that the moral of it was: This is how different things are now, happily, from those times when an incident like that would have been the signal for cries of defiance in the press of both countries." Today, "no one took this matter as anything but an occasion wherein we could show our trust in one another." Bryce asserted that "nothing . . . ought to be dearer to us than the maintenance of the most friendly and the most intimate relations with the great Republic across the Atlantic."[35]

Carter's and Bryce's favorable assessments of press opinion were echoed by Sir Percy Sanderson, Britain's consul general in New York. In a letter to Howard of January 24, which was sent on to Grey on the 26th, Sanderson described the editorials appearing up to then in the various New York papers as "throughout moderate in tone." These editorials, Sanderson related, had emphasized "the fact that the action of the Governor . . . was as unfavorably viewed by the general public in England" and "by the British Government as it was by the public of the United States," and had expressed "a consensus of opinion that the incident brought discredit on the Governor personally but would not in any way disturb the good relations between the two countries." Sanderson listed seven newspapers as sharing "substantially" this outlook.[36]

≪   ≫

The position of the press forms an interesting facet of the Swettenham affair, and, moreover, considerable historical significance attaches to it. First, the press in England and America willingly cooperated with the two governments in the rapid diplomatic defusing of the matter. Second, the editorial response of British and American journals to the Jamaica incident provides perhaps the single best window of the entire Roosevelt presidency on the thinking of opinion molders regarding the deepening of the Anglo-American special relationship. It provides such a good window, particularly insofar as the United States is concerned, on account of the peculiar nature of the incident.

The Swettenham incident was different in character from the Russo-Japanese War and the Moroccan crisis, where the Anglo-American element was largely invisible to the press and the public—different also from the Alaskan boundary dispute and the Newfoundland fisheries problem, which did involve national honor as well as conflicting interests but which involved the former in a relatively impersonal way. The Swettenham affair, featuring an egregious and gratuitous affront by a British colonial governor to a high-ranking American naval officer supplying emergency relief to the governor's devastated colony, was entirely a matter of national honor, and of a very intimate sort. In this sense it had more in common with the *Trent* affair of 1861 — in which an American naval officer forcibly removed two Confederate agents from a British ship, resulting in outbursts of passionate rhetoric on both sides of the Atlantic and almost in an Anglo-American war that would have assured the independence of the Confederacy — than it did with any other episode of the Roosevelt period. An encounter of the Swettenham-Davis type was bound to elicit the emergence of any bad feelings lingering beneath the surface.

Bradford Perkins contends that the "new spirit" of the Anglo-American rapprochement "most affected the political elite."[37] The reaction of the American press to the Swettenham incident is evidence that Perkins could easily have included the fourth estate under his "elite" umbrella.

A recurrent theme in the American press was condemnation of Swettenham combined with sympathy for Britons and Jamaicans. "The man who insulted Admiral Davis," one paper asserted, "humiliated only the country unfortunate enough to have such a person in its service at a time and place that enable him to misrepresent the people of England and Jamaica."[38] Another declared that Swettenham's letter "breathes contempt and hatred and shows a desire to wound," but that "the American people will not charge the offense of this official misfit upon the people of Kingston or lay them up against the British government."[39] A third claimed that "the American people are too sensible to hold the actions of Governor Swettenham against anyone but himself."[40] And a fourth, observing that the British press was doing "full justice" to Swettenham's "monumental" misdeed, urged that "we look the other way and appear not to listen as the thwacking takes place."[41]

A number of American newspapers chose to use the Swettenham incident as an opportunity to reaffirm Anglo-American solidarity. That the governor had made "a spectacle of himself," argued one, was "no reason why the two great nations he has so untowardly involved should go and do likewise."[42] Another saw Swettenham's "idiotic conduct" as serving "to develop afresh the mutual good feeling" between Britain and America.[43] Most notable in this regard was an editorial in the *New York Times* of January 24, titled "Lasting Peace with England." Referring only in passing to "Swettenham's escapade," this editorial focused instead on "the firm friendship between the English and the American people," averring that "Anglo-American amity," if at one time largely "talk, . . . has ripened into an enduring reality."[44]

The issue of February 9, 1907, of *Harper's Weekly* contained a very perceptive analysis under the title "Anglo-American Relations and the Swettenham Incident." This article described Swettenham as representative of England's "once great but long since decadent" landed interest, a class that "has been well-nigh ruined by the ultimate results of the repeal of the corn laws" in 1846, a class that favored the Confederacy in the Civil War and that continued still to entertain hostile feelings toward the United States. This essay also insightfully placed in historical perspective the American response to the Swettenham affair:

> The fact that the rebuff administered to Admiral Davis . . . should have evoked on the part of our national government and of the American press neither indignation nor resentment, but merely good-natured tolerance and amusement, bears witness to the magnitude of the change that has taken place in our attitude toward Great Britain in the eleven years that have elapsed since . . . Mr. Cleveland issued his Venezuela message. By a common impulse, the State Department and all of our influential newspapers combined to treat the offender as a crank, and declined to hold the British Ministry or the British people responsible for a foolish act of discourtesy and impertinence.

America, now a self-assured world power, had, the article went on, "outgrown the sensitiveness" of "the time . . . when we regarded Britons with habitual suspicion, and when a minor British official, or even an ordinary British subject, had it in his power to wound our national susceptibilities."[45]

A few American newspapers, naturally, expressed a contrary outlook that was either critical of Admiral Davis or dubious about the reality of Anglo-American friendship. "It would have been courteous as well as customary," said one, for Davis "to place all the American fleet at Swettenham's command."[46] Another claimed that Swettenham "speaks out the natural British feeling toward us. . . . Americans do not like Englishmen . . . and Englishmen do not like Americans."[47] But such views were decidedly atypical.[48]

The stance of the British press was, on the whole, similar to that of the American. Commendation of Davis was one theme. "The American Admiral's action in going to Kingston and offering help," one journal declared, "was what all Englishmen would wish a British Admiral to do in similar circumstances."[49] Swettenham, generally, was roundly condemned. "The standard of conduct which England expects from her Governors," another paper observed, "is, and should always be, a high one, and, unfortunately, Sir J. A. Swettenham fell far below it in a moment of irritation."[50] A third theme was the durability of the Anglo-American tie. "The incident can have no effect whatever," still another paper editorialized, "on the good relations between the British and American peoples."[51] The *London Times* addressed all three of these themes. "The most charitable explanation of the extraordinary wording of Sir Alexander Swettenham's communication," the *Times* remarked, "is that he was overwrought and unstrung by the terrible events of the last week." Whatever the case, "this lamentable close to a mission conceived in so admirable a spirit of international good will will certainly not lessen the gratitude of the unfortunate colony and of Englishmen all over the world either to Admiral Davis and his bluejackets or to the Government of the United States which sent them on their errand of mercy."[52]

Swettenham had few defenders in the British press—as John Carter had correctly reported in his letter to Root of January 25—even among the minority of newspapers critical of the conduct of the British government or of Admiral Davis. War Secretary Haldane's telegram to Root of January 21 was termed by one such journal "entirely superfluous," a "meddlesome indiscretion," and an "extraordinary breach of official etiquette."[53] Another suggested that Davis, despite his "praiseworthy efforts," had gone "beyond the necessities of the case and encroached too far on British authority."[54] One journal that did attempt to sustain Swettenham did so "on the ground that the idea of the British flag having to be upheld by American marines[55] was intolerably humiliating."[56]

In Jamaica itself, unsurprisingly, Swettenham was denounced practically with a single voice. The criticism offered by the *Jamaica Daily Telegraph* was presented in the preceding chapter. The *Jamaica Times*, in an editorial headed "The Governor's Inhumanity," suggested that Swettenham's "extraordinary behavior can only be explained by him having become drunken with power."[57] And the *Daily Gleaner*, in an angry open letter of February 12 to the "Elected Members of the Legislative Council," insisted that the American naval forces had come to the colony "on an errand of mercy" and had landed only when "requested to do so by Mr. Bourne." Swettenham, the *Daily Gleaner* charged, had been "unspeakably rude" to Jamaican officials as well as to Admiral Davis.[58] The governor's lukewarm support for an imperial loan for stricken Jamaica also incurred the *Daily Gleaner*'s wrath. "And now, in our hour of distress, when the future seems so dark for thousands of persons," warned a late February issue of this newspaper, "it almost appears as if we shall be forced to go to America for help—to America whose ships were practically ordered from our shores and who has been told that we need no assistance!"[59]

In contrast to the overall one-sidedness of editorial comment in the United States, Great Britain, and Jamaica, the position of the press in British colonies other than Jamaica was more varied. There there was considerably more sympathy and even some enthusiasm expressed for Swettenham. The *Singapore Free Press* asserted that Davis had overstepped his legitimate authority, and that "in his relations with Admiral Davis, Sir Alexander did a duty that had to be done."[60] The *Quebec Chronicle* argued "that the Governor could not have acted otherwise without lowering the dignity and prestige of the Empire."[61] Particularly pleased with Swettenham was the *Toronto Saturday Night*. "It was with a feeling of unholy glee," this journal declared, "that many a Canadian received the news that the Governor of Jamaica had requested the United States Rear-Admiral to withdraw his men to his ships and leave the control of Kingston in the hands of British authorities where it belonged." Swettenham "was Governor, and he governed." This was, claimed the *Saturday Night,* "the first exhibition of spunk that Canadians of the present generation have ever seen displayed" toward the United States "by any representative of British authority." Moreover, Swettenham had written "a very compact letter, not a redundant word in it, a very model of composition for use in the schools."[62]

But in the colonies too Swettenham was widely censured. The *Straits Times* found it "almost impossible to conceive of a condition of affairs that could warrant or justify" Swettenham's "offensive" letter to Davis. "It is deeply to be regretted," this paper went on, "that such an incident should have arisen out of Admiral Davis's friendly and succouring mission."[63] The *St. John's Evening Telegram* expressed the views of many newspapers in Newfoundland and Canada: "The American government acted promptly and generously in sending help by its war ships, and we cannot conceive that the generosity displayed should have been treated with a rude rebuff."[64]

On the whole, then, press reaction to the Jamaica incident, especially in the United States and Britain where it counted most (as well as in Jamaica itself), was decidedly favorable to Admiral Davis, critical of Governor Swettenham, and protective of the Anglo-American friendship. The press was very willingly in league with American and British political leaders pursuing damage-control diplomacy following the Swettenham incident. More important from a larger view, elite opinion molders in both countries showed themselves to be very much on board as the great rapprochement matured.

As January 1907 was passing into February, a few noteworthy developments were occurring with respect to the Swettenham incident. The British Colonial Office was struggling with a recalcitrant Swettenham to pin down the facts of the episode in advance of the opening of a session of Parliament. The full Davis Report came to the attention of Theodore Roosevelt, renewing the president's interest in the "closed" affair, quieting one of his chief concerns about it, and spurring his continuing engagement at the helm of American diplomacy relative to the incident. Swettenham, for his part, sent to the Colonial Office the first of a series of increasingly bizarre, pathetic, and angry letters in defense of his conduct during his encounter with Davis.

Swettenham had not complied readily with the request cabled by Elgin on January 24 for "a full report . . . by telegraph" on the landing of American naval forces in Kingston. His initial telegraphed reply was to "invite reference" to the very cable that had left the Colonial Office uncertain as to the circumstances of the landing.[65] Elgin cabled back the same day, the 26th: "I am anxious to know whether you have any complaint to make against Admiral Davis of a breach of international law or of courtesy. The same inquiry is being made for its own information by the American Government"—here Elgin was referring to the quest launched by Bacon through Carter, to be terminated by a disapproving Roosevelt on the 28th—"and no reply can be made." The Foreign Office, Elgin had been told by F. J. S. Hopwood, was "pressing for an immediate reply," so Elgin marked his telegram "most urgent."[66]

Nevertheless, Swettenham again responded with an evasive reference to his unclear earlier cable.[67] Elgin wired back with irritation: "I presume you duly received my cipher telegraph of yesterday marked most urgent."[68] The governor *still* resisted, cabling "I beg respectfully to recommend your Lordship's awaiting the receipt of a despatch which follows by next mail."[69] (This despatch, dated January 28, constitutes the main part of "Swettenham's report," cited often in chapter 6.) In the Colonial Office C. P. Lucas, seconded by Hopwood, noted that "a despatch would not be in time for the opening of Parliament."[70] Elgin tried again: "Matter most urgent. . . . I must ask that the main points in the promised despatch containing the explanations already pressed for may be sent immediately by telegram."[71]

In an effort to dilute his anti-American image, Swettenham momentarily changed the subject. A cable of the 28th asked Elgin to "convey thanks to Government of United States of America for supply of tents just received."[72] Sent from Cuba to help house Kingston's thousands of homeless, these tents indeed were, as Vice Consul William Orrett informed the State Department, "graciously accepted" by the governor.[73]

But on the main issue, Swettenham continued to be unhelpful. A second telegram of the 28th was rather vague on the question of authorization for the initial landing of American forces.[74] And a cable of January 30 stated simply: "Request that important secret and confidential despatch may be expected by next mail tomorrow," an entirely unrealistic prognostication.[75] By this point Winston Churchill was on record in favor of accepting Swettenham's resignation: "The sooner he is out of Jamaica the better."[76]

Meanwhile, the patient Lord Elgin tried yet again. "Parliament meets on the 12th of February," he cabled to Swettenham on February 1, "and in making preparation for that event it is necessary that I should as soon as possible have before me a complete and full statement of all the material circumstances of the case." The colonial secretary then asked the governor once more to telegraph the important portions of the promised despatch.[77]

At last Swettenham got the message. On February 3 he cabled at length (in two segments) most of the contents of the dispatch in question. But by using the word "suggestion," he still left unclear whether Admiral Davis had received proper authorization before landing an armed party at the penitentiary.[78]

It took several more days for the Colonial Office to sort out this matter to its satisfaction. A telegram to Swettenham of February 5 read: "May I understand that landing of armed party on 17th January at Penitentiary was not invited either by colonial secretary or by Wedderburn?"[79] Swettenham's cabled reply of the same day, although still somewhat ambiguous on the question, was accepted by the Colonial Office as sufficient to exonerate Davis. In the words of Olivier, "the admiral understood [Bourne] to authorise the landing of the armed party suggested by Mr. Wedderburn, and sent orders accordingly."[80]

⤝   ⤞

All this hair-pulling would have been unnecessary, of course, if the comprehensive Davis Report, with its fifty-four appendixes, had been available to the British government, as it was soon to be. But even in Washington it was not until the very end of January that this report emerged from the Navy Department. President Roosevelt was the first to see it, probably on January 31, and a copy was delivered to Secretary Root on February 2.

Roosevelt was truly delighted with the Davis Report. His reaction is captured well by this extract from a letter of February 1 from Navy Secretary Victor Metcalf to Admiral Davis: "The President directs that the Department express to you his heartiest commendation of all you did at Kingston. . . . He states that you upheld the best traditions of our navy in thus rendering distinguished service to humanity, and approves your entire actions [*sic*]."[81]

The appearance of the Davis Report perceptibly altered Roosevelt's outlook on the Swettenham incident. Up to then, a statesmanly wariness toward the possibility that embarrassment for the United States and awkwardness in Anglo-American relations could result if Davis's landing was permitted to become an issue had defined the parameters of TR's diplomacy. His goals had been to confine discussion to Swettenham's letter, to secure and respond warmly to a British apology, and to put the potentially messy affair neatly to rest and move on. Roosevelt had been very successful in attaining these objectives. Yet he knew that party politics in England might reopen debate on the incident, a prospect with which he was uncomfortable.

Reading the Davis Report eliminated much of this discomfort. Not that Roosevelt wanted to see the incident resuscitated, for he manifestly hoped it would not be. But now, for the first time, he was convinced that the American position was in all respects unassailable. He had never for a moment doubted that the American naval mission had been a noble act of generosity, but now he was sure also that Admiral Davis had landed under proper authority and that the mission had been as well executed as it had been well motivated. The naturally combative American nationalist TR, although by no means eager to do diplomatic battle with the United States' great friend England, was ready to do it if necessary. And he *was* eager to talk about the Swettenham affair with his closest American and British friends, now that he had the "inside story" and found it so appealing.

Roosevelt additionally decided that he wanted the Davis Report brought promptly to the attention of the British government. He believed that familiarity with this report would stiffen the British government's resolve to maintain its conciliatory policy and to keep a lid on the issue in the face of any parliamentary mischief-making. He passed the report along through several channels in an approach reminiscent of his employment of multiple messengers as he managed the diplomacy of the Alaskan boundary dispute.

One conduit was to be TR's friend George Otto Trevelyan. "In view of the affair at Kingston," Roosevelt wrote in a letter of February 4, "you may possibly be interested in the enclosed report of Admiral Davis with several appendices." Trevelyan, TR suggested directively, "might show the papers to Sir Edward Grey." Roosevelt had not allowed the papers to be made public in America, "because I did not think there was any object to be attained; but I am rather inclined to feel that your people ought to have the chance to look at them, . . . simply for their own information and without having them brought before them in any formal way." The president closed his letter by assuring Trevelyan (and, indirectly, the British government) that "the Swettenham business caused us nothing but amusement, and I send you these papers merely because under like circumstances I should like to know in an unofficial way the truth about any of our own people in similar position."[82]

Trevelyan proved to be a faithful messenger. On February 23 he wrote back to TR, describing himself as "much honoured by your letter" and the Davis Report as "admirably written, and in a fine spirit." Roosevelt's friend had already been in touch with Grey, to whom he was sending the report "at once," for Grey's own information and for transmission to Secretary Elgin.[83]

Arthur Lee was a second unofficial channel. Like Trevelyan, Lee received an assurance "that nobody here pays the slightest attention to the incident." Davis's report was being sent to Lee "for your own information merely." Roosevelt's letter, dated February 12, did not even hint that Lee ought to share the report with others.[84]

There was no need for any such hint. TR and Lee, very close friends that they were, understood each other extremely well. Roosevelt knew that Lee would handle the Davis Report in whatever way was most advantageous to the cause of Anglo-American unity, and Lee knew that Roosevelt expected him to do so. "I showed it privately to Sir Edward Grey," the Conservative M.P. Lee informed the president late in March, "and to many sensible men who had no means of knowing the facts and who had been misled by some of the yellow journals which had sought copy by espousing Swettenham's cause."[85]

Despite what Roosevelt had written to Trevelyan, there was to be an official channel as well. Secretary Root delivered the Davis Report to Chargé d'Affaires Howard on February 3, requesting, Howard told Grey in an accompanying letter of February 4, that it "might be treated as confidential." Root had "added that the President had thought . . . these papers . . . might interest His Majesty's Government, not only as giving Admiral Davis' side of the story, but also because they contained some criticisms of the Jamaican Administration which might possibly be of use." Howard had also been told of a U.S. decision, "in spite of great pressure by the press, not to publish them, in order to avoid reopening an affair which was formally closed."[86]

About a week later this question of publication suddenly became the focus of some rather frenzied diplomatic activity. Circulating rumors induced Howard to send a cable to Grey on February 10, well in advance of the arrival in London of Howard's letter of the 4th and the Davis Report: "Press to-day states that Governor's report is to be laid before Parliament. If this is true it will certainly force United States Government to publish Admiral Davis' report, which they are most anxious to avoid doing, in order to prevent polemics in press." For his part, Roosevelt "was determined not to publish it if he could possibly avoid doing so, as he wished the incident to be considered as closed and done with." Howard sought an "assurance, . . . which I could communicate to Secretary of State in case of necessity, that His Majesty's Government do not contemplate publishing any documents on the subject."[87]

Since a decision on publication was primarily the responsibility of the Colonial Office, Grey could not immediately give Howard and the United States the assurance they were seeking. So he tried to do the next best thing, cabling Howard on the 11th: "Publication of Governor's report not yet decided upon. You may assure Secretary of State that if papers are published I will submit an advance proof to the American Ambassador."[88] E. Gorst of the Foreign Office elaborated in a longer letter of the same date, sent to Howard on Grey's behalf. If a decision was made to publish any papers, Gorst wrote, "we should endeavor to publish nothing that might raise any controversy as to the action of the Admiral, or call it into question." Gorst had already spoken along these lines to Whitelaw Reid. "The Ambassador said he would communicate what I had said to his Government, and he thought there was every reason to hope it would be regarded as satisfactory."[89]

Reid acted quickly, telegraphing Root right away:

> Sir Edward Grey sent for me to-day in consequence despatch from
> Esmé Howard, mentioning President's uneasiness at rumor British
> Government about to publish Swettenham's report, which President
> thought might compel him to publish that of Admiral Davis. . . . Grey
> said their plan was to publish nothing which would put the President
> under any such necessity. They would feel bound to recognize
> Swettenham's good work [a reference to Swettenham's own efforts to
> deal with the earthquake], but they considered his letter improper, had
> required its withdrawal and felt fully justified in that course by all they
> had since learned. They were cordially grateful to United States for
> what it did and for disposition it showed. Parliament meets tomorrow.
> Government will praise Swettenham for courage and energy and
> express warm thanks to the United States for its action.[90]

By the next day, a consensus against any publication was taking shape in
the Colonial Office. After seeing Howard's telegram to Grey, Hopwood commented: "We must try to avoid publication." Both Churchill and Elgin endorsed
Hopwood's opinion.[91]

The Davis Report reached the Foreign Office—through the official channel
as it turned out—on February 18. Gorst read it most closely and found it "very
temperate in tone." Davis, Gorst remarked, had employed "all possible means to
regularise his position."[92]

Hardinge of the Foreign Office then wrote to Hopwood of the Colonial
Office at the urging of Grey. Hardinge informed Hopwood that the Davis
Report was coming "in a day or two, but, in the meanwhile Sir Edward Grey has
asked me to remind you that he has promised the U.S. Ambassador to let him
have an advance copy of any papers you may intend to present to Parliament."
Hardinge closed with a sentence reflecting Grey's ongoing desire to promote
Anglo-American harmony at every opportunity: "He wishes me to add that, if
the Colonial Office do not expect to publish anything he would be grateful if you
would let him know so that he may tell the U.S. Ambassador."[93]

Hopwood promptly assured Hardinge that "no Jamaica papers relating to
the 'incident' are to be published until they have been submitted to Foreign
Office." Better yet, "*we do not intend to publish any if we can avoid it.*" Hopwood cautioned, however, that Swettenham's unpredictable behavior eventually "may
force some publication."[94]

Hopwood's message was passed on to Reid, who telegraphed Root on
February 22. "Have just been informed by Sir Edward Grey," the ambassador
reported, "that present intention is not to lay papers before Parliament, but
should circumstances require them to alter this intention later, they will not fail
to submit them to me before doing so."[95]

By late February of 1907, the determined efforts of the governments of the two English-speaking powers had succeeded admirably in containing, if not quite yet in closing, the Swettenham incident. The leaders of these governments undoubtedly would have reacted skeptically to a prediction that the closure of the incident was still a number of months away.

CHAPTER

8

The Friendship Undiminished:
Theodore Roosevelt, the British Government,
and the Closing of the Incident

● ○ ●

Although President Roosevelt must have been pleased with the news that the British government was bent on blocking publication of provocative Jamaica incident papers, his feisty side came to the fore soon afterward in his dealings with the affair. Roosevelt commented in a letter of February 28 to Henry Cabot Lodge that "I was rather annoyed by an allusion to the Swettenham incident in a letter I have just received from Sir Edward Grey,[1] and I have written him in return a frank appreciation of Swettenham."[2]

Actually, Roosevelt's long letter to Grey—including the portion addressing the Swettenham incident—was for the most part characteristically diplomatic. "As to the Swettenham matter," he declared, "I trust I need hardly assure you that I did not care a rap about his letter, and that my only anxiety was at once to take such action as would prevent the more foolish among our own people from fancying that they had been insulted and doing something unwise in their turn." TR also expressed "very cordial sympathy" with Grey's position, citing as an example of "my own trials with the same type of man in the American service" that the "boorish" former U.S. ambassador to Venezuela, Herbert Bowen, had been "gratuitously insolent to Michael Herbert, then your Ambassador here—one of the sweetest tempered men I ever met." But, continuing with the Bowen analogy, Roosevelt then dropped a not very subtle hint: "I finally had to turn him out of the service." And Swettenham himself was charged with an "old-time *Saturday Review*, or *Blackwood's*, dislike of America." Least diplomatic was a handwritten footnote to the letter, comparing Swettenham after the earthquake to "a chicken without a head."[3]

One of the most interesting documents pertaining to the Swettenham affair is a letter of March 28 from Arthur Lee to Roosevelt. Lee described Swettenham as "merely an exaggerated type" of a "particular type of ass" whose "recognition was universal and instantaneous" — a characterization on which Lee elaborated humorously and poignantly at some length. What Lee, one of his nation's most thoughtful and enthusiastic proponents of the Anglo-American special relationship, found especially "lamentable" about the whole episode was "that this kind of fool — in an official position — however speedily he is recognised and repudiated, should have the power to convert what ought to have been a signal opportunity of drawing the two countries closer together into an occasion for even momentary friction — leading to explanations and apologies."

In a sense Lee functioned as one of the point men in Parliament on the Swettenham affair for both the British and the American governments. He had the distinction of having served in the previous government, was currently a member of the parliamentary opposition (from which any trouble over the incident would come), and was an able advocate for and vigilant guardian of England's friendship with the United States. "The subject of the 'Jamaica incident,'" he informed TR, "has been perpetually on the brink of coming up in Parliament for the last 2 months, and whilst I was most anxious that there should be no debate on the subject, (because at such times foolish people will say foolish things), I have been holding a watching brief throughout with a view to open intervention if necessary." But now, Lee asserted (a bit prematurely as it turned out), "there is very little chance of any parliamentary discussion of the incident."[4] (While Lee's report was essentially correct — for as yet there had been no serious agitation[5] — Grey had declared before Parliament in March that "the action of the American admiral was inspired by the single-minded motive of humanity," and that "any other construction placed upon his actions would be both unworthy and untrue." Grey was noncommittal on the question of whether any papers would be published.[6])

⫷   ⫸

Although Parliament was quiet on the Swettenham affair in February and March, Swettenham himself was anything but. On January 30 and 31, he had sent three lengthy secret dispatches to the Colonial Office. These letters were among the initial broadsides in what was to become a bitter and demeaning but also vigorous campaign of self-justification on the part of the governor. This barrage of telegrams and very long letters, continuing all the way into May, is really a story in its own right. It will be highlighted here but not presented at great length. Actually, as this campaign progressed ("deteriorated" is probably a more suitable word), it became more and more a fascinating psychological study of a disturbed and angry individual — although at the same time it did remain connected to the international diplomacy of the Jamaica incident.

The longest of the three secret letters offered a multitude of reasons for Swettenham's opposition to the landing of American naval forces in Jamaica. "The policy of the United States in these waters," he claimed, "is accretion not colonization," and Admiral Davis had been calculatedly advancing it. Plus there were Jamaicans interested in connecting their island with the United States, and "I believe my duty as Governor was to do my utmost to maintain the present dependency of Jamaica on the United Kingdom." In addition, "I deemed it most prudent to avoid a possibility I dreaded, viz., that of having an American sailor or marine arrested by negro Police or negro Soldiers, or worse still, having to apply to the Admiral to deliver up for trial on shore any one charged with an offence committed within Jamaican jurisdiction." Besides, "President Roosevelt having refused all foreign aid . . . for the sufferers by the San Francisco earthquake without any remonstrances from abroad, . . . I imagined that I was at liberty to exercise a similar privilege [*sic*]." And so it went.[7]

Another of the secret letters focused on a confidential memorandum issued by the Colonial Defence Committee in February 1906, declaring it "incumbent on the West Indian Colonies both in their own interests and for the maintenance of British prestige to be prepared to suppress disorder without the support of troops or warships." Ignoring the extraordinary situation brought about by the earthquake and the multifaceted character of the American relief mission, Swettenham requested that the United States government be informed of his "stringent instructions to be prepared to suppress disorder without the support of troops or war ships [*sic*]."[8]

The third dispatch accused Davis of deliberately usurping the governor's authority. "Under such trying circumstances," wrote Swettenham, "I submit that I acted with great forbearance." As for the notorious letter of January 18, its tone and language had been "mild" and unobjectionable.[9]

In five letters dated February 8 and February 22, Secretary Elgin responded to these and to Swettenham's prior communications, endeavoring to explain carefully and unprovocatively the position that the Colonial Office had assumed. Elgin rather falsely praised Swettenham for the "energy, courage and firmness" with which he had dealt with Kingston's emergency. The secretary was only moderately critical of the governor's failure to comply with earlier requests that he telegraph information promptly to the Colonial Office. Withdrawal of the letter of January 18 was necessary, for "thus, and thus only, could your own position and that of His Majesty's Government be regularised." There was common ground between them in that "I share your views as to the extreme undesirability of allowing foreign armed intervention in a British Colony." But the United States had acted with "genuinely friendly intent," had landed bluejackets only after obtaining what Admiral Davis had reasonably believed to be sufficient authorization, and would receive no complaint. As to the Colonial Defence Committee's memorandum, "it does not appear to me to be necessary that a communication in this sense should be made to the Government of the U.S., as that Government have not questioned the propriety of your action in declining their aid." Finally, Swettenham was offered the opportunity to withdraw his resignation; if he persisted in his decision to resign, "it will be my duty to accept it, though I shall do so with sincere regret."[10]

This attempt to placate and reason with Swettenham proved utterly fruitless. Whatever self-restraint and grasp of reality had been operating within the governor—never an abundance of either—began to desert him almost entirely when he received Elgin's letters of February 8. The governor's initial reaction was a very long and rude letter to Elgin dated February 26, focusing on a defense of Swettenham's dealings with the United States over the Panama Canal laborers issue.[11] He termed the words reportedly used about him by President Roosevelt "offensive and unjustifiable" and, incredibly, called for them to be "withdrawn, and an apology demanded for them." One rather ironic sentence denied that Swettenham was hostile toward "the United States of *North* America." Most astonishingly, he charged that "Rear-Admiral Davis's visit to Kingston with his squadron was an invasion of hostile territory, and consequently an act of war."[12] Back in the Colonial Office, this letter was "put by."[13]

Swettenham, it turned out, was just warming up. An even longer letter of February 28 opened by sharply insulting Elgin, as Swettenham requested "a patient, and if possible, as impartial a hearing as one in Your Lordship's position can give who is unused to judicial functions, and in addition labours under the immense disadvantage of having prejudged the case." On January 18, Swettenham contended, there had been exchanged two "perfectly friendly letters between two officers of different Governments on friendly terms." Several paragraphs later, however, he termed *Davis's* letter "extremely insolent." This letter of February 28 was encumbered by three irrelevant historical parallels, including an action taken in Africa by Henry Morton Stanley "under the pretext of an errand of mercy." H. C. Bourne and A. D. Wedderburn were accused of having "unwarrantably usurped" the governor's power "by permitting and inviting . . . intervention."[14] In a classic case of the pot calling the kettle black, Swettenham charged Elgin with "devoting . . . more care and attention to the false report of a quarrel and an alleged indiscreet letter than even to an earthquake which has wrought immense damage to life and property in this Colony." The governor reaffirmed his intention to resign in the face of his "unjust treatment," requesting "that as an act of tardy justice to myself Your Lordship will publish the whole correspondence," excepting one relatively unimportant secret dispatch.[15] In the Colonial Office, F. J. S. Hopwood's recommendation was "to leave the despatch to stand on its own demerits." Elgin agreed: "Certainly send no reply."[16]

Well before Swettenham's letter of February 28 reached London, he initiated an exchange of telegrams on the resignation and publication issues. He cabled to Elgin on March 1: "Request official publication of all correspondence. . . . Again tender my resignation."[17] On March 4 Elgin wired back: "I accept with regret your resignation and I will as soon as possible inform you of arrangements for your relief. His Majesty's Government are considering the question of how far publication of correspondence is consistent with public interests. I will communicate with you further on this point."[18] In a telegram of March 6, Swettenham sought to define his stance on publication with greater precision: "Referring to your telegram of 4th March, request official publication of my secret despatch of 28th February."[19]

The details of Swettenham's resignation were set forth in a series of communications between April 5 and April 12. H. C. Bourne, Jamaica's colonial secretary, would take over as interim governor May 3, on which date Sydney Olivier would embark from Britain for Jamaica to assume the governorship.[20]

Publication, of course, was a more sensitive and difficult issue. "When will correspondence be published?" Swettenham telegraphed on April 9.[21] After some deliberation, the government had arrived at a decision hardly designed to satisfy Swettenham. On April 13 Elgin cabled him the news: "Referring to your telegram of April 9, His Majesty's Government have decided that it is not in the public interest to publish any papers on the circumstances leading to your resignation, with exception of my long telegram of January 22 [ordering immediate withdrawal of the letter to Davis] and your two short telegrams January 23 [withdrawing the letter and applying to retire] arising thereout, together with text of letters as reported in your telegram of January 22. Papers will be published in a few days."[22] Swettenham's telegraphed reply of April 17 was predictable: "Respectfully but emphatically object to proposed selection of correspondence for publication as unjust; desire publication of entire correspondence."[23] The Colonial Office, of course, was unmoved. "Referring to your telegram of 17 April," read a cable dated April 22, "regret to inform you that decision of H.M.'s Government must be regarded as absolute and final in respect of publication."[24]

Meanwhile, as consultation with the United States prior to the publication of any papers had been promised in February, Grey cabled Ambassador James Bryce in Washington on April 12, listing the papers designated for publication. "We hope," Grey explained, "to prevent controversy extending beyond the question of the letter and its withdrawal. . . . You should inform Mr. Root" that Britain's "present intention is to publish nothing else."[25] Bryce spoke with Root, who had seen the papers, and then telegraphed back to Grey: "Secretary of State sees no objection to publication of documents mentioned in your telegram."[26] A parliamentary white paper titled *Correspondence Relating to the Resignation by Sir A. Swettenham of his Office as Governor of Jamaica* was then published, and on April 20 Ambassador Whitelaw Reid mailed two copies to Secretary Root.[27]

Parliament proved to be more an irritant than an obstacle in the implementation of the British government's policy of minimal publication. Winston Churchill spoke for the government on the Swettenham incident during April, skillfully parrying the opposition's thrusts. On the question of whether considerations other than age played a role in the governor's resignation, Churchill simply quoted Swettenham's telegram citing only age.[28] When asked whether Swettenham "was requested by the Colonial Office to withdraw his resignation," Churchill said that the governor had not been "requested" to rescind it but "had been given the opportunity of doing so if he wished." The under secretary of state for the colonies denied that any "action was taken upon a newspaper publication [of the January 18 letter] except in the event of that publication being accepted and endorsed by Sir A. Swettenham." When asked whether the British government would acknowledge that it had mistreated Swettenham and would apologize to him, Churchill stated merely: "The answer is in the negative." Churchill replied to a request for a full explanation of Admiral Davis's departure from Kingston by noting that "the propriety of Sir Alexander Swettenham's action in dispensing with the services of the contingent has not been called in question, and no useful purpose, but the reverse, would be served by setting forth the reasons for it."[29]

Publication was potentially the most problematic issue internationally that confronted the government in Parliament. On April 10 Churchill attempted to prepare the House of Commons for a limited publication of papers: "The correspondence affects other Governments besides our own, and it must be very carefully considered, from every point of view, by the Foreign Office as well as by the Colonial Office, before any decision can be come to in regard to publication."[30] The definitive rejection of a complete publication was issued on April 30. Sir Gilbert Parker, an opposition member of Parliament, asked Churchill "whether all the correspondence which passed between this Government and Sir Alexander Swettenham, in relation to the Admiral Davis incident and to his retirement, had been published, and, if not, whether he would lay it upon the table of the House." Here is Churchill's reply:

> No Sir. There is a considerable volume of correspondence upon the details of the incident . . . ; but His Majesty's Government have decided, after careful consideration of all the circumstances, that the public interest would not be served by its publication, either here or in the United States, and that such publication is wholly unnecessary to enable

a just opinion to be formed on the only point on which fault has been officially found with Sir A. Swettenham, viz., the propriety of his letter.[31]

April and May witnessed the final act of the indecorous exit of Governor Swettenham. On April 22, the date of the telegram informing Swettenham of the "absolute" finality of the government's decision on publication, another long letter, this one dated April 4, arrived at the Colonial Office. In this communication Swettenham returned to the Colonial Defence Committee memorandum theme of one of his letters of January 30, proffering a series of absurd arguments in support of his rejection of Admiral Davis's help (claiming at one point that he would have been obligated to turn down assistance even from the British navy). This letter's closing sentence read: "The policy the unfairness of which I am endeavouring to demonstrate seems to resemble that denounced in St. Matthew XXIII. 4."[32] No one in the Colonial Office believed the letter should be answered. After seeing the assessments of three lower-ranking officials, Churchill scribbled simply: "I shall do myself the pleasure of not reading it."[33]

In two more letters dated April 24, Swettenham continued to complain of willful mistreatment. He correctly pointed out that Elgin had informed him in a cable of February 8—designed to set the stage for three letters from the colonial secretary bearing the same date—of an intention to publish the two shorter of those three letters,[34] and that the government had reneged. Because a portion of one of Elgin's two letters intended for publication had briefly (in two sentences) addressed the issue of Davis's landing,[35] the government had apparently determined sometime afterward that it would be exposing itself to avoidable domestic and international complications by following through on what Elgin had told Swettenham. Still, the additional publication of those two letters alone would hardly have satisfied the governor, who now declared "my extreme unwillingness to cooperate in preventing the whole truth on [a] matter so closely affecting my honour and reputation from being made known." And he sought to bolster his position by accusing the government of a shameful policy of appeasement: "I respectfully submit that . . . it should be generally known how zealously His Majesty's present Ministers desire to placate the Government of the United States of North America, and what treatment British Governors are to expect from them in circumstances resembling mine."[36]

There was by this time full agreement in the Colonial Office "that further correspondence is useless." Churchill initiated an inquiry as to "whether the Official Secrets Act would have any bearing upon the course contemplated" by Swettenham. He was given an opinion that while the publication of documents marked secret would violate that law, "I doubt much if any jury would convict him."[37]

Swettenham saved his best for last. On May 2, his final day as governor of Jamaica, he dispatched to Elgin an extremely long letter—in the neighborhood of 5,000 words and accompanied by five enclosures—meant, it appears, to serve as his ultimate defense. Admiral Davis, "the pivot round which revolved all the machinery of intrigue," had sought "an opportune moment for carrying out his errand of armed intervention." Each minute Davis's forces were on shore "was attended with great danger to the peace of the Colony, and also to friendly international relations. It was my duty speedily to put an end to the danger,—courteously if possible: otherwise by all or any means in my power. I used all possible courtesy on the 17th. The result was a fresh and very discourteous landing on the 18th in the teeth of my objection." As for Swettenham's letter to Davis, it "was not discourteous." Moreover, it was "demi-official and not intended for publication, and thereby protected . . . from all criticism on account of tone or expression." In this protracted epistle, Swettenham displayed both his pettiness and his disdain for Americans by mentioning that Davis in his letter dated January 17 had misspelled thieves "theives" and by himself misspelling Vice Consul Orrett's name "Orret."

The Colonial Office could ignore most of Swettenham's letter of May 2. But officials in that office had to take notice when the outgoing governor renewed in a more explicit fashion the threat he had made on April 24. Elgin and

> Your Lordship's colleagues in the Ministry (probably conscious of the weakness of their case) are disposed to deny me the privilege, perhaps even the right, of having my defence laid before the public. I profoundly regret that this injustice to myself compels me to overcome the great reluctance which both sentiment and my past training inspire, to undertake *in a despatch intended for publication* the very disagreeable burden of criticising the conduct and letter of a high officer of a friendly Power on a visit to this Colony.[38]

The government did not seem to have a great deal of leverage over Swettenham at this point. Money, however, was a possibility. In a letter of April 25, Swettenham had betrayed concern over the amount of his pension.[39] It was Churchill who made the connection in his minute on the May 2 letter: "Sir Edward Grey should see. We may have an improper publication any day. But in that case I trust Sir A. Swettenham's pension will be withheld. No answer is needed to this despatch."[40]

This message undoubtedly was communicated to the retired governor, and perhaps it achieved the desired effect. Or maybe someone who knew Swettenham well—his brother Frank and C. P. Lucas are possibilities—convinced him that the publication of his whiny, recriminatory, bizarre letters would not enhance his reputation. Well into July at least,[41] and probably for many months afterward, there was worry within the Colonial and Foreign Offices that Swettenham might act on his threat. But in the end, for whatever reason, he did not.

What Sir Alexander Swettenham did was to try to get his story out by a much safer route—one that could endanger neither his pension nor (any further) his reputation. The chosen vehicle was a long letter from Frank Swettenham to the *London Times*, published on July 20. Like Sir Alexander's letters to Lord Elgin, Sir Frank's to the *Times* was encumbered by misleading information, unjustified charges, specious reasoning, and a failure to recognize the impropriety of the key letter; but unlike them, it was neither hysterical nor absurd. Frank blamed the *Times* for his brother's fate, omitted his brother's request for protection by American servicemen at the penitentiary, denied there had been any emergency in Kingston warranting outside assistance, asserted that the American government initially found nothing offensive in Alexander's letter, and implicitly scorned the Anglo-American special relationship. Throughout his letter (showing contempt through misspelling was evidently a part of the Swettenham family tradition), Frank rendered the admiral's name "Davies." (The *Times* defended itself to good effect simply by reprinting in full its editorial of January 21.)[42]

Sir Alexander's outrageous letters, meanwhile, remained buried among his private papers and in the archives of the Colonial and Foreign Offices. It would be the better part of a century before they would see the light of day.

From March 1907 on, the British government operated under the assumption that—insofar as it was able to manage properly the publication question—the Swettenham incident had ceased to be an issue in Anglo-American relations. This perspective was essentially correct, and yet to a certain extent it was overly optimistic. Great Britain never realized the latter point, nor could it have done so very easily.

Arthur Lee and George Otto Trevelyan, the two English friends whom Theodore Roosevelt employed in his Jamaica diplomacy, received no indication of the potential for further trouble (although TR's continuing interest in the affair must have been obvious to them). On April 8 Roosevelt, replying to Lee's informative and entertaining letter of March 28, sent his favorite British messenger these words on Swettenham and the Jamaica incident:

> You handled the Swettenham matter just as was necessary. To my immense amusement Swettenham himself has now turned into a most agreeable professional lover of America! The Secretary of the Navy

and various Senators made a stop at Jamaica on a trip on the *Dolphin*
recently, and they could not speak too highly of Swettenham's cor-
diality! I shall take the liberty of telling Admiral Davis what you so
kindly say of him.[43] I am sure, my dear fellow, I need not say to you,
what you, with your admirable sense of humor and broad-mindedness,
already realize, that the Swettenham incident was fundamentally
really a comic incident, and that, I regret to own, there are any number of Swettenhams in the American service who want but the chance
to develop their peculiar talents.[44]

The president sent similar news to Trevelyan on the morning of April 10 (the
significance of the time of day is seen below), relating that the party of
Americans visiting Jamaica in late March "all came away delighted" with
Swettenham. "Fortunately," TR added, "the incident is over without any trouble
having resulted."[45]

There were additional signals to the British government of an issue put
safely to rest. In response to inquiries from British officials regarding the cost of
relief supplies distributed in Jamaica by the United States, Roosevelt approved
a recommendation by Secretary of the Navy Victor Metcalf that—"in pur-
suance of" a law passed by Congress on January 18—"no charges . . . shall lie
against the Jamaican Government."[46] In a letter of May 1, Secretary Root
asked Ambassador Bryce "to advise the Jamaican Government . . . that no
charges lie against that Government for the stores in question."[47] Bryce passed
this message along to Grey, who in turn asked Bryce "to convey to the United
States Government an expression of cordial thanks for their generosity in this
matter."[48] Roosevelt's gesture of friendship here implicitly emphasized the unim-
portance of the Swettenham affair.

Finally, in May the British government compiled a second collection of
papers, this one called *Correspondence Relating to the Earthquake at Kingston
Jamaica, on 14th January, 1907.* It contained over 175 pieces of correspondence
but ignored the Swettenham incident entirely. On June 13 Grey gave Reid an
advance copy while remarking: "Your Excellency will observe that the volume
does not deal with the controversy between Sir J. A. Swettenham and Rear
Admiral Davis."[49] Reid approved the publication and transmitted the papers to
the State Department.[50] Here once more the Swettenham affair seemed to be a
thing of the past.

Even Reid, Roosevelt's highly communicative and dependable ambassador
in England, was by mid-April clearly under the impression that TR had put the
Swettenham incident behind him. In a six-page letter to the president of April
17, in a seven-page letter of May 1, and again in an eight-page letter of May 24
not a word was written about the matter.[51]

But a tactical error by the British government produced a brief eruption in the White House on April 10. Early that month the British government forwarded to Bryce in Washington a set of papers marked "Most Confidential" and headed "Correspondence relating to the landing of United States Naval forces at Kingston, Jamaica, and the resignation of Sir J. Alexander Swettenham of his office as Governor." These papers contained nearly all communications exchanged between Swettenham and Lord Elgin in January, including Swettenham's report of January 28 on the incident (although not his three more inflammatory secret dispatches of January 30-31). They also held much of the correspondence of February (but not Swettenham's particularly offensive letters of the 26th and 28th) and four telegrams of early March relating to Swettenham's resignation and his demand for the publication of papers. Bryce allowed Root access to this collection, and copies were made and retained by the State Department.

There seem to be two possible explanations for this rather extraordinary sharing of documents. One, by far the less likely, is that the British government was as late as early April still seriously contemplating a more extensive publication of papers and was seeking feedback from the United States. There is no evidence to substantiate this theory, and plenty—especially Elgin's messages to Swettenham and the private opinions registered by officials in the Colonial and Foreign Offices—to controvert it. Anyway, it is hard to believe that England could have imagined American acquiescence in any large-scale publication after the communications on the subject that had passed between London and Washington in February. The second possible explanation—almost certainly the correct one—is that Britain was at this time extremely confident about its relationship with the United States and was sending these papers to reciprocate the openhandedness evinced when the United States shared the Davis Report.

However, British officials had taken too literally statements by Roosevelt to the effect that "the Swettenham business caused us nothing but amusement,"[52] and they had misread or overlooked clues discernible in the letter to Grey of February 28 regarding the president's continuing capacity to be provoked by Swettenham and his defenders. The British did themselves no favor by making these documents available to Roosevelt, who had theretofore exhibited no overt desire to see them.

This substantial quantity of "most confidential" papers came to Roosevelt's attention on April 10. He studied them with great care (and evidently with his usual speed) that very day. Then, still on the 10th, he wrote a fairly long letter, focused exclusively on the Jamaica incident, to Secretary of State Root. This highly important letter, dormant in the Theodore Roosevelt Papers until very recently,[53] is quintessential Rooseveltian hands-on diplomacy and also demonstrates the persistence of TR's strong interest in the Swettenham affair, the president's nationalism, his pride in the American navy, his sense of honor, and the

limits beyond which he would not go in cultivating the Anglo-American special
relationship. In this letter Roosevelt analyzed Swettenham's correspondence
with the Colonial Office, finding it to contain contradiction and falsification. TR
characterized Swettenham's charge that the U.S. relief mission had been unin-
vited as a lie "with a comic side to it; for the implied complaint is the same as if
Governor Swettenham complained that some stranger had rescued his wife from
a burning building without having been introduced to her." He described
Swettenham's "letter of January 28th" [his "report"] as "distinctly offensive to
Admiral Davis" and to "the officers and men of the American fleet." The concluding paragraph combined instructions and analysis and is the most revealing
of the letter. The bulk of this paragraph follows:

> I have done everything in my power to make matters easy for the
> British Government in this affair; but I have not the slightest intention
> of permitting a record to be made which will seem to show that
> Admiral Davis was in the wrong and Swettenham in the right, or that
> the American Government is in any way to blame. These letters to and
> from Swettenham have been gathered and printed in permanent form
> by the British Government. I feel that we should in the same way
> gather and print, that is put in permanent form, all of the reports of
> Admiral Davis and the other officers in reference to the Swettenham
> affair, so that we can have them if necessity arises. . . . I am well aware
> that the British Government does not wish to agitate the matter and
> that it is only its factional opponents who, for unworthy reasons, are
> endeavoring to do so. But while I am delighted to be just as consider-
> ate of the British Government and of the feelings of the British people
> as is possible, I can not sanction such consideration being shown at the
> expense of our own officers and enlisted men of the squadron that went
> to Kingston on an errand of mercy. Swettenham's conduct has been
> preposterous from every standpoint. Our men acted admirably, and it
> would be a gross injustice to permit the record to be falsified.

The letter concluded with a handwritten postscript: "Only this morning I had
written Trevelyan that the Swettenham business was over! The British will be
pudding-headed fools if they revive it."[54]

Responding with alacrity to the president's aroused state, Root spoke with
Bryce the next day. The result was a telegram from Bryce to Grey: "Secretary
of State considers publication of Jamaica despatches would have most unfortunate effect here, and would oblige him to publish Admiral Davis' reports,
which he has hitherto resisted. Papers in question have now been returned to
me."[55] As he appears to have been intending to do anyway, Grey promptly
informed Bryce of the very limited publication of papers relating to Swettenham's

resignation planned by the British government.[56] The United States raised no objections. Root, meanwhile, seems to have assumed that the British decision on publication rendered inoperative Roosevelt's instructions to print the Davis Report in permanent form, and he neglected to carry them out.

Not only had the British government erred by providing the American government with the confidential papers, but the timing of their delivery had been ill-considered. It would have made more sense to have waited until England's ultimate position on publication had become clearer to the United States. Still, the arrival of these documents at the White House at *any* time would unquestionably have sparked some sort of private outburst on the part of the president.

Having clarified his policy and blown off steam at the same time, and having learned soon afterward that the British government was maintaining its conciliatory policy on the Swettenham incident, Roosevelt calmed down. And for several months the issue disappeared from his correspondence and probably from his concerns.

One final flare-up occurred; it came in August, when Frank Swettenham's letter in the July 20 edition of the *London Times* reached Roosevelt in Oyster Bay. Again the president was not "amused." On August 24 he wrote to the State Department, referring to his letter to Root of April 10 and quoting its entire concluding paragraph. TR then issued his instructions anew:

> I desire all the reports of Admirals Evans and Davis and of the various officers . . . to be gotten together, if it has not already been done, and either printed or prepared for publication. Governor Swettenham's brother, Mr. Frank Swettenham, has recently published in the London Times a most offensive and mendacious account of the case. I desire, for the sake of the good name of Admiral Davis, to have printed in some permanent form—tho of course not at present for general publication—material for a complete answer to these charges. Swettenham's case is now in the British Blue Book. Sooner or later it may see the light. When this occurs I wish to be able immediately to produce our whole case in answer.[57]

This time the State Department swung into action. The long-serving and highly competent Alvey A. Adee, then the acting secretary, wrote to Metcalf on September 4: "I have the honor to enclose copy of a letter from the President directing the assembling of matter concerning the Swettenham incident, with a view to its publication, for the reasons stated in this letter." Adee requested "copies of all . . . reports and correspondence" bearing on the affair "so that this Department may comply at the earliest practicable date with the President's directions."[58] Nine days later Adee was able to advise Roosevelt "of the receipt of a letter of the 7th instant" indicating that the Navy Department was fulfilling his request.[59] "Duplicate copies of all correspondence on file" in the Navy Department "relative to the Swettenham incident"—including the entire Davis Report and numerous other relevant documents—were delivered to the State Department on September 24.[60] Rather amazingly, however, these papers *still* were not put into "permanent form"; and apparently they never were.[61] Fortunately for the individuals responsible, Roosevelt did not ask to be shown the finished product he had twice requisitioned.

The diplomatic history of the Swettenham incident ends here. As noted, Swettenham's most contentious correspondence with his government was never published, and, therefore, neither were the major American documents. An article on the affair appearing on August 28 in the *Washington Post* evoked no official response either in Britain or in the United States.[62] By autumn, in both countries, there was little but silence.

⊰   ⊱

This awkward incident, which both governments had endeavored assiduously to "close" in January 1907, when it occurred, lingered for quite a bit longer. These many months witnessed recurrent bouts of irritation on the part of the formulator and manager of America's diplomacy, Theodore Roosevelt. But the president, consummate statesman that he was, channeled his irritation into outlets that often facilitated—and never impeded—the achievement of both his narrower and his broader policy objectives. The British government, for its part, dealt with the erratic behavior of the hostile and emotionally troubled governor of Jamaica about as well as it could have. Moreover, the incident was largely kept out of the public eye after January, enabling the two governments to bring it to a satisfactory resolution without undue political pressure or undue haste. Damage-control diplomacy, although proving to be a significantly more complex proposition than originally hoped and anticipated, was nonetheless ultimately a very successful one.

The diplomacy of the Swettenham incident provides an excellent window on the condition of the Anglo-American relationship by 1907 and on Theodore Roosevelt's perspectives on that relationship. By the end of 1906, Roosevelt had demonstrated in many ways his commitment to building and maintaining a strong informal alliance between the British Empire and the United States. The encounter between Admiral Davis and Governor Swettenham tested—in a way that no other episode of his seven-and-a-half-year presidency had tested or would test—the true depth of that commitment.

Before the Spanish-American War, Roosevelt had asserted that "every foot of American soil, including the nearest islands in both the Pacific and Atlantic, should be in the hands of independent American states, and so far as possible in the possession of the United States or under its protection."[63] If, as president, the nationalist TR had even the slightest inclination to reaffirm this outlook, the startling indecency of the governor of a British West Indian colony toward the commander of an American mission of mercy certainly afforded him a golden opportunity. That there was no such reaffirmation, even in private—that on the contrary there was a determination to isolate Governor Swettenham and to downplay the incident as an aberration—suggests how dramatically Roosevelt's attitude toward the British Empire in the Western Hemisphere had shifted over the preceding decade. Great Britain could keep Jamaica—and Trinidad and the Bahamas and British Guiana and, for that matter, Newfoundland and Canada—forever as far as TR was concerned. He had come to view the existence of these "local" British colonies as fully in harmony with the interests of the United States.

It is very doubtful that the president would have reacted the same way had the Jamaica incident occurred in 1902—or had a similar incident occurred in 1907 with another colonial power, even France. By 1907 Britain had demonstrated to Roosevelt's satisfaction that, uniquely among the powers, it was America's true, reliable, useful friend. It favored the status quo in most areas of the world, as the United States did, and, more generally, its interests and America's usually coincided. When Britain's interests had been in conflict with those of the United States, it had tended to yield to America, most notably over the Alaskan boundary in 1903. It, like the United States, was in Roosevelt's eyes more civilized than the other powers, and its colonial policy, like America's, was less selfish than theirs. It was an English-speaking nation that shared, at least in principle, America's attachment to the ideals of freedom and self-government. And, probably most important, it was the senior partner in an informal naval connection responsible for a favorable international balance of power. Anglo-American naval cooperation and supremacy served as a deterrent to the aggressive designs of rival powers and additionally ensured that the United States could uphold its vital interests should they be challenged.

Still, if the British government had not also looked at the maintenance of the Anglo-American partnership as a top foreign policy priority, the Swettenham incident could have severely impaired the friendship between the two countries. In January 1907 Theodore Roosevelt wanted and expected the British government to issue a suitable disavowal of and apology for Swettenham's behavior, and he intended to accept that disavowal and that apology in the friendliest possible spirit. But the strong feelings about the Swettenham situation exhibited by TR over the next several months provide convincing evidence that had the British government failed to respond in the expected manner—or even had it delayed in responding for any length of time—a serious breach with the Roosevelt administration would almost certainly have resulted. The publication by the British government of papers considered offensive by the president probably would have produced a somewhat less dramatic rift; but even here there would have been public anger and the publication with fanfare of the Davis Report, undoubtedly engendering feelings of estrangement on both sides of the Atlantic, especially in the United States. A further deterioration could easily have followed.

For Theodore Roosevelt the defense of America's "national honor" was absolutely a paramount objective. No other international imperative—not even maintaining the Anglo-American bond—ranked as high. Right from the beginning TR was most anxious that the Swettenham affair not be allowed to become an issue of national honor. He grasped very firmly the potentially explosive nature of "this little incident."[64] That no explosion occurred—not even a small one—is in large part a tribute to Roosevelt's deft diplomacy. But ultimately there were some key British decisions over which the president had little control and to which he could only react. To his great relief, these decisions conformed to his desires and expectations.

It is important to recognize that even the best of intentions on each side did not guarantee smooth sailing through the choppy waters of Swettenham incident diplomacy. A high quality of statesmanship in *both* countries was required as well. Such statesmanship was fortunately provided by Roosevelt, Grey, Howard, Elgin, Churchill, and others. Had the incident taken place during the Lansdowne-Durand period, it is not difficult to imagine all kinds of problems and a much less happy outcome.

In summation, the peculiarly sensitive Jamaica incident was truly a test for Great Britain and the United States. If the Anglo-American bond had been less solid than it seemed to be at the beginning of 1907—in particular, if Theodore Roosevelt's commitment to it had been shallower than his previous diplomacy and recent correspondence had suggested—the handling of the Swettenham affair would have uncovered any major weaknesses. There were no such weaknesses. Both nations passed the test with very high grades.

PART IV

Theodore Roosevelt and the
British Empire, 1907–1909:

A SEASONED FRIENDSHIP

Roosevelt and the British Empire:
Two Remaining Issues

● ○ ●

THE FINAL YEARS: AN INTRODUCTORY OVERVIEW

Barring a cataclysm," Theodore Roosevelt wrote to Henry Cabot Lodge in June 1908, "I am pretty well thru the great stress of my work as President, or at least the hardest work and most intense worry."[1] In a relative sense—despite a series of domestic policy battles with Congress, whose intensity was colorfully captured by Roosevelt's observation in a letter of January 1909 that "the period of stagnation continues to rage with uninterrupted violence"[2]—this was an accurate remark.

If limited to the realm of Anglo-American relations, such a declaration by the President would have been on target as early as the spring of 1907. The months between the clarification of Britain's Jamaica incident policy in April 1907 and the end of Roosevelt's presidency marked a calm and largely untroubled period of maturation for the already solid friendship between England and the United States. Some difficulties did occur in the early months of 1908 over divergent perceptions and priorities regarding the persisting issue of Japanese immigration to the American and Canadian west coasts, but this question was handled without any tension and posed no real threat to the special relationship. Roosevelt's final two years as president also witnessed the resolution of the long-intractable Newfoundland fisheries dispute. In addition, TR decisively quashed a potentially troublesome Anglo-American argument stemming from the 1908 Olympic games in London. No new conflicts of interest and no new international crises arose to jeopardize the partnership. Roosevelt remained very interested in the British Empire, and he thought and wrote a great deal about its problems and its future, according particular attention to India. Private affirmations of Anglo-American solidarity between Roosevelt and his English correspondents became ever more commonplace. The informal naval understanding continued to mature.

ROOSEVELT, BRITAIN, AND THE
JAPANESE IMMIGRATION PROBLEM

The hot-and-cold Japanese-American immigration-racism crisis of 1906-1909 —
introduced in chapter 4 — was the foreign policy issue that most greatly con
cerned and most fully engaged the energies of President Roosevelt during hi
last thirty months in office. Anglo-American diplomacy became an importan
subplot to the story of Japanese-American diplomacy in this period. Eve
when Britain was on the sidelines, Roosevelt regularly took the initiative t
update his closest British friends on his thoughts and actions pertaining t
Japanese-American tensions.

Throughout the long Japanese-American crisis, Roosevelt — whose "con
viction that these two nations could work together in friendship was neve
shattered"[3] — strove mightily to keep a handle on events. His task was comple
He was determined to treat Japan with the respect due a great power — whic
required modifying the conduct both of Californian legislators and o
Californian mobs — while still bringing to a halt the immigration into the Unite
States of Japanese laborers. He was equally determined to strengthen th
American navy and to do so in a manner that sent a clear message to Japanes
leaders without directly challenging or provoking them. A stronger navy, TF
was convinced, would render war both less likely and more winnable.

The first half of 1907 found Roosevelt making every effort to secure a
informal "gentlemen's agreement" that would "mutually" exclude Japanese an
American laborers from each other's country. War rumors in February and
war scare in June prompted by anti-Japanese mob activity in California in Ma
added a sense of urgency to the president's endeavor.

During these months Roosevelt shared his thinking on the unfolding crisis
and his frustrations as well, with British correspondents. "With infinite labor an
against every kind of opposition," he wrote to John St. Loe Strachey in February
"I am gradually working out the most satisfactory solution of which the Japanes
business was capable." The settlement envisioned by TR, he told Sir Edward Gre
that same month, "satisfies California without bringing a break with Japan.
Under such a settlement, "we shall treat the Japanese who are here on an exac
equality with the people of Europe," but Japanese laborers, who "make up th
enormous bulk of possible immigrants, shall not be admitted." To point out tha
the Japanese immigration problem directly concerned the British Empire as wel
as the United States, Roosevelt remarked to Strachey that "the attitude o
Australia toward Japanese immigration is exactly that of California."[4]

In March Roosevelt managed to prevent provocative discriminatory law
from being passed by the California legislature, writing several long and persua

sive letters to Governor James Norris Gillett as a central aspect of this campaign.[5] Then, for a brief period, Roosevelt relaxed, assuming incorrectly that an informal gentlemen's agreement hammered out in February would be fully honored by the Japanese government and that Californian provocations would cease.[6] But much to the president's dismay, anti-Japanese mob activity in San Francisco soon reinvigorated the crisis. Roosevelt was exaggerating very little if at all when he declared in a letter of May 23 to his Japanese friend, Baron Kentaro Kaneko, that "nothing during my Presidency has given me more concern than these troubles."[7] Later in this letter Roosevelt renewed his push for the implementation of the gentlemen's agreement. Dealing with "conditions not as I would like them to be but as they are, the best thing to do is to prevent the laboring classes of either country from going in any numbers to the other."[8] Several weeks later Roosevelt updated the British government on the state of affairs through a frank letter to Cecil Spring Rice: "The San Francisco mob bids fair, if not to embroil us with Japan, at any rate to arouse in Japan a feeling of rankling anger toward us that may at any time bear evil result. . . . I am doing everything I can to meet the just grievances of the Japanese, to atone for and remedy any wrong. But I am also doing everything I can to keep the navy at the highest point of efficiency!"[9]

By the time he mentioned the navy to Spring Rice, Roosevelt had already made a major decision that was very quickly to become an important element in his policy toward Japan: to send the entire American battleship fleet on a "practice cruise" to the Pacific—later transformed by TR into a voyage around the globe. The president spent much of his time during the summer of 1907 planning the details of this cruise, evaluating U.S.-Japanese relations including the likelihood of war, and pushing for Japan's prompt adherence to the gentlemen's agreement.

From the very beginning of the crisis, Roosevelt had been watching for an opportunity to bring to bear Britain's influence on its ally Japan in the cause of promoting a conciliatory Japanese policy toward the United States. (Clearly he was not deterred by his failure to persuade England to lean on Japan as the Treaty of Portsmouth was being negotiated during the summer of 1905; rather, he was encouraged both by the British Empire's own Oriental immigration concerns and by recent developments in Anglo-American relations.) A severe anti-Japanese riot in Vancouver, British Columbia, on September 7 provided just such an opportunity. This riot, Roosevelt wrote to Strachey immediately upon learning of its occurrence, "shows once again how like the problems are that our two countries have to meet. . . . All such disorders must be punished rigorously; but it is idle to blind ourselves to the fact that the English-speaking commonwealths of the seacoasts on the Pacific . . . ought not to be asked to submit to . . . the unchecked immigration of Asiatics, . . . and that if asked they will refuse."[10]

A few days later TR wrote with some satisfaction to Henry Cabot Lodge:

It is only a few months since the English papers were commenting with complacency upon the bad effects of the federal Constitution of our Republic, the lawlessness of the national character, and contrasting it with the British Empire. Now a much worse outbreak has occurred in Vancouver than anything that has occurred in San Francisco. It will do good in two ways. In the first place it will bring sharply home to the British public the fact that the British commonwealths along the Pacific will take precisely the same attitude as the American States along the Pacific; and in the next place, it will bring Japan toward a realization of the fact that in this matter she will have to face the same feeling in the British Empire which she does in the American Republic.

And while the behavior of the Canadian and American mobs was "indefensible, . . . the attitude which is back of the movement is in each case sound."[11]

When unacceptable levels of immigration from Japan to the United States continued into November, Roosevelt urged Secretary of State Elihu Root to remind the Japanese that "British Columbia, New Zealand, and the Australian commonwealths"—colonies of Japan's "staunchest ally, England—. . . take precisely the same position as our own Pacific Coast States take." Root was instructed to define the problem as "economic" and to explain "that our aim is to settle it in a way that will prevent friction and the disruption of the friendly relations" between the United States and Japan.[12]

The early months of 1908 marked the most active phase of Anglo-American diplomacy related to the Japanese-American crisis. Roosevelt's diplomatic strategy centered on impressing Japan with American naval power—the "Great White Fleet" having begun its fourteen-month voyage in December 1907—and working through Canadian officials and British friends in an effort to persuade the British government to weigh in with Japan on the immigration issue.

Canada achieved its own gentlemen's agreement with Japan between November 1907 and January 1908. But Prime Minister Sir Wilfrid Laurier was neither enthusiastic about the terms of this agreement nor optimistic that Japan would honor its commitment to limit sharply the immigration of Japanese laborers to British Columbia. So when Roosevelt extended a third-party invitation to Canada's knowledgeable commissioner of labor and immigration, William L. Mackenzie King, to visit Washington "to discuss 'matters of common interest,'" Laurier consented. On January 25 King arrived in the United States and met with the president, who expressed the view that "England's interests and ours are one in this matter" and encouraged King to travel to Britain to convey to the government there "the serious and immediate nature" of the immigration question. A word from England to Japan, "spoken in a friendly way to an ally, . . . might go far." King then returned to Canada, where he found Prime

Minister Laurier in accord with TR "that the United States and Canada had common interests in the Pacific."[13]

On January 31 King went back to Washington carrying Laurier's pledge to cooperate with the United States. Pleased with the Canadian stance, Roosevelt opened up and explained to King the linkage between the cruise of the American battle fleet and U.S. diplomacy toward Japan. Despite a recent promising turn in Japanese-American negotiations, a trip to England by King remained highly desirable; it could "help Japan realize, through its ally Great Britain, that agreements must be kept and immigration restricted."[14]

The next day Roosevelt wrote to Laurier describing a luncheon meeting he had had with King and James Bryce, the British ambassador, at which Bryce "was as interested as I had previously been in Mr. King's statement" that "the feeling in Western Canada . . . is at least as strong as . . . in California, Oregon and Washington." Bryce "cordially agreed that it would be a good thing to have Mr. King go to the other side to explain matters fully to the Imperial Government, which Mr. King tells me is what you propose to have him do. It seems to me that this course is eminently wise. I have spoken with entire freedom and frankness to Mr. King" and have shown him "the documents concerning our own negotiations, so that he will be able to speak with full knowledge to the Imperial authorities." Roosevelt also expressed great satisfaction that the American and Canadian governments were cooperating so closely on this matter.[15]

Roosevelt then proceeded to write Arthur Lee a long letter focused primarily on the Japanese immigration problem and his belief that Anglo-American cooperation could help resolve it. He began by praising Mackenzie King as "a very capable, resolute fellow" who had acquired and shared with Roosevelt documents showing that "immigration was really completely under the control" of the Japanese government, which had "deliberately overissued" passports.[16] The Canadian commissioner, Roosevelt recounted, had stressed British Columbia's and Alberta's emphatic opposition to Japanese immigration. He had also "thanked me very earnestly for having sent our fleet to the Pacific." The president had then told King "that the Japanese had given us at last the most positive and unequivocal assurance that the flood of emigration to America would be stopt, and that we had informed them plainly that we could no longer accept excuses, and that if" immigration did not diminish sharply "it would be but a short while before Congress passed laws restricting this immigration."

King, Roosevelt continued, would now be going to London to inform the government there "in detail as to the actual condition of sentiment in British Columbia and in western Canada generally, and of the identity of this sentiment with that obtaining in our western . . . States, and of the great desirability that the United States and the British Empire should work together in this matter."

Bryce had endorsed King's transatlantic diplomatic mission, following which Roosevelt had asked the ambassador "if he would not also cable Sir Edward Grey expressing the hope that certain leaders of the opposition might be likewise fully informed." The trusted Lee's own marching orders followed: "I told King that I should write you, in absolute confidence, of our interview, and asked him to call on you when he reaches London. For fear there is some miscue I should be much obliged if you would look him up. Do not show this letter to anyone, except that in strict confidence you can show it to Grey, Balfour, and Strachey, if . . . you feel sure they will understand my writing." The first secretary of the American embassy, John Carter, would be informed "that I have written you," and Lee was urged to speak with him as well.

The president closed his letter to Lee on a note of cautious optimism and with a plug for Anglo-American unity. Recent breakthroughs in American and Canadian negotiations with Japan had improved the prospects for "a peaceable and satisfactory solution." Still, Japan might once again fail to honor its under-takings. "Under such circumstances," Roosevelt proclaimed, "the Empire of Great Britain and . . . the United States" in tandem "should convince the Japanese that . . . our peoples have nothing but the friendliest and most respectful feeling for Japan, but that . . . , in the interest of lasting peace and good will between Japan and the English-speaking peoples, it is imperative that all immigrants of the working class from Japan should be kept out of English-speaking countries."[17]

Only a few days after writing his letter to Lee, a surprised Roosevelt was informed that the British government was unwilling to pursue a joint Anglo-American policy on the Japanese immigration question. On February 6 Bryce outlined Grey's position to Root: "that Japan had never mentioned to Great Britain its immigration difficulties with the United States, and for Britain to approach Japan on the part of the United States would imply doubt whether Japan intended to keep its assurances. If Japan raised the subject . . . or if further difficulties arose, Grey would then 'bear in mind' the views of the President." According to Charles Neu, the British government balked because it considered TR's "dark portrayal of Japanese-American relations" to be exaggerated. Japan, Grey and his associates believed, "was engaged in the difficult task of postwar consolidation" and viewed "conflict with the United States" as "unthinkable." (Moreover, Britain's Liberal leaders were attempting "to conceal" from their "sensitive ally" their own lack of enthusiasm for the Anglo-Japanese alliance that they had inherited from their Conservative predecessors.) Thus, while Roosevelt had assumed correctly "that any clear choice between the Anglo-Japanese Alliance and Anglo-American friendship could only be decided" by the British government "in favor of the latter," British officials simply did not see themselves "confronting that choice in the early months of 1908."[18]

Although he certainly could not have been pleased with Grey's stance, Roosevelt received the news without any apparent anger. A recent sharp decline in Japanese immigration to the United States and new assurances from the Japanese government undoubtedly were reducing the president's sense of urgency. In addition, the progress of his Great White Fleet was absorbing much of his attention and helping to keep his mood upbeat.

Nonetheless, the difference between Roosevelt's reaction to Grey's rebuff in February 1908 and his reaction to Britain's unwillingness actively to support his diplomacy during the Russo-Japanese peace negotiations of 1905 is noteworthy. During the period June-August 1905, TR had recurrently complained directly to the British government and, employing less diplomatic language, to trusted American correspondents about British unhelpfulness. While he had endeavored successfully during those months to criticize British policy without undermining the Anglo-American relationship, criticize it he did. Unless something important had changed by 1908 in his attitude toward England, one would anticipate at a minimum finding negative references about British policy in some private letters to American friends. But no such references are to be found.

Allowing that the contrasting circumstances explain some of the difference, it still seems reasonable to contend that Roosevelt's more favorable overall disposition toward Britain and its government in 1908 as compared with 1905 is a significant part of the explanation. The British rationale for inaction in the more recent case was more readily accepted by a president who perceived it as emanating from a government that was both more credible and unquestionably friendlier to the United States. The effects of events since 1905 — including but certainly not limited to the replacement of Lansdowne's ministry by Grey's — were being manifested in 1908.

Hence, when Roosevelt met with Bryce on February 14, he expressed agreement with Grey's position "that a British attempt to influence Japan might be harmful." Roosevelt now redefined his objective as "the adoption of a similar attitude on the question of Asiatic immigration." Concerned about an ongoing Japanese military buildup, he also told Bryce that if tensions were to rise later and pose a threat of Japanese-American war — perhaps late in the spring — England and the United States could avert it "by the simultaneous use of firm warnings." In essence, as Neu suggests, Roosevelt "had swiftly adjusted to Great Britain's refusal to act and now sought to pave the way for future collaboration if Japanese-American relations deteriorated. Such an occurrence was unlikely, but worth providing for."[19]

Although accommodating Grey's reluctance to lean on Japan, TR persisted in his efforts to influence British policy. When Mackenzie King paid a third visit to Washington prior to traveling to London, the president stressed once more "the importance of convincing British statesmen how uncertain the future was." The immigration picture remained cloudy, and war remained a distinct possibility. "Only if Japan understood the common interest of the United States and Great Britain in the Pacific" could peace be assured. Roosevelt was interested, he told King, in "some kind of convention between the English-speaking peoples, whereby . . . it would be understood on all sides that the Asiatic peoples were not to come to the English-speaking countries to settle, and that our people were not to go to theirs."[20] Similarly, on March 7 Roosevelt wrote to Arthur Lee—who had replied very supportively to TR's letter of February 2—emphasizing the common interests with regard to Asiatic immigration of "Canada, Australia, and the United States."[21]

Roosevelt's mention of Australia was no passing thought, for Australia was coming to play an important part in his policy toward Japan. Early in February Australian Prime Minister Alfred Deakin had made known informally his desire to have the American battle fleet pay a visit to his self-governing colony. Actually, Deakin's "irregular action" displeased British officials because, as Neu remarks, it "emphasized the conflict between Great Britain's obligations to the Anglo-Japanese Alliance and to its empire."[22] But this displeasure never came to the attention of the American government; in a letter to TR dated March 5, King Edward VII enthusiastically endorsed the Australian invitation.[23] The president accepted without hesitation, for "such a visit would symbolize the unity of the English-speaking peoples of the Pacific."[24]

Then, later in March, there occurred an important break in the Japanese-American crisis. While Roosevelt again was worrying about recent Japanese immigration figures, Japan too extended an invitation to the American battle fleet. The president agreed to the visit—"of course we shall go," he stated in a letter to Lee[25]—and the air of tension eased considerably.

Therefore, the international climate was relatively calm during Mackenzie King's visit to Britain, which began on March 18. A couple of weeks later, Arthur Lee reported to Roosevelt on King's mission. Lee himself had played a major role, doing "everything I could to prepare the ground for him," with King having seen "pretty well everyone, on both sides of politics, who has any influence." The president's friend then proceeded to paint a very rosy picture of the substance of King's visit: "He has so far found no difference of opinion as to your main principle that a complete halt should be called in the immigration of labourers into English speaking countries from Japan . . . *and vice-versa*, and that, if necessary, the English-speaking communities should cooperate to make this exclusion effective." In Lee's perception, "practically every responsible person over here" held such a view. His letter's only important disclaimer was not very emphatic: "What definite steps the Govt., and Sir E. Grey, are prepared to take at the present moment I do not know—but Grey (when I spoke to him) expressed himself as most anxious to cooperate with you." Lee pledged to help "keep the opposition leaders fully acquainted with your views" and to assist Roosevelt's policy in any way TR desired.[26]

It was a sign of Roosevelt's adjustment to Grey's earlier refusal to counsel Japan and of the president's diminished sense of urgency when, after thanking Lee "heartily for all you have done in connection with Mackenzie King," he declared: "The visit has achieved just what I hoped." Moreover, "the trip of our fleet has had a most beneficial effect," with Japan's invitation a particularly encouraging development. Thus, "there isn't anything more to do just at the moment." Still, the immigration of Japanese laborers remained too high, so "no one can tell when the situation will grow acute."[27]

Roosevelt hoped that he had persuaded the British leadership "of the seriousness of the immigration problem" and had "prepared the way for . . . collaboration if a crisis came with Japan." Considering Grey's skepticism about the likelihood of war between Japan and the United States, it is questionable, as Neu argues, whether TR had attained even this more limited objective. But at the same time, as Neu also points out, "in a showdown between the United States and Japan, Great Britain could only side with the great power across the Atlantic whose aid might be crucial in maintaining Europe's increasingly precarious balance of power."[28] By emphasizing to Britain's leaders common Canadian and American interests regarding Japanese immigration and by alerting them to the possibility of a sudden Japanese-American explosion, Roosevelt probably ensured that the British government would not be caught off guard and would be able to act in accord with its interests should Japanese-American relations worsen dangerously.

In April, well before the Great White Fleet traversed the Pacific, one of the major objectives of the cruise was achieved. Roosevelt had intended that the cruise would engender public support for an expanded naval building program and thereby help him win needed congressional votes for the construction of additional battleships. He gained authorization and funding for two of the four battleships he had requested, plus two per year in the future. The president expressed his satisfaction in a letter to Henry White: "I knew I would not get thru two and have those two hurried up unless I made a violent fight for four. Moreover they have now, as a result of the fight, announced . . . a steady policy . . . of building two ships a year—a great gain."[29] This success increased the likelihood that Roosevelt would achieve another major objective of the voyage: impressing Japan with the naval power of the United States and, in the process, diminishing the chances of war. Indeed, the world cruise constituted a classic— perhaps *the* classic—example of Big Stick diplomacy in action. Roosevelt was expressing one of his most fundamental beliefs when—with Japan clearly in mind—he told a Naval War College audience on July 22 that "diplomacy rests on the substantial basis of potential force."[30]

Meanwhile, during the late spring and early summer of 1908, the Japanese government finally began to assert effective control over the immigration of Japanese laborers to the United States. Even the cautious Grey lent an indirect hand by reminding Japan in July "of the importance of restricting immigration to Canada."[31] Roosevelt's concerns began to subside.

In August and September the American battle fleet visited New Zealand and Australia. The people of both self-governing colonies reacted with "the utmost enthusiasm"; indeed, the fleet was met with receptions that "surpassed even those on the Pacific Coast."[32] As Japan's invitation to the fleet had eliminated any conflict between the Australian invitation and the imperatives of the Anglo-Japanese alliance, Britain also responded with genuine satisfaction. Bryce was "delighted," he told TR, by the "splendid reception your fleet has had in Australia. It seems to me that one of the best results of this wonderful Pacific voyage has been the heartiness of the greetings exchanged between your sailors and our people there."[33] To this latter remark Roosevelt replied: "I quite agree."[34]

Notwithstanding the great success of the stopovers in Australia and New Zealand, the most important diplomatic event of the world cruise was still ahead. As Neu observes, it was the October visit to Japan that Roosevelt was anticipating as "the culmination of his bold project. A warm welcome would seal America's friendship with Japan and confirm beyond all doubt" the wisdom of the whole venture. As it turned out, the Japanese greeting was "wildly . . . enthusiastic."[35] As he wrote to George Otto Trevelyan, Roosevelt was "extremely pleased."[36]

The signing of the Root-Takahira Agreement in late November of 1908 constituted a climactic triumph for Theodore Roosevelt's Japanese policy. With the immigration problem having finally been brought under control, and with Japan's grand welcome for the United States' battleship fleet having bolstered Japanese-American relations, the two governments proceeded to negotiate an understanding wherein each recognized and pledged to respect the vital interests of the other in East Asia and the Pacific. It was implicit in the Root-Takahira Agreement that where Japan's predominant position in southern Manchuria clashed with America's Open Door policy in China, the former would take precedence. Neu accurately evaluates this agreement as "the natural culmination" of Roosevelt's Far Eastern policy—as "an expression of his desire for a complete accommodation with Japan."[37]

The Root-Takahira Agreement was well-received in England. Foreign Secretary Grey was "gratified" that America's public policy toward Japan was now so similar in substance to his own country's.[38] Writing on December 1, Arthur Lee saw the agreement as "splendid and a real knock-out for the mischief-mongers on both sides of the Atlantic" who have tried "to use Japan as a wedge with which to drive England and America apart." Lee went on to declare that "for this consummation, as for so many other happy solutions, we feel very grateful, here, to you and to Root."[39]

Responding to Lee on December 20, TR expressed complete accord with his friend's assessment. The president perceived the Root-Takahira Agreement as "an admirable thing all around." He saw it playing a part in "keeping England and America closer together . . . ; which, as you know, is something I always have peculiarly at heart." Roosevelt then added a note of self-congratulation: "My policy of constant friendliness and courtesy toward Japan, *coupled with sending the fleet around the world,* has borne good results!"[40]

Roosevelt faced one final challenge to his policy of promoting friendly U.S.-Japanese relations. Anti-Japanese agitation in California brought several discriminatory bills before the state legislature early in 1909. TR fought vigorously to prevent the enactment of any such legislation, writing repeatedly to Governor Gillett in an effort to enlist him (and then to convey appreciation for his help) in the struggle.[41] This approach—successful two years earlier—once again proved to be well-considered and enabled the president to achieve his objective of blocking the offensive legislation.

Toward the end of this unwelcome flare-up, Roosevelt shared these sober reflections with Lee: "The thing that gives me serious uneasiness is the friction with Japan. I have been reluctantly forced to the conclusion that it is indispensable for the Japanese to be kept from coming in any numbers as settlers to the United States, the feeling in our western States on this point being as strong as it is in Australia and British Columbia."[42]

⊰   ⊱

Developments in Japanese-American relations during the period 1907-1909 did no damage to the Anglo-American friendship. While Roosevelt energetically sought British diplomatic support for the United States on the Japanese immigration issue early in 1908, he accepted without apparent dismay Britain's unwillingness to become directly involved. The president's frequent assertions in his meetings and correspondence of closely similar Anglo-American interests regarding Japanese immigration generally found a receptive audience among Britons, Canadians, and Americans alike. The immigration-racism crisis actually served to broaden the ties between the British Empire and the United States, because the world cruise of the Great White Fleet that grew out of tensions with Japan brought the American navy to New Zealand and Australia, where it was welcomed with very great enthusiasm. Most significantly, Roosevelt's impressive success in overcoming numerous obstacles in his quest to achieve a friendly understanding between the United States and Japan aligned American and British Far Eastern policies more closely than ever before. Partisans of Anglo-American harmony — TR foremost among them — had no cause for regret or worry.

ROOSEVELT, BRITAIN, AND THE PERSISTING
CHALLENGE OF THE NEWFOUNDLAND FISHERIES

"The Newfoundland business and similar matters are mere child's play compared with this Japanese business, from the standpoint of its ultimate importance," Roosevelt declared in July 1907 in a letter to Secretary of State Root.[43] Despite the admirable sense of proportion reflected in this statement, the Newfoundland fisheries problem required and received much attention from British and American diplomats during the final two years of Roosevelt's presidency. Ambassador to Britain Whitelaw Reid, who played a significant role in support of the efforts of Roosevelt and Root to find a solution, commented in September 1908 on "the extreme difficulty surrounding every phase of this petty and long drawn out negotiation."[44]

The most important developments in fisheries diplomacy took place during the spring and summer of 1907. In the spring Newfoundland's premier, Sir Robert Bond, was in England agitating the issue. "Since he has been here," Reid reported to TR on May 1, "he has broken out into speeches and interviews in which he appeals to Parliament and the British public against . . . the modus vivendi" of 1906, "and practically insists that the King's sanction shall be given to Newfoundland legislation undertaking to nullify our rights under the treaty of 1818." One such speech had "produced . . . a profound sensation."[45]

Spurred by Bond's vigorous lobbying, Foreign Secretary Sir Edward Grey presented a detailed proposal to Reid on June 20. Grey despaired of a permanent solution at this time, because on the most "vital point of principle . . . — the application of the Newfoundland regulations to American fishermen —. . . there does not seem to be any immediate prospect of agreement." He therefore put forward a "temporary solution," most of whose provisions, including bans on purse seines (very large fishing nets able to be closed in the manner of drawstring purses) and on the employment of citizens of Newfoundland as fishermen on American vessels, were in conflict with the American stance.[46]

Grey's letter, despite its friendly tone, was a troubling development in the eyes of the Roosevelt administration. In essence, Grey was advocating the replacement of the modus vivendi of 1906 with another one decidedly less favorable to the United States. At this point Roosevelt and Root moved dramatically both to break the immediate impasse and to achieve a permanent settlement—by proposing that all outstanding issues be resolved through binding arbitration.

The American government presented its position in a letter of July 12 from Reid to Grey. After thanking Grey for acknowledging "the moderation and fairness with which Mr. Root has stated the American side of the case" and expressing in turn U.S. "appreciation of your conduct of the discussion," the ambassador firmly rejected the foreign secretary's proposal: "With the utmost desire to find in your last letter some practicable basis for an agreement, we are unable to perceive it. Acquiescence in your present proposals would seem to us equivalent to yielding all the vital questions in dispute, and abandoning our fishing rights on the coast of Newfoundland under the treaty of 1818." Reid proceeded to identify his government's major objections to the British plan, concluding that "the task of reconciling" the two countries' positions "seems hopeless."

Then, suddenly, Reid shifted gears: "In this conviction my Government authorizes me and I now have the honour to propose a reference of the pending questions under the treaty of 1818 to arbitration before The Hague Tribunal." Reid noted hopefully that the British ambassador to the United States, James Bryce, had "recently suggested some form of arbitration." As an added incentive, the reference of the fisheries problem "to The Hague Tribunal might prove an important step in promoting the spread of this peaceful and friendly method of adjusting differences among all civilized countries of the world."

In the meantime, while awaiting the outcome of the arbitration proceedings, Reid recommended "the continuation in force . . . of the modus vivendi I had the honour of arranging with you last year." In 1906 this agreement had "resulted in voluntary arrangements by which our fishermen gave up purse-seines" but "did . . . employ Newfoundland fishermen." Such a trade-off, Reid made very clear, was as far as the United States was prepared to go with regard to the coming fishing season, and Britain ought to agree to it.[47]

In letters dated July 17 and July 19, Reid reported to Roosevelt that "no doubt . . . the British authorities were a little surprised . . . by our proposal for arbitration," to which the ambassador was optimistically anticipating an affirmative reply: "I don't see how they can refuse it."[48] Reid then broadened the discussion, initiating an illuminating dialogue with Roosevelt on the arbitration concept in general and on their assessment of the relative significance of the fisheries dispute. Reid expected to "lose a part at least of what we think we have a right to; . . . arbitrators are so rarely judicial that their decisions are nearly always in the nature of a compromise," and thus "the side that has the least merit

is sure to gain a good deal that it is not entitled to. To this extent I fully agree with
the views of Senator Lodge." Lodge and others, however, were overestimating
"the importance to the United States of this Newfoundland fishery question."[49]

Reid's analysis found a receptive audience. Roosevelt considered arbitration
a useful and desirable device for resolving international disagreements, but
only those that did not involve questions of vital interests, national honor, or territorial integrity.[50] The Newfoundland fisheries, TR apparently believed,
involved none of these:

> In this Newfoundland business I quite take your view. I have never
> felt that the matter was of such vital importance to us, or that our
> rights were so clear, that we could afford to take an extreme position
> in reference to it—such a position as we took on the Alaska boundary
> business, for instance. Therefore, as I hold precisely your views on
> arbitration—namely, that tho it is superior as a rule to war, it is a
> method which has peculiar attractions for the side that is wrong—I felt
> that this was properly a case in which we could afford to give this ini-
> tial advantage to England. . . . *I do not want to jeopardize bigger things else-*
> *where* by insisting on our rights here up to the point of bringing
> ourselves face to face with some very uncomfortable difficulty.[51]

The foregoing quotation also demonstrates the fundamental consistency of
Roosevelt's outlook on the fisheries controversy since he first had to deal with
it in 1905. The United States, he believed all along, was partially responsible for
the problem, and it would be foolish to allow this relatively minor and ambiguous dispute to damage the Anglo-American friendship in any way. In such a situation, arbitration by the Hague Tribunal seemed an entirely suitable vehicle
for resolution.

Ambassador Reid was pleased to report on August 9 that "our proposal for
arbitration . . . is accepted orally; and Sir Robert Bond, in spite of his opposition
to it" at the time it was presented, "has made no difficulty." Moreover, Grey had
agreed to renew the modus vivendi of 1906 for the 1907 fishing season, although
this agreement "has to be kept confidential yet on account of their desire to get
. . . Bond to consent to it rather than override him by an act of Parliament."[52]
During the following weeks, the British government did its best to placate
Bond—in Reid's words, "to humor his desire to seem as if he had not been
beaten"—but the renewed modus vivendi did indeed take effect.[53]

As it turned out, Roosevelt's conciliatory and inspired arbitration proposal
did pave the way for the amicable resolution of the aged Anglo-American conflict over the Newfoundland fisheries. Again in 1908 Reid had to struggle with
the British government to renew the modus vivendi—an annoyance the ambassador attributed to the continuing agitation of "the cantankerous and narrow"

Bond[54]—but the opposition of Newfoundlanders and their leader could not stem the tide. As the calendar turned and the negotiations moved toward a climax, the perspective of the British government was captured very well by the *London Times:* "Of all international questions now outstanding, these fishery disputes are probably the oldest and the most complicated. They have been a source of constant and dangerous friction. An agreement has now nearly been reached, *thanks greatly to the fact that the United States has approached the question in a more moderate spirit than ever before,* and it would be a thousand pities . . . if old wounds so nearly healed were to be opened again."[55] A second *Times* editorial declared: "We count upon the leaders and the people of our oldest colony to recognise . . . the obligations and responsibilities of Imperial partnership."[56]

Early in 1909, with the grudging assent of Newfoundland, the United States and Great Britain formally arranged to have the fisheries question submitted to a five-judge panel at The Hague. As Roosevelt and Reid were anticipating, the tribunal's verdict, rendered in 1910, was a compromise between the claims of the two sides.[57] Regardless, this previously intractable dispute with the best and most important friend of the United States had finally been laid to rest in a satisfactory manner. It marked yet another triumph for Roosevelt's statecraft.

❧ 10 ❧

Roosevelt and the Troublesome
Olympic Games Controversy of 1908

● ○ ●

The 1908 summer Olympic games in London were the scene of great controversy and bitterness between British and American athletic officials and (to a lesser extent) athletes. Large numbers of citizens in both England and the United States shared in the controversy and bitterness. Potential diplomatic repercussions soon became apparent to thoughtful partisans of the Anglo-American special relationship.

✠   ✠

"It should have been called the Battle of Shepherds Bush. The firing didn't die down until years afterward." So remark John Kieran and Arthur Daley in *The Story of the Olympic Games* at the beginning of their chapter on the 1908 Olympics.[1] While the 400-meter race of July 23 and the marathon of July 24 became the focus of Anglo-American contention, there was plenty of buildup to these climactic events. "Since the beginning of the [modern] Olympic games [in 1896]," noted the *New York Times* on July 25, "the great rivalry has been between England and America." And, lamentably, "disputes . . . seem to be inseparable from athletic contests when both Englishmen and Americans take part."[2]

Most of the problems sprang from the fact that the British Olympic Committee arranged, conducted, and officiated at the games. A number of nations besides the United States lodged vigorous protests at various points. Indeed, "so great was the uproar and so widespread the protests over the way some of the British officials handled their parts of the program" that, following the 1908 games, the International Olympic Committee transferred authority and responsibility "to the international sports governing bodies in each particular sport."[3]

Prior to July 23, American athletes and officials were upset for many reasons, including: the absence of the American flag from the new stadium at Shepherd's Bush during the opening ceremony; the participation of a Canadian runner considered by the United States to be a professional; "the coaching of British athletes by enthusiastic British officials who were judging the contests" while members of the American Olympic Committee were barred from the field; the rules for the pole vault competition; and the classification as "ordinary footwear" of the ground-gripping "monstrous boots" worn by the English tug-of-war team.[4]

On the other side, naturally, British officials angrily rejected American accusations of favoritism. Moreover, Britons tended to find American behavior at the games obnoxious, as David Wallechinsky points out in *The Complete Book of the Olympics:* "Many British sports enthusiasts were disgusted by the exuberant displays of the Americans whenever a U.S. athlete won an event." A London newspaper condemned "'the blowing of a new squeaking instrument of torture [probably a kazoo]'" and declared that "'the Americans made themselves a nuisance and behaved in a manner which is happily quite foreign to the athletic grounds of England.'"[5] Such disaffection was undoubtedly exacerbated by British frustration over American success in the games: Overall the United States won fifteen of the twenty-seven track and field events compared with ten victories for the British Empire (eight for Britain and one each for Canada and South Africa).

The well-prepared explosion occurred on July 23, two days before the end of the track and field games, with the running of three Americans and one Briton in the 400-meter final. "The unfortunate series of disputes which has arisen since the opening of the Olympic games," began the account of the *New York Times,* "culminated this afternoon in an occurrence which threatened to wreck the inter-Olympic meetings." The *Times* described "an uproar . . . such as seldom or never was witnessed on an athletic field."[6] More than eighty years later, Wallechinsky asserted that "few events in Olympics history have caused as much controversy as the final of the 1908 400 meters in London."[7]

With "some of the less conservative London newspapers" predicting foul play on the part of the three American runners, the 400-meter race began with tension unusually high.[8] British officials were "stationed . . . every 20 yards around the track" to guard against American misdeeds. In the homestretch, the British participant, Lieutenant Wyndham Halswelle, moved to the outside in an effort to pass the leader, American John Carpenter, but Carpenter "ran wide and kept Halswelle from taking the lead."[9] While Carpenter thus did apparently obstruct Halswelle's path, whether he did so by intent — and whether he "elbowed" his rival "severely" in the process[10] — were and have ever since been questions lacking definitive answers. The race was not videotaped, and no photographs of the crucial moments were brought forward. The *New York Times* reported "no signs of a deliberate foul," whereas the *London Times* found "palpable ... interference," claiming that "the Americans had run the race on a definite and carefully thought-out plan."[11]

In either case, numerous British officials suddenly "leaped out on the track."[12] They "yelled 'foul' and 'no race' and broke the tape before Carpenter reached it." Chaos ensued among officials, athletes, and spectators, as people shouted at one another "for a half hour before the track could be cleared. Carpenter was disqualified and the race was ordered rerun without him two days later, this time with strings laid out to divide the lanes."[13] The American Olympic Committee lodged a formal protest and "passed a resolution ordering the men not to run."[14] On July 25, therefore, Halswelle ran alone.

At a minimum, it seems fair to conclude, British officials acted too hastily. They could and should have permitted the runners to complete the race, after which they could have investigated allegations of American misconduct and issued their ruling.[15] Yet even a more carefully considered disqualification of Carpenter probably would not have prevented an angry American reaction. For "whatever may be the facts in the unfortunate episode, both the English and the Americans firmly believe that their men are absolutely right and the others wholly wrong."[16]

It was in this charged atmosphere that the marathon was run the next day. It was "an inspiring contest" — "the most thrilling athletic event" of modern times, according to the *New York Times*.[17] The weather for this race — 26 miles and 385 yards from Windsor Castle to the finish line in front of Queen Alexandra's box in the Olympic stadium — was warm and muggy. The British contestants harmed their prospects by expending too much energy early in the race. About a half-mile from the stadium, Dorando Pietri, an Italian, passed Charles Hefferon, a South African, for the lead.

But Pietri, "urged on by the well-meaning but overzealous crowd," had "picked up his pace too early." When he entered the stadium, he "appeared dazed and headed off in the wrong direction. Track officials rushed to his aid and pointed him the right way. But after going only a few yards, he collapsed on the track."[18] Following a moment of indecision, doctors and officials helped Pietri to his feet. As he proceeded deliriously toward the finish line, Pietri fell repeatedly, receiving assistance each time.

Meanwhile, the South African Hefferon had "developed stomach cramps" after ill-advisedly accepting a drink of champagne two miles from the stadium, and near the entrance to the stadium he was passed by John Hayes, a twenty-two-year-old American who had been running a carefully paced race. When

Hayes entered the stadium ahead of Hefferon, recounts Wallechinsky, "this was too much for the British officials. When Dorando [Pietri] started to collapse for a fifth time, just short of the finish, . . . the head organizer of the race caught him and carried him across the line."[19] Hayes crossed the line thirty-two seconds later. Next came Hefferon, and after him two more Americans.

Initially, British officials declared Pietri, who had to be removed from the track on a stretcher, the winner. Italy's flag "was hoisted to the top of the pole with the Stars and Stripes under it."[20] The United States immediately protested "on the ground that [Pietri] received assistance, and the protest was finally sustained," Pietri being disqualified.[21] The key word is "finally," for "some hours" of heated discussion passed before the judges reversed their decision, which "only added fuel to the flames that had been raging. . . . It was a good thing," assert Kieran and Daley, "that the meet ended the next day."[22]

Leading American and British newspapers did their best to downplay the turmoil. On July 25 the *New York Times* anticipated that "the bitter feeling of the Americans caused by the disqualification of Carpenter in the 400-meter race . . . will subside" as a result of Hayes's triumph in the marathon.[23] The next day the same paper predicted optimistically that "time will soften the asperities caused by the conflict of judgment, and the Olympic games of 1908 will always be pleasantly remembered."[24] For its part, the *London Times* declared a bit disingenuously that "Englishmen will rejoice in the victory of an American, and in the splendid display made by the representatives of the United States in this [marathon] race. . . . Although we naturally feel some regret that the English runners . . . did not make a better appearance on our own ground, it is at least some satisfaction to our national pride that . . . the Anglo-Saxon stock" dominated the marathon. Even more disingenuously, this same editorial contended that the 1908 games had served to strengthen international friendship, and that the British officials' "evident impartiality will have impressed all competitors that their cause could not be in fairer hands."[25]

A separate *New York Times* news article of July 26 painted a more realistic picture. While praising the temperate tone of London's newspapers, this article commented on the extremely strained relations between British and American athletic officials, whose acrimonious exchanges were likely to "drag on." Moreover, "despite the conservatism of the press, the English public is imbibed with a fierce prejudice against American athletes. . . . The Olympiad, . . . while an athletic success, . . . has been a deplorable failure . . . as a means of promoting international friendship."[26]

And indeed, American athletic officials, despite their team's achievements, were in no sense prepared to let bygones be bygones. The first of them to return to the United States, Captain Charles Dieges, publicly characterized the British managers of the games as "incompetent and prejudiced. . . . The British Amateur Athletic Association," Dieges claimed, "did all it could to prevent our men from winning. All through the two weeks we got the rawest kind of deals."[27] Some of the American athletes themselves "were outspoken in their opinion that the English officials were . . . poor sports," who "discriminated against the Americans."[28]

The American carrying the heaviest grudge was James E. Sullivan, the United States' foremost amateur athletic official. Sullivan was the U.S. commissioner to the Olympic games and also president of the Amateur Athletic Union. Upon arriving back in the United States on August 7, Sullivan issued an extremely inflammatory declaration. He condemned sharply and at length British handling of the 400-meter and marathon races. He characterized "the government of amateur sport . . . in England" as "a joke," contending that England was becoming "athletically degenerate." Most provocatively, Sullivan spoke glowingly of "the American boys who went into *the enemy's country* and realized such glorious results."[29]

☒   ☒

President Theodore Roosevelt was well aware of the Anglo-American athletic estrangement growing out of the fourth Olympiad. On July 26 the *New York Times* correctly identified Roosevelt, the honorary president of the American Committee of the Olympic Games, as "a staunch admirer of amateur athletics" who "has followed the progress of the American athletes" at the London games.[30] At the same time, however, Roosevelt's view of the proper place of athletics in the lives of the people of his era was rather more complicated than the foregoing quotation suggests. Therefore, it seems advisable to explore TR's thinking on this subject before looking into his handling of the Anglo-American Olympics controversy.

As Arnaldo Testi points out in a recent essay in the *Journal of American History*, Roosevelt looked upon organized sports as "an area where young males could learn to confront life properly."[31] Before an audience at Georgetown College in June 1906, the president declared: "I believe in athletics . . . chiefly because of the moral qualities that they display. I am glad to see the boy able to keep his nerve in a close baseball game, able to keep his courage under the punishment of a football game or in a four-mile boat race; because . . . this means that he is going to keep his nerve and courage in more important things."[32] Sports served this purpose only for participants who strove hard to realize fully their potential, whatever that potential might be: "High proficiency in sport is not necessary in order to get good out of it; altho . . . it is in every way bad to show a slipshod indifference to high proficiency, an unwillingness or inability to put one's whole heart into the contest."[33] While TR heartily approved of baseball and football as games in which "the moral qualities . . . are all the time called into play," he expressed even greater enthusiasm for "the hardy out-of-door sports of the wilderness."[34] Experiencing sports as a spectator was fine with Roosevelt, but only up to a point: "To obtain rest and enjoyment by looking at other men practise an interesting sport is entirely proper," but "excessive indulgence" in this activity distorted "the perspective of life" and was "noxious."[35]

Roosevelt applied the philosophy of sports as a healthy means of building character to his own life. He regularly engaged in vigorous physical recreation, counting riding, hunting, hiking, climbing, rowing, swimming, camping, tennis, boxing, and wrestling among his pastimes. "I am not really good at any games," TR wrote in February 1909. "Perhaps in my time I came nearer to being fairly good as a walker, rider, and rifle-shot than in any other way; but I was simply an average good man even in these three respects." Roosevelt attributed his proficiency as a hunter to "three causes: first, common sense and good judgment; second, perseverance"; and third, steadiness under pressure.[36] These qualities, honed by his hunting and other sporting experiences, were all of central importance to the extraordinary success of Roosevelt's career. Throughout his years in politics, especially during his presidency, TR also valued his various outdoor activities as "a diversion and as a means of refreshing me for doing double work in serious governmental business."[37]

But there was invariably an implied or expressed caveat to Roosevelt's affirmations of enthusiasm for athletics. Sports for TR were always a means, never an end. "In their proper place they are very good indeed," he stated, but they "are only good in their proper place."[38] Roosevelt elaborated in a letter of 1903 to Theodore, Jr., a secondary school student at the time: "I am delighted to have you play football. I believe in rough, manly sports. But I do not believe in them if they degenerate into the sole end of anyone's existence." The president cautioned his oldest son not "to sacrifice standing well in your studies to any overathleticism; and above all, I need hardly tell you that character counts for a great deal more than either intellect or body in winning success in life. *Athletic proficiency is a mighty good servant, and like so many other good servants, a mighty bad master.*"[39] Sports, Roosevelt was firmly convinced, should never be regarded as "the serious business of life."[40]

Athletics were certainly not important enough to be permitted to endanger international goodwill. "I do not believe in these international matches," the president declared in a letter to Whitelaw Reid after reading the ambassador's account of the Olympics fiasco. "Where the feeling is so intense it is almost impossible that there should not be misunderstandings."[41]

⫸   ⫷

The Anglo-American Olympics controversy engaged the energies of President Roosevelt far more than he would have preferred. While Roosevelt sought and ultimately was able to expend these energies behind the scenes, he felt obliged on several occasions to write lengthy letters on the subject of the Olympics dispute. These letters, particularly two of October and November 1908 to Theodore A. Cook, a member of the British Olympic Council, risked exposing the president's interest and involvement. Roosevelt seems to have taken this risk only after carefully considering its ramifications *and* the ramifications of the alternatives. In addition, for a brief period in late November, it appeared that the British government had decided to take part in the controversy—a challenge to which Roosevelt responded vigorously.

Upon receiving a telegram from Commissioner Sullivan apprising him officially of the American successes in the track and field games, TR cabled back on July 27: "Heartiest congratulations to you and team. Wish I could shake hands with each man."[42] Shortly afterward, however, the celebration of American athletic accomplishments would take a back seat to the pursuit of Rooseveltian-style damage-control diplomacy.

On August 11 Ambassador Reid wrote a long letter, of which more than half was devoted to the Olympics matter, to President Roosevelt. In this letter Reid identified the *contrast* between the way British officials handled the 400-meter race and the way they handled the marathon as "the real point which impressed Americans who kept cool." Regarding the former contest, "under the theory that the rules must be strictly enforced," Carpenter "was immediately pronounced disqualified. . . . There was no meeting of the committee, no hearing of testimony, no question of what [Carpenter] had to say for himself, and no explaining of how he succeeded in interfering with the man behind him, who had ample room to pass on one side, if not on the other—provided he was capable of passing."

Reid then proceeded to offer a detailed description and analysis of the finish to the marathon, averring that Dorando Pietri had been "carried across the line . . . like a child held by its nurse and learning to walk." The ambassador continued: "Then tremendous cheers went up, and the Italian flag, under the authority of the committee, was hoisted, to indicate that this man, who had conspicuously broken the plain rules five or six times in the face of everybody in the Stadium, and with the obvious connivance of the committee itself, was the real winner." Moreover, "the British committee did not . . . correct its obvious and flagrant error until the American committee was forced into the invidious position of protesting. . . . *Not till then* was the British committee shamed into recognizing the violation of rules which it had been so swift to denounce and punish the day before; not till then was the Italian flag reluctantly brought down and the American flag hoisted."

Thus the glaring contrast: "The same justice was not meted out by the committee to an American, who *may* have inadvertently broken the rules, . . . and to an Italian, who broke them again and again, under the eyes of everybody. . . . I don't believe anybody who calmly considered the circumstances could doubt that the Americans had cause to complain of the committee and of the crowd *on one day or the other.*"

Switching gears, Reid offered up some criticisms of the American athletes and officials. The athletes were "often bad losers," and "some of them seemed to have chips on their shoulders." There was also, as Reid illustrated, a shortage "of courtesy and etiquette." And American officials had in addition failed utterly "in getting the facts fairly before the British public."

Yes, American athletes did do "magnificently" in the games themselves. "All the same," Reid declared, "I do not believe it a good thing to subject international friendship to strains of this sort. There has been bitterness enough developed in a day over these races to come near counterbalancing the diplomacy of years. . . . The best hope we can cherish now is that, as in the case of most college quarrels over athletics, the thing will be forgotten in a few months."[43]

Roosevelt was "particularly pleased" with Reid's "full and convincing statement. . . . I agree with every word." TR doubted that Carpenter "intended to commit a foul" and viewed "the conduct of the English judges" as "so bad that we . . . will never be sure that Carpenter committed a foul even unwittingly." Similarly, Roosevelt considered "the conduct of the judges and of the British public in connection with the Marathon race very bad indeed." Still, the issue was unimportant, and the president, like Reid, preferred to disregard it: "My idea is that in public there shall nothing whatever be said about the matter . . . and that the talk shall be permitted to die down."[44]

Actually, Roosevelt appears to have formulated his outlook on the Olympics dispute, and on how it should be handled, prior to receiving Reid's letter—probably through reading newspaper accounts at the summer White House in Oyster Bay. When TR wrote to Reid on August 20, he stated that Reid's letter of August 11 had "just come."[45] Yet on August 18 the president had already written a very long letter to George Candee Buell in which he had given full expression to his thinking on the Olympics controversy.[46]

Buell, an American, had sparked Roosevelt's lengthy epistle by writing TR in support of the British position. Buell had enclosed English newspaper clippings and an "extract from [an] American in London" as documentation.[47] Roosevelt's sharp retort assailed British officials' conduct in the tug-of-war as well as in the 400-meter and marathon races. TR closely analyzed Buell's newsaper clippings, identifying instances both of prejudiced commentary and of outright misrepresentation. Concerning the marathon, Roosevelt charged British officials with "a scandalous partiality which ought to cause you very grave doubts before accepting their verdict in the case of Carpenter." It was, TR asserted, "hard not to draw an uncharitable conclusion" about British handling of the two events at the center of the dispute. Roosevelt clearly indicated his belief that Buell had been naive: "It is nonsense to talk about 'the public knowing the truth about the running of Carpenter,' by which you apparently mean that the public should accept as gospel the blackguardly article of that English paper, *The Sportsman*."

Aroused as his nationalism and sense of fair play were by Buell's mailing, Roosevelt attempted to place the Olympics issue in its proper perspective before closing his reply: "I never should have stated my views at all, even privately, except in answer to a letter such as yours, and I state them to you for your private information merely. . . . It would be improper, ungenerous, unwise and tend to no good purpose to make any such statement as this in public." Just as Carpenter was "a gentleman of good character," the British officials were "entirely honorable men" (whose judgment was unfortunately impaired by the great excitement" under which they were operating). Thus, "I should deprecate in the strongest way any kind of public criticism of the British judges." The president was determined "to refrain from every statement which will tend to cause international bitterness, and simply to congratulate the American team, which . . before an unfriendly audience and with unfriendly surroundings nevertheless scored so signal a triumph."[48]

Meanwhile, arrangements were made for a gala victory parade in New York City on August 29 and for the American Olympic team to visit President Roosevelt at Sagamore Hill on August 31. On August 30 the *New York Times* claimed that "fully a quarter of a million New Yorkers turned out to witness the parade and celebration," climaxed by a reception at City Hall, "the like of which has never been witnessed in this country."[49]

In advance of the gathering in Oyster Bay, Roosevelt communicated with Commissioner Sullivan. "There has been too much talk about the matter," the president insisted in a letter of August 24, and "nothing is to be gained by more talk. We won a remarkable victory anyhow, and for us to make complaints of unfair treatment does us no good whatever, gains us no support anywhere, and simply causes us to be regarded rather contemptuously as confirmed kickers." A dignified celebration—free of negative statements—was now in order.[50]

TR was in a buoyant spirit as he and Edith received the American athletes at Sagamore Hill. Roosevelt offered "words of welcome and congratulation" to each individual athlete, afterward telling the team that "I think I could come pretty near

passing a competitive examination on your records and feats." When Sulliva
raised the issue of British misconduct, the president seized the opportunity t
counsel his visitors: "We don't need to talk, we've won. . . . You fellows have wo
a place for all time. I feel like giving you the advice I gave my regiment when it dis
banded. 'Remember,' I said, 'that you're heroes for ten days, but when that tim
is up drop the hero business and go to work.'"[51] A *New York Times* editorial c
September 2 lauded Roosevelt for his "wise words of counsel. . . . Wholly sincer
in his admiration of the men, . . . Mr. Roosevelt is the only President we have eve
had who could talk to athletes . . . like one of themselves."[52]

By this time, Roosevelt had recognized that Sullivan was something of a loos
cannon who posed a potentially serious obstacle to the quiet withering away o
the Anglo-American Olympics controversy. The president decided to try to co
opt the outspoken commissioner through flattery and through the sharing of con
fidences—with strings explicitly attached. Early in September TR expressed "m
appreciation of the disinterested work for the United States which you have don
so well."[53] He also sent Sullivan "a copy of that letter"—probably Reid's c
August 11 (less likely Roosevelt's to Buell of August 18), to which Roosevel
apparently had referred privately while the Olympians were at Sagamore Hill
One can assume that Roosevelt wanted Sullivan to read not only Reid's criticism
of British officiating but also Reid's swipes at American behavior and the ambas
sador's attempt to put the dispute in perspective. "You can show it to three or fou
intimate friends," TR continued, "but do not show it to anyone who will tal
about it, and take especial care that no hint of it gets into the papers."[54]

Undoubtedly Roosevelt was now hoping that he would be obliged to say an
write nothing more about the Olympics dispute. Notwithstanding the strong pri
vate opinions laid out in his letter to Buell, Roosevelt viewed the controversy a
insignificant and as an unwelcome menace to Anglo-American harmony.

So much was this the case that the president chose to let pass entirely withou
comment some remarks by Arthur Lee that were considerably at variance with hi
own perspective. In a letter of September 6, Lee noted the "great satisfaction here
over "your advice to the Olympic games winners. I was delighted to see," he wen
on, "that you discouraged the talk about 'unfair treatment by the British judges
That was of course the veriest nonsense," for which Lee faulted "the Irish
American agitator." The disagreement over the 400-meter race Lee attributed t
"a misunderstanding of our rules of track racing," under which, he contended, "th
judges had no alternative but to disqualify Carpenter." Still, Lee perceived th
Olympics affair as "a great pity" and was "coming round to the view that, on th
whole, these international athletic or sporting contests are more likely to caus
friction than good feeling, & might well be discontinued."[55] There was not a hin
of discord in Roosevelt's self-restrained reply. "I am glad you like what I said t

the Olympian athletes on their return," he wrote to his friend. "Aside from the compliments, it amounted in effect to nothing more than that they should 'keep their heads shut.' I quite agree with you that international athletic contests are rarely of benefit."[56] As this and earlier letters make clear, TR just wanted the Olympics controversy to die a natural death, the sooner the better.

Unexpectedly, however, Roosevelt was the recipient of an extraordinarily presumptuous five-page letter dated September 8 from Theodore A. Cook of the British Olympic Council.[57] Its essence is captured by the following excerpt:

> I was obliged to publish the facts about the 400-metre race in our Stadium in July; and I did so with the full knowledge that neither yourself nor any other of the best Americans conversant with the best sport [sic] would countenance what Carpenter had done. I could easily forgive him. But it is only right to tell you that if some of the incidents that occurred in our games are not forgotten, it is not likely that American athletes will be welcomed again on English tracks.

Cook then referred to a current ban on American crews "at Henley. It would be a thousand pities if that ban were extended to other sports."

Cook did offer praise for the American team — "a finer set of athletes than your boys I never saw" — blaming "what their managers dictated" for the difficulties. James Sullivan and the American team's manager, Matt Halpin, were singled out for particularly sharp condemnation. Sullivan and Halpin were guilty of unfair accusations against British Olympic officials, and Sullivan's "self-imposed absence . . . from the dinner given by the Amateur Athletic Association, and from that given by the government," seemed "impossible in anyone representing you and all you stand for." In his final sentence Cook declared: "I write personally and not officially, because I can speak more freely in a private letter about such matters."[58]

Truly amazed by what he had read, Roosevelt replied to Cook on October 20 with a seven-page letter of his own. As perhaps the single most important document relating to Roosevelt's handling of the Olympics controversy, this letter merits close scrutiny.

Roosevelt began by expressing relief "that your letter is a personal one," for "if any letter like yours were published it would awaken bitter resentment." Roosevelt's letter also was "purely personal" and "not for publication," although he did authorize Cook to share it with his colleagues "if they know of your letter, and if you are sure that they will treat this letter as confidential."

TR then revealed his great displeasure: "I do not think you are aware of the offensiveness of your language; indeed, your sending me the letter at all is a gratuitous and officious act, to be excused only by the apparent fact that you mean well." Cook's offensive language "and your evident ignorance that it is offensive, both indicate an attitude of mind which, if shared by your colleagues who had charge of the Olympic Games, goes far to explain much of the trouble that occurred."

Roosevelt was particularly incensed by Cook's remarks pertaining to the banning of American athletes: "If the attitude . . . you betray . . . represents the general attitude of the men interested in British sport, I most emphatically hope that American athletes will not again appear on English tracks; and I am quite indifferent as to whether they are barred out, because I should protest in any event against their going."

Next Roosevelt took up an analysis of the 400-meter race. Carpenter was a "man of excellent reputation." Moreover, published predictions of American foul play had been "an outrage: If the circumstances had been reversed, if the British athletes had been in America, and such a publication had been made in an American paper, and there had followed such action as actually did follow on the part of the judges," many Britons "would at once have said that the whole affair was a put-up job, and that the accusation made in advance that there would be foul play was simply intended to cover a decision that there was foul play, without regard to the merits of the case." As it was, "the breaking of the tape" constituted "gravely reprehensible conduct" by the judges. "Whether Carpenter was or was not guilty, your officials certainly were guilty of misconduct as grave as that of which he was accused," displaying "a bias which makes their decision one to be accepted with great caution."

The president then turned to a central theme of his earlier correspondence with Reid and Buell: "In literally inexplicable contrast to what had been done in the Carpenter case," British officials ignored and even abetted flagrant rules violations in the marathon and declared Pietri the winner, not reversing their decision "until they had forced the Americans to protest on behalf of Hayes." To drive home this point, TR quoted in full more than three pages of Reid's letter of August 11, identifying the author as "a very prominent American who was present at the games, but was not connected in any way with the management."

Finally, Roosevelt endeavored to encapsulate both his reason for writing and his larger view of the controversy in his closing paragraph:

> I have publicly deprecated any expression of criticism or resentment on the part of the American athletes or their managers. I have advised them all to accept the decisions in each case without complaint, and to keep their mouths shut, and say nothing against the judges or officials. I gave this advice both in the interest of sport, and because I felt that the trouble would only grow worse with discussion, and that for the sake of the good feeling between the two countries it

was highly undesirable to rake up and keep alive what had been done. If your letter were a public one I should not answer it at all, for several reasons; among others, because I do not feel that anything whatever is to be gained from any standpoint by further public discussion of this matter. But neither do I feel like permitting you and your colleagues, if you are speaking for them, to think that I acquiesce in the strictures that you make upon the American athletes, and in your assumption that the skirts of the British officials were clean, and that the wrong was entirely on the side of my countrymen. I do not understand exactly why you wrote to me. As you have written me I send you this answer, which, let me repeat, is not for publication. The whole incident has made me very gravely doubt the wisdom of encouraging international athletic competitions.[59]

Transparently, Cook's letter had aroused TR's nationalism, and one can wonder whether Roosevelt, as he claimed, would really have refrained from replying had the letter been public. Official silence in the face of such a provocation would have required enormous restraint from a president not disposed to be seen as "acquiescing in" unjust criticisms of Americans by foreigners. Roosevelt's response would naturally have taken a different shape, but that there would have been a response seems most likely.

As it was, even by writing privately to Cook, Roosevelt risked public exposure of his involvement in a controversy of which he had been determined to steer clear. TR hardly knew his new British correspondent; indeed, the content and tone (and even the mere fact) of Cook's letter offered substantial grounds for doubting the Briton's judgment. Roosevelt's insistence on confidentiality certainly provided no guarantee (although he clearly did sense—correctly as it turned out—that Cook was an honorable man). Yet—and this is the key point—the president evidently preferred public exposure of his engagement with the controversy to "permitting you and your colleagues" (he assumed Cook had collaborated with others on the letter) "to think that I acquiesce" in the views expressed by Cook. Such exposure would of course be unfortunate and detrimental to the realization of Roosevelt's goal of having the dispute peter out quietly, and in the process would complicate Anglo-American relations, at least in the short run. But it would be no disaster; the controversy, after all, was over sports, not over national honor or vital interests, and Roosevelt was confident he could find a way to deal with exposure of his involvement if it became necessary for him to do so. In essence, after calculating the risks and finding them acceptable, he succumbed to a nearly irresistible urge. He stated his case and took his chances.

Actually, Roosevelt seems to have been rather pleased with his letter to Cook. For with his reply on November 6 to a letter from Sullivan,[60] in whose

trustworthiness and discretion he apparently had gained confidence, TR
included "a copy of a letter I sent to one of the English Olympic people who, as
I thought quite unwarrantably, wrote me." There was the usual insistence on
privacy: "Of course I do not want any use made of this letter of mine and it is
only for your eye, because, as you know, I have felt that the best way was to
keep entirely quiet about the business."[61]

Meanwhile, in late October or early November, Cook completed a draft of
a thirty-six-page pamphlet titled "The Americans at the Olympic Games," com-
missioned by the British Olympic Council and intended for publication. This
pamphlet resembles a detailed lawyer's presentation both defending the British
Olympic Council and attacking leading American Olympic officials — Sullivan,
Gustavus Kirby, and Joseph Maccabe in particular. Numerous "witnesses,"
including several Americans and many Canadian and continental European
Olympic officials, are quoted in support of the British case. Cook vigorously
upholds British conduct across the board — in the 400-meter race (where a foul
was "beyond question"), the marathon, the tug-of-war, the certification of the
Canadian runner challenged by the United States, and other specific controversies, and in the overall administration of the games. "English fair play" is a
continuous theme. The attack on Sullivan and his associates is wide-ranging,
extremely bitter, and in places sarcastic. They are the purveyors of "malevolent
mendacities." Sullivan has been "striving to shelter" his "unpardonable conduct
under the plea that he represents the President of the United States." The pamphlet had to be prepared in order "to show these gentlemen up in their true
colours, and to demonstrate that they have deliberately deceived their countrymen by fabricating falsehoods for purposes best known to themselves."[62]

On November 2 Cook sent Roosevelt the "first rough proofs" of his pamphlet,[63] along with a six-page letter replying to TR's letter of October 20. Cook
explained that his first letter "was only directed to the White House because the
Honorary President of the American Olympic Committee was also the President
of the United States; and because" Sullivan, Kirby, and Maccabe, "members of
your Executive Committee, are the gentlemen chiefly responsible for the misrepresentations published in the American Press, uttered at public dinners,
and printed in pamphlet form, misrepresentations which have never yet been
contradicted by any other member of the American Olympic Committee." In
addition, "I felt confident that you had not been fully informed of the facts."

Cook then attempted to justify his forthcoming pamphlet. "We have hitherto
remained silent under a storm of obloquy and abuse" emanating from the
United States, and "our continued silence has been misconstrued." Cook
acknowledged "that we may have committed many involuntary errors" in
administering an international gathering "of such dimensions and of so delicate

n intricacy," but he argued "that it is impossible any longer to take continued accusations of deliberate dishonesty lying down." Roosevelt's letter, moreover, convinces me that if, from its Honorary President downwards, the American Olympic Committee still sees no reason to disavow the public utterances of three of its members — if, from the President . . . down to the million unknown readers of the papers, the American people still believe these misrepresentations — then, it is time to speak out on our side."

Roosevelt had professed ignorance of the charges against Sullivan contained in Cook's earlier letter. "I felt sure that this was so," Cook now declared rather snidely, "and I look forward very much to the results of wider knowledge."

Roosevelt could hardly have been pleased with what he had read to this point. But whatever degree of displeasure he may have been feeling was more than offset by a paragraph on the letter's final page:

> I have considered very carefully the question of showing your letter to Lord Desborough [the chairman of the British Olympic Council] or any of my colleagues. I have come to the conclusion that for the present, at all events, it will be better to preserve its purely personal and private nature in the strictest possible sense, and to disclose not a word of it to anyone. In view of its importance, I should prefer to leave to you any subsequent decision as to the use of it, in any way you may desire; and I hold myself entirely at your disposition to that effect. Until you inform me of your wishes, it will remain entirely confidential to myself.[64]

President Roosevelt now seized what he saw as an excellent opportunity both to contribute to the defusing of the controversy and, especially, to extricate himself from the somewhat perilous position into which he had decided to put himself by writing to Cook on October 20. In a reply dated November 17, TR characterized Cook's letter of November 2 as "frank and manly," this time studiously ignoring the more "offensive" passages. Roosevelt claimed not to have seen a single article sharply "attacking you and your colleagues . . . since the return of the team." And neither Sullivan, nor Kirby, nor Maccabe "has had any influence at all upon me. What I wrote to you in my letter was based upon the statements of two Americans of the very highest character who were present at the games, but whose names . . . I do not think it desirable to mention." Following is by far the most important portion of this letter:

> I have declined to be drawn into the matter in any shape or way, and I am exceedingly pleased that you have decided not to show my letter to Lord Desborough or any of your colleagues. Naturally, I thought you might be writing with their knowledge. As this proves not to be

the case I would far rather that the letter went no further, and that the incident be treated as at an end. As you rightly say, international goodwill is more important than any number of games. *Thruout the time I have been President I have steadily striven for a better sympathy and understanding between the United States and Great Britain, and to have me take any part whatever in this exceedingly unfortunate controversy would simply tend to undo just what I have been striving to accomplish.*

Roosevelt then sought to drive home his determination to disengage by asking Cook to "understand . . . why I do not read thru the rough draft" of the pamphlet: "I do not desire to know anything about it."[65]

Cook proved more than obliging. He had "received with great pleasure" TR's letter of November 17. "It was never my desire in the least to draw you into controversy," Cook proclaimed, "and as one indication . . . I now have the honour to return you your original letter of October 20th, which has never left my hands or been seen by anyone else." And "I shall never trouble you with the subject again."[66] This time there was no response from the president; yet unquestionably he was extremely grateful to his overly earnest—but also incredibly discreet—British correspondent. Theodore Cook thus stands as a minor hero in the story of Theodore Roosevelt's continuing success in promoting Anglo-American friendship.

As it turned out, keeping Commissioner Sullivan on board proved more difficult than working with Cook. This was a problem Roosevelt had needlessly created for himself; it had been an uncharacteristically imprudent act, offering no discernible potential benefits, when TR sent Sullivan a copy of his letter to Cook of October 20. Sullivan, himself still deeply embroiled in the Olympic controversy, naturally wanted to employ Roosevelt's letter on behalf of his cause and also wanted to know what Cook had written about him to Roosevelt.[*] Roosevelt was therefore compelled to restate emphatically his initial requirement: "No, you must not publish that letter or show it to anyone. . . . If you begin showing it to members of your committee I am afraid it will get out." And regarding Cook's criticisms of Sullivan, TR felt obliged to prevaricate: "What Cook said about you was merely a general expression of disapproval, with no specific charges."[68]

But Sullivan, looking upon Roosevelt's letter to Cook much as a newly licensed teenage boy might look upon a parent's Jaguar he is forbidden to drive, persisted. He really wanted to use the letter now; as a second choice, he wanted to use it when TR left the presidency. So on November 17, just two days after writing the letter quoted in the preceding paragraph, Roosevelt wrote to Sullivan once more. "Let me repeat," he began, "that I do not want you to show that copy of my letter to Cook to anyone, or to leave it where by any pos-bility it can be seen." This was no temporary demand: "When I leave the office I shall still have associations with the Presidency from the mere fact that I once held the position. One of my great aims is . . . international goodwill, and I cannot afford to be drawn in any way into this controversy." The president also expressed some irritation and indirectly admonished Sullivan, who was clearly relishing the fight he was in: "I do wish that this controversy could have been avoided, but at any rate I see no good, no point whatever, to be gained by going on with it now."[69]

These two letters from TR to Sullivan were written at a particularly intense point in the transatlantic athletic officials' slugfest. On November 6 the Amateur Athletic Association (AAA) of Great Britain had notified the Amateur Athletic Union (AAU) of the United States of the disqualification from future competition in Britain of John Carpenter. At its annual meeting on November 16, the AAU formally refused to recognize Carpenter's disqualification. The AAU also reelected Sullivan, "contrary to all precedents," for a third term as its president and officially endorsed his actions at the 1908 Olympic games. Sullivan's sometimes petty annual address featured a long and detailed enumeration of alleged British misdeeds at the games. And the AAU adopted a resolution "that hereafter no athlete registered with the Amateur Athletic Union be given permission to compete in any international competition . . . over which the Amateur Athletic Association has jurisdiction."[70]

Not to be outdone, the next day the AAA published a long "official statement" (which Cook was including at the end of his pamphlet) in the *London Times*, whose purpose was "emphatically to refute," point by point, various charges leveled by American officials against British management of the Olympiad. The British responses included such phrases as "a deliberate lie," "this bogus interview," and "a disgraceful falsehood." As to the AAU breaking off relations with the AAA, there was this bit of one-upmanship: "Although the A.A.U. of America have repeatedly asked to enter into a working agreement with the A.A.A., the latter body have always respectfully declined. There are, therefore, no athletic relations to break off."[71]

In replying on November 19 to a letter from Sullivan dated the preceding day, Roosevelt endorsed, albeit unenthusiastically, the resolution of the AAU terminating athletic relations with the AAA. "In view of what you tell me about the English Amateur Athletic Association writing you," TR declared, "you could not refrain from action."[72]

Then occurred a turn of events that briefly drew Roosevelt into a more visible participation in the controversy. From the onset of the trouble in July through mid-November, there had been no government-to-government contact regarding the Anglo-American Olympics dispute and no open involvement by

either government. Any such involvement, TR had believed all along, would b
inappropriate and potentially damaging. Toward the end of November, howeve
the British embassy in Washington began serving as a conduit for the dissemi
nation of the arguments being put forward by British athletic officials.

In Roosevelt's eyes this was an alarming development indeed. It gave, for th
first time, a clear diplomatic dimension to the problem. In the interest of pre
serving the Anglo-American special relationship, it no longer seemed advisabl
to the president to let hotheaded U.S. athletic officials handle the American sid
of the matter on their own. TR now wanted greater input—although still behin
the scenes.

Thus, on November 23 an unhappy Roosevelt sent a "private" request t
Sullivan to "send me any statements . . . in reference to the attack or statemer
published by the British people and sent out thru the Embassy here." Or even be
ter, "why don't you bring on any statement yourself, and take lunch with me?"

November 25 and 26 were the climactic days of Roosevelt's Olympia
diplomacy. Most important and telling was a stern reprimand issued by TR t
his friend James Bryce, the British ambassador to the United States, on th
25th. Here the president not only offered his perspectives on the relativ
insignificance of the Olympics dispute but in the process endeavored to smothe
in its infancy the new and troubling diplomatic dimension. He fervently hope
it was not too late.

"Please treat this note as informal and unofficial," Roosevelt began. "
greatly regret that your government thought that their Embassy in Washingto
ought to put forth such a statement . . . on behalf of the British officials in th
Olympic Games. I should most emphatically have refused any request from th
corresponding American officials to secure the publication of any similar state
ment in England thru the American Embassy." Clearly Roosevelt was extremel
upset: "Absolutely no good whatever comes, or can come, from any action b
any official of either the British or American Government in this matter. On th
contrary, harm has come already from the publication made by the Britis
Embassy, and further harm will come if either the American or the Britis
Government takes any part whatsoever in this exceedingly unfortunate affai
Moreover," he went on (one imagines him composing fast and furiously),

> such action gives it an entirely unwarranted importance. I thoroly
> believe in athletics, but it is absurd to attach to them such portentous
> importance as would warrant the interference of the governments of
> the two countries to settle whether an American fouled an Englishman
> in the four hundred metre race, or whether the British officials behaved
> unfairly in the Marathon race. It is even more preposterous for the offi-
> cials of the two governments to allow themselves to be made the solemn

instruments of calling the attention of the public to a bitter controversy as to which given set of officials has or has not behaved badly; as to whether certain American or certain British papers have or have not published slanderous articles. The quarrel has been most regrettable, most unfortunate. Not the slightest good can come . . . from what would in any event be the rather absurd course of getting the two governments embroiled in the effort to nicely apportion the rights and wrongs of the various controversies. Such being the case, it seems to me exceedingly unwise to take any action which amounts to a provocation to continue the quarrel, and gives it an immense advertisement.

Already, Britain's serious misstep was causing complications for TR. Members of the AAU understandably have "asked this government to take some action in response to what they regard as the official action of the British Embassy." The president was doing his best to resist: "My present intention is to positively refuse to be drawn in any way into the controversy . . . , because I am convinced that the surest way to cause friction is to keep alive the discussion, and that from the point of view of international good relations the wisest possible thing to do for those in power in the two countries, is to say nothing whatever."

Roosevelt assured Bryce that for "these athletic rows"—here TR illustrated by discussing the long Harvard-Yale athletic estrangement following a football game in the mid-1890s—"time and silence are the only sure remedies." He warned that should "either government" foolishly assume any responsibility "for anything said in the matter," there "may finally result . . . an amount of irritation and damage ludicrously disproportionate to the original cause."[74]

As TR indicated to Bryce, Sullivan had indeed requested direct presidential action in a letter of November 24.[75] But before giving serious consideration to a public role, Roosevelt was absolutely determined to give the British government, through Bryce, the chance to get the message and back away from the controversy. So he replied firmly—and negatively—to Sullivan's request in a "purely personal" letter of November 25. Roosevelt was "exceedingly sorry" about the continued public discussion of the dispute. But "in any event, let me again impress upon you that I must not be brought in any way into the affair." TR sought to mollify the frustrated commissioner by offering in the near future to "speak to you at some length about the affair, but purely for your private information."[76]

In a letter dated November 26, Roosevelt endeavored to bring Ambassador Reid up to date. "I am afraid by direction of the Government at home," TR asserted, "the British Embassy here . . . did a very foolish thing in publishing, and getting the papers to circulate, the acrid protest of the British Olympic officials against the American officials and athletes. It of course immensely advertises the quarrel, and gives precisely the opportunity which I had hoped would not be given for the anti-British people to write bitter articles." Roosevelt summed up what he had told Bryce. Concerning the substance of the controversy, Roosevelt had come to the view that there had been "discreditable" behavior on both sides, with "each side . . . blind to its own misdeeds and clamorously unjust about the misdeeds of the other."[77]

Roosevelt did not dispatch his letter to Reid right away. Instead, or so it would appear from Roosevelt's letter, he visited with Bryce the evening of the 26th, received a letter from Reid either late on the 26th or early on the 27th, and added a "P.S." to his letter to Reid on the 27th before sending it off.[78]

From Bryce Roosevelt had been surprised but also relieved to learn "that the Government had not communicated with the British Embassy." Thus, the British government had *not* chosen to become involved in the Olympics controversy; rather, Bryce himself had been guilty of "slack management." And Roosevelt implied clearly that he had persuaded Bryce of his error, meaning that there would be no further participation in the dispute by either government.[79]

Reid had enclosed with his letter, dated November 18, the AAA's "official statement" in the *London Times* of November 17, discussed earlier. The AAA's statement had strengthened Reid's belief "that our people have used some language which . . . was at least unwise." He singled out for criticism "our Irish-American friend, Mr. Sullivan," against whom the feeling in Britain "has become extremely bitter." But Reid's primary concern was that "prolonging a discussion" was likely "to embitter relations which the Government has been constantly trying to make more friendly."[80]

In the "P.S." to his letter to Reid, Roosevelt noted with satisfaction "how exactly your view of the course to follow in the matter of the athletic squabble coincides with what I had already written above." Manifestly uplifted by his encounter with Bryce, the president closed his commentary on the Olympics issue with a little humor: "As you say, I think both sides have been to blame, and it is a case for the application of one of my favorite anecdotes—that of the New Bedford whaling captain who told one of his men that all he wisht from him was 'silence, and damn little of that.'"[81]

While British and American athletic officials would continue well into the future to do verbal battle, the date November 26, 1908, marks the conclusion of the Olympics controversy as a potential menace to ongoing Anglo-American amity. For it was on the 26th that Roosevelt held his pivotal meeting with Bryce, just as it was on the 26th that Theodore Cook wrote TR a reassuring letter, enclosing with it Roosevelt's long letter to him of October 20, "which has never left my hands or been seen by anyone else."[82] In a letter to Roosevelt of December 21, Reid said he "was sorry to hear . . . about the encouragement given to the prolongation of the dispute" but was hoping "that recent occurrences have caused it to be quite forgotten."[83] Roosevelt was happy to be able to report back optimistically on January 6, 1909: "I think that the Olympic game squabble is dying a natural death."[84]

✄   ✄

The 1908 Olympics controversy marked a troublesome episode for Theodore Roosevelt. It constituted a most unwelcome intrusion as he continued to cultivate Anglo-American harmony during the final year of his presidency. He really wanted nothing to do with it, and yet he found himself privately taking part just the same. For while this dispute was over an issue Roosevelt considered unworthy of governmental attention, it aroused passions among segments of the populations of both Britain and the United States—and particularly among athletic officials—that made it difficult to ignore. And TR certainly did not ignore it.

Roosevelt's perspectives on the substance of the controversy—although not on its relative insignificance and the need to minimize it—did shift somewhat over the key period August-November 1908. Throughout most of this period, he held a decidedly partisan American view, displayed most vividly in his letters to George Buell and Theodore Cook of August 18 and October 20, respectively. By late November, however, as evidenced by his letter to Whitelaw Reid of November 26, he was professing a somewhat less one-sided outlook. This shift was probably influenced by Reid's reports of American misconduct, by Cook's pamphlet (which TR may have looked over despite the denial in his letter of November 17), and, especially, by what Roosevelt came to see as the relentless and excessive combativeness of James Sullivan and his associates. TR was very tired of the controversy by late November and considered officials in both countries responsible for its persistence. If he continued to believe that American athletes had been discriminated against in London, he no longer had much sympathy for their managers.

The Olympics controversy of 1908 did pose a threat to the Anglo-American partnership, as Roosevelt acknowledged in his correspondence on several occasions. Yet the threat was not quite on the level of that posed by the Jamaica incident of 1907. The differences are instructive. Most obviously, the Olympics dispute centered around allegations of mistreatment of American sportsmen by athletic officials not connected to the British government, while the Jamaica affair entailed a flagrant insult to the American navy by a British colonial governor. These were far from equivalent cases in Roosevelt's view. The "national honor" was potentially at issue in Jamaica in 1907—not so in London in 1908. President Roosevelt immediately seized the reins of American diplomacy pertaining to the Jamaican episode and grasped them tightly throughout; in sharp contrast, he considered diplomacy on *any* governmental level to be inappropriate to the Olympics situation (although he did keep a close eye on it and intervened decisively on November 25 and 26). It is suggestive that the Olympics dispute elicited only one brief exchange (which was not initiated by the president) in Roosevelt's extensive, frank, and intimate correspondence with his very close English friend, Arthur Lee, during the period from July 1908 through March 1909, whereas Jamaica had been a major topic in their letters during the early months of 1907. The Olympics controversy was less dangerous and, to TR at least, far less interesting.

Still, the Olympics affair did challenge Roosevelt's diplomatic acumen. He understood that he had to try to minimize it—had to try from behind the scenes to nudge it to a close. While he performed very well and, as usual, achieved a successful outcome, this was not quite his finest hour as a diplomatist. It is hard to find fault with his dealings with Theodore Cook. Roosevelt responded in an appropriate and measured way—and only after thoughtfully calculating the risks and benefits—to Cook's initial provocation, and interacted with him very deftly from that point forward. And with Bryce, when the chips were down, TR was a virtuoso. But sending a copy of his first letter to Cook to James Sullivan on November 6 was a careless, pointless mistake that compromised Roosevelt's position and forced him repeatedly during November to reiterate his demand for Sullivan's confidentiality and also to flatter the petty and self-important commissioner, whose antics TR was coming increasingly to find gratuitous and distasteful. Roosevelt did, however, manage to prevent Sullivan from revealing the letter; the president's error produced inconvenience and annoyance but not failure. In the final analysis, Roosevelt's handling of the Olympics controversy helped keep the Anglo-American partnership on course and stands as yet another instance of his highly impressive statecraft.

Roosevelt and the British Empire: Intimate Last Years

● ○ ●

ENGLAND, GERMANY, AND THE EPISODE OF THE TWO INTERVIEWS

Theodore Roosevelt's sharply contrasting perspectives on Britain and Germany—perspectives that had largely crystallized by 1906—became firmer still between 1907 and 1909. During this period his growing concerns about Germany's intentions brought him into ever greater sympathy with the government and people of Great Britain.

As a means of maintaining cordial relations with Germany, Roosevelt did continue his habit of insincerely flattering the kaiser. "I have entire confidence in your genuine friendliness to my country," TR told the German ruler in January 1907. "Primarily owing to your attitude, the relations of the two countries have been placed on an excellent footing."[1] Two years later he sought again "to assure" the kaiser "how much I have appreciated the unvarying friendship you have shown this country during the years that I have been President." William II was "the most influential and powerful of living men; and your hearty good will to America has been of real moment to my fellow countrymen."[2] (Roosevelt was decidedly more honest when he expressed grief and lament in August 1908 upon the death of Ambassador Speck von Sternburg, "my intimate personal friend . . . who showed such intelligent good will for America."[3]) Feigned affection and admiration of this sort played right into what Raymond A. Esthus calls the kaiser's "appalling naiveté in his relations with Roosevelt."[4]

Roosevelt's worries about the direction of German foreign policy were exacerbated by a report he received from John St. Loe Strachey following the latter's visit to Germany and France. "The general conclusion I formed in Berlin," Strachey informed TR in a letter of February 11, 1907, "was not altogether optimistic as regards peace." Although the kaiser "is no doubt in a sense quite sincere when he represents himself as in favor of peace, he might be willing to engage in war for reasons of *pure policy,* which would seem detestable — I can use no other word — to an English or American statesman." Strachey had learned "that the Germans genuinely believed two years ago, when our fleet went into the Baltic, that we intended to attack them and destroy them" — because in reverse circumstances "they would not have hesitated for a moment to destroy" the British fleet "before it became a real danger." German statesmen, Strachey discovered, simply "cannot believe that British statesmen are not also moved by similar feelings." And if such notions "govern German action and if they regard war as some time or other inevitable, one cannot feel very safe."

In contrast, Strachey found "French statesmen as well as the French people" to be "extremely pacific. . . . That they will ever provoke a war or attack Germany is I feel sure out of the question." But in the wake of the Moroccan crisis, the French people and their leaders were "exceedingly pessimistic" about Germany's designs.[5]

The president replied on February 22 that he was "profoundly imprest with what you described in both Berlin and Paris. I regret greatly to say that in its essentials I think your belief as to the foreign policies of the two countries is justifiable." Strachey's accurate characterization of *"the German attitude toward war,* which is fundamentally the Bismarck attitude, *is one that in the progress of civilization England and America have outgrown;* and for the sake of civilization I hope that other nations will also outgrow it."[6] In a long and thoughtful discourse on the armaments limitation issue contained in a letter to Foreign Secretary Sir Edward Grey that same month, this was Roosevelt's most significant declaration — really his bottom line: "For the free and civilized powers [read the United States, Great Britain, and France] to agree to a limitation which would leave them helpless before a military despotism or barbarism [read Germany, Russia, and Japan] is not to be considered."[7] When Arthur Lee wrote to TR that December about concerns shared by Britons over the "enormous additions" Germany was making to its navy, he was addressing a receptive audience.[8]

Encouraged by Roosevelt's false flattery, however, a misled (and self-deluded) William II futilely endeavored during the closing months of 1907 and throughout most of 1908 to establish a German-Chinese-American alliance to oppose what had in effect become an Anglo-Franco-Russo-Japanese "quadruple entente" ranged against Germany. Roosevelt's response, outlined clearly by Esthus, was "to parry the Kaiser's scheme." It took the Root-Takahira Agreement of November 1908 to prove definitively to the German government the hopelessness of the kaiser's project.[9]

⊀ ⊁

By 1908 there was little that German diplomats could have done to modify, much less to alter, the pro-British thrust of Roosevelt's policy toward the Anglo-German rivalry. But the bungling kaiser managed to find a way to create an even worse situation for Germany in this regard.

What might be called the "episode of the two interviews" began when *New York Times* journalist William B. Hale conducted an interview with William II in July 1908. The kaiser's remarks during this two-hour meeting were so indiscreet and inflammatory that on August 8, Oscar King Davis, a representative of the *Times*, traveled to Oyster Bay to solicit Roosevelt's opinion on how the matter ought to be handled.

The president's alarmed reaction comes through clearly in a letter he wrote to Secretary of State Elihu Root that very day. This interview, declared TR, "would invite an international explosion if made public." The kaiser had erroneously claimed that the United States, Germany, and China were about to conclude an arrangement designed to oppose Japan in East Asia. William also had displayed "intense bitterness" toward Britain and had "said that very shortly Germany would have to go to war with her, and that he believed the time had nearly come, and that England was a traitor to the white race, as had been shown by her alliance with Japan." Regarding the Russo-Japanese War, the kaiser had argued that Russia had been resisting "the yellow peril" on behalf of "the entire white race." He had gone on to predict a U.S.-Japanese war "within a year or two," stating "that he was glad we were preparing for it." And for its part, Britain's Australian colony "would welcome our fleet to show that she repudiated England's Japanese policy." Astonished by these extraordinary declarations, Roosevelt had "told Davis that I should reprobate in the strongest manner such a conversation being made public."[10] Roosevelt had in addition offered the following sardonic observation to Davis, according to the latter's own notes: "They say the Emperor and I are alike, and have a great admiration for each other on that account. I do admire him, very much as I do a grizzly bear."[11]

While the president was certain that the publication of the Hale interview could do great harm, he did feel obliged to bring it to the attention of British leaders. (Unbeknownst to TR, as Esthus explains, in late August the Foreign Office received from the *London Times*, "which had a working agreement with the *New York Times* for exchange of information, . . . an accurate summary of the Hale interview."[12]) Roosevelt considered the matter extremely delicate and endeavored to handle it with the utmost discretion. So in mid-October he wrote a letter to Arthur Lee, by this time without question TR's closest British friend, and sent it by diplomatic pouch to Henry White, by now his ambassador to

France and "the man . . . of all the people in Europe . . . in whom I have the most implicit trust." White was instructed to travel to London to deliver Roosevelt's letter to Lee, "letting him read it as often as he likes, but yourself seeing that it is destroyed immediately thereafter and that no copy is kept of it."[13]

Although not liking to be "a stirrer up of strife," TR wrote to Lee, "I have been persistently telling so many Englishmen that I thought their fears of Germany slightly absurd and did not believe that there was need of arming against Germany." Thus, "perhaps it is incumbent upon me now to say that I am by no means as confident as I was in this position." Directing that the information contained in this letter should be shared with "no one save . . . Balfour and Grey," the president referred to the kaiser as "very jumpy" and noted that "more than once in the last seven years I have had to watch him hard and speak to him, with great politeness, but with equal decision, in order to prevent his doing things that I thought against the interests of this country." Roosevelt then turned to the interview conducted by Hale, "a very honorable fellow whom I know well," in which the kaiser "spoke . . . with astounding frankness." TR detailed the contents of the interview, including William's statement "that he regarded war between England and Germany as inevitable and as likely soon to take place." The kaiser, Roosevelt related, "spoke very bitterly of the King, saying that he and all those immediately around him were sunk in ignoble greed and lookt at life from a purely stock market standpoint, and that he and they hated me virulently," blaming TR's economic policies for diminishing the value of their American investments.

Roosevelt went on to praise Hale for showing the notes of his interview to German Foreign Ministry officials, who "nearly went thru the roof, and protested most emphatically that the utmost damage would result from its publication." The president recounted his meeting with Oscar Davis, remarking that he had "earnestly urged" Davis to suppress the interview, "stating that it would undoubtedly create a general panic and would cause extraordinary bitterness between England and Germany." He had also invoked the self-interest of the *Times* by arguing that "the Emperor was absolutely certain to repudiate" any report on the interview, which could prove detrimental to the newspaper's reputation. Naturally Roosevelt was pleased that no publication had as yet occurred.[14]

Eleven days later, on October 28, Roosevelt's effort to shield the British public from the kaiser's highly provocative statements was dealt a severe blow by the publication in the *London Daily Telegraph* of a second interview, this one given by the kaiser to an anonymous British interviewer. In this second case—in sharp contradiction to the first—William "described himself as an ardent friend of Britain who had advised the British on how to win the Boer War and was now restraining the German people, whose prevailing sentiment was not friendly to

England." As Esthus narrates, the publication of this interview produced "amazement in Britain and a storm of protest in Germany." Britons believed only the "ominous admission that the German people were unfriendly to England," while in his home country "the Kaiser was attacked . . . vigorously" and as a result "promised not to talk politics again without his Chancellor's advice."

At this bizarre and unexpected turn, Roosevelt decided to pull back his letters to White and Lee. One reason was an aversion "to further inflaming the Anglo-German rivalry" at such a dangerous time. Probably even more important, "the Kaiser had been so humbled by the reaction to the *Daily Telegraph* interview that he could do no immediate mischief against England."[15] Whitelaw Reid assessed the matter in these words in a letter to Roosevelt of November 3: "If the Emperor had sat up nights for a month to devise the best way of discrediting himself at home and abroad, he could not have hit upon a more successful method. . . . In the language of the Southern negro, commenting on his son's experience with the hind legs of a mule: 'Bill'll never be so handsome again, but he'll know a heap sight more.'"[16] Three weeks later the ambassador expanded on his largely optimistic appraisal: "To me the essential thing in the whole affair" is "that really some good comes out of it. The English are impressed" by the kaiser's apparent desire, however clumsily expressed in the *Daily Telegraph* interview, to evince friendliness for their country. They were also encouraged by the favorable disposition toward them of German government officials and journalists and of the German public. Reid described "the present attitude of the English towards the German Government and people" as "a curious mingling of good-will and sympathy in their embarrassments." The ambassador was confident "that whatever may be the outcome of the present troubles, the relations between England and Germany are sure to be better for a few months, at any rate, than they have been for years past."[17] Roosevelt agreed with Reid, predicting "that for some years to come the Kaiser will not be a source of serious danger as regards international complications."[18] On November 23, therefore, TR wrote to Lee, informing his friend that "current publications have rendered it unnecessary" for White to deliver to Lee the "exceedingly confidential" presidential letter dated October 17.[19]

While drawing back from his plan to give British leaders a complete written account of Hale's interview, Roosevelt does appear to have conveyed "its substance orally to Ambassador Bryce." For on November 18, as Esthus recounts, "Bryce sent to Grey a private letter giving an accurate summary of the Hale interview."[20] (Like TR, Bryce seems to have been unaware that the British government had learned the substance of the Hale interview more than two months earlier.)

Despite the shock of the *Daily Telegraph* interview, Roosevelt took pride in his handling of the whole episode. "Did I tell you of the Kaiser's interview with . . .

Hale last summer," he asked his oldest son in a letter of November 20, "and of my part in helping to prevent" its publication? "It was," he contended, "a far worse interview than the one that was actually published in the English paper" and "would have had far worse effects." TR provided a comparative analysis of the two interviews to illustrate his point.[21]

It should be noted that the suppression of the Hale interview was ultimately only partial. Elements of the interview were reported in the December 1908 edition of the American publication *Nineteenth Century.* Some copies of this article found their way to London. Reid admitted to Roosevelt in a letter of December 21 that, along with many Britons, he was "full of curiosity as to just what did happen" with regard to the Hale interview.[22] In his reply of January 6, 1909, the president was forthcoming, there being "no reason why I should not tell you what happened." Hale's interview "contained not only the *Century* matter (which, altho foolish, was not very harmful excepting for two pages of attack on the Catholic church)"; it also contained more explosive declarations — including William's prognostication of an Anglo-German war — which TR detailed for Reid, as he had previously done for Root and (until shifting course) for Lee. Roosevelt additionally informed his ambassador of the O. K. Davis visit. And TR emphatically denied rumors that he had had any part in arranging for Hale to interview the kaiser. While clearly less worried than he had been a few months earlier about the potential repercussions of a full exposure of the Hale interview, Roosevelt nevertheless instructed Reid to "use the greatest care in letting anyone know what I have told you."[23]

During a meeting with King Edward VII a couple of weeks later, Reid "was glad," he wrote to the president, "to be able to assure him that Mr. Hale had not gained access to the Emperor through your introduction." Reid reported that he had found the king less than fully informed about the contents of the Hale interview and determined to look beyond the episode of the two interviews and to continue "his friendly effort to . . . maintain good relations" with Germany.[24]

Welcome though it was, this lull in Anglo-German tension had no discernible effect on Roosevelt's deep-rooted wariness of German intentions. In retrospect — from the vantage point of international power politics and American self-interest — one might be tempted to view Roosevelt's perspectives and policies on the Anglo-German rivalry and the Anglo-American special relationship as logical almost to the point of being self-evident. It is therefore important to emphasize — as David Fromkin does in his ambitious and impressive recent book about the great transition in American foreign policy in the middle decades of the twentieth century and the people who oversaw that transition — that Theodore Roosevelt's understanding of the balance of power was highly unusual among American political figures of his era. More particularly, TR "was one of the few who saw that the growing power of Germany would one day threaten the United States, and that it would be in America's interest to back Great Britain against Germany."[25]

ROOSEVELT AND IMPERIAL MATTERS:
FOCUS ON BRITISH INDIA

Continuity marked Theodore Roosevelt's outlook on imperial matters throughout his presidency. During his final two years in office, the themes were familiar ones. At various times, TR lauded the American record in the Philippines, worried about slow population growth in Australia, and reflected hopefully but with some uncertainty and concern about the future direction of civilization. Roosevelt's last six or seven months as president, however, did see a noticeable shift in focus, with British rule in India receiving far more of his attention than it had ever received before. This increased presidential attention to India, as it turned out, had a highly salutary impact on the Anglo-American relationship.

During the second half of the second term of his presidency, Roosevelt's observations on American administration of the Philippines had a very recognizable ring. "We are training a people in the difficult art of self-government" with great success, he contended in a letter of April 1907 to Andrew Carnegie. "We have acted in a spirit of genuine disinterestedness, of genuine and single-minded purpose to benefit the islanders . . . , a spirit wholly untainted by . . . silly sentimentality."[26]

Great Britain, despite its many extraordinary imperial accomplishments, had nowhere met with quite such success. "In international affairs," Roosevelt wrote in February 1908 to Boston lawyer and Republican politician Grafton Dulany Cushing, "we have shown our ability to hold our own against the strong; while no nation has ever behaved towards the weak with quite the disinterestedness and sanity combined which we have shown as regards Cuba and the Philippines."[27] The comparison was more explicit when TR resurrected an earlier theme in a letter of August 1907—written in reaction to "Bishop Brent's sudden attack on the American Government of the Philippines"—to Silas McBee. "We have stayed . . . in the Philippines . . . literally for the islanders' good and not for our own, and with as lofty a national purpose of performance of duty as has ever been seen—a realized purpose, too." In stark contrast, he asserted, "the English in the Malay provinces . . . have from the standpoint of the natives done infinitely worse . . . ; or, to speak more exactly, whereas we have greatly helped the natives, they have ruined them."[28]

Actually, at the time he wrote to McBee, Roosevelt was feeling pessimistic about his country's staying power in the Philippines. As Secretary of War William Howard Taft was preparing to depart for the Philippines "to open the new Filipino assembly, the first major instrument of self-government for the Islands," a rather gloomy letter from the president came his way. "It has been everything for the islands and everything for our own national character that we should have taken them and have administered them with . . . really lofty and disinterested efficiency," Roosevelt proclaimed. To his great regret, however, "it is impossible . . . to awaken any public interest in favor of giving them tariff advantages"; likewise, "it is very difficult to awaken any public interest in providing any adequate defense of the islands." Lacking such adequate defenses, TR went on with an oft-cited remark, "the Philippines form our heel of Achilles.[29] They are all that makes the present situation with Japan dangerous." Considering the manifest unwillingness of the American people to "accept the Philippines" over the long haul "simply as an unremunerative and indeed expensive duty, . . . we shall have to be prepared for giving the islands independence of a more or less complete type much sooner than I think advisable."[30] McBee too read of "our heel of Achilles."[31]

But with the progress of the Great White Fleet, congressional authorization and funding of new battleships, and the relaxation of tensions with Japan, Roosevelt's pessimism waned in 1908, and his Philippines policy remained on a fixed course. In a speech delivered in January 1909, he confidently asserted that "we are constantly giving to the people of the Philippines an increasing share in, an increasing opportunity to learn by practice, the difficult art of self-government. . . . We are leading them forward steadily in the right direction."[3]

Theodore Roosevelt never wavered in his belief that human racial, religious, and ethnic groups advanced along the path of civilization at differing rates but always with difficulty. He was interested in learning about the stages of development of peoples everywhere, including in such remote places (psychologically, if not geographically) as Haiti and Liberia.[33] He was intrigued by Cecil Spring Rice's impression of a "growth in Persia among the Mohammedans of a belief in toleration," which seemed to TR "to mark the possibility of an evolution which will make Mohammedanism a working creed for modern civilization." He cautioned, however, that "at present it is impossible to expect moral, intellectual and material well-being where Mohammedanism is supreme."[34]

Nor did Roosevelt ever doubt that enlightened imperial rule by a more "civilized" foreign power accelerated the civilization process and therefore served the interests of the native inhabitants. "In spite of all its defects," he contended early in 1909, such rule "is in a very large number of cases the prerequisite condition to the moral and material advance of the peoples who dwell in the darker corners of the earth." Algeria, for example, was "far better off in every way under French rule than it was . . . before the French came . . . , and it is far better off in every way than . . . Morocco," which "continues to enjoy much the same kind of independent self-government" as prevailed in Algeria prior to the French takeover.[35] "I wish to heaven, not in your interest but in the interest of all civilized mankind," he thus told Ambassador Jean Jules Jusserand in August 1908, "that France could take all Morocco under its exclusive charge."[36] Similarly, Roosevelt cited "the enormous advantages conferred by the English occupation of the Soudan [*sic*], if not on the English themselves, certainly on the natives and on humanity at large."[37] In keeping with his belief that imperial rule should be conducted generously and in the interest of the indigenous population, TR praised British treatment of Negroes in Jamaica and criticized it in southern Africa.[38]

There was another strong conviction that Roosevelt never abandoned. The English-speaking peoples, he was certain, were the most advanced of all peoples and stood in the vanguard in "the great work of uplifting mankind."[39] Hence, TR remained worried about the small Australian population. "If the rate of increase . . . continues no greater than in the past ten years," he argued in a letter to Strachey of September 1907, "it would be the end of this century before Australia has doubled in population. Under such circumstances the yellow peril which they dread might be a very real peril indeed for them." Consequently, Roosevelt reasoned, the colony should end its highly restrictive immigration policy: "Where their birth rate is so low they should encourage in every way the kind of immigration that they can assimilate and digest."[40] Roosevelt wrote much the same thing to Spring Rice a few months later, although with a diminished sense of foreboding: "I very much wish that Australia would either encourage European immigration or would see a higher birth rate among its own citizens. It is not pleasant to realize how slowly the scanty population of that island continent increases. But as long as Great Britain retains her naval superiority and Australia is part of the British Empire Australia is safe."[41]

What were the long-range prospects for the progress of civilization? Roosevelt confessed to being concerned and quite uncertain, but on balance he inclined toward optimism and in any case was determined to do his part. "By the middle of this century," he remarked in a letter of November 1908 to William Sidney Rossiter, who had sent him some "rather melancholy" tables, "it looks as if all the civilized races would have stopt increasing. Of course, . . . it is perfectly possible that we may have gotten aroused to the moral side of the matter (when I say 'we' I mean the civilized peoples) and the tendency may be changed; but it certainly is a very curious and lamentable tendency now."[42] To Jusserand TR offered these reflections on the subject: "We cannot any of us tell whither civilization is tending, or what may be the strength or even the direction of the great blind forces working all around us. But I very cordially agree with Lord Acton that we are in honor bound to do right *because* it is right." As for himself, Roosevelt fully intended to carry out his "duty to lead efficiently, as well as in the right direction."[43]

⊰ ⊱

British India was experiencing serious unrest during the closing months of Theodore Roosevelt's presidency. Indeed, according to Elting E. Morison and his associates, "not since the Mutiny" in 1858 "had India witnessed the violence that broke out in the last months of 1908."[44] The turmoil in India was sparked by intensifying communal rivalries within the colony and by the frustration experienced by Hindu nationalists, in particular the more extreme among them, over the perceived unresponsiveness of Great Britain to their demands for change. John Morley, the Liberal secretary of state for India, attempted with notable success to restore stability by implementing a program of constitutional adjustment, the Morley-Minto reforms, which moved British policy toward the position of the more moderate nationalists by significantly increasing the political role of the native population.[45]

In August 1908 Ambassador Reid brought the British government's great concerns about India's travails to Roosevelt's attention and launched the president into a period of intensified contemplation and active private and public discussion of British rule in India. "Morley is troubled and anxious about India," Reid related. "The trouble is that the Babu is educated enough to want self-government after the English pattern, but hasn't character enough to be capable of it."[46]

"I am much interested," TR replied, "in what Morley said to you about India." Roosevelt's analysis, much less crude than Reid's, was that "the Indian Babu . . . receives what is in many ways a peculiarly bad training. He is fitted by his education only to hold public office or to practice as a lawyer in the courts under English control." However, only "a limited proportion can hold public office, and the remainder including almost all of the lawyers, find the path of agitation against the government almost the only one open to them, and it is rendered congenial by the bitterness they feel because of the aspirations which their education has kindled and which cannot be gratified." In general, Roosevelt thought, "the problem of the control of thickly peopled tropical regions by self-governing northern democracies is very intricate."[47]

In November the British writer and editor Sydney Brooks took the initiative in trying to draw Roosevelt into a public endorsement of British rule in India. Brooks informed the president that "people in England, and especially some of them in high places," were "disturbed . . . by what looks like a regular campaign of attack upon British rule in India in the American press." While acknowledging that "British rule in India has its faults" and required significant alterations "if it is to do as much good in the future as it has done in the past," Brooks believed firmly that the "prejudice . . . created in the American mind" by the press was mostly "groundless and wrong-headed." During the current crisis in India, Brooks claimed, British leaders would "greatly value . . . the moral support and sympathy of the American people." For his part, Brooks had undertaken "to do what I can do to lay the impartial truth of the situation before the American people"; two major essays of his on the subject were scheduled for publication in *Harper's Weekly* in December and January.[48] He framed his request of Roosevelt in these words: "I know that if you could find occasion to say a public word of approval of British rule in India it would do more than anything else to set opinion straight and would be very greatly appreciated over here."[49] (Actually, it was the *British* anti-imperialist press and its impact on *British* public opinion that *most* troubled Brooks and British leaders, and which they hoped a supportive speech by President Roosevelt would primarily help to counteract. This was their real, hidden, agenda.)

Roosevelt was somewhat surprised by, but also receptive to, Brooks's remarks and suggestion. "I did not realize that any considerable number of our papers had been attacking England on the subject of India," TR declared in a letter of November 20, "and I am sorry to learn it. . . . English rule in India has been one of the mighty feats of civilization, one of the mighty feats to the credit of the white race during the past four centuries, the time of its extraordinary expansion and dominance." Undoubtedly the British had "committed faults, . . . tho I do not know them—my business being to know the faults we have committed in the Philippines ourselves," for which "I am steadily trying to advance and perfect remedies." Roosevelt did not pass up this opportunity to remind Brooks that some British writers—in the *Saturday Review*, of which Brooks was editor, and elsewhere—"have been very foolish in the effort to be caustic about our work in the Philippines." As to Brooks's request, the president was amenable but withheld a definitive commitment: "I do not want to force a speech on the subject, but if I get the chance I shall certainly speak very strongly."[50]

His exchange of letters with Brooks apparently induced Roosevelt to worry more about and pay closer attention to the situation in India. His desire to weigh in knowledgeably and effectively on the matter is evident in letters to Reid and John Morley of November 26 and December 1, respectively.

"I do not like what I hear about India," TR told his ambassador. "It looks to me as if a very ugly feeling was growing up there. How do the British authorities feel about it? Are they confident that they can hold down any revolt?"[51]

By writing to Morley, Roosevelt was seeking information directly from the source. He made his inquiry of the secretary of state for India in extremely sympathetic and supportive terms:

> I grow concerned now and then at what I hear about the unrest in India. I know very little about it save that I realize the immensity of the burden which England has to bear . . . ; a burden that is now on your shoulders. . . . English rule in India has marked one of the signal triumphs of civilization. I do not suppose that there is any serious menace to it, and I am sure that you will be able gradually to work reform where reform is needed, without permitting yourselves to be overwhelmed by any reform movement gone crazy. If you feel at liberty, do tell me simply for my private information, what the situation in India really is. You will be telling it to a well-wisher.[52]

A presidential speech addressing British rule in India was evidently in the works.

Not yet sure of Roosevelt's intentions, Brooks played his best cards as he renewed his campaign in a letter of December 12. He had shared Roosevelt's letter of November 20 with Morley, "who was much gratified by it." Brooks was sure that if Morley "were in a position to do so, he would very warmly second the suggestion I made to you about saying a word of public approval of what the British have accomplished in India." In addition, Brooks endeavored to engage more fully the president's interest and concern by offering up a Philippines connection: "I fully appreciate what you say about not wanting to force a speech" on India, he remarked, "but I was rather hoping that some reference to it might come in naturally when you were treating of your own problems in the Philippines and of your own work and purpose in that archipelago." Moreover, Brooks contended plausibly, "the East is becoming more homogeneous in sentiment & sympathies with every year that passes & the repercussion of an explosion at Calcutta would very quickly . . . make itself felt at Manila."[53]

On December 21 Reid responded to Roosevelt's inquiries of the preceding month. The ambassador began by reiterating his belief—which he claimed was shared by the Britons "most familiar with Indian affairs"—that "the present Indian agitator" had the "English education" but not "the stability of character" to qualify him to play a leading governmental role. Reid had spent some time with Morley and had found him "distinctly despondent . . . about English rule in India." Morley believed, nonetheless, "that there was absolutely no honorable way for England to relax her hold; and was equally sure that if she ever did, either through choice or on compulsion, the result for India would be infinitely worse." Morley had recently given before the House of Lords a statesmanly and "courageous" speech on India—a speech receiving "practically universal approval"—of which Reid was sending "a full report" to Roosevelt: "You will observe that he is, for a Liberal, strikingly emphatic against . . . giving India Parliamentary institutions, in anything like our sense. At the same time, he does propose measures for Indian representation in Executive Councils, etc., which impress both sides here as quite advanced, and as really opening a new chapter in Indian rule." Morley's speech, Reid remarked, had served to lessen "the general apprehension."[54]

A week later Roosevelt gave Brooks the answer he was looking for. The Earl of Warwick had visited TR and had, like Brooks, urged a presidential speech on India—and had done so, Roosevelt was convinced, at the behest of the British government.[55] The president had then "asked Bryce to come down, and found that he was very anxious that I should speak along the lines you mention." Ambassador Bryce had also "entirely agreed with me that it would not do to make a statement confined to India, and that it must come in in the course of some other speech. Accordingly I shall bring in the subject when I speak at a Methodist missionary meeting some three weeks hence." Roosevelt had shared a draft of this speech with Bryce, "who had no suggestions to make and seemed pleased, so I trust it will be satisfactory. It certainly represents exactly what I believe."[56]

In addition to Bryce, Roosevelt had asked Secretary of State Root to "go over the draft of what I propose to say to the Methodists on January 18th."[57] TR then informed President-Elect Taft of his intention "to give the English a good word for their work in India. . . . This I know will meet your hearty approval."[58] And in early January Roosevelt thanked Reid for his letter of December 21, noting the British government's desire that he speak "to correct the tendency here among well-meaning but foolish people to feel that the English rule in India is an iniquity. I shall do so in a speech a fortnight hence."[59]

It had taken quite awhile, but on January 8 Morley at last replied to Roosevelt's letter of December 1. "About India, what can I say to you?" Morley wrote. "I don't know how to begin, and if I once began, I should never know how to end." So he simply sent the president a copy of his recent speech in the House of Lords (as Reid had done two weeks before) and referred him to "the King's proclamation on November 1, last," the fiftieth anniversary of the end of East India Company rule and the establishment in its place of crown government in India. The news that Roosevelt was going to speak about India, Morley declared, caused him to "rejoice."[60]

Brooks too played a part in preparing TR for his upcoming speech through the publication in mid-December of the first of his two *Harper's Weekly* articles on India. "I like your article," Roosevelt told him.[61] Brooks's article highlighted the fifty years of crown government in India, acknowledging imperfections but emphasizing accomplishments, particularly "an absolute and unbroken internal peace, . . . a sure and constant growth of material prosperity, . . . a rapid multiplication of the accessories of a well-organized state," and a "constant tendency . . . to widen the area of public employment for Indians. . . . On the whole," the article concluded, "I do not see how any dispassionate critic can deny that British rule in India has been an immense civilizing and beneficent influence."[62]

Naturally, Brooks was delighted to learn of Roosevelt's scheduled speech, which, he stated in a letter of January 13, "will be of inestimable service in putting American opinion on the right track." Brooks also sought to clarify his own role, which, he sensed correctly, TR suspected had been at least slightly misrepresented. Although Brooks had known "that the good people at the India Office" would approve of his initiative, "the idea of asking you to speak . . . was entirely my own and was acted upon without consultation with anyone." He therefore considered himself "under a personal as well as a national debt of gratitude to you for the decision you have reached."[63]

The evening of January 18, 1909, at the celebration of the African Diamond Jubilee of the Methodist Episcopal Church, President Roosevelt delivered a long speech extolling the contribution of enlightened imperial rule to the advance of civilization in general and to an improved quality of life for native populations in particular. He sought to illustrate this point by looking specifically at French rule in Algeria, British rule in India, and American rule in the Philippines. He then accorded extended attention to the positive impact on African populations of Christian missionary work, singling out for praise the achievements over seventy-five years of the Methodist Episcopal Church and encouraging the continuation of Methodist missionary activity in Africa.

Only a relatively small group of insiders—including Morley and others in the British government—knew that the approximately 15 percent of Roosevelt's address that focused on British India was the speech's principal raison d'être. The president's remarks on this topic were unambiguously laudatory, even celebratory.

"In India," Roosevelt began with trumpets blaring, "we encounter the most colossal example history affords of the successful administration by men of European blood of a thickly populated region in another continent." Even the achievements of the Roman Empire did not match up. Mistakes had been made along the way, of course, "but on the whole there has been a far more resolute effort to do justice, a far more resolute effort to secure fair treatment for the humble and oppressed" under British rule than ever before in India's history. "England does not draw a penny from India for English purposes; she spends for India the revenues raised in India; and they are spent for the benefit of the

Indians themselves." Indeed, British rule in India had been a liberating experience for the Indian masses, who were receiving "incalculable benefits" and "are far better off than ever before, and far better off than they would now be if English control were overthrown or withdrawn." If the British were to leave, "the whole peninsula would become a chaos of bloodshed and violence; all the weaker peoples, and the most industrious and law-abiding, would be plundered and forced to submit to indescribable wrong and oppression." Certainly there were "reforms to be advanced"; Roosevelt had "no question that there is being made and will be made a successful effort to accomplish these reforms. But," he stressed, "the great salient fact is that the presence of the English in India . . . has been for the advantage of mankind." In sum, "every wellwisher of mankind, every true friend of humanity, should realize that the part England has played in India has been to the immeasurable advantage of India, and for the honor and profit of civilization, and should feel profound satisfaction in the stability and permanence of English rule."[64]

The next day, January 19, the *London Times* published verbatim the entire India portion of Roosevelt's speech. The same issue included an editorial brimming with satisfaction and appreciation. "We have long been conscious," declared the *Times*, that British rule in India was "a monument . . . to our highest qualities as a nation. . . . But it is new to us to have its greatness, moral and political, proclaimed in unhesitating accents by the Chief Magistrate of the people whose esteem and good opinion we prize beyond those of any other foreigners." Roosevelt's praise was all the more meaningful in that "it comes from a statesman who has himself borne his share of the 'white man's burden,' and who has learnt, in bearing it, how heavy is the load." On the plane of Anglo-American relations, Roosevelt's "testimony . . . is an impressive proof of the happy change which has taken place of late years in the relations of the American people to us"—a change so far-reaching as to render it "possible for the President of the United States to express in a public speech his unstinted admiration of the British administration of alien races."[65]

Expressions of gratitude of a more personal character were not long in coming. Ambassador Bryce thanked Roosevelt in a note of January 19, and the following day he passed along the thanks of two of the most important British government officials concerned with India and the image of British rule there, Morley and Foreign Secretary Grey. Roosevelt's "eloquent speech," according to Grey, would be "most highly appreciated both in England and in India," and Morley "wishes that a similar message should be conveyed to you from him."[66] TR replied to Bryce with a brief note on January 21. While Roosevelt was "very glad that Grey and Morley liked what I said, . . . nobody owes me any credit or appreciation in the matter. I felt that it ought to be said, and particularly at this time, when there was the agitation in India, and when there were foolish people here, and worse than foolish people in other countries, who lookt with mischievous pleasure on that agitation." Roosevelt was "more than pleased" if he had "been of the least use in the matter."[67]

Morley weighed in right away on his own behalf. "It seems like thanking a juryman for an acquittal," he commented wittily on January 22, "but I must say to you how great a service your Indian speech renders to all of us who are wrestling with Indian difficulties." The speech had been not only a great "encouragement . . . to us at the helm" but also a blow to those "wrong-headed" radicals who condemn "strong measures against bombs, murder-clubs, and other anarchist delights." Roosevelt's "splendid vindication," Morley asserted, "will tend powerfully to abate misgivings that haunt some minds. . . . We are greatly indebted."[68]

Sydney Brooks, of course, offered his appreciation as well: "All England . . . beamed" upon reading Roosevelt's remarks, which were "immense . . . in my little campaign for the enlightenment of American opinion. Whenever a voice is raised in the American Press against British rule in India I smother it in quotations from your speech."[69]

Whitelaw Reid and Arthur Lee perhaps best captured the magnitude of the impact of Roosevelt's speech on the Anglo-American special relationship. "The other day the King sent for me," Reid wrote on January 22, "and almost the moment I entered the room began telling me how heartily he appreciated what you said in your recent speech about the English in India. *The same feeling is expressed everywhere. I am sure nothing has been done since I have known England . . . that has been so gratefully received, or has so encouraged their cordial feeling towards us.*"[70]

Lee developed this theme much more fully in a letter to TR of January 29. "I cannot tell you," he wrote, "what pleasure your whole-hearted tribute to our work" in India "has given to everyone with whom I have come in contact . . . , and moreover you chose a moment to say what you did which made your testimony of quite peculiar value to us." During this "very anxious and critical time," Keir Hardie, a leader among Britain's "domestic agitators, . . . was actually slandering our Indian administration to American audiences." Earlier, when Hardie "was in India . . . preaching disloyalty there, one of his favourite themes was the 'indignation of the American people' at the tyranny of British rule, and I have no doubt whatever that the Babu agitators were persuaded that you and the U.S. govt. deeply sympathised with their aspirations to drive us out of the country." So in America and in India, as well as in Britain, Roosevelt's speech had constituted a sharp setback for Hardie and his anti-imperialist cause.

Lee then identified a new and important aspect of the contribution of TR's speech to the consolidation of the Anglo-American bond. Not only had the speech "laid us" collectively "under a deep obligation," but

I, personally, have additional reasons for being grateful for it. There are a number of excellent people over here (some of them friends of my own) who have fallen victim to the journalistic wiles of the Wilhelmstrasse, and who could not be persuaded that your real sympathies were not "pro-German" (in the sense of being "anti-British"). I have from time to time reasoned gently with those whose ignorance on this point was apt to cause mischief, but I was often met by the reply that "if what I said was true—why was it that you never make any *public* references to England of a friendly character"? This was, of course, a perfectly puerile argument, because good friends do not need to slobber over each other in public, but none the less it was worth while to give the final quietus to this sort of misunderstanding, and your speech (apart from its more serious significance) has convinced the "doubting Thomases" as nothing else could. So I am delighted on that ground also.[71]

Roosevelt was "glad" to read Lee's observations. In a letter of February 7, he attributed the timing of his speech to "Keir Hardie's coming over here, and the knowledge I had of the unrest in India, and my further knowledge of the fact that agitators in England and agitators in India both sometimes traded on supposed American support of the Indian agitation. . . . If I did any good," TR offered with more modesty than he felt, "I am pleased."[72]

Although Roosevelt's letter did not refer specifically to Lee's insights regarding the speech's effect on the perceptions of numerous leading Britons, undoubtedly it was these insights that "pleased" TR the most. For he would be vacating the presidency in a month, and he wished to leave Anglo-American relations in the healthiest possible condition in every single respect.

EXPRESSIONS OF ANGLO-AMERICAN UNITY

President Roosevelt's correspondence with his British friends during 1907-1909 provides a crystal clear window on the depth of his devotion to the Anglo-American special relationship in the closing years of his presidency. The pattern of intimacy in private letters sharply in evidence by 1906 persisted—indeed attained new levels—between 1907 and 1909. Examples abound; what follows is a selected sampling.

Roosevelt and his close English friend John St. Loe Strachey—accurately labeled by David Burton as "the most sentimental" of TR's British correspondents "in matters pertaining to Anglo-American friendship"[73]—continued their mutual advocacy of Anglo-American unity and their like-minded exchanges on the domestic and international issues of the day. "It is curious how in our two governments parallel problems always arise" and "how exactly you and I agree

on most of the great questions which are fundamentally the same in both coun
tries," Roosevelt declared in letters of February and September 1907.[74] The sec
ond of these was written largely in reply to a letter from Strachey lauding TR fo
giving "a lead to all those here as well as in America who are determined, on th
one hand to fight socialism, and on the other to hold the trusts and combines i
check."[75] When Strachey soon afterward proposed to dedicate his book *Problem*
and Perils of Socialism to Roosevelt, the president was "greatly pleased."[76]

A series of letters to George Otto Trevelyan in 1908 indicates further that
strong Anglo-American tie had become a fundamental assumption—a matter o
course—for Theodore Roosevelt. On New Year's Day, TR commented at lengt
and with satisfaction on a Trevelyan volume on the American Revolution
Battles such as Yorktown, Roosevelt observed, normally necessitate "centurie
. . . before the wound not only scars over but becomes completely forgotten, and
the memory becomes a bond of union and not a cause of division. It is our busi
ness to shorten the time as much as possible; and no one has done better work
toward this end than you."[77] On June 19 Roosevelt bared his soul in a long let
ter to Trevelyan rationalizing his refusal to seek a third consecutive term as pres
ident. This may be the most illuminating of TR's many letters addressing this
topic—and it was written not to an American but to a Briton.[78] In November
Trevelyan was among the first people to whom Roosevelt wrote after the pres
idential election. (This upbeat letter expressed unbounded—later to prove
unfounded—optimism regarding William Howard Taft's performance in the
presidency.)[79] And the high value Roosevelt attached to Trevelyan's good opin
ion of him permeated a letter of December 1, the following sentence in partic
ular: "I know that your legislative and administrative soul will go out in
sympathy to me when I mention my pride in the fact that at the close of my
administration, in spite of a panic, in spite of the purchase of Panama and of the
beginning of the construction of the canal, in spite of having embarked on var
ious schemes that need money, I yet leave the finances a good deal better off than
when I found them."[80]

The notion that the British and American people shared common faults and
faced common perils is especially evident in Roosevelt's letters to the often
gloomy Cecil Spring Rice. "The love of pleasure, . . . the growth of extravagance
and luxury among the upper classes, and a certain frivolous habit of mind and
failure to fix the relative values of things," TR wrote in July 1908, "are very dan
gerous and very marked among the English-speaking peoples, as well as in
France. . . . Such growth does . . . contain the possibility of national disaster."[8]
While agreeing several months earlier that "the governing class in England" had
"no real foreign policy," Roosevelt insisted that "our people tend to have even
less." Moreover, "the capitalist and educated classes are those least to be trusted

n this matter." Roosevelt had "fought, not very successfully, to make our people understand" the necessity of coupling freedom "with military strength" in order to ensure the survival of the former. It was "astounding," he told a receptive Spring Rice, "how shortsighted many people in your country and mine . . . are where war is concerned."[82]

A particularly harmonic exchange of correspondence took place during the winter of 1908 between Roosevelt and King Edward VII. "I feel very strongly," proclaimed the American president, "that the real interests of the English-speaking peoples are one, alike in the Atlantic and the Pacific."[83] "I entirely agree," replied the British monarch, "and I look forward with confidence to the cooperation of the English speaking races becoming the most powerful civilising factor in the . . . world."[84] In a similar spirit, TR shared with John Morley in December 1908 the view that "the great progress of mankind has been made in and through countries like England and the United States, where the democratic movement of the kind that we believe in has been strongest."[85]

Roosevelt also displayed his attachment to Britain in correspondence with various Americans. In letters to Elihu Root, he wholeheartedly endorsed Britain's insistence at the second Hague Conference "upon maintaining its own great naval superiority" and noted approvingly that the immigration to the United States of a diverse array of nationalities "has diminished what used to be the one feeling of hostility, that against England."[86] TR praised William W. Rockhill for providing him with information on Tibet that Roosevelt considered important to Britain and had shared with the British government; "if we can do a good turn to England in this matter I shall be glad."[87] And Roosevelt at times looked to British examples when advocating progressive legislation for the United States.[88]

Nor were Britain's colonies excluded from direct expressions of presidential affection. In two letters to Canadian Prime Minister Sir Wilfrid Laurier in 1908, Roosevelt referred to "the great and wonderful country at the head of whose government you stand" and to "the close bonds of friendship and mutual aims which exist between Canada and the United States."[89]

For their part, the British were recognizing not only Roosevelt's eminence as a naturalist and international stature but also, undoubtedly, his proven affinity for their country and empire when Lord George Nathaniel Curzon invited TR to Oxford to present the Romanes lecture.[90] The invitation extended in August 1908 by Curzon, Oxford's chancellor (and a former viceroy of India), was notably flexible and open-ended: Roosevelt could "deliver this lecture on any subject congenial to you—at any future date when you may be in England." Roosevelt, Curzon claimed, "would meet with such a reception . . . as no British Prime Minister ever has done."[91]

The president accepted immediately. "I can think of few things which would rather do than to deliver the Romanes lecture," he declared. "It is an honor that I sincerely appreciate." Moreover, TR had been hoping to visit England in 1910 following a long African trip devoted to hunting big game and collecting specimens and yet had "rather a horror of ex-Presidents traveling around with no real business. . . . This invitation . . . will give me the excuse desire to spend a fortnight in England and see certain of my friends."

Near the end of Roosevelt's letter of acceptance can be found an extremely (and probably inadvertently) revealing sentence: "I much desire to talk over with you certain matters connected with both India and the Empire; and certain dangers which your people and our people alike have to face and which believe we have the power to overcome if only we choose to exercise reasonable forethought, reasonable care, for the national honor in the future."[92] As a writer generally very attentive to the words he employed, Roosevelt's use of "the national honor" in a collective Anglo-American sense—however hastily he may have constructed this particular letter—should not be dismissed as a simple slip-up. While Roosevelt unquestionably remained—and would always remain—an American nationalist, his ever closer identification of British and American interests and values seems to have led him to become by 1908 something of an *Anglo*-American nationalist as well. A significant evolution clearly had taken place.

Roosevelt's grateful and enthusiastic reply to Curzon's invitation, it might be added, was more than mere politeness. In a letter written the same day, August 18, to Henry Cabot Lodge, Roosevelt said of the Romanes lecture: "I regard it as an honor to be asked and moreover, as something right in my line."[93]

⊰   ⊱

Immediately after relinquishing the presidency in March 1909, Theodore Roosevelt embarked on a dramatic fifteen-month trip that took him to eastern and northeastern Africa, to several countries in continental Europe (including major visits to Italy, France, Norway, and Germany), and finally to Great Britain. The African portion of the journey was by far the longest, lasting about eleven months. While Roosevelt had initially thought primarily in terms of a hunting expedition, the purpose of the voyage expanded early in the planning stage to include a large-scale scientific component—the collection of a huge quantity of mammal and bird specimens for the Smithsonian Institution, which in turn agreed to cover some of the costs of the trip.

It was the British Empire that hosted Roosevelt during his many months in Africa (aside from "an excursion into the Belgian Congo to shoot the giant eland"[94]). His lengthiest stay by far was in British East Africa, and he and his very large party also spent a substantial amount of time hunting and gathering in Uganda. The Sudan and Egypt were the former president's final stops in Africa.

As TR's great-grandson Tweed Roosevelt points out in a 1992 essay, the trip was planned "methodically and painstakingly," the president "ignoring no detail, however small."[95] Indeed, during the closing year of his presidency, TR's correspondence on the subject of his upcoming adventure was truly "voluminous."[96] Seeking advice and assistance, Roosevelt wrote a large quantity of letters to knowledgeable and influential Britons. They, on the whole, were very generous in their responses. Ambassador Whitelaw Reid also very actively and assiduously performed an essential function as both an adviser and an intermediary.

Among other Britons, Roosevelt requested counsel and aid from Colonel John Henry Patterson, author of the 1908 book *The Man-Eaters of Tsavo;* Edward North Buxton, writer and veteran African hunter; Frederick Courteney Selous, big-game expert and writer; General Sir Francis Reginald Wingate, governor-general of the Sudan and sirdar of Egypt; and Lord Crewe, who had recently become secretary of state for the colonies. TR frequently indicated his gratitude for their efforts on his behalf. "I cannot too warmly express my appreciation of what the Colonial Office and my English big game friends have done for me in the matter of the African trip," he declared in a letter to Sydney Brooks; "Wingate . . . has been more than nice about everything," Roosevelt informed Henry White.[97]

As for Reid, not only did he labor diligently to help make arrangements for Roosevelt's trip; he also assumed the role of TR's adviser on matters of etiquette. In response to TR's preference to spend the English leg of his journey visiting with friends, while avoiding "wearisome and fantastic ceremonies," Reid offered this advice in a letter of August 11: "I am sure you could not come to London, make the visits to Trevelyan, Arthur Lee and others . . . and not see . . . the King and Queen. I am perfectly sure that a failure to see them would puzzle and hurt them, and would probably be regarded as discourteous." On the other hand, "everybody will understand your desire not to make a spectacular trip; and I will take pains to feel the ground a little in a quiet way, in order to make up my mind how far you can abstain from what is usual . . . without arousing criticism and perhaps resentment."[98] Roosevelt also apprised Reid that he did "not want to take any but the very simplest outfit of civilized clothing to Africa."[99] A disapproving ambassador admonished his boss to "reconsider that plan!" For "your associates will be almost exclusively English people for nearly a year . . . ; and even in the heart of Central Africa I think you will find the average Englishman . . . dressing for dinner very much as he would at home." Reid urged TR to bring along "a dress suit, with an odd dinner jacket, a frock coat, and the necessary linen; . . . there will hardly be a week during your absence when you won't wish you had" these items.[100] A reluctant Roosevelt yielded (although not without a fuss and not quite entirely): "You make me very melancholy as to what you say about my clothes in Africa; but I suppose I shall have to carry all that you suggest, excepting that I think I shall take in place of the regular frock coat a black cutaway coat, so that on emergencies [*sic*] I can wear this without that atrocity and horror—a top hat."[101]

One other prominent Briton who extended himself to advise and assist Roosevelt in advance of the African adventure was Winston Churchill. Ambassador Reid endeavored to facilitate the efforts of Churchill, toward whom the president, as seen in chapter 5, was ill-disposed.

Actually, over the final two years of Roosevelt's presidency, Reid carried on a low-key campaign to reshape Roosevelt's perspective on Churchill into a more generous and more accurate one. Just after Churchill had so skillfully defended the government's handling of the Jamaica incident before Parliament in April 1907, Reid opened a letter to TR by dissenting "mildly from your crisp judgment on Winston Churchill as a cad," and by noting "the very unusual promotion just given him as a member of the Privy Council." Young (thirty-two), "self-assertive," and "powerful on the stump"—and "increasingly important" to the Liberal party—Churchill's "rise in public estimation and in actual power in the House of Commons has been as great as that of any other member, perhaps greater." (Reid did soften his endorsement a little by relating an episode where Churchill was "still lingering at the Casino long after midnight and losing money heavily in gambling.")[102] Several months later, in summing up for TR the fortunes "this season" of various prominent British political figures, Reid wrote that Churchill "has by sheer dint of pertinacity and speaking power . . . made himself much too important in his party to be quarrelled with."[103] Roosevelt was noncommittal, stating only: "I am particularly interested in the sketch you give of the reputations won and the successes and failures on both sides in the session of Parliament that has just closed."[104] But Reid had not made much headway; in a letter of May 1908 to his oldest son, Roosevelt described Churchill, who had obtained his first cabinet post the previous month, as "a rather cheap character."[105]

In August 1908 Reid described to Roosevelt a recent encounter with Churchill at a party: "Winston volunteered to say that you ought to go into the preserves, and that he would be glad to make out suggestions for an itinerary. He has hunted all through that region himself." Almost apologetically, the ambassador then added: "While I remembered your candid opinion of the young man, I thought it better not to discourage his helpful disposition. So I shall no doubt have a letter from him by and by."[106]

This time Roosevelt really did appear to mellow. "What you say about Churchill's talking to you is interesting," he replied, "and whatever my present opinion of him, I suppose it will have to be altered if he does give me any useful suggestions!"[107] But in the meantime, TR's distaste for Churchill held steady.[108]

For his part, Churchill was truly eager to help Roosevelt and in the process to cultivate a friendly relationship with him. "Winston Churchill sends me the accompanying copy of his book about his recent hunting trip through Africa, which he has had specially bound for you," Reid informed TR in a letter of December 23, 1908. "He asks me to add that it would be a great pleasure to him if he could be of any service to you . . . in regard to your East African expedition."[109]

It now became evident that Reid's campaign had been in vain. Roosevelt opened his letter of reply with these words: "I do not like Winston Churchill but I suppose I ought to write to him. Will you send him the enclosed letter if it is all right?"[110] While the president's letter to Churchill was certainly gracious and proper, it lacked the high degree of warmth and enthusiasm with which TR normally would have expressed his appreciation for a personal gift of this sort. "Thru Mr. Reid," he began, "I have just received the beautiful copy of your book, and I wish to thank you for it." Roosevelt had read every chapter "with a great deal of interest, . . . especially the one describing how you got that rare and valuable trophy, a white rhinoceros head. Everyone has been most kind to me about my proposed trip to Africa. I trust I shall have as good luck as you had." Churchill was given no encouragement to continue corresponding.[111]

Roosevelt would have his way. There would be no further correspondence between him and Churchill,[112] no real relationship. In England in 1910 TR even snubbed the future great prime minister. "I have refused to meet Winston Churchill," he wrote to Lodge, "being able to avoid causing any scandal by doing so."[113]

There is a certain irony in Roosevelt's severe misjudgment of Churchill. If Roosevelt, who was ordinarily a highly astute judge of character, had lived into the middle and late 1930s, he would undoubtedly have become an avid admirer of—and could very conceivably have become an American counterpart to—the courageous, embattled Briton, whose situation was in some respects analogous to that of Roosevelt himself in 1915 and 1916. In a footnote to TR's letter to his son of May 23, 1908, cited previously, the editors of *The Letters of Theodore Roosevelt* offer insightful commentary. They refer to Churchill's "caustic restlessness" and to "the difficulties under which men of brilliance, insight, vigor, and independence must labor" as members of political parties "when they have come to distrust the party responses to prevailing conditions." The editors then put forward the following assertion: "Possessing the Churchillian talents, although perhaps in lesser degree, and the Churchillian defects, although perhaps to a greater extent, Roosevelt may in 1908 have come more naturally by his skepticism of the Churchillian personality than he would have four years or thirty-two years later."[114]

⊀ ⊁

A close reading of the letters written and received by Theodore Roosevelt during 1907-1909 lends itself readily to the conclusion that, excepting relatives, Roosevelt's single most intimate correspondent in the final years of his presidency was an Englishman, Arthur Lee. As has been seen in earlier chapters, TR engaged Lee's services in significant ways in managing the Durand problem, the Jamaica incident, and the crisis in U.S.-Japanese relations; and in each case Lee rendered faithful and valuable service. And prior to the publication of the kaiser's *Daily Telegraph* interview, Roosevelt had selected Lee as his British confidant and agent in what the president considered the highly delicate and explosive matter of the Hale interview. Lee's exemplary work in support of the president's policies not only reflected very favorably on Lee's intelligence, personality, and discretion; it was also a direct outgrowth of the intimate personal relationship that had developed between him and President Roosevelt.

A revealing portrait of the depth of the Roosevelt-Lee friendship can be found in the two men's correspondence on the subject of—a portrait. In a letter of December 13, 1907, Lee introduced Roosevelt to "the great Hungarian Portrait painter, Philip László, . . . a real genius" who "has painted practically every crowned head & celebrity in Europe," and who "has an unequalled gift of depicting character"—plus a "delightful personality" and "the inestimable merit of working at lightning speed." As László would soon be in the United States, Lee asked "a great favour" of TR: to permit László to "paint a sketch portrait of you—for me. . . . I should prize it more than I can say." László "would . . . come to you at any time that suited your convenience," and the First Lady would receive "a replica of the picture—if you are pleased with it." This was not, as Lee recognized, the sort of request that anyone other than a very special friend could reasonably make of the President of the United States.[115]

Although "touched at your wanting my picture for yourself, . . . painted by a real genius," Roosevelt initially was noncommittal, citing "the pressure there is upon me to have my picture painted and . . . the small amount of time at my disposal."[116] Lee, in reply, again praised László's speed and personality and declared: "I *do* realise very clearly that my request was no slight one. . . . But my conscience is blunted by the fact that I do want your portrait so *very* much, and because I feel László is the one living artist who can make a success of it."[117] "All right," TR wrote in a letter of February 2, 1908, "László shall paint that picture, and that is all there is about it."[118] Lee then thanked the president heartily and informed him that "László . . . will arrive in Washington on . . . *March 9 or 10*, & will . . . await your convenience."[119]

The portrait—reproduced on the page opposite this one—was a complete success. On March 21 the president sent Lee a brief note, telling his friend "that

Portrait of President Theodore Roosevelt. Painted by Philip László in March 1908.
Courtesy of the Theodore Roosevelt Association.

I think it the best portrait that has ever been made of me."[120] An extremely appreciative Lee was "delighted" and also "much relieved to know that you apparently bear me no ill will for having exposed you to the ordeal of sitting! I know well what an infliction it is, and that your friendship for me should have stood the strain shows that it has all the staying power that I could wish for." He was "of course immensely anxious to see the portrait," which would soon "occupy the place of honour in my house." Lee thanked Roosevelt again — "more than I can say — . . . for helping me to possess what I so greatly desired."[121] Roosevelt, in his turn, assured Lee that "the obligation is altogether mine"; not only were he and Edith entirely pleased with the portrait, but "I took a great fancy to László himself, and it is the only picture which I really enjoyed having painted."[122]

Lee was thrilled with the painting. He found it "absolutely convincing as a likeness, . . . almost uncannily . . . alive, . . . vibrating with suppressed energy," and a "penetrating . . . psychological study." It will, he told TR, "always be a vivid and living reminder of your friendship." The portrait, Lee added, was serving a public as well as a private purpose. By early May many had already visited Lee's home to see it, and Lee claimed that Britons were "immensely interested to know what you really look like, as, so far, they have seen nothing but caricatures — and bad ones at that. So I feel that good work has been done all round." Now Lee would arrange "to have the portrait reproduced in the best way possible" and would "send several copies for you and your family."[123]

In the meantime, Lee asked Roosevelt to give him "the great pleasure and satisfaction of accepting . . . the accompanying gift" — "Seats of the Mighty," a painting by Bruseius Simons. Lee was aware that Roosevelt was fond of this painting, and "I know of noone who has occupied the 'Seats of the Mighty' so honorably to himself, and so usefully to his country, as you have done."[124] Roosevelt was "overwhelmed" when this gift arrived at Sagamore Hill. "Upon my word," he declared, "I feel almost uncomfortable, for . . . my admiration of that picture must have been really too open" when "I first saw it in your house. . . . Great tho the value of the gift is, I prize infinitely more the spirit that lay behind it. . . . It will always be one of my most cherished possessions."[125] It would be "kept . . . in the north room, . . . my favorite and special room," where "we shall inlay it in the panel."[126] Lee and his wife were "very happy . . . that we have been able to send you something that you really care about."[127]

At the beginning of December, Lee shipped Roosevelt fifty-three reproductions of the László portrait, which he had arranged to have made in Germany "in the best way possible. . . . They seem to me . . . to preserve the spirit and technique of the original as far as is possible in a mono-tone." Lee asked TR to sign three of the reprints and to return them to him, expressing the hope that "you may be able to find some use for the remaining 50."[128] Roosevelt agreed with Lee's estimation of the reproductions and thanked him for taking "such infinite pains to get them." Promptly sending three signed reprints to Lee, the president intended to give "Root and Mrs. Lodge and my sisters and my daughter, copies, for Christmas. But," he added, "I feel very selfish about the pictures and regard them as altogether too valuable to be distributed save in the most sparing and cautious way."[129]

In no regard was Arthur Lee a presumptuous person. He had a highly developed sensitivity to the meanings and nuances and impact of words, a highly refined sense of propriety, and an equally acute sense of timing. Anyway, Theodore Roosevelt was not one to countenance presumptuousness. The deep and special friendship that reverberates throughout the Lee-Roosevelt correspondence surrounding the László portrait was entirely genuine.

For Lee, not surprisingly, the approach of Roosevelt's voluntary retirement from the presidency was disconcerting. "I must confess," Lee wrote to TR in December 1907, "to a somewhat sad and blank feeling when I look beyond March 1909 and realise what your resignation of the helm may entail"; and naturally "one of my chief anxieties is the effect it may have upon Anglo-American relations."[130] But Lee knew his American friend well, so he was not engaging in idle chatter or wishful thinking when he consoled himself several months later with these words: "Of course we all look upon your retirement as merely temporary, and expect to see you return in due time, like a giant refreshed, to run another course." In this same letter, Lee thanked Roosevelt for being an "inspiration . . . to me, in common with thousands of others, who are trying, however feebly and ineffectively, to do the right thing in their own spheres of politics."[131]

On September 6, 1908, with Roosevelt's retirement now a foregone conclusion, Lee devoted well over half of an eight-page letter to TR's upcoming trip. In essence he lobbied Roosevelt to make Lee's home his base in 1910 during the British leg of his journey. Lee assured TR of privacy and comfort for his traveling party and whatever arrangements for visitors he would prefer. "We have only one rule in our household," Lee stated. "Any friends who stay with us must do exactly what they like . . . and not expect to be 'entertained' except when they ask to be!" And "it would be a great delight to us to have you for as long as you could stay."[132] The president wrote back immediately that he and Edith "shall be delighted to accept your more than kind invitation," and he gave Lee some preliminary information about his plans and desires for his time in Britain.[133] And indeed, when TR and some members of his family visited England in May and June of 1910, the Lees hosted the Roosevelts both in their London residence and at Chequers Court, their country abode.[134] The former president was entirely satisfied with the arrangements.[135]

The Roosevelt-Lee correspondence during the last couple of years of Roosevelt's presidency is rich in vivid discussion of the Anglo-American special relationship. Much of this discussion has been cited earlier in various contexts. One major topic to which Roosevelt and Lee accorded a great deal of attention during this period—just as they had done previously—was British and American naval power. Because this issue was at the core of President Roosevelt's strategic vision for the partnership that he labored so assiduously and skillfully to build between the British Empire and the United States, these particular Roosevelt-Lee exchanges seem a suitable focus for the close of this study.

Roosevelt did not equivocate when he wrote to Lee during the summer of 1908. "Do you know," he stated, "I think I have become almost as anxious as you are to have the British fleet kept up to the highest point of efficiency" and in its "present position of relative power. . . . It is a great guaranty for the peace of the world."[136]

That autumn the president expressed himself even more emphatically: "I do not believe that the British Empire has any more intention of acting aggressively than has the United States, and I believe that in one case as in the other a powerful fleet is not only in the interest of the nation itself, but is in the interest of international peace, and therefore to be desired by all who wish to see the peace of the world preserved." Roosevelt was "now striving to have us build up our fleet," whose "mere existence," he believed, would serve both to maintain "peace between Japan and ourselves" and to deter challenges to the Monroe Doctrine. "In exactly the same way," he concluded, "I feel that Britain's great navy is a menace to no Power, . . . and I hope to see it maintained in full efficiency."[137]

Lee's absolute belief in the sincerity of Roosevelt's endorsements of British naval supremacy, and his total confidence in the breadth and sophistication of Roosevelt's understanding of international relations (and of domestic politics in Great Britain), come sharply into focus in a letter of January 29, 1909. Lee was preparing to continue his defense in Parliament of "our traditional 'Two Power standard' of Naval strength"—meaning the maintenance of a fleet "equal to that of the two next strongest powers, whoever they may be, and wherever they may be situated"—against an "artful" campaign by "the 'peace-at-any-price' Radicals" to undermine it by calling for the formal exclusion of the United States from the standard. "They fancied they had rather got me in a hole over this—knowing that I was a friend of America—but my reply was of course obvious. The whole virtue of the Two Power standard rests in the universality of its application, and without that it is bound to give offence." After briefly elaborating with reference to France, Japan, and Germany, Lee remarked upon "a concerted effort" by opponents of the standard "to persuade the British Public that there is great indignation in America . . . that we do not exclude your Navy from our 'Two

Power' Formula." While he doubted that "there is any feeling of resentment, or even concern, on the part either of the United States Government or the American people," he "naturally" was interested in Roosevelt's assessment of the matter. Lee "of course" would not quote the president "in any shape or form, but I should feel much greater confidence in handling the subject if I were fortified by your opinion."[138]

Roosevelt provided that opinion without delay—and without ambiguity—in a letter of February 8. TR did "not believe this country can possibly take any offense at your argument if you make it as you outline it in your letter to me; and most emphatically there will be no justification for taking offense." He then spelled out his position in one extremely long sentence:

> Your stand should be that you are urging a permanent policy; that it is not a policy aimed at any nation; that it is not meant to bring on war, but to avoid war, and that it is consistent with the most genuine feeling of friendship for, and desire to keep on friendly terms with, all other nations; that in particular you have the very heartiest feeling of friendship for the United States, and would laugh at any thought of trouble between the two great English-speaking peoples; but that if England discriminates in favor of any one nation, she can do it only by giving offense to other nations, and thereby transforming into a just objection to the policy what is now an objection without any real merit whatever; that if you in parliament specifically except America you will rightly be asked why you do not specifically except any one of several other powers, with all of which England is and hopes to remain on the friendliest terms, and that then you would be asked why you regard any power as possibly hostile; in short, that this is simply a policy for the preservation and defense of the Empire, entirely impersonal, and that for the very reason that it is not aimed at any nation, you think it would be grossly improper specifically to name any nation either as excepted or included; for if you named any given nation as excepted from the policy, it would be equivalent to stating that other friendly nations were really those against which the policy was directed.

So there you have it, Arthur![139]

The perspective that Theodore Roosevelt had developed by 1905 or 1906 on Anglo-American naval power clearly had become an article of faith for him by the end of his presidency in 1909. A large and efficient American navy, crucial in its own right, was also the junior member of an informal two-power alliance responsible for an international balance of power decidedly favorable to American—and Anglo-American—interests. It was the president's firm conviction that the Royal Navy was the United States' friend, its strength an asset to world peace and American security.

The foregoing analysis of the correspondence between Theodore Roosevelt and Arthur Lee has been offered as an illustration of the extraordinarily harmonious condition of the Anglo-American relationship during the period 1907-1909. For there existed between these two individuals a very close *personal* friendship that was deeply rooted in and inextricably linked to a very close *international* friendship. A personal friendship so intimate and so full—with so few important subjects either off limits or open only for superficial discussion—could hardly have been realized between TR and any non-British foreigner, even Jean Jules Jusserand. Under President Roosevelt's guidance, the United States and Great Britain forged a unique international partnership, and the personal bond between Roosevelt and Lee grew and flourished largely on that account.

— Epilogue and Conclusion —

● ○ ●

While Theodore Roosevelt's administration and British leaders constructed in the first decade of the twentieth century a solid foundation for a lasting friendship between the English-speaking powers, troubled times, as it turned out, were not far off. In the eyes of former President Roosevelt—who was to die at the age of sixty on January 6, 1919, shortly after the armistice—the events of World War I completely validated his presidential foreign policy, providing irrefutable proof of the enormous importance to both countries and to the world of a permanent special relationship between Great Britain and the United States.[1] But despite Roosevelt's strenuous opposition during and immediately following the war, Woodrow Wilson and his successors devalued the Anglo-American partnership (a process actually begun by TR's own hand-picked successor, William H. Taft), which in effect ceased to function in the 1930s.

Fortunately, the period of disaffection was of limited duration. The revival, beginning in 1939, of close cooperation between Britain and the United States ultimately extricated the world from the clutches of the most unimaginable tyranny. In the post - World War II era, with the British Empire shrinking dramatically and the United States now incontestably the senior partner, the Anglo-American connection has remained strong—despite what was widely perceived in Britain to be an American betrayal during the Suez crisis of 1956, and despite British concerns about a dangerous lack of sophistication in American anti-communism during the 1950s and 1960s. The 1980s and 1990s have witnessed a renewed affirmation of Anglo-American unity, manifested most strikingly in a common approach to North Atlantic Treaty Organization missile deployments and in solidarity during the Falklands War of 1982, the bombing of Libya in 1986, and, most impressively, the war against Iraq in 1991. One might argue that to a significant extent, the twentieth century has indeed been, as Theodore Roosevelt forecast in 1901 (although undoubtedly with a very different script in mind), "the century of the men who speak English."[2]

⚔   ⚔

Theodore Roosevelt was genuinely friendly toward England and became increasingly so as his presidency progressed. A common language certainly facilitated the bonding process, giving Britain an advantage over its rivals for TR's affection. But Roosevelt's perceptions of a common history, a common duty to extend civilization, a common attachment to the principles of freedom and self-government, and, above all, common strategic interests were the truly decisive elements.

It needs to be added, however, that there was always at least a small measure of ambivalence in the president's attitude toward Great Britain. Alongside his commitment to "the English-speaking peoples," Roosevelt was an *American* nationalist. Especially in the early part of his presidency, he was ready to get into scraps with Britain—even to the point of risking military engagement—when fundamental American interests or U.S. honor were at issue; and throughout his time in office (although less so toward the end), he would express irritation when the conduct of British diplomacy did not meet with his approval. He also decried what he saw as the increasing "flabbiness" of British (as of American) society, a problem that rendered England less formidable as an informal ally and added urgency to Roosevelt's naval building program. TR had little patience with Britons who criticized the United States or who attempted to elevate Britain's image at America's expense, just as he had little patience with American expatriates residing in England. In his correspondence with American friends, Henry Cabot Lodge in particular, the president often indicated displeasure with Britain or with some of its leaders or citizens.

With most parts of the British Empire President Roosevelt did not display much concern. It is not even clear that he kept abreast of developments in the majority of England's vast holdings. When he wrote between 1901 and 1907 about the dependent areas of the empire, he usually dealt with Egypt, where he approved of the British performance, and Malaya, about which he was critical. On several occasions (but only in private letters to American friends) he harshly denounced British behavior in Malaya in response to what he considered totally groundless charges by a British writer of American misconduct in the Philippines. TR turned his attention to the empire's crown jewel, India, only during the final year of his presidency—but then he made up for lost time by effusively praising the performance and accomplishments of the ruling British. When Roosevelt discussed the self-governing portions of the empire, where his interest was generally much keener, he normally focused on Canada and Newfoundland, with which diplomatic complications persisted throughout his presidency, and Australia, whose low birth rate, TR believed, cast a large shadow over the prospects for the continued ascendancy of the English-speaking peoples. Still, taken as a whole—as so many of his letters and his India speech of January 18, 1909, definitively demonstrate—Roosevelt viewed the British Empire as a great positive force, indispensable to world peace and to the advancement of civilization.

Crucial to the viability of a partnership between Britain and the United States under TR was that both countries were, on the whole, status quo powers in a changing world. Both backed the open door in China, the existing situation in the Pacific, a stable balance of power on the European continent, and continued British naval supremacy. Early in Roosevelt's presidency the British acquiesced in American hegemony in the Caribbean and quickly came to see it as a positive good. Both English-speaking powers trained a wary eye on Germany, Japan, and Russia and sought to understand, to limit, and to contain those countries' ambitions. Roosevelt's estimation of these three powers vacillated as circumstances changed, but suspicion was never very far beneath the surface.

President Roosevelt's thinking on the international balance of power was subtle and sophisticated. Certainly Frank Ninkovich's 1986 essay portraying TR as hostile to the balance-of-power principle widely misses the mark.[3] But it would be equally inaccurate to argue that TR saw "balance" as the key to stabilizing all areas of potential great power conflict. He did indeed desire such balance where the contenders for advantage were Germany and Russia, or Germany and Japan, or, as in Manchuria, Russia and Japan. But when Great Britain or the United States was a party to a dispute with another power, balance was the president's *minimum* objective. A better guarantee of peace, Roosevelt believed, was an *im*balance decidedly favorable to England or America or the two of them combined, depending on the situation. Being the world's most civilized and most righteous countries, Britain and the United States could be counted on not to abuse a position of military superiority, and such superiority would meanwhile ensure against miscalculation or adventurism on the part of a more selfish, less civilized, less mature power. A preponderance of British or American strength—especially naval strength—in any region of the globe constituted a safeguard, not a danger. The balance of power that Roosevelt desired was thus a very skewed sort of balance, but one that was entirely consistent with his worldview.

Once the difficult Alaskan boundary dispute was resolved in America's favor—as TR, convinced that the national honor of the United States was at issue, had insisted that it must be—the path was clear for Britain and the United States to pursue their mutual agenda. There could be no formal alliance, of course; Roosevelt was not only an American nationalist but also an extremely adept politician. Anyway, the unwritten partnership operated much as an alliance would have done—but at little political cost, and without tying the president's hands. It perfectly suited his purposes.

The informal understanding between Roosevelt's America and the British Empire was secured by the end of 1903 and increased in solidity over the next few years. Yet at the end of 1906, it was still unclear just how far the president would be willing to go in tolerating offensive British actions that, if taken by other powers, would surely bring forth from TR either private threats or public expressions of indignation (or both), and would contain real potential for escalation. The very awkward Swettenham affair of 1907 posed this question pointedly. Roosevelt and British leaders overcame a variety of obstacles (among them TR's own sensitivities about the episode) and together succeeded in minimizing this incident; and their success in this endeavor dramatized the depth that the Anglo-American bond had attained. Indeed, Anglo-American relations during 1907-1909 were extremely intimate—an intimacy that fostered and was both strengthened and personified by the extraordinary friendship of Roosevelt and Arthur Lee. In the aftermath of the Jamaica incident, no one could doubt any longer that the British Empire occupied a unique and privileged place in President Roosevelt's foreign policy.

⨎   ⨎

Roosevelt's highly successful cultivation of a deep-rooted Anglo-American friendship might briefly be placed in the larger context of the United States' first twentieth-century presidency.[4] For TR's presidency was replete with important domestic and foreign policy achievements—the former including major innovations in the areas of corporate regulation, consumer protection, and, especially, safeguarding the environment. Without depreciating any of President Roosevelt's accomplishments, it can be asserted with conviction that the establishment of a special relationship between the United States and the British Empire should be counted as very prominent among them.

⨎   ⨎

The subtitle of this book is *A Study in Presidential Statecraft.* The narrative may have persuaded some readers (and reconfirmed for others) that Theodore Roosevelt was truly a masterful statesman. Closely attentive to both the details and the larger framework of his diplomacy, Roosevelt was almost uniformly successful in dealing with specific foreign policy challenges and in advancing his broader objectives. He kept his country at peace while consistently upholding what he defined as its vital interests, and he was directly responsible for restoring or preserving peace between other powers. Moreover, his statesmanship significantly enhanced the United States' image in the world.

The centerpiece of Rooseveltian statecraft was the cultivation of an Anglo-American special relationship. The protection of major U.S. interests, the promotion of international stability and peace, and the moral imperative of advancing civilization all required, Roosevelt was convinced, a solid connection between Great Britain and the United States. While U.S. relations with each of the other powers were also highly important to Roosevelt, he pursued these relations in the context of the building of a strong partnership between England and the United States. TR desired and developed amicable relations with both Germany and Japan—a testament to his diplomatic dexterity—but the special relationship with Britain always took precedence.

The execution of Rooseveltian statecraft was as impressive as its conception. The path to Anglo-American harmony and cooperation was strewn with obstacles. Moreover, TR had to overcome these obstacles as an American nationalist, meaning that in some circumstances he would need to induce certain British concessions or behaviors in order to keep the Anglo-American relationship on a forward track. Employing his signature brand of informal, personal diplomacy, he induced such concessions and behaviors extremely effectively—most notably in managing the Alaska boundary quarrel and the Jamaica incident. Even when British conduct disappointed him—such as in the cases of the Anglo-German attack on Venezuela, the Russo-Japanese peace negotiations, the first phase of the Moroccan crisis, and the U.S.-Japanese tension over the immigration-racism problem—Roosevelt endeavored to avoid unnecessary Anglo-American discord, always keeping his larger objectives in focus. The president's reasonableness and sense of proportion were most vividly on display as he empathized with the British government's predicament during the Newfoundland fisheries controversy and labored successfully to achieve a compromise solution. All in all, Roosevelt's performance in building the Anglo-American special relationship was remarkably adept.

Taken together, the conception, execution, and results of Theodore Roosevelt's diplomacy with regard to the British Empire lead compellingly to a very favorable evaluation. Indeed, an example of higher-quality presidential statecraft in American history would be difficult to identify. As the end of the 1990s approaches, one can even speculate that later historians will consider the United States' greatest practitioner of statecraft in the twentieth century to have been the century's first president.

— Notes —

● ○ ●

Preface

1. In the 1980s such a trend among scholars was confirmed in two presidential performance polls conducted by David L. Porter and the *Chicago Tribune*. From his "near great," seventh-place rankings in the Arthur M. Schlesinger, Sr., polls of 1948 and 1962, Roosevelt advanced to fifth and fourth in the Porter and *Tribune* surveys, respectively, achieving "great" status in each case. See David L. Porter, "American Historians Rate Our Presidents," in William D. Pederson and Ann M. McLaurin, eds., *The Rating Game in American Politics* (New York, 1987), 33-37.

2. Howard K. Beale, *Theodore Roosevelt and the Rise of America to World Power* (Baltimore, 1956); William H. Harbaugh, *The Life and Times of Theodore Roosevelt* (New York, 1961); Charles E. Neu, *An Uncertain Friendship: Theodore Roosevelt and Japan, 1906-1909* (Cambridge, MA, 1967), vii.

3. In William Tilchin, "The Rising Star of Theodore Roosevelt's Diplomacy: Major Studies from Beale to the Present," *Theodore Roosevelt Association Journal*, 15, 3, Summer 1989, 2-24, this writer defines "major studies" as works "whose principal focus is the foreign policy of Theodore Roosevelt as president, and whose area of inquiry is not overly narrow" (p. 2). The article identifies—and then proceeds to review in some depth—the following group of major studies: Beale, *TR and the Rise of America*; David H. Burton, *Theodore Roosevelt: Confident Imperialist* (Philadelphia, 1968); Raymond A. Esthus, *Theodore Roosevelt and the International Rivalries* (Claremont, CA, 1970); Frederick W. Marks III, *Velvet on Iron: The Diplomacy of Theodore Roosevelt* (Lincoln, NE, 1979); William C. Widenor, *Henry Cabot Lodge and the Search for an American Foreign Policy* (Berkeley, 1980); Richard H. Collin, *Theodore Roosevelt, Culture, Diplomacy, and Expansion: A New View of American Imperialism* (Baton Rouge, 1985); and Serge Ricard, *Théodore Roosevelt et la justification de l'impérialisme* [Theodore Roosevelt and the Justification of Imperialism] (Aix-en-Provence, France, 1986). All those from Burton through Collin depict Roosevelt's diplomacy more favorably than does *TR and the Rise of America*. And Ricard too would soon emphatically join the chorus. One of the principal themes of Ricard's highly ambitious and important *Théodore Roosevelt: principes et pratique d'une politique étrangère* [Theodore Roosevelt: Principles and Practice of a Foreign Policy] (Aix-en-Provence, 1991) is TR's "extraordinary effectiveness in diplomacy" (p. 249). (Except where otherwise indicated, all translations of Ricard's writings found in this book are the author's.)

4. William N. Tilchin, "Theodore Roosevelt," in Frank W. Thackeray and John E. Findling, eds., *Statesmen Who Changed the World: A Bio-Bibliographical Dictionary of Diplomacy* (Westport, CT, 1993), 487.

5. Henry F. Pringle, *Theodore Roosevelt: A Biography* (New York, 1931). According to Dewey W. Grantham, Jr., Pringle regarded TR as nothing more "than a 'violently adolescent

person.'" Grantham, "Theodore Roosevelt in American Historical Writing, 1945-1960," *Mid-America*, 43, 1, January 1961, 5n. In an interesting evaluation and contextual analysis of this popular book, Collin cites its "convincing dramatic unity" and contends that well into the future "Pringle's portrait of the impulsive imperialist will remain a part of the Roosevelt image." Collin, "Henry F. Pringle's Theodore Roosevelt: A Study in Historical Revisionism," *New York History*, 52, 2, April 1971, 164, 168. Evidence of the potency of Pringle's lingering impact can be found in Frederick W. Marks III, "Theodore Roosevelt and the Righting of History," *Theodore Roosevelt Association Journal*, 12, 1, Winter 1986, 8-12. Marks surveyed eighteen high school history texts published between 1962 and 1985 for their portrayal of Roosevelt's diplomacy and "was shocked" by what he discovered. Marks grades most of the accounts he read with an "F" and laments: "One would never have gathered from *any* of the publications in question that during TR's 7½ years in the White House he became the world's premier statesman" (p. 8). (Emphasis in original.)

6. Elting E. Morison, John M. Blum, and Alfred D. Chandler, the editors of *The Letters of Theodore Roosevelt* (8 vols., Cambridge, MA, 1951-1954), are able to account for well over 100,000 letters. See Vol. III, p. v. One hundred thousand letters can be divided up into an awe-inspiring average of more than 4½ per day over Roosevelt's entire lifetime.

7. These "superbly edited" volumes, wrote Dewey W. Grantham, Jr., in 1961 in his distinguished historiographical essay, provide "a magnificently documented record of Roosevelt's life and career," and have "proven an extraordinary stimulus to historians and biographers interested in the Roosevelt era." Grantham, "TR in American Historical Writing," 32. Lewis L. Gould, writing thirty years later, observes, similarly, that this "excellent" collection "made modern writing about Roosevelt a much easier task." Gould, *The Presidency of Theodore Roosevelt* (Lawrence, KS, 1991), xi.

8. Marks, "TR and the Righting of History."

9. See, for example, Marks, *Velvet on Iron*, 172.

10. As examples of the former, see Esthus, *TR and the International Rivalries*, 39, 65, 134; Widenor, *Lodge*, 158-59; and Collin, *TR, Culture, Diplomacy, and Expansion*, 175-76. As examples of the latter, see Beale, *TR and the Rise of America*, 160; and Burton, *TR: Confident Imperialist*, 35-37, 167.

11. Raymond A. Esthus, *Theodore Roosevelt and Japan* (Seattle, 1966), which presages some portions of his *TR and the International Rivalries*, and Charles E. Neu, *Uncertain Friendship* both focus on it. The latter is a probing and insightful study that evaluates the impact of domestic politics in both the United States and Japan on the course of diplomacy, assesses the development of American naval strategy in the context of the president's perspectives on relations with Japan and a variety of other contemporary factors (internal, technological, and diplomatic), ably captures the complexities and shifts over time in U.S.-Japanese relations, and presents a revealing microcosmic look at the operation of Roosevelt's foreign policy.

12. See note 3.

13. Bradford Perkins, *The Great Rapprochement: England and the United States, 1895-1914* (New York, 1968).

14. This book is a revised and expanded version of William Neal Tilchin, "Theodore Roosevelt and the British Empire, 1901-1907," Ph.D. diss., Brown University, 1992.

15. Gould, *Presidency of TR*, x.

16. Marks, *Velvet on Iron*, passim. Ricard, however, is also correct when he points out in *TR: principes et pratique* that TR often forsook patience, courtesy, and empathy in his dealings with weaker nations, such as Colombia and China. See, for example, pp. 24, 253, 311, 359-62.

17. See Beale, *TR and the Rise of America*, 55-80.

18. Ricard, *TR: principes et pratique*, 240-41.

19. TR to Sterling Edwin Edmunds, December 1, 1904, Morison et al., eds., *The Letters of Theodore Roosevelt*, IV, 1055.

20. John Milton Cooper, Jr., *The Warrior and the Priest: Woodrow Wilson and Theodore Roosevelt* (Cambridge, MA, 1983), 110-11.

21. Burton, "Three Roosevelt Women," *Theodore Roosevelt Association Journal*, 21, 2, Spring-Summer 1996, 5.

22. TR, comments Thomas G. Dyer, was "conscious of the power and importance of language," and "he often stressed the necessity for precision when discussing any serious matter." Dyer, *Theodore Roosevelt and the Idea of Race* (Baton Rouge, 1980), 24.

23. Burton makes this point specifically in reference to TR's correspondence with his closest English friends: "The intense personal convictions of the proponents of Anglo-American solidarity, convictions they often felt the need to explain and elaborate in detail, were more likely to be written fully and frankly in private letters to men of kindred views than [to be expressed] in public pronouncements." Burton, "Theodore Roosevelt and His English Correspondents: The Intellectual Roots of the Anglo-American Alliance," *Mid-America*, 53, 1, January 1971, 13.

24. Edmund Morris, *The Rise of Theodore Roosevelt* (New York, 1979).

25. Morris, "'A Few Pregnant Days': Theodore Roosevelt and the Venezuelan Crisis of 1902," *Theodore Roosevelt Association Journal*, 15, 1, Winter 1989, pp. 2, 13n. In this article Morris tests TR's integrity by closely investigating Roosevelt's most historiographically controversial claim—that he had issued Germany an ultimatum over its Venezuelan intervention of 1902-1903. Roosevelt convincingly passes this rigorously administered test.

26. Collin, *TR, Culture, Diplomacy, and Expansion*, 202.

Chapter 1

1. W. David McIntyre, *The Commonwealth of Nations: Origins and Impact, 1869-1971* (Minneapolis, 1977), 20.

2. A "protectorate" was in essence a colony under another name. As Eric A. Walker explains it, "a protectorate still might not be strictly speaking part of the Crown's dominions nor its inhabitants anything more than 'British protected persons'; . . . but, for practical purposes and in the eyes of foreign governments, it was a possession in which British officials exercised powers over everyone, powers which varied according to the vigour of the native institutions, but usually equalled and sometimes surpassed the effective authority of officials in a Crown Colony." Walker, *The British Empire: Its Structure and Spirit, 1497-1953* (Cambridge, MA, 1956), 103.

3. Concise discussions of all the events and developments mentioned in this paragraph can be found in Alexander DeConde, *A History of American Foreign Policy* (3rd ed., 2 vols., New York, 1978), I, 79-281 passim.

4. Bradford Perkins, *The Great Rapprochement: England and the United States, 1895-1914* (New York, 1968).

5. Quoted in Ernest R. May, *Imperial Democracy: The Emergence of America as a Great Power* (New York, 1961), 40.

6. Quoted in Perkins, *Great Rapprochement*, 29. Whitelaw Reid, ambassador to Britain during the second half of Theodore Roosevelt's presidency, was likewise premature when—in two "strongly anglophile" speeches delivered in England in 1897 after representing the United States as ambassador extraordinary on special mission to Queen Victoria's Diamond

Jubilee—he referred joyously to Anglo-American "solidarity" and "cultural unity."
Bingham Duncan, *Whitelaw Reid: Journalist, Politician, Diplomat* (Athens, GA, 1975), 175.

7. This is the period to which Charles S. Campbell, Jr., devotes his well-researched and thorough *Anglo-American Understanding, 1898-1903* (Baltimore, 1957).

8. Campbell, *Anglo-American Understanding*, 44.

9. The impact on Theodore of his father's decision might have been profound. David McCullough suggests that it may have been "the glaring single flaw in the life of an idolized father and one he would feel forever compelled to compensate for." McCullough, *Mornings on Horseback* (New York, 1981), 57. John Milton Cooper, Jr., sees it as *the* overriding factor in Roosevelt's eagerness to see battle in the Spanish-American War. Cooper finds "a trail of clues," among them a 1907 speech in which TR declared: "I did not intend to have to hire somebody else to do my shooting for me." Cooper, *The Warrior and the Priest: Woodrow Wilson and Theodore Roosevelt* (Cambridge, MA, 1983), 12-13.

10. Quoted in McCullough, *Mornings on Horseback*, 287.

11. Reviewing *The Winning of the West* during the 1890s, the eminent historian Frederick Jackson Turner approvingly asserted that Roosevelt "has made use of widely scattered sources not heretofore exploited; and with graphic vigor he has portrayed the advance of the pioneer into the wastes of the continent." Harvey Wish, ed., *Theodore Roosevelt, "The Winning of the West": Selections* (Gloucester, MA, 1976), xxi. According to William H. Harbaugh, writing in 1961, "it stamped its author as a historian of genuine distinction: of brilliant, though uneven, literary power; of broad, and often acute, comprehension; and of extraordinary narrative force." Harbaugh, *The Life and Times of Theodore Roosevelt* (3rd ed., New York, 1975), 61. John A. Gable claimed in 1975 that this study "still stands as an important work on the history of the American frontier." Gable, "Introduction: Theodore Roosevelt as Historian and Man of Letters," Theodore Roosevelt, *Gouverneur Morris* (reprint, Oyster Bay, NY, 1975), x. And John Milton Cooper wrote in 1983 of "a distinguished historian" who "dug deeply in original sources and probed the past with insight and imagination." Cooper, *The Warrior and the Priest*, 33.

12. Cooper is on track when he claims that "no diplomatic dispute of the day, no matter how minor, failed to arouse his belligerency." Cooper, *The Warrior and the Priest*, 35.

13. Quoted in Harbaugh, *Life and Times of TR*, 106.

14. Quoted in James T. Patterson, *America in the Twentieth Century: A History* (3rd ed., New York, 1989), 77.

15. See Peter Karsten, "The Nature of 'Influence': Roosevelt, Mahan and the Concept of Sea Power," *American Quarterly*, 23, 4, October 1971, 585.

16. Ibid., 588.

17. Ibid., 598. TR's private assessments of Mahan were at times quite unflattering. For example, the president wrote these words to James Jeffrey Roche in March 1906: "I was as disappointed as you with Mahan's *War of 1812*. He is a curious fellow, for he cannot write in effective shape of the navy or of the fighting of his own country." TR to Roche, March 7, 1906, Elting E. Morison, John M. Blum, and Alfred D. Chandler, eds., *The Letters of Theodore Roosevelt* (8 vols., Cambridge, MA, © 1951-1954 by the President and Fellows of Harvard College), V, 173. *The Letters of Theodore Roosevelt* are hereinafter cited as *Letters of TR*. (Harvard University Press has graciously granted the author permission to reproduce the quotations from this source that appear in this book.)

18. Howard K. Beale, *Theodore Roosevelt and the Rise of America to World Power* (Baltimore, 1956), 2.

19. TR to Cecil Spring Rice, August 5, 1896, and Spring Rice to Edith Carow Roosevelt, July 1898, quoted in David H. Burton, "Theodore Roosevelt and His English Correspondents:

A Special Relationship of Friends," *Transactions of the American Philosophical Society*, 63, 2, March 1973, 7.

20. Cecil Spring Rice to Stephen Spring Rice, September 15, 1901, in Stephen Gwynn, ed., *The Letters and Friendships of Sir Cecil Spring Rice* (2 vols., London, 1929), I, 346.

21. Arthur Lee to TR, April 2, 1901, quoted in Burton, "Special Relationship of Friends," 11.

22. Burton, "Theodore Roosevelt and His English Correspondents: The Intellectual Roots of the Anglo-American Alliance," *Mid-America*, 53, 1, January 1971, 17.

23. Ibid., 22.

24. TR to Henry Cabot Lodge, two letters, December 20 and 27, 1895, *Letters of TR*, I, 500, and Albert Bushnell Hart and Herbert Ronald Ferleger, eds., *Theodore Roosevelt Cyclopedia* (revised 2nd ed., Westport, CT, 1989), 623.

25. *TR Cyclopedia*, 623.

26. TR to Spring Rice, November 25, 1898, quoted in Beale, *TR and the Rise of America*, 93.

27. TR to William Archer, August 31, 1899, quoted in ibid., 89.

28. TR to Lee, July 25, 1900, quoted in ibid., 93.

29. TR to James Bryce, March 31, 1898, quoted in ibid., 176.

30. TR to Alfred Thayer Mahan, March 18, 1901, quoted in ibid., 176.

31. TR to Lee, March 18, 1901, *Letters of TR*, III, 20.

32. TR to Lee, April 24, 1901, *Letters of TR*, III, 66.

33. Campbell, *Anglo-American Understanding*, 195.

34. TR to Lee, April 24, 1901, *Letters of TR*, III, 64; TR to Spring Rice, March 2, 1900, quoted in Beale, *TR and the Rise of America*, 104.

35. TR to John St. Loe Strachey, March 8, 1901, *Letters of TR*, III, 9.

36. TR to Strachey, January 27, 1900, *Letters of TR*, II, 1144.

37. TR to Lee, March 18, 1901, *Letters of TR*, III, 20.

38. TR to Spring Rice, July 3, 1901, *Letters of TR*, III, 109.

39. TR to Lee, January 30, 1900, quoted in Burton, "Special Relationship of Friends," 39.

40. TR to George von Lengerke Meyer, April 12, 1901, quoted in Beale, *TR and the Rise of America*, 395. This view, expressed early in his vice presidency, reflected TR's outlook years before as assistant secretary of the navy. In a letter of that time to William W. Kimball, he declared: "Germany is the power with whom I look forward to serious difficulty." TR to Kimball, December 17, 1897, quoted in Richard H. Collin, *Theodore Roosevelt, Culture, Diplomacy, and Expansion: A New View of American Imperialism* (Baton Rouge, 1985), 123-24. Even more telling was a belligerently anti-German letter to Spring Rice dated August 13, 1897. See Serge Ricard, *Théodore Roosevelt: principes et pratique d'une politique étrangère* [Theodore Roosevelt: Principles and Practice of a Foreign Policy] (Aix-en-Provence, France, 1991), 243-44.

41. Ricard, *TR: principes et pratique*, 219.

42. TR to Bryce, March 31, 1898, *Letters of TR*, II, 807.

43. TR to Lee, November 25, 1898, quoted in Burton, "Special Relationship of Friends," 37.

44. TR to Elihu Root, September 2, 1899, quoted in ibid., 9.

45. TR to Strachey, November 19, 1900, *Letters of TR*, II, 1425.

46. TR to Spring Rice, March 16, 1901, *Letters of TR*, III, 16. For example, see Beale, *TR and the Rise of America*, 81; Charles E. Neu, *An Uncertain Friendship: Theodore Roosevelt and Japan, 1906-1909* (Cambridge, MA, © 1967 by the President and Fellows of Harvard College), 12; and Ricard, *TR: principes et pratique*, 244-45. (Harvard University Press has graciously granted the author permission to reproduce the quotations from Neu's *Uncertain Friendship* that appear in this book.)

47. TR to Lodge, June 19, 1901, *Letters of TR*, III, 97.

48. TR to Spring Rice, August 5, 1896, quoted in Beale, *TR and the Rise of America*, 261.
49. TR to Spring Rice, August 11, 1899, quoted in Burton, "Special Relationship of Friends," 27.
50. TR to Spring Rice, March 16, 1901, *Letters of TR*, III, 16.
51. TR to George Ferdinand Becker, July 8, 1901, *Letters of TR*, III, 112.
52. TR to Anna Roosevelt Cowles, December 17, 1899, quoted in Beale, *TR and the Rise of America*, 95, and in Thomas G. Dyer, *Theodore Roosevelt and the Idea of Race* (Baton Rouge, 1980), 149.
53. Dyer, *TR and the Idea of Race*, 168, 30.
54. Ibid., 56.
55. Ricard, *TR: principes et pratique*, 248. Similarly, Roosevelt defined American patriotism inclusively as a common allegiance to a flag and "an unfailing adherence to the same democratic ideals" (p. 248).
56. Dyer, *TR and the Idea of Race*, 28, 68.
57. Campbell, *Anglo-American Understanding*, 234.

Chapter 2

1. Neu, *Uncertain Friendship*, 13.
2. Lewis L. Gould, *The Presidency of Theodore Roosevelt* (Lawrence, KS, 1991), 174.
3. Beale, *TR and the Rise of America*, 458.
4. Hermann Speck von Sternburg to TR, October 9, 1901, Theodore Roosevelt Papers, reel 20, Library of Congress, Washington, D.C., and Harvard College Library, Cambridge, MA; TR to Sternburg, October 11, 1901, *Letters of TR*, III, 173.
5. TR to Theodore Roosevelt, Jr., October 4, 1903, *Letters of TR*, III, 614. For a discussion of Roosevelt's thinking on sports, see chapter 10, pp. 191-92.
6. TR to John St. Loe Strachey, June 20, 1902, and July 18, 1902, quoted in Burton, "Special Relationship of Friends," 39.
7. Abbott Lawrence Lowell to TR, June 12, 1903, TR Papers, reel 34.
8. TR to Lowell, June 13, 1903, *Letters of TR*, III, 488.
9. Speech before the Hamilton Club, Chicago, April 10, 1899, in John Allen Gable, ed., *The Man in the Arena: Speeches and Essays by Theodore Roosevelt* (Oyster Bay, NY, 1987), 41.
10. TR to Albert Henry George Grey, April 1, 1902, *Letters of TR*, III, 251.
11. Hamilton Club speech, April 10, 1899, in Gable, ed., *Man in the Arena*, 41.
12. Annual message of December 3, 1901, quoted in David H. Burton, *Theodore Roosevelt: Confident Imperialist* (Philadelphia, 1968), 84.
13. Speech delivered in Hartford, Connecticut, August 22, 1902, quoted in Willis Fletcher Johnson, ed., *Theodore Roosevelt: Addresses and Papers* (New York, 1909), 64; TR to George F. Hoar, December 23, 1902, *Letters of TR*, III, 395.
14. TR to James Francis Tracey, December 17, 1902, *Letters of TR*, III, 393.
15. Ricard, *Théodore Roosevelt et la justification de l'impérialisme* [Theodore Roosevelt and the Justification of Imperialism] (Aix-en-Provence, France, 1986), 254.
16. TR to Maria Longworth Storer, December 8, 1902, *Letters of TR*, III, 391.
17. Burton, *TR: Confident Imperialist*, 18-19.
18. Beale, *TR and the Rise of America*, 143.
19. TR to Arthur Lee, April 24, 1901, *Letters of TR*, III, 64.
20. Joseph Choate to TR, September 28, 1901, quoted in Campbell, *Anglo-American Understanding*, 234-35.
21. TR to John Hay, September 30, 1901, *Letters of TR*, III, 154.
22. TR to Hay, October 5, 1901, *Letters of TR*, III, 161.

23. TR to Choate, October 9, 1901, *Letters of TR*, III, 170.

24. TR to Henry Cabot Lodge, October 19, 1901, *Letters of TR*, III, 179.

25. Lee to TR, December 17, 1901, quoted in Burton, "Special Relationship of Friends," 42, 11.

26. Sir Julian Pauncefote to Lord Lansdowne, December 19, 1901, quoted in Warren G. Kneer, *Great Britain and the Caribbean, 1901-1913: A Study in Anglo-American Relations* (East Lansing, MI, 1975), x.

27. TR to Lee, December 31, 1901, *Letters of TR*, III, 214.

28. TR to Hay, July 1, 1902, *Letters of TR*, III, 284. The acquisition by the United States of the Panama Canal Zone in November 1903—which featured U.S. naval support for a successful Panamanian uprising against Colombian rule, followed by a U.S.-Panamanian treaty extremely favorable to the United States—has ever since been the single most controversial episode in Theodore Roosevelt's diplomacy. Historians long assumed that ex-President Roosevelt had gratuitously stirred the pot by boasting in a speech delivered in California on March 23, 1911: "I took the Canal Zone." But a careful analysis presented by James F. Vivian in 1980 strongly suggests that TR committed no such faux pas. Instead, Vivian demonstrates, Roosevelt more likely claimed rather innocuously that he "took a trip to the Isthmus" and that he "started the canal." Vivian, "The 'Taking' of the Panama Canal Zone: Myth and Reality," *Diplomatic History*, 4, 1, Winter 1980, 95-100. Be that as it may, the incorrectly attributed quote did reflect Roosevelt's true perspective. For in a letter of June 1908 to George Otto Trevelyan, TR wrote proudly about "taking Panama." TR to Trevelyan, June 19, 1908, *Letters of TR*, VI, 1087.

29. TR to Sternburg, October 11, 1901, *Letters of TR*, III, 172.

30. Beale, *TR and the Rise of America*, 30.

31. Raymond A. Esthus, *Theodore Roosevelt and the International Rivalries* (Claremont, CA, 1970), 38.

32. Collin, *TR, Culture, Diplomacy, and Expansion*, 96.

33. TR to Hay, January 18, 1902, *Letters of TR*, III, 219.

34. TR to Hay, February 15, 1902, *Letters of TR*, III, 230.

35. TR to Whitelaw Reid, March 3, 1902, *Letters of TR*, III, 237.

36. TR to Hay, November 7, 1901, *Letters of TR*, III, 190.

37. TR to Andrew Dickson White, December 17, 1901, *Letters of TR*, III, 208.

38. TR to A. D. White, January 16, 1902, *Letters of TR*, III, 218.

39. TR to Sternburg, unsent letter, March 6, 1902, *Letters of TR*, III, 239.

40. TR to Sternburg, March 8, 1902, *Letters of TR*, III, 242.

41. William C. Widenor, *Henry Cabot Lodge and the Search for an American Foreign Policy* (Berkeley, 1980), 167.

42. Beale, *TR and the Rise of America*, 81.

43. Ricard, *TR: principes et pratique*, 412, 247.

44. Collin, *TR, Culture, Diplomacy, and Expansion*, 171.

45. Esthus, *TR and the International Rivalries*, 39.

46. TR to Choate, October 9, 1901, *Letters of TR*, III, 170.

47. John St. Loe Strachey to TR, September 23, 1901, and TR to Strachey, October 15, 1901, quoted in Burton, "Special Relationship of Friends," 15.

48. TR to Lee, December 31, 1901, *Letters of TR*, III, 214.

49. Quoted in Campbell, *Anglo-American Understanding*, 250-51n.

50. Beale, *TR and the Rise of America*, 421.

51. Campbell, *Anglo-American Understanding*, 274. Pauncefote had died in May 1902, and his successor, Sir Michael Herbert, did not arrive in the United States until October.

52. TR to Sternburg, October 11, 1901, *Letters of TR*, III, 172.

53. Annual message of December 3, 1901, quoted in Kneer, *Britain and the Caribbean*, 7.

54. Kneer, *Britain and the Caribbean*, 28n.

55. Ibid., 18-19.

56. Herbert to Lansdowne, November 13, 1902, quoted in ibid., 22.

57. Colonial Office to Foreign Office, February 19, 1902, quoted in ibid., 30n.

58. Herbert to Lansdowne, November 19, 1902, quoted in ibid., 26.

59. Lansdowne to Herbert, December 4, 1902, quoted in ibid., 26.

60. Henry White to Hay, December 15, 1902, and December 17, 1902, quoted in ibid., 36.

61. Herbert to Lansdowne, December 16, 1902, quoted in Esthus, *TR and the International Rivalries*, 41.

62. See Frederick W. Marks III, *Velvet on Iron: The Diplomacy of Theodore Roosevelt* (Lincoln, NE, 1979), 43-44, for a coherent and plausible explanation.

63. Kneer, *Britain and the Caribbean*, 35.

64. Quoted in ibid., 39.

65. Quoted in ibid., 38.

66. Ricard, *TR: principes et pratique*, 280n.

67. See Dexter Perkins, *A History of the Monroe Doctrine* (Boston, 1941), 214-20; Marks, *Velvet on Iron*, 38-47, 49-50, 52-54; and Edmund Morris, "'A Few Pregnant Days': Theodore Roosevelt and the Venezuelan Crisis of 1902," *Theodore Roosevelt Association Journal*, 15, 1, Winter 1989, 2-13. For a survey of the literature of the controversy, see Ricard, *TR: principes et pratique*, 279-80n.

68. Ricard, *TR: principes et pratique*, 279-94. Ricard has also published in English an abbreviated version of his well-conceived "second phase" theory. Ricard, "The Anglo-German Intervention in Venezuela and Theodore Roosevelt's Ultimatum to the Kaiser: Taking a Fresh Look at an Old Enigma," in Serge Ricard and Hélène Christol, eds., *Anglo-Saxonism in U.S. Foreign Policy: The Diplomacy of Imperialism, 1899-1919* (Aix-en-Provence, France, 1991), 65-77. Lewis Gould, whose important *Presidency of TR* was published the same year as Ricard's *TR: principes et pratique*, was not convinced by either Marks or Morris or any earlier advocates that an ultimatum was really issued. Gould, *Presidency of TR*, 77-79. It would be interesting to know whether Gould's conclusion would have been different had he had access to Ricard's account before completing his manuscript.

69. Kneer, *Britain and the Caribbean*, 40.

70. Herbert to Lansdowne, December 19, 1902, quoted in ibid., 40.

71. TR to William Howard Taft, December 26, 1902, *Letters of TR*, III, 399. For the other letters, see pp. 396-98.

72. TR to George Wheeler Hinman, December 29, 1902, *Letters of TR*, III, 399-400.

73. Herbert to Lansdowne, December 29, 1902, quoted in Campbell, *Anglo-American Understanding*, 292.

74. Quoted in Campbell, *Anglo-American Understanding*, 292.

75. TR to Theodore Roosevelt, Jr., February 9, 1903, *Letters of TR*, III, 423.

76. Herbert to Lansdowne, February 7, 1903, quoted in Kneer, *Britain and the Caribbean*, 52.

77. See ibid., 54-56.

78. Herbert to Lansdowne, February 25, 1903, quoted in ibid., 60-61.

79. TR to Lodge, June 29, 1903, quoted in Campbell, *Anglo-American Understanding*, 300; TR to Reid, June 27, 1906, *Letters of TR*, V, 319.

80. TR to Cecil Spring Rice, November 1, 1905, *Letters of TR*, V, 63. Until lately, this letter was believed to be Roosevelt's first recorded reference to his private ultimatum to Germany. (There were to be at least thirteen more such references between 1905 and 1917. See

Morris, "'Pregnant Days,'" 3-5.) In 1991, however, Ricard brought to light a report from French ambassador Jean Jules Jusserand to his government on a conversation he had with Roosevelt on May 15, 1905. The president told Jusserand that he had employed "stern language" with the kaiser during the Venezuelan crisis, but that "the thing was hushed up." Jusserand to Théophile Delcassé, May 16, 1905, quoted in Ricard, *TR: principes et pratique*, 281. (Ricard's translation, as provided in "TR's Ultimatum to the Kaiser: Taking a Fresh Look," 67.)

81. TR to H. White, August 14, 1906, *Letters of TR*, V, 358-59.
82. Quoted in Campbell, *Anglo-American Understanding*, 299.
83. TR to Hay, March 13, 1903, *Letters of TR*, III, 446. (Emphasis in original.)
84. TR to Hay, April 22, 1903, *Letters of TR*, III, 465.
85. TR to Hay, August 9, 1903, *Letters of TR*, III, 549.
86. TR to Henry Clay Taylor, September 15, 1903, *Letters of TR*, III, 602.
87. Burton, "Theodore Roosevelt and the 'Special Relationship' with Britain," *History Today*, 23, 8, August 1973, 530. (Emphasis added.)
88. Campbell, *Anglo-American Understanding*, 240.
89. Lee to TR, December 17, 1901, quoted in Burton, "Special Relationship of Friends," 44.
90. Campbell, *Anglo-American Understanding*, 302.
91. TR to Lodge, January 28, 1909, *Letters of TR*, VI, 1497.
92. TR to Elihu Root, March 29, 1902, quoted in Collin, *TR, Culture, Diplomacy, and Expansion*, 178.
93. TR to Lodge, January 28, 1909, *Letters of TR*, VI, 1492.
94. TR to Hay, July 10, 1902, *Letters of TR*, III, 287-88.
95. TR to Hay, July 16, 1902, *Letters of TR*, III, 294-95.
96. TR to Strachey, July 18, 1902, quoted in Burton, "Special Relationship of Friends," 44.
97. Strachey to TR, August 18, 1902, quoted in ibid., 44.
98. TR to Hay, January 14, 1903, *Letters of TR*, III, 405.
99. TR to George Frederick William Holls, February 3, 1903, *Letters of TR*, III, 418.
100. Holls to Strachey, February 10, 1903, quoted in Campbell, *Anglo-American Understanding*, 308.
101. As to historians, see, for example, Campbell, *Anglo-American Understanding*, 311-12, and Elting E. Morison et al., *Letters of TR*, III, 448n.
102. Campbell, *Anglo-American Understanding*, 311.
103. TR to Elihu Root, Henry Cabot Lodge, and George Turner, March 17, 1903, *Letters of TR*, III, 448-49.
104. Quoted in Campbell, *Anglo-American Understanding*, 321.
105. Time was hardly the fundamental problem. In a letter to Henry White of April 10, 1903, Hay quoted a private messenger who had come to Washington representing Laurier: "Sir Wilfrid knows, and all of us know, that we have no case." Quoted in ibid., 333n.
106. Lansdowne to Herbert, June 16, 1903, quoted in ibid., 321.
107. Lodge to TR, June 23, 1903, quoted in ibid., 322.
108. Lodge to TR, June 27, 1903, TR Papers, reel 34.
109. TR to Hay, June 29, 1903, *Letters of TR*, III, 507.
110. TR to Lodge, July 8, 1903, in Henry Cabot Lodge, ed., *Selections from the Correspondence of Theodore Roosevelt and Henry Cabot Lodge, 1894-1918* (2 vols., New York, 1925), II, 38.
111. TR to Lodge, July 16, 1903, quoted in Campbell, *Anglo-American Understanding*, 323; also in Lodge, ed., *Correspondence of TR and Lodge*, II, 39. (Emphasis in original.)
112. Campbell, *Anglo-American Understanding*, 326-27.
113. Oliver Wendell Holmes to TR, July 14, 1903, TR Papers, reel 35.
114. TR to Holmes, July 25, 1903, *Letters of TR*, III, 529-31.

115. Joseph Chamberlain to Arthur Balfour, August 8, 1903, quoted in Marks, *Velvet on Iron*, 62.

116. TR to Hay, July 29, 1903, *Letters of TR*, III, 532-33.

117. TR to Lodge, August 6, 1903, *Letters of TR*, III, 545.

118. TR to Turner, August 8, 1903, quoted in Campbell, *Anglo-American Understanding*, 327.

119. TR to Root, August 8, 1903, *Letters of TR*, III, 546.

120. Lodge to TR, August 8, 1903, TR Papers, reel 308.

121. TR to Hay, September 15, 1903, *Letters of TR*, III, 601.

122. On September 20 Hay himself wrote an important letter to Henry White, who transmitted its contents directly to Balfour. From his own perspective (and perhaps mildly over-accentuating his own role), the secretary of state, a man thoroughly trusted and respected by the British leadership, ably outlined the president's position: "The President, at my earnest persuasion, consented to this Tribunal, because I felt sure we could convince any great English lawyer, that our contention was just. He was not so sanguine, but agreed to try the experiment, to enable the British Government to get out of an absolutely untenable position, with dignity and honor. If the Tribunal should disagree he will feel he has done his utmost, and will make no further effort to settle the controversy. He will hold the territory, as we have held it since 1867, and will emphasize the assertion of our sovereignty, in a way which cannot but be disagreeable to Canadian amour propre. And all the labor of the last few years, to bring about a closer friendship between the two governments will have gone for nothing.

"And this, after I have heard from Laurier, and Pauncefote, directly, *that they know they have no case.*" Quoted in Campbell, *Anglo-American Understanding*, 333. (Emphasis in original.)

123. TR to Hay, September 21, 1903, *Letters of TR*, III, 603.

124. See TR to Lodge, January 28, 1909, *Letters of TR*, VI, 1495.

125. TR to Root, October 3, 1903, *Letters of TR*, III, 613.

126. Lodge to TR, September 24, 1903, TR Papers, reel 37.

127. TR to Lodge, October 5, 1903, *Letters of TR*, III, 616.

128. Choate to Hay, telegram, October 15, 1903, and Hay to Choate, telegram, October 16, 1903, Campbell, *Anglo-American Understanding*, 336, 339.

129. See above, p. 42.

130. TR to Lodge, Root, and Turner, telegram, October 20, 1903, quoted in Campbell, *Anglo-American Understanding*, 347n.

131. TR to Holmes, October 20, 1903, *Letters of TR*, III, 634.

132. TR to Theodore Roosevelt, Jr., October 20, 1903, *Letters of TR*, III, 635.

133. Between July and October 1903, inclusive, not a single piece of correspondence passed between Roosevelt and Cecil Spring Rice, Arthur Lee, John St. Loe Strachey, or George Otto Trevelyan. See *Index to the Theodore Roosevelt Papers* (3 vols., Manuscript Division, Reference Department, Library of Congress, Washington, D.C., 1969), II, 647, and III, 1109, 1135, 1190.

134. TR to Spring Rice, November 9, 1903, *Letters of TR*, III, 650-51.

135. Lee to TR, November 22, 1903, TR Papers, reel 38.

136. TR to Lee, December 7, 1903, *Letters of TR*, III, 665-66.

137. TR to Spring Rice, November 1, 1905, *Letters of TR*, V, 63.

138. TR to Philander Chase Knox, February 8, 1909, *Letters of TR*, VI, 1511.

139. TR to Alfred Thayer Mahan, June 8, 1911, quoted in Campbell, *Anglo-American Understanding*, 347.

140. Kneer, *Britain and the Caribbean*, 99.

141. Collin, *TR, Culture, Diplomacy, and Expansion*, 186.

142. Widenor, *Lodge*, 133.
143. Henry Kissinger, *Diplomacy* (New York, 1994), 41.
144. TR to Sternburg, October 11, 1901, *Letters of TR*, III, 172.
145. Annual message of December 3, 1901, quoted in Beale, *TR and the Rise of America*, 192.
146. Beale, *TR and the Rise of America*, 192.
147. Neu, *Uncertain Friendship*, 12.
148. Beale, *TR and the Rise of America*, 192.
149. Choate to Hay, February 12, 1902, quoted in Campbell, *Anglo-American Understanding*, 255.
150. H. White to Lodge, February 26, 1902, quoted in Beale, *TR and the Rise of America*, 153.
151. Campbell, *Anglo-American Understanding*, 255.
152. Beale, *TR and the Rise of America*, 194.
153. Hay to TR, April 25, 1903, quoted in ibid., 153-54.
154. TR to Hay, July 14, 1902, *Letters of TR*, III, 293.
155. TR to Hay, May 22, 1903, *Letters of TR*, III, 478. (Emphasis added.)
156. TR to Francis Butler Loomis, July 1, 1903, and TR to Hay, July 1, 1903, *Letters of TR*, III, 508, 509.
157. TR to Hay, July 18, 1903, *Letters of TR*, III, 520.
158. TR to Hay, July 29, 1903, *Letters of TR*, III, 532.
159. TR to Albert Shaw, June 22, 1903, *Letters of TR*, III, 497-98.
160. TR to Holls, July 4, 1903, *Letters of TR*, III, 509.

Chapter 3

1. Esthus, *TR and the International Rivalries*, 41-42.
2. TR to Elihu Root, February 16, 1904, *Letters of TR*, IV, 731.
3. Henry White to TR, February 5, 1904, TR Papers, reel 41.
4. TR to White, February 17, 1904, *Letters of TR*, IV, 732.
5. Cecil Spring Rice to TR, February 11, 1904, in Gwynn, ed., *Spring Rice*, I, 395.
6. TR to Spring Rice, March 19, 1904, *Letters of TR*, IV, 760-61.
7. Hermann Speck von Sternburg to TR, March 24, 1904, quoted in Esthus, *TR and the International Rivalries*, 44.
8. TR to Spring Rice, June 13, 1904, *Letters of TR*, IV, 830-33.
9. See Gwynn, ed., *Spring Rice*, I, 419-23.
10. TR to John Hay, July 26, 1904, *Letters of TR*, IV, 865.
11. See TR to Captain John Elliott Pillsbury, July 29, 1904, and TR to Hay, July 29, 1904, *Letters of TR*, IV, 869.
12. TR to Sternburg, August 15, 1904, *Letters of TR*, IV, 896.
13. Spring Rice to Hay, August 31, 1904, in Gwynn, ed., *Spring Rice*, I, 426.
14. TR to Hay, September 19, 1904, *Letters of TR*, IV, 946.
15. TR to Spring Rice, November 9, 1904, in Gwynn, ed., *Spring Rice*, I, 434.
16. Spring Rice to TR, December 7, 1904, in Gwynn, ed., *Spring Rice*, I, 438-40.
17. Russia was then on the verge of its chaotic and bloody, but inconclusive, Revolution of 1905.
18. TR to George von Lengerke Meyer, December 26, 1904, *Letters of TR*, IV, 1079-80.
19. See ibid., 1079.
20. TR to White, December 27, 1904, *Letters of TR*, IV, 1082.
21. Roosevelt's diplomacy during 1905 was partly designed to ensure that Japan's priorities would be those which seemed the most logical to him. "The President," Charles Neu observes, "encouraged Japanese continentalism in an effort to limit Japanese ambitions in the Pacific." Neu, *The Troubled Encounter: The United States and Japan* (New York, 1975), 44.

22. TR to Spring Rice, December 27, 1904, *Letters of TR*, IV, 1084-85, 1087-88. (Emphasis added.)

23. Sternburg to TR, December 29, 1904, TR Papers, reel 51. It might be mentioned that, due to his large handwriting, a fifteen-page letter from Sternburg is about the equivalent of most six or seven-page letters.

24. TR to Sternburg, January 12, 1905, *Letters of TR*, IV, 1100-1101.

25. See TR to Sternburg, telegram, January 18, 1905, *Letters of TR*, IV, 1106-7.

26. Sir Mortimer Durand to Lord Lansdowne, telegram, January 23, 1905, and letter, January 26, 1905, quoted in Esthus, *TR and the International Rivalries*, 50-51.

27. Esthus, *Double Eagle and Rising Sun: The Russians and Japanese at Portsmouth in 1905* (Durham, NC, 1988), 19-20.

28. John Hay Diary, entries dated January 29, January 30, and February 2, 1905, quoted in Beale, *TR and the Rise of America*, 155.

29. George Monger, *The End of Isolation: British Foreign Policy, 1900-1907* (London, 1963), 182.

30. TR to Meyer, February 6, 1905, *Letters of TR*, IV, 1115-16.

31. TR to Charlemagne Tower, February 16, 1905, *Letters of TR*, IV, 1122.

32. TR to George Otto Trevelyan, March 9, 1905, *Letters of TR*, IV, 1134.

33. TR to King Edward VII, March 9, 1905, *Letters of TR*, IV, 1136.

34. Monger, *End of Isolation*, 183.

35. Durand to Lansdowne, March 19, 1905, quoted in ibid., 185.

36. TR to Hay, April 2, 1905, *Letters of TR*, IV, 1157.

37. TR to Samuel R. Gummeré, March 31, 1905, quoted in Beale, *TR and the Rise of America*, 360.

38. William Howard Taft to TR, April 5, 1905, TR Papers, reel 53.

39. TR to Taft, April 8, 1905, *Letters of TR*, IV, 1159.

40. TR to Whitelaw Reid, April 28, 1906, *Letters of TR*, V, 230-51. Howard Beale is convinced, following "a checking of the sources," that Roosevelt was "an amazingly accurate reporter in this instance." Beale, *TR and the Rise of America*, 389n. Lewis Gould comments along similar lines. Gould, *Presidency of TR*, 323n. And Serge Ricard remarks more generally in reference to this letter that Roosevelt's "practice of gathering together the pertinent documents of an important negotiation and of confiding its details to a (a few) privileged person(s) has considerably facilitated the historian's task." Ricard, *TR: principes et pratique*, 375n.

41. TR to Reid, April 28, 1906, *Letters of TR*, V, 230-31.

42. Gould, *Presidency of TR*, 190.

43. TR to Sternburg, April 20, 1905, *Letters of TR*, IV, 1166.

44. TR to Taft, April 20, 1905, *Letters of TR*, IV, 1161-62, 1165.

45. Beale, *TR and the Rise of America*, 362.

46. Esthus, *TR and the International Rivalries*, 58.

47. Lansdowne to Arthur Balfour, April 27, 1905, quoted in ibid., 58.

48. TR to Reid, April 28, 1906, *Letters of TR*, V, 231.

49. Spring Rice to Edith Carow Roosevelt, April 26, 1905, in Gwynn, ed., *Spring Rice*, I, 469.

50. A hint of frustration came through in a letter of May 15 from Roosevelt to Lodge. "It always amuses me," TR declared, "to find that the English think that I am under the influence of the Kaiser." He then referred to these misled Britons as "heavy-witted creatures." *Letters of TR*, IV, 1181.

51. TR to Spring Rice, May 13, 1905, *Letters of TR*, IV, 1177-78.

52. TR to Meyer, May 22, 1905, *Letters of TR*, IV, 1189.

53. Sternburg to TR, May 31, 1905, quoted in TR to Reid, April 28, 1906, *Letters of TR*, V, 232.

54. TR to Reid, April 28, 1906, *Letters of TR*, V, 234.

55. Reid to TR, telegram, June 5, 1905, TR Papers, reel 54.

56. TR to Reid, telegram, June 6, 1905, *Letters of TR*, IV, 1207.

57. Esthus, *TR and the International Rivalries*, 59.

58. Sternburg to TR, June 11, 1905, quoted in TR to Reid, April 28, 1906, *Letters of TR*, V, 235-36.

59. TR to Reid, April 28, 1906, *Letters of TR*, V, 236.

60. Sternburg to TR, June 18, 1905, quoted in TR to Reid, April 28, 1906, *Letters of TR*, V, 238.

61. Maurice Rouvier to Jean Jules Jusserand, June 23, 1905, quoted in TR to Reid, April 28, 1906, *Letters of TR*, V, 237. (Author's translation.) Jusserand's pivotal role during the first stage of the Moroccan crisis is highlighted particularly well by Ricard. See *TR: principes et pratique*, 377-85.

62. TR to Reid, April 28, 1906, *Letters of TR*, V, 238.

63. TR to Henry Cabot Lodge, June 16, 1905, *Letters of TR*, IV, 1221. (Emphasis added.)

64. Reid to TR, June 17, 1905, TR Papers, reel 55.

65. Reid to TR, June 23, 1905, TR Papers, reel 55.

66. TR to Sternburg, June 25, 1905, *Letters of TR*, IV, 1256-57. (Emphasis added.)

67. Esthus, *TR and the International Rivalries*, 61.

68. See Monger, *End of Isolation*, 203-4.

69. TR to Reid, April 28, 1906, *Letters of TR*, V, 240.

70. Jusserand to Rouvier, June 28, 1905, quoted in TR to Reid, April 28, 1906, *Letters of TR*, V, 241. (Author's translation.)

71. Sternburg to TR, June 28, 1905, quoted in TR to Reid, April 28, 1906, *Letters of TR*, V, 241.

72. Esthus, *TR and the International Rivalries*, 82.

73. See Ricard, *TR: principes et pratique*, 382-85.

74. TR to Lodge, July 11, 1905, *Letters of TR*, IV, 1273.

75. TR to Taft, April 20, 1905, *Letters of TR*, IV, 1162-63.

76. TR to Trevelyan, May 13, 1905, *Letters of TR*, IV, 1174.

77. TR to Lodge, May 24, 1905, *Letters of TR*, IV, 1192.

78. TR to Spring Rice, May 26, 1905, *Letters of TR*, IV, 1194.

79. TR to Lodge, June 5, 1905, *Letters of TR*, IV, 1202-3, 1206.

80. TR to Kermit Roosevelt, June 11, 1905, *Letters of TR*, IV, 1210.

81. Monger, *End of Isolation*, 199, 206.

82. TR to Spring Rice, June 16, 1905, *Letters of TR*, IV, 1234.

83. TR to Lodge, June 16, 1905, *Letters of TR*, IV, 1230, 1232-33.

84. Reid to TR, June 17, 1905, TR Papers, reel 55. (Emphasis in original.)

85. TR to Reid, June 30, 1905, *Letters of TR*, IV, 1258.

86. TR to Reid, July 7, 1905, *Letters of TR*, IV, 1265-66. (Emphasis added.)

87. Spring Rice to the Secretary of State, July 10, 1905, in Gwynn, ed., *Spring Rice*, I, 474-77. (Emphasis in original.)

88. In 1895, to be precise, such a combination had deprived the Japanese of the major fruits of their victory in the Sino-Japanese War.

89. TR to Spring Rice, July 24, 1905, *Letters of TR*, IV, 1283-85.

90. TR to Reid, July 29, 1905, *Letters of TR*, IV, 1292-93.

91. George Kennan to TR, March 30, 1905, TR Papers, reel 53.

92. TR to Kennan, May 6, 1905, *Letters of TR*, IV, 1169. (Emphasis added.)

93. Lodge to TR, June 29, 1905, quoted in Beale, *TR and the Rise of America*, 156.

94. Taft to Root, telegram, July 29, 1905, quoted in ibid., 157.

95. TR to Taft, telegram, July 31, 1905, *Letters of TR*, IV, 1293.

96. Ricard, *TR: principes et pratique,* 355.

97. TR to Reid, August 3, 1905, *Letters of TR,* IV, 1298. Having only recently secured a conference on the Moroccan question, and with his Russo-Japanese peacemaking entering its most important and intense phase, Roosevelt also reflected in general terms in this letter on his extraordinary activity as an international mediator: "In all these matters where I am asked to interfere between two foreign nations all I can do is this. If there is a chance to prevent trouble by preventing simple misunderstanding, or by myself taking the first step or making some suggestion about it when it has become a matter of punctilio with the two parties in interest that neither of them should take the first step, then I am entirely willing and glad to see if I can be of any value in preventing the misunderstanding from becoming acute to the danger point. If, however, there is a genuine conflict of interest which has made each party resolute to carry its point even at the cost of war, there is no use of my interfering, and I do not try and never shall try in such case unless I am myself willing in the last resort to back up my action by force."

98. TR to Durand, August 23, 1905, *Letters of TR,* IV, 1310-11.

99. TR to White, August 23, 1905, *Letters of TR,* IV, 1313.

100. Lansdowne, Foreign Office minute, quoted in Monger, *End of Isolation,* 215.

101. TR to William II, telegram, August 27, 1905, *Letters of TR,* IV, 1317.

102. TR to William Woodville Rockhill, August 29, 1905, *Letters of TR,* IV, 1327.

103. Durand to TR, August 31, 1905, quoted in TR to Lodge, September 2, 1905, *Letters of TR,* V, 9.

104. TR to Durand, September 8, 1905, quoted in Beale, *TR and the Rise of America,* 305.

105. TR to Reid, September 11, 1905, *Letters of TR,* V, 18.

106. TR to Reid, September 16, 1905, *Letters of TR,* V, 29.

107. TR to Arthur Lee, September 21, 1905, quoted in Burton, "Special Relationship of Friends," 45.

108. TR to John St. Loe Strachey, September 11, 1905, quoted in ibid., 45.

109. Strachey to TR, September 9, 1905, quoted in ibid., 47.

Chapter 4

1. TR to George von Lengerke Meyer, February 6, 1905, *Letters of TR,* IV, 1115.

2. TR to George Otto Trevelyan, March 9, 1905, *Letters of TR,* IV, 1134.

3. TR to Leonard Wood, March 9, 1905, *Letters of TR,* IV, 1136.

4. William Sowden Sims to TR, July 5, 1906, TR Papers, reel 65.

5. TR to Sims, July 7, 1906, *Letters of TR,* V, 333-34. And see chapter 2, p. 35.

6. TR to Charles William Eliot, September 22, 1906, *Letters of TR,* V, 421.

7. TR to David Bowman Schneder, June 19, 1905, *Letters of TR,* IV, 1240-41.

8. TR to Cecil Spring Rice, June 16, 1905, *Letters of TR,* IV, 1233-34.

9. See chapter 3, note 21.

10. TR to William Howard Taft, October 7, 1905, *Letters of TR,* V, 49.

11. TR to Spring Rice, November 1, 1905, *Letters of TR,* V, 61.

12. Esthus, *TR and the International Rivalries,* 65.

13. TR to Wood, January 22, 1906, *Letters of TR,* V, 135.

14. TR to Whitelaw Reid, June 27, 1906, *Letters of TR,* V, 320.

15. TR to Kentaro Kaneko, October 26, 1906, *Letters of TR,* V, 473.

16. While Roosevelt had recently abandoned his fight to impose simplified spelling on an unwilling nation, he had decided to "continue using the new spelling . . . in my own correspondence." TR to James Brander Matthews, December 16, 1906, *Letters of TR,* V,

527. An illuminating and entertaining account of TR's unsuccessful foray into the field of orthographic reform is provided by Serge Ricard, "'2 Mutch is 2 Mutch': The Spelling Reform Controversy in the Early Twentieth Century," in Ricard, ed., *L'éducation aux États-Unis: mythes et réalités* [Education in the United States: Myths and Realities] (Aix-en-Provence, France, 1992), 177-93. Disapproving American congressmen and private citizens were joined by the British press: "In those days of Anglo-American honeymooning, . . . the *London Times* . . . deplored the 'inconsiderate' and 'unconcerted' nature" of Roosevelt's undertaking (p. 184).

17. TR to Sir Edward Grey, December 18, 1906, *Letters of TR*, V, 528-29.

18. TR to John St. Loe Strachey, December 21, 1906, *Letters of TR*, V, 532.

19. TR to Reid, September 19, 1905, *Letters of TR*, V, 32.

20. TR to Spring Rice, November 1, 1905, *Letters of TR*, V, 63.

21. Esthus, *TR and the International Rivalries*, 108-9. Serge Ricard also emphasizes Roosevelt's "effective" — indeed "decisive" — impact "on the course of the negotiations" at Algeciras. Ricard, *TR: principes et pratique*, 385.

22. TR to Henry White, August 23, 1905, *Letters of TR*, IV, 1313.

23. Elihu Root to White, November 28, 1905, quoted in Beale, *TR and the Rise of America*, 371-72.

24. Esthus, *TR and the International Rivalries*, 65.

25. White to TR, April 8, 1906, TR Papers, reel 64.

26. TR to Meyer, February 1, 1906, *Letters of TR*, V, 145.

27. See Root to Speck von Sternburg, February 19, 1906, in TR to Reid, April 28, 1906, *Letters of TR*, V, 243.

28. Sternburg to TR, February 22, 1906, quoted in TR to Reid, April 28, 1906, *Letters of TR*, V, 244.

29. TR to Oscar Solomon Straus, February 27, 1906, *Letters of TR*, V, 168.

30. TR to Reid, March 1, 1906, *Letters of TR*, V, 169-70.

31. Esthus, *TR and the International Rivalries*, 98.

32. Root to Sternburg, March 7, 1906, quoted in TR to Reid, April 28, 1906, *Letters of TR*, V, 245.

33. Monger, *End of Isolation*, 274-78.

34. Root to Sternburg, March 17, 1906, quoted in TR to Reid, April 28, 1906, *Letters of TR*, V, 248. (Emphasis added.)

35. TR to Reid, April 28, 1906, *Letters of TR*, V, 249.

36. TR to Reid, April 28, 1906, *Letters of TR*, V, 242-43.

37. There had, however, been a Franco-American "misunderstanding" relating to Roosevelt's proposal of February 19 and the French preference for one-country police administration in most Moroccan ports. For this misunderstanding TR and even Jusserand blamed the French government on account of its failure to apprise Roosevelt clearly and in a timely manner of its position; but the president, Ricard argues, made a couple of important "unilateral decisions" and thus was also partly at fault. Ricard, *TR: principes et pratique*, 387-88.

38. TR to Reid, April 28, 1906, *Letters of TR*, V, 251.

39. TR to Reid, June 27, 1906, *Letters of TR*, V, 318. (Emphasis added.)

40. TR to White, April 30, 1906, *Letters of TR*, V, 251.

41. White to TR, April 8, 1906, TR Papers, reel 64.

42. TR to White, April 30, 1906, *Letters of TR*, V, 251-52.

43. White to TR, April 8, 1906, TR Papers, reel 64.

44. TR to Reid, June 27, 1906, *Letters of TR*, V, 318-20.

45. TR to Jean Jules Jusserand, April 25, 1906, *Letters of TR*, V, 221.

46. TR to Andrew Carnegie, August 6, 1906, *Letters of TR*, V, 345-46.

47. TR to Reid, August 7, 1906, *Letters of TR*, V, 348-49.
48. TR to White, August 14, 1906, *Letters of TR*, V, 358-59.
49. TR to Trevelyan, August 18, 1906, *Letters of TR*, V, 366.
50. Grey to TR, December 4, 1906, TR Papers, reel 70.
51. TR to Grey, December 18, 1906, *Letters of TR*, V, 528.

Chapter 5

1. Campbell, *Anglo-American Understanding*, 268.
2. TR to Nicholas Murray Butler, August 29, 1904, *Letters of TR*, IV, 913.
3. John Hay to TR, September 22, 1904, TR Papers, reel 48.
4. TR to Hay, September 24, 1904, *Letters of TR*, IV, 952.
5. TR to Charles Warren Fairbanks, November 12, 1904, *Letters of TR*, IV, 1031.
6. TR to Henry Cabot Lodge, November 12, 1904, *Letters of TR*, IV, 1031.
7. TR to Winthrop Murray Crane, November 12, 1904, *Letters of TR*, IV, 1032.
8. TR to Lodge, January 6, 1905, *Letters of TR*, IV, 1094. Between November 1904 and January 1905, arbitration treaties were negotiated between the United States and Britain, France, Germany, Japan, Italy, Mexico, Austria-Hungary, Spain, Portugal, Switzerland, Norway, and Sweden. These treaties, as described by Elting E. Morison and his associates, "provided for arbitration, before the Hague Court, of any matters involving either interpretation of treaties or legal differences that did not affect the vital interests, honor, or independence of the contracting parties. Before submitting questions to the court, the nations involved were to conclude a 'special agreement' defining the dispute and the procedure of arbitration." Morison et al., *Letters of TR*, IV, 1092n. Here again Lodge incurred the president's displeasure by proposing an amendment that in effect would necessitate a *separate* treaty, requiring Senate ratification, before *each* arbitration undertaken. Such an amendment rendered the treaties a "sham" and a "farce," Roosevelt insisted in letters to Lodge and others. See TR to John Coit Spooner, January 6, 1905; to Lodge, January 6, 1905; to Andrew Carnegie, February 6, 1905; to Ernest Hamlin Abbott, February 6, 1905, in *Letters of TR*, IV, 1093, 1094, 1114, 1117. An exasperated TR vented his frustration to Hay late in January: "I am getting to take your view of the Senate under stress of seeing the way they are handling the arbitration treaties." TR to Hay, January 28, 1905, *Letters of TR*, IV, 1112. When the Senate adopted Lodge's amendment on February 11, an angry Roosevelt withdrew the treaties. Hay's successor, Elihu Root, later persuaded Roosevelt to support watered-down arbitration treaties as preferable to none at all. In 1908 the United States entered into twenty-four bilateral arbitration treaties—each requiring endorsement by two-thirds of the Senate prior to any arbitration proceeding.
9. TR to Silas McBee, February 16, 1905, *Letters of TR*, IV, 1122.
10. DeConde, *History of American Foreign Policy*, I, 365. The Anglo-American Convention of 1818 had "forever" granted fishing rights—somewhat restricted but still profitable—to American fishermen in Newfoundland waters. Various controversies had brought various adjustments—on balance favorable to the United States—over the succeeding decades. A regularly renewed modus vivendi dating from 1888 was still in effect when 1905 began.
11. TR to Lodge, May 15, 1905, *Letters of TR*, IV, 1181.
12. Lodge to TR, August 16, 1905, TR Papers, reel 58.
13. TR to Lodge, August 19, 1905, *Letters of TR*, IV, 1305-6.
14. To others Roosevelt wanted it clear that this and other disagreements between himself and Lodge did not affect his opinion of the senator's work in any fundamental way. On February 23, 1906, he shared these thoughts with Lyman Abbott: "Lodge is a man of very

strong convictions, and this means that when his convictions differ from mine I am apt to substitute the words 'narrow' and 'obstinate' for 'strong'; and he has a certain aloofness and coldness of manner that irritate people who don't live in New England. But he is an eminently fit successor of Webster and Sumner in the senatorship from Massachusetts. . . . He and I differ radically on certain propositions, as for instance on the pending [railroad] rate bill and on the arbitration treaties of a couple of years ago; but I say deliberately that during the twenty years he has been in Washington he has been on the whole the best and most useful servant of the public to be found in either house of Congress." *Letters of TR,* V, 163. But that Roosevelt's assessment of Lodge had incurred at least a mild diminution is suggested by a comment in TR's letter of August 6, 1906, to Andrew Carnegie. Regarding the president's unsuccessful fight for his arbitration treaties early in 1905, Roosevelt attacked the Senate as "often a dangerous body as regards its dealings with foreign affairs" and referred to Senator Orville H. Platt of Connecticut—who unlike Lodge had upheld Roosevelt's position—as "the very best man in the Senate." *Letters of TR,* V, 346.

15. TR to Lodge, September 6, 1905, *Letters of TR,* V, 13.
16. TR to Lodge, November 1, 1905, *Letters of TR,* V, 67.
17. TR to Whitelaw Reid, June 27, 1906, *Letters of TR,* V, 320.
18. TR to George Otto Trevelyan, September 9, 1906, *Letters of TR,* V, 401.
19. TR to Sir Edward Grey, December 18, 1906, *Letters of TR,* V, 529.
20. TR to Arthur Lee, January 5, 1907, TR Papers, reel 344.
21. TR to Charles William Eliot, April 4, 1904 (sent not to Eliot but to Arthur Twining Hadley, April 6, 1904), *Letters of TR,* IV, 769.
22. TR to Kermit Roosevelt, November 11 and 14, 1906, *Letters of TR,* V, 495.
23. TR to Cecil Spring Rice, January 18, 1904, *Letters of TR,* III, 699.
24. See pp. 93-94.
25. TR to Carl Schurz, September 8, 1905, *Letters of TR,* V, 16.
26. TR to Andrew Carnegie, August 6, 1906, *Letters of TR,* V, 345.
27. TR to Trevelyan, September 12, 1905, *Letters of TR,* V, 22.
28. TR to Frederick Scott Oliver, August 9, 1906, *Letters of TR,* V, 352.
29. TR to Joseph Gurney Cannon, September 12, 1904, *Letters of TR,* IV, 939-41.
30. TR to Reid, September 11, 1905, *Letters of TR,* V, 20.
31. TR to Reid, January 23, 1906, *Letters of TR,* V, 138.
32. TR to Lodge, April 30, 1906, *Letters of TR,* V, 253-56.
33. TR to Trevelyan, November 23, 1906, *Letters of TR,* V, 498-99.
34. TR to Florence Lockwood La Farge, September 25, 1905, *Letters of TR,* V, 35.
35. TR to Reid, September 11, 1905, *Letters of TR,* V, 19-20.
36. TR to Trevelyan, March 9, 1905, *Letters of TR,* IV, 1134-35.
37. Kneer, *Britain and the Caribbean,* 225.
38. TR to Alice Roosevelt Longworth, June 24, 1906, *Letters of TR,* V, 312-13.
39. TR to Reid, June 27, 1906, *Letters of TR,* V, 320.
40. Trevelyan to TR, August 28, 1906, TR Papers, reel 67; TR to Trevelyan, September 9, 1906, *Letters of TR,* V, 400. However, when he actually met Balfour in England in 1910, Roosevelt found him to be one of "the most charming men whom I ever met" and "a brilliant man." TR to David Gray, October 5, 1911, *Letters of TR,* VII, 405-6, 415.
41. TR to Lodge, September 12, 1906, *Letters of TR,* V, 408.
42. TR to John St. Loe Strachey, October 25, 1906, *Letters of TR,* V, 468.
43. TR to Spring Rice, January 18, 1904, *Letters of TR,* III, 699.
44. TR to Rudyard Kipling, November 1, 1904, *Letters of TR,* IV, 1008.

45. TR to Spring Rice, July 24, 1905, *Letters of TR*, IV, 1286.
46. Lodge to TR, June 29, 1905, quoted in Beale, *TR and the Rise of America*, 147-48.
47. TR to Trevelyan, November 23, 1906, *Letters of TR*, V, 499.
48. TR to Strachey, February 12, 1906, *Letters of TR*, V, 152.
49. Strachey to TR, March 10, 1906, quoted in Burton, "Special Relationship of Friends," 15.
50. Strachey to TR, August 26, 1906, quoted in ibid., 16.
51. TR to Oliver, August 9, 1906, *Letters of TR*, V, 350-51.
52. TR to Finley Peter Dunne, November 23, 1904, *Letters of TR*, IV, 1042.
53. TR to George von Lengerke Meyer, February 6, 1905, *Letters of TR*, IV, 1115.
54. TR to Reid, September 11, 1905, *Letters of TR*, V, 19.
55. TR to Spring Rice, December 27, 1904, *Letters of TR*, IV, 1085, 1087.
56. TR to Spring Rice, May 13, 1905, and June 16, 1905, *Letters of TR*, IV, 1178, 1234.
57. TR to Hay, February 27, 1905, and TR to King Edward VII, March 9, 1905, *Letters of TR*, IV, 1128, 1135-36.
58. TR to Lodge, May 24, 1905, *Letters of TR*, IV, 1192-93.
59. TR to Trevelyan, May 13, 1905, *Letters of TR*, IV, 1174.
60. Lee to TR, May 24, 1905, TR Papers, reel 54.
61. TR to Lee, June 6, 1905, *Letters of TR*, IV, 1207. (Emphasis added.)
62. TR to Strachey, September 2, 1905, quoted in Burton, "Special Relationship of Friends," 36.
63. "More than ever before," George Monger contends, British foreign policy under Grey "fell into the control of one man." *End of Isolation*, 256.
64. TR to Strachey, February 12, 1906, *Letters of TR*, V, 152.
65. Henry White to TR, April 8, 1906, TR Papers, reel 64.
66. TR to Trevelyan, November 23, 1906, *Letters of TR*, V, 500.
67. TR to William Sowden Sims, October 13, 1906, *Letters of TR*, V, 455.
68. TR to Theodore Roosevelt, Jr., May 14, 1904, *Letters of TR*, IV, 798.
69. Reid to TR, June 19, 1906, TR Papers, reel 65.
70. Lee to TR, October 14, 1906, TR Papers, reel 69.
71. TR to Lee, October 15, 1906, *Letters of TR*, V, 458.
72. Lee to TR, October 16, 1906, TR Papers, reel 69.
73. TR to Grey, October 22, 1906, *Letters of TR*, V, 464.
74. Reid to TR, October 24, 1906, TR Papers, reel 69.
75. TR to Reid, November 6, 1906, *Letters of TR*, V, 488.
76. Grey to TR, December 4, 1906, TR Papers, reel 70.
77. TR to Grey, December 18, 1906, *Letters of TR*, V, 527, 529.

Chapter 6

1. Bradford Perkins gives the Swettenham incident only one paragraph—a rather misleading one at that—in *The Great Rapprochement: England and the United States, 1895-1914*, p. 275. Warren G. Kneer does likewise—though more accurately—in *Great Britain and the Caribbean, 1901-1913: A Study in Anglo-American Relations*, pp. 117-18. In his wide-ranging and penetrating *Theodore Roosevelt and the Rise of America to World Power*, Howard K. Beale deals with the Jamaica incident in exactly one concise sentence (p. 143). Two major books of the 1990s on Roosevelt's diplomacy—Richard H. Collin, *Theodore Roosevelt's Caribbean: The Panama Canal, the Monroe Doctrine, and the Latin American Context* (Baton Rouge, 1990), and Serge Ricard, *Théodore Roosevelt: principes et pratique d'une politique étrangère*—neglect it altogether, as do most other works on TR's foreign policy, and as does Lewis L. Gould's probing and detailed *The Presidency of Theodore Roosevelt*.

2. *Harper's Weekly*, February 9, 1907, 187.

3. The Jamaica incident and its diplomatic aftermath are first recounted in William Neal Tilchin, "Theodore Roosevelt and the British Empire, 1901-1907," Ph.D. diss., Brown University, 1992, 238-353. A briefer version is provided in William N. Tilchin, "Theodore Roosevelt, Anglo-American Relations, and the Jamaica Incident of 1907," *Diplomatic History*, 19, 3, Summer 1995, 385-405.

4. William H. Orrett to Robert Bacon, telegram, January 14, 1907, quoted in Orrett to Bacon, January 20, 1907, Numerical and Minor Files of the Department of State, 1906-1910, General Records of the Department of State, Record Group 59 (hereinafter RG 59), 4001/30, National Archives, Washington, D.C.

5. *New York Times*, January 16, 1907.

6. *Kingston Gleaner*, January 18, 1907.

7. Nicholas R. Snyder to Bacon, January 19, 1907, RG 59, 4001/28.

8. Snyder to Bacon, January 22, 1907, RG 59, 4001/13.

9. Orrett to Elihu Root, telegram, January 21, 1907, RG 59, 4001/16.

10. Root to Sir Edward Grey, January 16, 1907, and TR to King Edward VII, January 16, 1907, RG 59, 3892.

11. *Jamaica Daily Telegraph*, January 22, 1907.

12. Orrett to Root, telegram, January 22, 1907, RG 59, 4001/16; Sir J. Alexander Swettenham to Lord Elgin, telegram, February 2, 1907, Colonial Office: Jamaica: Original Correspondence, 1689-1951, Record Class CO (hereinafter simply CO) 351, 19/4392, Public Record Office, Kew, England.

13. Frederick Van Dyne to Assistant Secretary of State, January 15, 1909, RG 59, 4001/154.

14. Theodore Roosevelt, annual message of 1906, quoted in Colonial Office to Foreign Office, February 27, 1907, CO 137, 655/5046.

15. TR to George Otto Trevelyan, November 23, 1906, *Letters of TR*, V, 499.

16. Elgin to Swettenham, telegram, January 16, 1907, in *Jamaica. Correspondence Relating to the Earthquake at Kingston, Jamaica, on 14th January, 1907. Presented to both Houses of Parliament by command of His Majesty. June, 1907*, in Foreign Office: General Correspondence: Political, 1906-1963, Record Class FO (hereinafter simply FO) 371, 358/18547, Public Record Office.

17. Root to Esmé Howard, January 16, 1907, RG 59, 3892/2.

18. Victor H. Metcalf to R. D. Evans, telegram, January 16, 1907, Navy Department papers in RG 59, 4001/147-48.

19. Swettenham to Elgin, telegram, January 16, 1907, CO 137, 655/2214.

20. Swettenham to G. W. E. Griffith, telegram, January 15, 1907, FO 371, 358/4432.

21. Swettenham to Elgin, January 30, 1907, CO 137, 655/5665. See also Swettenham to colonial under secretary, June 13, 1907, FO 371, 358/23710.

22. Griffith to Grey, January 23, 1907, FO 371, 358/4432.

23. Foreign Office to Colonial Office, February 14, 1907, FO 371, 358/4432.

24. Evans to secretary of the navy, January 16, 1907, Navy Department papers in RG 59, 4001/147-48.

25. Griffith to Swettenham, telegram, January 16, 1907, quoted in Griffith to Elgin, February 4, 1907, CO 137, 655/6222.

26. Evans to Charles Magoon, telegram, January 16, 1907, FO 371, 358/4432.

27. Magoon to Griffith, January 17, 1907, FO 371, 358/4432.

28. Howard to Grey, telegram, January 16, 1907, FO 371, 358/1806.

29. Howard to Root, January 16, 1907, RG 59, 3892/8.

30. Howard to Grey, telegram, January 16, 1907, FO 371, 358/1807; Howard to Root, January 17, 1907, RG 59, 4001/2.

31. Navy Department to Evans, telegram, January 17, 1907, quoted in J. E. Pillsbury to Charles H. Davis, telegram, January 17, 1907, Navy Department papers in RG 59, 4001/147-48.

32. See Metcalf to TR, April 23, 1907, FO 371, 358/17129.

33. G. A. Converse to Evans, telegram, January 17, 1907, Navy Department papers in RG 59, 4001/147-48.

34. Metcalf to Evans, telegram, January 17, 1907, quoted in Pillsbury to Davis, telegram, January 17, 1907, Navy Department papers in RG 59, 4001/147-48.

35. Evans to Davis, telegram, January 17, 1907; see also Evans to commanding officer, USS *Yankton*, January 17, 1907, Navy Department papers in RG 59, 4001/147-48.

36. E. A. Anderson to Evans, January 19, 1907, Navy Department papers in RG 59, 4001/147-48.

37. Anderson to Evans, January 29, 1907, Navy Department papers in RG 59, 4001/147-48.

38. Anderson to Evans, January 19, 1907, Navy Department papers in RG 59, 4001/147-48.

39. Anderson to Davis, January 17, 1907, in Naval Records Collection of the Office of Naval Records and Library, Record Group 45, entry 307, "Navy Department, Bureau of Navigation. Copies of Correspondence to and from the Department Relating to the Kingston Disaster. From January 15, 1907 to February 18, 1907," National Archives. (Emphasis added.)

40. "Report of Rear Admiral C. H. Davis, U.S.N., with appendix of reports from other officers in relation to the situation at Kingston subsequent to the earthquake" (hereinafter Davis Report), p. 2, Navy Department papers in RG 59, 4001/147-48.

41. Swettenham to Elgin, January 28, 1907, CO 137, 655/5617; Davis Report, 2.

42. Neither the British nor the American government would ever conduct a formal investigation of the Swettenham incident that was about to occur. However, the archival resources in London and Washington pertaining to the matter are ample. Foremost among these materials is the extensive report prepared within days of the episode by Admiral Davis. Attached to Davis's report were fifty-four appendixes, over half consisting of the reports of other officers participating in the relief mission. The great preponderance of the available evidence tends to corroborate Davis's depiction of his experience in Kingston. Theodore Roosevelt's friend Arthur Lee, one of the first Britons to see the report, was persuaded that it contained "the facts" and described the admiral's behavior in Jamaica as "magnificent throughout." Lee to TR, March 28, 1907, TR Papers, reel 72. Winston Churchill, then the under secretary of state for the colonies and an important contributor to the resolution of the affair, was particularly impressed. "The report of the American Admiral," Churchill observed to his colleagues in the Colonial Office, "seems to justify & explain entirely his actions & motives. They do credit to him." Churchill, minute, March 6, 1907, CO 137, 660/6854. See also Evans to secretary of the navy, January 23, 1907, in Naval Records Collection, RG 45, entry 307. The Davis Report, as one would expect, omits some secondary points that would add little to the admiral's case and is somewhat misleading and self-serving in a couple of places. But its fundamental integrity seems beyond dispute.

The report of Governor Swettenham, contained in a letter to Colonial Secretary Elgin of January 28 (CO 137, 655/5617) and in subsequent letters and telegrams, is, in contrast, extremely unreliable. Important omissions are frequent, and outright falsehoods are not uncommon. As an aid in sorting out the affair, Swettenham's report is as often a hindrance as an asset.

43. Davis Report, 3.

44. Ibid., 3-4.

45. Among the many provisions allotted for distribution were 561 pounds of milk, 560 of bread, 550 of flour, 529 of preserved meat, 350 of biscuits, 214 of coffee, 210 of tomatoes, 207 of sugar, 200 of salt pork, 119 of butter, and 110 of rice. Order issued January 17, 1907, Davis Report, Appendixes K and K1.

46. H. C. Bourne to Swettenham, January 20, 1907, and A. D. Wedderburn to Bourne, January 20, 1907, CO 137, 655/4972.

47. Davis to Evans, January 29, 1907, in Naval Records Collection, RG 45, entry 307.

48. Davis Report, 4.

49. Ibid., 4-5.

50. See note 42, second paragraph.

51. Swettenham to Elgin, January 28, 1907, CO 137, 655/5617.

52. Davis Report, 5.

53. Ibid., 7.

54. Ibid., 5.

55. J. L. Sticht, Davis Report, Appendix B2.

56. See Swettenham to Elgin, January 28, 1907, CO 137, 655/5617. In the documents pertaining to the Jamaica incident, there are innumerable examples of Swettenham's unsympathetic, obsessive, domineering, petty nature. His personal trial and sentencing of the ringleaders of the prison mutiny (to "fifteen lashes each," later "reduced to ten each") —at a time when leadership to combat the far-reaching horror of the earthquake was badly needed—is a very revealing one. Swettenham to Elgin, January 17, 1907, in CO 137, 655/5617.

57. Davis to Evans, January 17, 1907, Davis Report, Appendix G.

58. Evans to Navy Department, telegram, January 18, 1907, RG 59, 4001/8.

59. Orrett to secretary of state, January 17, 1907, RG 59, 4001/25.

60. Davis Report, 6.

61. Swettenham to Elgin, January 28, 1907, CO 137, 655/5617.

62. C. P. Lucas, minute, January 30, 1907, CO 137, 655/3699.

63. Swettenham to Elgin, January 28, 1907, CO 137, 655/5617.

64. Davis Report, 6-7.

65. Ibid., 7-8.

66. Davis to Swettenham, January 17, 1907, Davis Report, Appendix C, and many other sources. (Emphasis added.) See Tilchin, "TR and the British Empire, 1901-1907," 263-64, for the complete text of this letter.

67. Swettenham to Elgin, January 28, 1907, CO 137, 655/5617.

68. Davis Report, 8.

69. Ibid., 8-9.

70. Swettenham to Davis, January 18, 1907, Davis Report, Appendix C1.

71. Davis Report, 9.

72. Swettenham's hostility, however, does not seem to have been *completely* under control. Gunner R. E. Cox, while engaged in blasting walls the morning of the 18th, was called over to Headquarters House to see Swettenham. "You Americans," Cox quoted the governor as saying, "have not authority to do work of any kind in the city. The walls, no matter what their condition remain the property of their owners and the civil authorities are able to do this work when called upon." Davis Report, Appendix A7.

73. J. N. A. Marshall to Swettenham, January 18, 1907, CO 137, 655/4972. Marshall, like Swettenham, seems to have been far more concerned with upholding his own prerogatives

than with addressing the needs of the local population. Issuing a rather incredible indict-
ment, Paymaster E. F. Hall of the *Indiana* observed that "very few of the Colonial or British
troops appear anywhere except at their camp, which is beautifully located, away from the
scene of action and its discomforts. At no place have I seen any of these troops . . .
engaged in cleaning the streets, removing the dead, or seeing that other persons performed
such work, the heaviest part of which has fallen to our officers and men since their
arrival." Davis Report, Appendix B3.

74. Intentionally or otherwise, Swettenham's denial of the Milke incident was as inaccurate as
his letter was scornful. See "Original Declaration of Mr. Oswald Milke," January 23,
1907, enclosed in Orrett to Bacon, January 25, 1907, RG 59, 4001/48-50.

75. Swettenham to Davis, January 18, 1907, Davis Report, Appendix C2, and many other
sources.

76. Swettenham to Elgin, January 28, 1907, CO 137, 655/5617.

77. Davis to Evans, January 29, 1907, in Naval Records Collection, RG 45, entry 307.

78. Davis Report, 9.

79. Davis Report, 7, 9. Detailed evidence of the efficiency and contributions of the American
hospital can be found in the fifteen-page report of Medical Inspector H. E. Ames and in
the eleven-page report of Surgeon O. D. Norton. See Davis Report, Appendixes E, E1.

80. Davis Report, 9.

81. Ibid., 9-10.

82. Davis to Orrett, January 19, 1907, and Davis to commanding officer of USS *Celtic*,
January 19, 1907, Davis Report, Appendixes D, D1.

83. Swettenham to Elgin, January 18, 1907, CO 351, 19/4149.

84. Davis Report, 10.

85. *New York Times*, January 21, 1907.

86. Swettenham to Davis, January 19, 1907, RG 59, 4001/97.

87. Swettenham to Root, telegram, January 20, 1907, RG 59, 4001/7.

88. Swettenham to Elgin, telegram, January 21, 1907, CO 137, 655/2651.

89. Swettenham to Elgin, telegram, January 21, 1907, CO 137, 655/2744.

90. The most compelling evidence that Swettenham probably sensed trouble ahead for himself is a long letter he wrote to C. P. Lucas, his "intimate friend" in the Colonial Office
(Lucas's phrase in minute of January 24, 1907, in CO 137, 655/2972), on January 19.
The subject of this letter was the dispute with the United States over the hiring of
Jamaican laborers for work on the Panama Canal. Its conclusion that America had "no
legitimate cause of complaint against the Government of Jamaica" was not very per-
suasive. Still, Swettenham's conduct with regard to the canal laborers question was, as
the governor seems to have realized, less clearly objectionable than was his letter to
Admiral Davis. So on the very day of Davis's departure from Jamaica, with the earthquake recovery effort continuing to require the governor's undivided attention,
Swettenham spent a large chunk of time addressing a long-simmering controversy
entirely lacking in urgency. It is difficult to avoid the impression that he was seeking both
to create a diversion and to strengthen his own position in the eyes of his superiors.
Afterward, it apparently occurred to Swettenham that the Colonial Office would see the
connection and suspect his motivation. In a follow-up letter of January 28, he referred
to his letter of January 19 as "dated the 16th," the day before Davis's arrival.
Swettenham to Lucas, January 19, 1907; Swettenham to Elgin, January 28, 1907, CO
137, 655/5046. When Elgin later noted the discrepancy, Swettenham offered this plausible but dubious explanation: "I regret that I misquoted the date having forgotten (in the

absence of any office copy) that it had been delayed after completion." Elgin to Swettenham, February 27, 1907, CO 137, 655/5046; Swettenham to Elgin, April 4, 1907, FO 371, 358/24398.

91. C. W. Tait to Davis, January 19, 1907, as published in the *Kingston Gleaner,* January 19, 1907.
92. Norton, Davis Report, Appendix E1.
93. Ames, Davis Report, Appendix E.
94. W. N. McDonnell, Davis Report, Appendix E5.
95. W. Pitt Scott, Davis Report, Appendix A3. (Emphasis in original.)
96. *Jamaica Daily Telegraph,* January 22, 1907.
97. Scott Henry Perky to TR, January 23, 1907, RG 59, 4001/83-85.
98. *New York Times,* January 23, 1907.
99. George Solomon to *Jamaica Daily Telegraph,* January 28, 1907.
100. Vernon E. Grosett to *Jamaica Daily Telegraph,* January 28, 1907.
101. Davis to Tait, January 19, 1907, as published in the *Kingston Gleaner,* January 19, 1907.
102. Davis Report, 11-14.
103. Beehler to Navy Department, telegram, January 20, 1907, in Naval Records Collection, RG 45, entry 307.
104. R. W. Meade to secretary of the navy, March 4, 1895, Navy Department papers in RG 59, 4001/147-48.
105. F. Napier Broome to Meade, March 5, 1895, Navy Department papers in RG 59, 4001/147-48.

Chapter 7

1. *New York Times,* January 21, 1907.
2. Lord Elgin to J. Alexander Swettenham, two telegrams, January 21, 1907, CO 137, 655/2557.
3. R. B. Haldane to Elihu Root, telegram, January 21, 1907, RG 59, 4001/6.
4. Sir Edward Grey to Esmé Howard, telegram, January 21, 1907, British correspondence in RG 59, 4001.
5. Howard to Robert Bacon, January 21, 1907, RG 59, 4001/12.
6. *New York Times,* January 22, 1907.
7. Bacon to Haldane, telegram, January 21, 1907, RG 59, 4001/6.
8. See Howard to Grey, telegram, January 21, 1907, FO 371, 358/2580.
9. Bacon to Howard, January 22, 1907, FO 371, 358/2735. (Emphasis added.)
10. *New York Times,* January 24, 1907.
11. John R. Carter to Root, telegram, January 22, 1907, RG 59, 4001/15.
12. Bacon to Carter, telegram, January 24, 1907, RG 59, 4001/15. (Emphasis added.)
13. Elgin to Swettenham, telegram, January 22, 1907, *Jamaica. Correspondence Relating to the Resignation by Sir A. Swettenham of his Office as Governor of Jamaica. Presented to Both Houses of Parliament by Command of His Majesty. April, 1907,* 1-2, British correspondence in RG 59, 4001.
14. Swettenham to Elgin, telegram, January 22, 1907, CO 137, 655/2891.
15. Swettenham to Elgin, telegram, January 22, 1907, CO 137, 655/2890.
16. Winston Churchill, minute, January 23, 1907, CO 137, 655/2890.
17. Sydney Olivier, minute, January 23, 1907, CO 137, 655/2891.
18. F. J. S. Hopwood, minute, January 23, 1907, CO 137, 655/2891.
19. Swettenham to Elgin, telegram, January 23, 1907, *Jamaica. Correspondence Relating to Resignation of Swettenham, April, 1907,* 4.
20. Swettenham to Elgin, telegram, January 23, 1907, in ibid., 4.

21. Elgin to Swettenham, telegram, January 24, 1907, CO 137, 655/2972.

22. Foreign Office to Howard, telegram, January 24, 1907, FO 371, 358/2795.

23. Howard to Bacon, January 24, 1907, RG 59, 4001/23. It is indicative of the British government's emphasis on avoiding any complications in wrapping up the incident that neither the Foreign Office's telegram to Howard nor Howard's note to Bacon included Swettenham's qualifier ("At the instance of the Secretary of State for the Colonies"). The omission was commented on by Swettenham's friend in the Colonial Office, C. P. Lucas, in a minute of February 11: "I think—with all deference—that the governor had a right to expect that his retraction would be made in the terms which he most carefully employed and would have good reason to resent that other terms were used." Minute in CO 351, 19/FO5176.

24. Charles Hardinge to Grey, January 24, 1907, FO 371, 358/2795.

25. Howard to Grey, January 24, 1907, FO 371, 358/3865.

26. Bacon to Carter, telegram, January 24, 1907, RG 59, 4001/22A.

27. See Carter to Grey, January 25, 1907, and Hardinge to Carter, January 25, 1907, FO 371, 358/3400.

28. Carter to Root, telegram, January 25, 1907, RG 59, 4001/24.

29. Carter to Root, telegram, January 27, 1907, RG 59, 4001/26.

30. Unattributable note, January 28, 1907, RG 59, 4001/26.

31. Root to American embassy in London, telegram, January 28, 1907, RG 59, 4001/26.

32. Root to Howard, January 29, 1907, RG 59, 4001/23. (Emphasis added.)

33. *Jamaica Daily Telegraph*, January 31, 1907.

34. Carter to Root, January 25, 1907, RG 59, 4001/69.

35. James Bryce, speech to Reform Club, Manchester, January 25, 1907, quoted in *New York Times*, January 26, 1907.

36. Sir Percy Sanderson to Howard, January 24, 1907, and Howard to Grey, January 26, 1907, FO 371, 358/5357.

37. Perkins, *Great Rapprochement*, 6.

38. *New York Evening Mail*, quoted in *Jamaica Daily Telegraph*, January 31, 1907.

39. The *Commercial*, quoted in ibid.

40. The *Courier-Journal*, quoted in ibid.

41. *New York Globe*, quoted in ibid.

42. The *Evening Times*, quoted in ibid.

43. The *Evening Star*, quoted in ibid.

44. *New York Times*, January 24, 1907.

45. *Harper's Weekly*, February 9, 1907, 187.

46. *New York Press*, quoted in *Jamaica Daily Telegraph*, January 31, 1907.

47. The *Inter-Ocean*, quoted in ibid.

48. The same was true among important American political figures. On January 22, the quixotic, anti-navalist Republican Senator Eugene Hale sent a note to Secretary Root: "Events down there are showing that we should think twice before taking possession of a foreign town and undertake [*sic*] to establish order. What would have happened if Great Britain had sent a fleet into San Francisco and taken charge there?" Robert Bacon appended a note of his own to Root, then still in Canada: "This is the only disagreeable thing we have heard from our own people." RG 59, 4001/17.

49. *London Morning Post*, quoted in *Jamaica Daily Telegraph*, January 31, 1907.

50. *London Daily Mail*, quoted in ibid.

51. *London Tribune*, quoted in ibid.

52. *London Times,* January 21, 1907.
53. *London Daily Graphic,* quoted in *Jamaica Daily Telegraph,* January 31, 1907.
54. *Pall Mall Gazette,* as reported in *Jamaica Daily Telegraph,* January 26, 1907.
55. "I note in the public press," Admiral R. D. Evans wrote to Secretary of the Navy Victor H. Metcalf on January 29, "that the men landed at Kingston are frequently referred to as marines. . . . The landing parties of every nature were composed entirely of bluejackets under the command of naval officers." Naval Records Collection, RG 45, entry 307.
56. *London Globe,* as reported in *Jamaica Daily Telegraph,* January 26, 1907.
57. *Jamaica Times,* January 26, 1907.
58. *Daily Gleaner,* February 12, 1907.
59. *Daily Gleaner,* February 27, 1907.
60. *Singapore Free Press,* April 5, 1907.
61. *Quebec Chronicle,* as reported in *Jamaica Daily Telegraph,* January 31, 1907.
62. *Toronto Saturday Night,* January 26, 1907.
63. *Straits Times,* January 22, 1907.
64. *St. John's Evening Telegram,* quoted in *Jamaica Daily Telegraph,* January 31, 1907.
65. Swettenham to Elgin, telegram, January 26, 1907, CO 137, 655/3153.
66. Elgin to Swettenham, telegram, January 26, 1907, and Hopwood, minute, January 26, 1907, CO 137, 655/3153.
67. Swettenham to Elgin, telegram, January 27, 1907, CO 137, 655/3264.
68. Elgin to Swettenham, telegram, January 27, 1907, CO 137, 655/3264.
69. Swettenham to Elgin, telegram, January 27, 1907, CO 137, 655/3216.
70. Lucas and Hopwood, minutes, January 28, 1907, CO 137, 655/3216.
71. Elgin to Swettenham, telegram, January 28, 1907, CO 137, 655/3216.
72. Swettenham to Elgin, telegram, January 28, 1907, CO 137, 655/3498.
73. William H. Orrett to Bacon, January 28, 1907, RG 59, 4001/77.
74. Swettenham to Elgin, telegram, January 28, 1907, CO 137, 655/3699.
75. Swettenham to Elgin, telegram, January 30, 1907, CO 137, 655/3942; see Olivier, minute, January 30, 1907, CO 137, 655/3942.
76. Churchill, minute, January 30, 1907, CO 137, 655/3699.
77. Elgin to Swettenham, telegram, February 1, 1907, CO 137, 655/3942.
78. Swettenham to Elgin, telegram, February 3, 1907, CO 137, 655/4571 and 4574.
79. Elgin to Swettenham, telegram, February 5, 1907, CO 137, 655/4574.
80. Swettenham to Elgin, telegram, February 5, 1907, and Olivier, minute, February 7, 1907, CO 137, 655/4713.
81. Metcalf to Charles H. Davis, February 1, 1907, Navy Department papers in RG 59, 4001/147-48.
82. TR to George Otto Trevelyan, February 4, 1907, *Letters of TR,* V, 579.
83. Trevelyan to TR, February 23, 1907, TR Papers, reel 72.
84. TR to Arthur Lee, February 12, 1907, TR Papers, reel 344.
85. Lee to TR, March 28, 1907, TR Papers, reel 72.
86. Howard to Grey, February 4, 1907, FO 371, 358/5361.
87. Howard to Grey, telegram, February 10, 1907, FO 371, 358/4525.
88. Grey to Howard, telegram, February 11, 1907, FO 371, 358/4525.
89. E. Gorst to Howard, February 11, 1907, FO 371, 358/4865.
90. Whitelaw Reid to Root, telegram, February 11, 1907, RG 59, 4001/89.
91. Hopwood, February 12, 1907, with endorsements by Churchill, February 15, and by Elgin, February 16, minutes in CO 351, 19/FO5406.

92. Gorst, minute, February 18, 1907, FO 371, 358/5361.
93. Hardinge to Hopwood, February 20, 1907, FO 371, 358/5361.
94. Hopwood to Hardinge, February 21, 1907, FO 371, 358/5361. (Emphasis added.)
95. Reid to Root, telegram, February 22, 1907, RG 59, 4001/102.

Chapter 8

1. No such letter survives either in the Theodore Roosevelt Papers or in the papers of the Foreign Office touching on the Jamaica incident.
2. TR to Henry Cabot Lodge, February 28, 1907, TR Papers, reel 345.
3. TR to Sir Edward Grey, February 28, 1907, *Letters of TR*, V, 601-2.
4. Arthur Lee to TR, March 28, 1907, TR Papers, reel 72.
5. On March 14 M.P. Jesse Collings had agitated briefly by asking "if it is in accordance with international law and international etiquette for the admiral of a Foreign ship to land an armed force in a British Colony without the permission of the Governor of that Colony." The Foreign Office answered "in the negative," but also remarked that "if . . . the Right Honorable member is referring to the Jamaica incident, . . . the American Admiral understood that he had received sufficient authority for landing his men." FO 371, 358/8570.
6. Reported to Elihu Root by John R. Carter, March 15, 1907, RG 59, 4001/119.
7. J. Alexander Swettenham to Lord Elgin, January 30, 1907, CO 137, 655/5669.
8. Swettenham to Elgin, January 30, 1907, CO 137, 655/5670.
9. Swettenham to Elgin, January 31, 1907, CO 137, 655/5671.
10. Elgin to Swettenham, three letters dated February 8, 1907, CO 137, 655/4574; and Elgin to Swettenham, two letters dated February 22, 1907, CO 137, 655/5666 and CO 137, 655/5669-71.
11. Actually, the British government did support Swettenham's position on Jamaican labor for canal work. It was "part of a considered policy . . . approved by Lord Elgin's predecessors and endorsed by him," E. Gorst of the Foreign Office informed Ambassador James Bryce in a letter of March 11, and Bryce should be prepared to uphold it. "It is, however, unnecessary," Gorst tellingly added, "that you should initiate a discussion on this subject." CO 137, 661/9312.
12. Swettenham to Elgin, February 26, 1907, FO 371, 358/11510. (Emphasis added.)
13. Elgin, minute, March 20, 1907, CO 137, 656/9294.
14. Swettenham would elaborate on this point in a letter to Elgin of March 18, citing a colonial regulation prohibiting the type of communication Bourne had had with Davis, and asserting that Wedderburn carried no more weight than "other unofficial bystanders" present when Bourne and Davis met. FO 371, 358/17343.
15. Swettenham to Elgin, February 28, 1907, FO 371, 358/11510.
16. F. J. S. Hopwood, minute, March 21, 1907, and Elgin, minute, March 23, 1907, CO 137, 656/9976.
17. Swettenham to Elgin, telegram, March 1, 1907, CO 351, 19/7809.
18. Elgin to Swettenham, telegram, March 4, 1907, British correspondence in RG 59, 4001.
19. Swettenham to Elgin, telegram, March 6, 1907, CO 351, 19/8352.
20. See Elgin to Swettenham, April 5, 1907, FO 371, 358/17343; Elgin to Swettenham, telegram, April 6, 1907, FO 371, 358/17343; Swettenham to Elgin, telegram, April 8, 1907, CO 351, 19/12496; Elgin to Swettenham, April 12, 1907, FO 371, 358/17343.
21. Swettenham to Elgin, telegram, April 9, 1907, CO 351, 19/12601.
22. Elgin to Swettenham, telegram, April 13, 1907, FO 371, 358/17343.
23. Swettenham to Elgin, telegram, April 17, 1907, CO 351, 19/13683.

24. Elgin to Swettenham, telegram, April 22, 1907, CO 137, 657/13683.
25. Grey to Bryce, telegram, April 12, 1907, FO 371, 358/11684.
26. Bryce to Grey, telegram, April 14, 1907, FO 371, 358/11912.
27. Whitelaw Reid to Root, April 20, 1907, RG 59, 4001/124-25.
28. Winston Churchill addressing Parliament, April 10, 1907, FO 371, 358/17343.
29. Churchill addressing Parliament, April 30, 1907, FO 371, 358/17343.
30. Churchill addressing Parliament, April 10, 1907, FO 371, 358/17343.
31. Sir Gilbert Parker and Churchill addressing Parliament, April 30, 1907, FO 371, 358/17343. The next day Whitelaw Reid endeavored to reshape, by rendering more multidimensional, Roosevelt's view of Churchill. The ambassador was not successful. See discussion of Reid to TR, May 1, 1907, TR Papers, reel 73, in chapter 11, pp. 230.
32. Swettenham to Elgin, April 4, 1907, FO 371, 358/17343. St. Matthew XXIII. 4. reads as follows: "For they bind heavy burdens and grievous to be borne, and lay *them* on men's shoulders; but they *themselves* will not move them with one of their fingers." (Emphasis in New Testament.)
33. Churchill, April 27, 1907, and others, minutes in CO 137, 657/14271.
34. Elgin to Swettenham, telegram, February 8, 1907, CO 137, 655/4574.
35. Elgin to Swettenham, February 8, 1907, CO 137, 655/4574.
36. Swettenham to Elgin, two letters, April 24, 1907, FO 371, 358/17343 and 24398.
37. Churchill, May 13, 1907, and others, minutes in CO 137, 657/16456.
38. Swettenham to Elgin, May 2, 1907, FO 371, 358/24398. (Emphasis added.)
39. Swettenham to Elgin, April 25, 1907, CO 351, 19/16461.
40. Churchill, minute, May 25, 1907, CO 137, 658/17940.
41. See P. S. C., minute, July 22, 1907, FO 371, 358/24398.
42. Frank Swettenham to *London Times*, and editorial response, *London Times*, July 20, 1907.
43. Davis had clearly gained favor with the president through his performance in Jamaica and the report he had submitted. On April 10 Roosevelt told Lodge that Davis would replace his commander, Admiral Evans, if the latter chose to retire. See TR to Lodge, April 10, 1907, *Letters of TR*, V, 645-46. As it turned out, Davis retired in August 1907 and Evans did so a year later.
44. TR to Lee, April 8, 1907, *Letters of TR*, V, 644.
45. TR to George Otto Trevelyan, April 10, 1907, TR Papers, reel 345.
46. Victor H. Metcalf to TR, April 23, 1907, and TR's approval, April 23, 1907, in FO 371, 358/17129. The law of January 18 authorized the president "to use and distribute among the suffering and destitute people of the Island of Jamaica, such provisions, clothing, medicines, and other necessary articles belonging to . . . the naval establishment as may be necessary for the purpose of succoring the people who are in peril and threatened with starvation on said island in consequence of the recent earthquake and attending conflagration."
47. Root to Bryce, May 1, 1907, FO 371, 358/17129.
48. Bryce to Grey, May 9, 1907, FO 371, 358/17129; Bryce to Root, July 6, 1907, RG 59, 4001/137.
49. Grey to Reid, June 13, 1907, FO 371, 358/18547.
50. Reid to Root, June 17, 1907, RG 59, 4001/132-33.
51. Reid to TR, April 17, 1907, May 1, 1907, and May 24, 1907, TR Papers, reels 73-74.
52. TR to Trevelyan, February 4, 1907, *Letters of TR*, V, 579. (See chapter 7, p. 148.)
53. It was first published in Tilchin, "TR and the British Empire, 1901-1907," 344-45, where its complete text is reproduced.

54. TR to Root, April 10, 1907, TR Papers, reel 345.
55. Bryce to Grey, telegram, April 11, 1907, FO 371, 358/11649.
56. Grey to Bryce, telegram, April 12, 1907, FO 371, 358/11684. (See above, p. 157.)
57. TR to Department of State, August 24, 1907, TR Papers, reel 346.
58. Alvey A. Adee to Metcalf, September 4, 1907, RG 59, 4001/140.
59. Adee to TR, September 13, 1907, RG 59, 4001/143.
60. Metcalf to Root, September 24, 1907, RG 59, 4001/147-48.
61. See W. I. [or T.] G. [or C.] to Robert Bacon, January 26, 1909, RG 59, 4001/140.
62. Bryce sent a copy of this article to Grey. The ambassador thought the *Post*'s decision to run such an article at that time may have been due to Admiral Davis's recent retirement. Bryce to Grey, August 31, 1907, FO 371, 358/30617.
63. Quoted in Frank Ninkovich, "Theodore Roosevelt: Civilization as Ideology," *Diplomatic History*, 10, 3, Summer 1986, 235.
64. See chapter 7, p. 140.

Chapter 9

1. TR to Henry Cabot Lodge, June 24, 1908, *Letters of TR*, VI, 1096.
2. TR to Kermit Roosevelt, January 10, 1909, *Letters of TR*, VI, 1473.
3. Neu, *Uncertain Friendship*, 19.
4. TR to John St. Loe Strachey, February 22, 1907, *Letters of TR*, V, 597; TR to Sir Edward Grey, February 28, 1907, *Letters of TR*, V, 600.
5. See TR to James Norris Gillett, March 9, March 11, March 12, and March 14, 1907, *Letters of TR*, V, 608-10, 610-14, 614-15, 618-19.
6. "Both the President and Secretary of State," Charles Neu explains, "accepted the assurances of the Japanese government and did not yet understand how complex the task of stopping the immigration of Japanese laborers would be. Nor did they foresee how even a trickle of immigrants would feed the growing anti-Japanese movement in California. In retrospect, . . . the Gentlemen's Agreement of February, 1907, only began the task of keeping Japanese laborers out of the United States. But to Roosevelt and Root it seemed, in the spring of 1907, to have largely ended it." *Uncertain Friendship*, 77-78.
7. Roosevelt made similar statements in several other letters. See TR to Elihu Root, July 13, 1907, *Letters of TR*, V, 717; to Lawrence O. Murray, July 13, 1907, V, 719; to William Kent, January 22, 1909, VI, 1478-79; to William Howard Taft, February 13, 1909, VI, 1519.
8. TR to Kentaro Kaneko, May 23, 1907, *Letters of TR*, V, 671-72.
9. TR to Cecil Spring Rice, July 1, 1907, *Letters of TR*, V, 699.
10. TR to Strachey, September 8, 1907, *Letters of TR*, V, 787-88.
11. TR to Lodge, September 11, 1907, *Letters of TR*, V, 790.
12. TR to Root, November 19, 1907, *Letters of TR*, V, 851-52.
13. Neu, *Uncertain Friendship*, 184-85, 194.
14. Ibid., 194.
15. TR to Wilfrid Laurier, February 1, 1908, *Letters of TR*, VI, 917-18.
16. This letter, as Charles Neu points out, exaggerated the degree of Canadian initiative and understated the degree of American initiative behind Mackenzie King's visits to the United States and the subsequent coordination of Canadian and American policy. Neu ponders the reasons for Roosevelt's seemingly gratuitous "prevarications," speculating that perhaps the president, ever mindful of the potential domestic political consequences of his actions in foreign policy, was "providing against the contingency of a future public debate [in England, most likely] over King's mission and his role in it." *Uncertain Friendship*, 196-97.

It is possible nevertheless that Roosevelt's manner of orchestrating King's visits to Washington and London may have been sufficiently deft and indirect to validate—if only in a technical sense—the claims he later put forward in a letter to Whitelaw Reid: "that Mackenzie King had come down here from Laurier without my knowing anything whatever about the circumstances; that he saw me without any suggestion on my part; and that I was informed he was to go to London before I entered into any correspondence with Laurier in the matter." TR to Reid, March 30, 1908, *Letters of TR*, VI, 985.

17. TR to Arthur Lee, February 2, 1908, *Letters of TR*, VI, 919-21.

18. Neu, *Uncertain Friendship*, 197-201.

19. Ibid., 202-4.

20. Ibid., 204-5.

21. Lee to TR, February 21, 1908, TR Papers, reel 81; TR to Lee, March 7, 1908, *Letters of TR*, VI, 965.

22. Neu, *Uncertain Friendship*, 230-31.

23. King Edward VII to TR, March 5, 1908, TR Papers, reel 81. However, the British government did act to prevent Canadian authorities from extending a similar invitation to the fleet. British opposition to such a visit evaporated when Japan invited the fleet to its shores. England then proposed a visit by the fleet to British Columbia—a proposal declined by the United States government, which was eager to move the fleet across the Pacific.

24. Neu, *Uncertain Friendship*, 205.

25. TR to Lee, April 8, 1908, *Letters of TR*, VI, 996.

26. Lee to TR, March 31, 1908, TR Papers, reel 82. (Emphasis in original.)

27. TR to Lee, April 8, 1908, *Letters of TR*, VI, 995-96.

28. Neu, *Uncertain Friendship*, 208-10.

29. TR to Henry White, April 27, 1908, *Letters of TR*, VI, 1017-18.

30. Quoted in *Letters of TR*, VI, 1108n. Several months later Roosevelt declared in a letter to Whitelaw Reid: "The foreign policy in which I believe is in very fact the policy of speaking softly and carrying a big stick. I want to make it evident to every foreign nation that I intend to do justice; and neither to wrong them nor to hurt their self-respect; but that on the other hand, I am both entirely ready and entirely able to see that our rights are maintained in their turn." TR to Reid, December 4, 1908, *Letters of TR*, VI, 1410.

31. Neu, *Uncertain Friendship*, 208.

32. TR to Reid, August 20, 1908, *Letters of TR*, VI, 1188; Neu, *Uncertain Friendship*, 258. In Sydney on August 20, according to the *New York Times*, "half a million people assembled to give the visitors a royal welcome." Prime Minister Deakin claimed "that for months past the hearts of the people of New South Wales have throbbed with pleasurable anticipation of this visit." *New York Times*, August 20, 1908.

33. James Bryce to TR, August 29, 1908, TR Papers, reel 84.

34. TR to Bryce, September 7, 1908, *Letters of TR*, VI, 1210. Referring happily to "our kinsmen on the other side of the globe," a *New York Times* editorial attached strategic importance to the growing Australian-American connection: "As our battleships, carrying a message of peace around the world, dropped anchor in the broad harbor of Sydney, the cheers and salutes from the shores had a significance which will not be missed by the nations." *New York Times*, August 20, 1908.

35. Neu, *Uncertain Friendship*, 269-70.

36. TR to George Otto Trevelyan, November 6, 1908, *Letters of TR*, VI, 1330.

37. Neu, *Uncertain Friendship*, 318.

38. Reid to TR, November 24, 1908, TR Papers, reel 86.

39. Lee to TR, December 1, 1908, TR Papers, reel 86.

40. TR to Lee, December 20, 1908, *Letters of TR*, VI, 1432. (Emphasis in original.)

41. See TR to Gillett, telegrams of January 16, January 26, January 27, February 4, February 6, and February 10, 1909, and letters of January 16 and January 26, 1909, *Letters of TR*, VI, 1477-78, 1483-86, 1502, 1505, 1517. See also TR to Philip Ackley Stanton, telegrams of February 6 and February 8, 1909, *Letters of TR*, VI, 1505-6, 1509-10.

42. TR to Lee, February 7, 1909, *Letters of TR*, VI, 1508. For an in-depth presentation of TR's views on Japanese-American relations as his presidency wound down, see TR to Philander Chase Knox, February 8, 1909, *Letters of TR*, VI, 1510-14. Roosevelt was very worried about the future and offered detailed advice to the incoming administration on how best to deal with the multifaceted challenges inherent in managing this crucial and delicate relationship.

43. TR to Root, July 13, 1907, *Letters of TR*, V, 718-19.

44. Reid to TR, August 22, 1908, TR Papers, reel 84. Taking an even longer view, in January 1909 the *London Times* lamented that "the fisheries question . . . has been for a century . . . a source of international friction which is always present, and which has sometimes threatened to become virulent." *London Times*, January 21, 1909.

45. Reid to TR, May 1, 1907, TR Papers, reel 73.

46. Grey to Reid, June 20, 1907, TR Papers, reel 74.

47. Reid to Grey, July 12, 1907, TR Papers, reel 75.

48. Reid to TR, two letters, July 17 and 19, 1907, TR Papers, reel 75.

49. Reid to TR, July 19, 1907, TR Papers, reel 75.

50. William N. Tilchin, "Theodore Roosevelt," in Frank W. Thackeray and John E. Findling, eds., *Statesmen Who Changed the World: A Bio-Bibliographical Dictionary of Diplomacy* (Westport, CT, 1993), 483. See TR to Lodge, January 6, 1905, *Letters of TR*, IV, 1094; TR to Lyman Abbott, June 8, 1905, IV, 1208; TR to Grey, February 28, 1907, V, 601.

51. TR to Reid, July 29, 1907, *Letters of TR*, V, 732-33. (Emphasis added.)

52. Reid to TR, August 9, 1907, TR Papers, reel 76.

53. Reid to TR, August 28, 1907, TR Papers, reel 76. Actually, Bond fought hard against the American proposal for arbitration as well as the renewal of the modus vivendi. But "he was unable to affect the [modus vivendi], or, ultimately, to prevent the arbitration." Morison et al., *Letters of TR*, V, 790n.

54. Reid to TR, August 22, 1908, TR Papers, reel 84. As late as January 1909, a *New York Times* editorial described Bond as "irreconcilable" and as "unalterably opposed to an agreement satisfactory to England and the United States." *New York Times*, January 20, 1909.

55. *London Times*, January 25, 1909. (Emphasis added.)

56. *London Times*, January 27, 1909.

57. Alexander DeConde concisely highlights the tribunal's decision: "The most important feature of the award sustained Britain's right to make and enforce local fishing regulations, but the regulations had to be reasonable. If the United States contested their reasonableness, then the objections would go to a permanent mixed fishery commission that would determine who was right." In addition, "the tribunal ruled that bays less than ten miles wide at the mouth were inshore waters and hence closed to American fishermen. When the mouth exceeded ten miles, the area of local jurisdiction was three miles along the shore of the bay and Americans could fish in the bay beyond the three-mile limit." *History of American Foreign Policy*, I, 364-65.

Chapter 10

1. John Kieran and Arthur Daley, *The Story of the Olympic Games, 776 B.C. to 1964* (Philadelphia, 1965), 63.

2. *New York Times*, July 25, 1908.

3. Kieran and Daley, *Olympic Games*, 65-66.

4. Ibid., 63-64, 67.

5. David Wallechinsky, *The Complete Book of the Olympics* (Boston, 1992), 98.

6. *New York Times*, July 24, 1908.

7. Wallechinsky, *Complete Book of Olympics*, 20.

8. Kieran and Daley, *Olympic Games*, 69.

9. Wallechinsky, *Complete Book of Olympics*, 20.

10. *London Times*, July 24, 1908.

11. *New York Times*, July 24, 1908; *London Times*, July 24, 1908.

12. Kieran and Daley, *Olympic Games*, 69.

13. Wallechinsky, *Complete Book of Olympics*, 20.

14. *New York Times*, July 24, 1908.

15. Carpenter insisted on his innocence: While "I certainly ran wide," the charges of "'boring' or pocketing" were "ridiculous. . . . We just raced him off his feet and he could not stand the pace." *New York Times*, July 24, 1908.

16. *New York Times*, July 24, 1908.

17. *New York Times*, July 25, 1908.

18. Wallechinsky, *Complete Book of Olympics*, 54.

19. Ibid., 55.

20. Kieran and Daley, *Olympic Games*, 72.

21. *London Times*, July 25, 1908. Pietri, who recovered quickly from his exhaustion, became the object of immense sympathy and admiration, especially in Britain. On July 25 he "was presented with a special gold cup by the Queen." Wallechinsky, *Complete Book of Olympics*, 55.

22. Kieran and Daley, *Olympic Games*, 72.

23. *New York Times*, July 25, 1908.

24. *New York Times*, July 26, 1908.

25. *London Times*, July 25, 1908.

26. *New York Times*, July 26, 1908.

27. *New York Times*, July 31, 1908.

28. *New York Times*, August 2, 1908.

29. *New York Times*, August 8, 1908. (Emphasis added.) Many Americans, of course, were put off and embarrassed by such talk. The *Outlook*, for example, criticized American officials' "sneering, quarrelsome, and unsportsmanlike assertions" and expressed "regret that the American record in London should have been marred by querulous talk." *Outlook*, 89, 14, August 1, 1908, 739.

30. *New York Times*, July 26, 1908.

31. Arnaldo Testi, "The Gender of Reform Politics: Theodore Roosevelt and the Culture of Masculinity," *Journal of American History*, 81, 4, March 1995, 1522.

32. TR, address to Georgetown College, June 14, 1906, *TR Cyclopedia*, 31.

33. TR, statement of February 1, 1909, quoted in *Letters of TR*, VI, 1500n.

34. TR, *Harper's Weekly*, December 23, 1893, p. 1236, in *TR Cyclopedia*, 581; TR, 1905, *TR Cyclopedia*, 582.

35. TR, *Outlook*, October 21, 1911, p. 409, in *TR Cyclopedia*, 581.

36. TR, statement of February 1, 1909, quoted in *Letters of TR*, VI, 1500n.

37. TR to Speck von Sternburg, July 19, 1902, *Letters of TR*, III, 297.

38. TR, February 15, 1904, foreword to *The Master of the Game* by Edward, second Duke of York, *TR Cyclopedia*, 31.

39. TR to Theodore Roosevelt, Jr., October 4, 1903, *Letters of TR*, III, 614. (Emphasis added.)

40. See, for example, TR, annual message as governor, Albany, January 3, 1900, *TR Cyclopedia*, 32; TR, 1905, *TR Cyclopedia*, 582; TR to Theodore Roosevelt, Jr., November 27, 1908, *Letters of TR*, VI, 1387.

41. TR to Whitelaw Reid, August 20, 1908, *Letters of TR*, VI, 1190.

42. James E. Sullivan to TR, telegram, July 25, 1908, and TR to Sullivan, telegram, July 27, 1908, TR Papers, reel 428.

43. Reid to TR, August 11, 1908, TR Papers, reel 84. (Emphasis in original.)

44. TR to Reid, August 20, 1908, *Letters of TR*, VI, 1190.

45. TR to Reid, August 20, 1908, *Letters of TR*, VI, 1186.

46. Although "just come" conceivably could have meant two or three days ago, it probably had not. Roosevelt was not prone to imprecision in his use of language. And his letter to Buell contained information not offered by Reid—for example, a reference to "stimulants administered to the Italian" during the marathon. TR to George Candee Buell, August 18, 1908, *Letters of TR*, VI, 1182.

47. Neither Buell's letter nor the enclosures accompanying it survive in the Theodore Roosevelt Papers. There is no mystery, because Roosevelt's letter to Buell contains this sentence: "I re-enclose you these papers as you request." TR to Buell, August 18, 1908, *Letters of TR*, VI, 1183.

48. TR to Buell, August 18, 1908, *Letters of TR*, VI, 1181-85.

49. *New York Times*, August 30, 1908.

50. TR to Sullivan, August 24, 1908, TR Papers, reel 350.

51. *New York Times*, September 1, 1908.

52. *New York Times*, September 2, 1908.

53. TR to Sullivan, September 3, 1908, TR Papers, reel 351.

54. TR to Sullivan, September 1, 1908, TR Papers, reel 351.

55. Arthur Lee to TR, September 6, 1908, TR Papers, reel 84.

56. TR to Lee, September 17, 1908, TR Papers, reel 351.

57. It is almost certain that Roosevelt received Cook's letter *after* writing to Lee on September 17. Cook mailed his letter to the White House, to which TR did not return from Oyster Bay until September 23. It does seem likely that Roosevelt's response to his close friend Lee would have mentioned or at least referred obliquely to Cook's letter had TR seen it beforehand.

58. Theodore A. Cook to TR, September 8, 1908, TR Papers, reel 84.

59. TR to Cook, October 20, 1908, TR Papers, reel 351.

60. Between August 1908 and January 1909, Sullivan wrote a number of letters to Roosevelt. Very strangely, however, while the Theodore Roosevelt Papers contain eleven letters from TR to Sullivan written during these months (with Roosevelt usually specifying that he is replying to a letter from Sullivan), this collection appears to contain *none* of Sullivan's letters to the president. None of Sullivan's letters from these months is listed in the *Index to the Theodore Roosevelt Papers*. Perhaps these letters were accumulated in a separate file, which then somehow was lost to the historical record.

61. TR to Sullivan, November 6, 1908, TR Papers, reel 352.

62. Cook, annotated rough proofs of "The Americans at the Olympic Games," sent to TR, November 2, 1908, TR Papers, reel 85.

63. On November 12 Cook mailed TR page proofs, projecting December 5 as the date of publication. Cook to TR, November 12, 1908, TR Papers, reel 85.

64. Cook to TR, November 2, 1908, TR Papers, reel 85.

65. TR to Cook, November 17, 1908, TR Papers, reel 352. (Emphasis added.)

66. Cook to TR, November 26, 1908, TR Papers, reel 86.

67. Sullivan to TR, November 13, 1908, referred to in TR to Sullivan, November 15, 1908, TR Papers, reel 352.

68. TR to Sullivan, November 15, 1908, TR Papers, reel 352.

69. TR to Sullivan, November 17, 1908, TR Papers, reel 352.

70. *New York Times,* November 17, 1908.

71. *London Times,* November 17, 1908.

72. TR to Sullivan, November 19, 1908, TR Papers, reel 352.

73. TR to Sullivan, November 23, 1908, TR Papers, reel 352.

74. TR to James Bryce, November 25, 1908, *Letters of TR,* VI, 1381-82.

75. Sullivan to TR, November 24, 1908, referred to in TR to Sullivan, November 25, 1908, TR Papers, reel 352.

76. TR to Sullivan, November 25, 1908, TR Papers, reel 352.

77. TR to Reid, November 26, 1908, *Letters of TR,* VI, 1384.

78. The visit with Bryce the evening of November 26 is corroborated by TR to Theodore Roosevelt, Jr., November 27, 1908, *Letters of TR,* VI, 1387.

79. TR to Reid, November 26, 1908, *Letters of TR,* VI, 1385. It appears as if Bryce, while a large improvement over Durand, had never quite measured up to Roosevelt's standards and expectations for a British ambassador to the United States. The following remark in a letter of July 1907 to Cecil Spring Rice is suggestive: "Bryce is doing well, but you would do even better, and naturally I would give anything if you could be here." TR to Spring Rice, July 1, 1907, *Letters of TR,* V, 699.

80. Reid to TR, November 18, 1908, TR Papers, reel 86.

81. TR to Reid, November 26, 1908, *Letters of TR,* VI, 1384-85.

82. See above, p. 202. Actually, Cook did violate his pledge that "I shall never trouble you with the subject again," for on January 4, 1909, he wrote to Roosevelt once more. Cook excused himself, as follows: "I had hoped that I should not be obliged to mention the Olympic Games to you again, and I still have no desire whatever to 'draw you into any controversy', though I must point out that I only address you as President of the American Olympic Committee." Sullivan, Gustavus Kirby, and Joseph Maccabe were continuing to infuriate British athletic officials—in Cook's case, to the point where he could not restrain himself, despite his earlier promise, from disclosing and illustrating this fact to Roosevelt. TR Papers, reel 87. The president did not reply to Cook's letter.

83. Reid to TR, December 21, 1908, TR Papers, reel 87. Reid starkly displayed some of his prejudices and class biases in this letter when he derisively remarked upon the marathon contestants—"an Italian pastry cook," "an Irish-American clerk in a dry goods shop," and "the Indian"—who had turned professional after the Olympic games.

84. TR to Reid, January 6, 1909, *Letters of TR,* VI, 1465.

Chapter 11

1. TR to William II, January 8, 1907, *Letters of TR,* V, 542-43.

2. TR to William II, December 26, 1908, *Letters of TR,* VI, 1441. See also TR to William II, April 4, 1908, *Letters of TR,* VI, 992-93.

3. TR to Hermann Von Hatzfeldt-Wildenburg, telegram, August 24, 1908, *Letters of TR*, VI, 1196-97.

4. Esthus, *TR and the International Rivalries*, 120.

5. John St. Loe Strachey to TR, February 11, 1907, TR Papers, reel 71. (Emphasis in original.)

6. TR to Strachey, February 22, 1907, *Letters of TR*, V, 596. (Emphasis added.)

7. TR to Sir Edward Grey, February 28, 1907, *Letters of TR*, V, 600-601.

8. Arthur Lee to TR, December 13, 1907, TR Papers, reel 80.

9. Esthus, *TR and the International Rivalries*, 123-27.

10. TR to Elihu Root, August 8, 1908, *Letters of TR*, VI, 1163-64.

11. Oscar King Davis, *Released for Publication: Some Inside Political History of Theodore Roosevelt and His Times, 1898-1918* (Boston, 1925), quoted in Esthus, *TR and the International Rivalries*, 127.

12. Esthus, *TR and the International Rivalries*, 130.

13. TR to Henry White, October 17, 1908, *Letters of TR*, VI, 1292.

14. TR to Lee, undelivered letter, October 17, 1908, *Letters of TR*, VI, 1292-94.

15. Esthus, *TR and the International Rivalries*, 128-29.

16. Whitelaw Reid to TR, November 3, 1908, TR Papers, reel 85.

17. Reid to TR, November 24, 1908, TR Papers, reel 86.

18. TR to Reid, November 26, 1908, *Letters of TR*, VI, 1384.

19. TR to Lee, November 23, 1908, *Letters of TR*, VI, 1378-79.

20. Esthus, *TR and the International Rivalries*, 129-30.

21. TR to Theodore Roosevelt, Jr., November 20, 1908, *Letters of TR*, VI, 1371.

22. Reid to TR, December 21, 1908, TR Papers, reel 87.

23. TR to Reid, January 6, 1909, *Letters of TR*, VI, 1466-67.

24. Reid to TR, January 22, 1909, TR Papers, reel 87.

25. David Fromkin, *In the Time of the Americans: FDR, Truman, Eisenhower, Marshall, MacArthur — The Generation That Changed America's Role in the World* (New York, 1995), 28.

26. TR to Andrew Carnegie, April 5, 1907, *Letters of TR*, V, 640.

27. TR to Grafton Dulany Cushing, February 27, 1908, *Letters of TR*, VI, 955.

28. TR to Silas McBee, August 27, 1907, *Letters of TR*, V, 775.

29. For example, see Neu, *Uncertain Friendship*, 142, and Collin, *TR, Culture, Diplomacy, and Expansion*, 149.

30. Morison et al., *Letters of TR*, V, 742n; TR to William Howard Taft, August 21, 1907, *Letters of TR*, V, 761-62.

31. TR to McBee, August 27, 1907, *Letters of TR*, V, 776.

32. TR, "Address of the President at the celebration of the African Diamond Jubilee of the Methodist Episcopal Church, Washington, D.C., January 18, 1909," pp. 28-29, Theodore Roosevelt Collection, Harvard College Library, Cambridge, MA. Quoted by permission of the Houghton Library, Harvard University.

33. See TR to Harry Hamilton Johnston, July 11, 1908, *Letters of TR*, VI, 1125-26. As "the outgrowth of immigration movements from our colored populations," Liberia could be seen as a special case. But Roosevelt chose to downplay the connection: "Beyond a paternal interest, the United States has no organic relation with or responsibility to that Government." Address to Methodist Episcopal Church, January 18, 1909, p. 48.

34. TR to Cecil Spring Rice, July 1, 1907, *Letters of TR*, V, 698.

35. TR, Address to Methodist Episcopal Church, January 18, 1909, pp. 12-13, 16-17.

36. TR to Jean Jules Jusserand, August 3, 1908, *Letters of TR*, VI, 1148.

37. TR, Address to Methodist Episcopal Church, January 18, 1909, pp. 10-11.

38. See TR to Johnston, July 11, 1908, *Letters of TR*, VI, 1126. Harry Hamilton Johnston, an explorer and leading colonial official in Africa and a student of Negro populations worldwide, agreed but inserted a qualifier. In Jamaica and indeed "in most parts of the British Empire the Negro is dealt with most considerately." But "what you have been told about . . . Southern Africa is *quite correct*. . . . It is only fair to say," Johnston added, "that this extraordinary attitude towards all the coloured races is practically confined to the Transvaal, Orange State, and above all to Natal. It is completely absent from Cape Colony." Johnston to TR, August 6, 1908, TR Papers, reel 84. (Emphasis in original.)

39. See chapter 2, pp. 24-25.

40. TR to Strachey, September 8, 1907, *Letters of TR*, V, 787.

41. TR to Spring Rice, December 21, 1907, *Letters of TR*, VI, 869.

42. TR to William Sidney Rossiter, November 19, 1908, *Letters of TR*, VI, 1366-67.

43. TR to Jusserand, August 3, 1908, *Letters of TR*, VI, 1148. (Emphasis in original.)

44. Morison et al., *Letters of TR*, VI, 1383n.

45. Morley's program is outlined in detail in Sydney Brooks, "The Briton and the Native in India," *Harper's Weekly*, January 16, 1909, 16.

46. Reid to TR, August 22, 1908, TR Papers, reel 84.

47. TR to Reid, September 3, 1908, *Letters of TR*, VI, 1206.

48. Brooks, "Fifty Years of British Rule in India" and "The Briton and the Native in India," *Harper's Weekly*, December 19, 1908, p. 22, and January 16, 1909, p. 16.

49. Brooks to TR, November 11, 1908, TR Papers, reel 85.

50. TR to Brooks, November 20, 1908, *Letters of TR*, VI, 1370.

51. TR to Reid, November 26, 1908, *Letters of TR*, VI, 1384.

52. TR to John Morley, December 1, 1908, *Letters of TR*, VI, 1402.

53. Brooks to TR, December 12, 1908, TR Papers, reel 86.

54. Reid to TR, December 21, 1908, TR Papers, reel 87.

55. See TR to Lee, December 20, 1908, and TR to Brooks, December 28, 1908, *Letters of TR*, VI, 1433, 1443.

56. TR to Brooks, December 28, 1908, *Letters of TR*, VI, 1443-44.

57. TR to Root, December 26, 1908, *Letters of TR*, VI, 1441.

58. TR to Taft, December 29, 1908, *Letters of TR*, VI, 1447.

59. TR to Reid, January 6, 1909, *Letters of TR*, VI, 1465.

60. Morley to TR, January 8, 1909, TR Papers, reel 87.

61. TR to Brooks, December 28, 1908, *Letters of TR*, VI, 1443.

62. Brooks, "Fifty Years of British Rule," 22.

63. Brooks to TR, January 13, 1909, TR Papers, reel 87.

64. TR, Address to Methodist Episcopal Church, January 18, 1909, pp. 17-24.

65. *London Times*, January 19, 1909.

66. James Bryce to TR, two letters, January 19 and 20, 1909, TR Papers, reel 87.

67. TR to Bryce, January 21, 1909, *Letters of TR*, VI, 1478.

68. Morley to TR, January 22, 1909, TR Papers, reel 87.

69. Brooks to TR, February 13, 1909, TR Papers, reel 88.

70. Reid to TR, January 22, 1909, TR Papers, reel 87. (Emphasis added.)

71. Lee to TR, January 29, 1909, TR Papers, reel 88. (Emphasis in original.)

72. TR to Lee, February 7, 1909, *Letters of TR*, VI, 1507.

73. Burton, "Special Relationship of Friends," 35.

74. TR to Strachey, two letters, February 22 and September 8, 1907, *Letters of TR*, V, 597, 786.

75. Strachey to TR, August 26, 1907, TR Papers, reel 76.

76. TR to Strachey, March 14, 1908, *Letters of TR*, VI, 971.

77. TR to George Otto Trevelyan, January 1, 1908, *Letters of TR*, VI, 882.

78. TR to Trevelyan, June 19, 1908, *Letters of TR*, VI, 1085-90. In this letter one senses genuine regret on the part of Roosevelt—a recognition that he had been rash and misguided in forswearing any third-term ambitions on the heels of his landslide victory in 1904. True, TR argued that on balance he was doing the right thing, emphasizing "the risk of creating a bad precedent" and focusing on "the men whom Abraham Lincoln called 'the plain people'" and a determination to avoid "shattering their faith in my personal disinterestedness." Nonetheless, it is possible to read the following lines as the most revealing of the letter: "At times I have felt a little uncomfortable as to whether my announced decision had been wise. . . . There is very much to be said in favor of the theory that the public has a right to demand as long service from any man who is doing good service as it thinks will be useful; and during the last year or two I have been rendered extremely uncomfortable both by the exultation of my foes over my announced intention to retire, and by the real uneasiness and chagrin felt by many good men because, as they believed, they were losing quite needlessly the leader in whom they trusted, and who they believed could bring to a successful conclusion certain struggles which they regarded as of vital concern to the national welfare. . . . Therefore, when I felt obliged to insist on retiring and abandoning the leadership, now and then I felt ugly qualms as to whether I was not refusing to do what I ought to do, and abandoning great work on a mere fantastic point of honor."

79. TR to Trevelyan, November 6, 1908, *Letters of TR*, VI, 1328-30.

80. TR to Trevelyan, December 1, 1908, *Letters of TR*, VI, 1397-98.

81. TR to Spring Rice, July 21, 1908, *Letters of TR*, VI, 1138.

82. TR to Spring Rice, December 21, 1907, *Letters of TR*, VI, 871.

83. TR to King Edward VII, February 12, 1908, *Letters of TR*, VI, 940.

84. Edward VII to TR, March 5, 1908, TR Papers, reel 81.

85. TR to Morley, December 1, 1908, *Letters of TR*, VI, 1401.

86. TR to Root, July 2, 1907, *Letters of TR*, V, 700, and TR to Root, July 2, 1908 (a coincidence), *Letters of TR*, VI, 1104.

87. William Woodville Rockhill to TR, June 30, 1908, TR Papers, reel 83; TR to Rockhill, September 7, 1908, *Letters of TR*, VI, 1210-11.

88. See TR to Henry Lee Higginson, March 28, 1907; TR to William Emlen Roosevelt, May 27, 1907; and TR to James Speyer, August 30, 1907, *Letters of TR*, V, 634, 674, 777. Actually, TR's chief concern about internal British politics was a tendency "to go too far," whereas in America the bigger danger to societal stability was posed by "the reactionaries and unscrupulous men of vast wealth." TR to Theodore Roosevelt, Jr., November 20, 1908, *Letters of TR*, VI, 1371-72.

89. TR to Sir Wilfrid Laurier, two letters, February 1 and December 24, 1908, *Letters of TR*, VI, 918, 1437.

90. The Romanes lecture was "founded in 1891 by George John Romanes, eminent British physiologist," and "was offered annually to naturalists of great reputation." Morison et al., *Letters of TR*, VI, 1177n.

91. Lord George Nathaniel Curzon to TR, August 3, 1908, TR Papers, reel 84.

92. TR to Curzon, August 18, 1908, *Letters of TR*, VI, 1177-78.

93. TR to Henry Cabot Lodge, August 18, 1908, *Letters of TR*, VI, 1180. Roosevelt's Romanes lecture on June 7, 1910, was titled "Biological Analogies in History." According to William H. Harbaugh, "it was not an intellectual success." *Life and Times of TR*, 358.

94. Tweed Roosevelt, "Theodore Roosevelt's African Safari," in Natalie A. Naylor, Douglas Brinkley, and John Allen Gable, eds., *Theodore Roosevelt: Many-Sided American* (Interlaken, NY, 1992), 428.

95. Ibid., 415.

96. Morison et al., *Letters of TR*, VI, 978n.

97. TR to Brooks, November 20, 1908, and TR to White, September 10, 1908, *Letters of TR*, VI, 1369, 1230. See also TR to Lee, September 2, 1908, and TR to Spring Rice, September 17, 1908, *Letters of TR*, VI, 1205, 1242.

98. TR to Lee, August 7, 1908, *Letters of TR*, VI, 1159-60; Reid to TR, August 11, 1908, TR Papers, reel 84.

99. TR to Reid, December 4, 1908, *Letters of TR*, VI, 1410.

100. Reid to TR, December 21, 1908, TR Papers, reel 87.

101. TR to Reid, January 6, 1909, *Letters of TR*, VI, 1466.

102. Reid to TR, May 1, 1907, TR Papers, reel 73.

103. Reid to TR, August 28, 1907, TR Papers, reel 76.

104. TR to Reid, September 6, 1907, *Letters of TR*, V, 785.

105. TR to Theodore Roosevelt, Jr., May 23, 1908, *Letters of TR*, VI, 1034.

106. Reid to TR, August 11, 1908, TR Papers, reel 84.

107. TR to Reid, August 20, 1908, *Letters of TR*, VI, 1186.

108. See TR to Trevelyan, November 6, 1908, *Letters of TR*, VI, 1329.

109. Reid to TR, December 23, 1908, TR Papers, reel 87.

110. TR to Reid, January 6, 1909, *Letters of TR*, VI, 1465.

111. TR to Winston Leonard Spencer Churchill, January 6, 1909, *Letters of TR*, VI, 1467.

112. The *Index to the Theodore Roosevelt Papers* lists approximately two dozen letters exchanged by Roosevelt and "W. Churchill" after January 1909 (Vol. I, 197). But in every case the individual in question was one of two Americans named William Churchill and (coincidentally) Winston Churchill. The latter, a devoted political supporter of Roosevelt, wrote or received the great majority of these letters.

113. TR to Lodge, June 4, 1910, *Letters of TR*, VII, 87. See also TR to David Gray, October 5, 1911, *Letters of TR*, VII, 406. An indirect compliment was the most Roosevelt would allow himself. "I have never liked Winston Churchill," the former president remarked to Arthur Lee shortly after the outbreak of World War I in 1914, "but in view of what you tell me as to his admirable conduct and nerve in mobilizing the fleet, I do wish that if it comes in [*sic*] your way you would extend to him my congratulations on his action." TR to Lee, August 22, 1914, *Letters of TR*, VII, 810.

114. Morison et al., *Letters of TR*, VI, 1034n.

115. Lee to TR, December 13, 1907, TR Papers, reel 80.

116. TR to Lee, December 26, 1907, *Letters of TR*, VI, 875.

117. Lee to TR, January 11, 1908, TR Papers, reel 80. (Emphasis in original.)

118. TR to Lee, February 2, 1908, *Letters of TR*, VI, 919.

119. Lee to TR, February 21, 1908, TR Papers, reel 81. (Emphasis in original.)

120. Lee to TR, March 21, 1908, TR Papers, reel 348.

121. Lee to TR, March 31, 1908, TR Papers, reel 82.

122. TR to Lee, April 8, 1908, *Letters of TR*, VI, 995.

123. Lee to TR, two letters, May 4, 1908, and July 10, 1908, TR Papers, reels 82, 83.

124. Lee to TR, July 10, 1908, TR Papers, reel 83.

125. TR to Lee, August 7, 1908, *Letters of TR*, VI, 1158-59.

126. TR to Lee, September 2, 1908, *Letters of TR*, VI, 1205.

127. Lee to TR, September 6, 1908, TR Papers, reel 84.

128. Lee to TR, December 1, 1908, TR Papers, reel 86.

129. TR to Lee, December 20, 1908, *Letters of TR*, VI, 1432.

130. Lee to TR, December 13, 1907, TR Papers, reel 80.

131. Lee to TR, July 10, 1908, TR Papers, reel 83.

132. Lee to TR, September 6, 1908, TR Papers, reel 84; see also Lee to TR, January 29, 1909, and March 1, 1909, TR Papers, reel 88.

133. TR to Lee, September 17, 1908, TR Papers, reel 351.

134. As noted by the editors of *The Letters of Theodore Roosevelt*, "Lee gave Chequers Court . . . to the nation to serve as the official country seat for the Prime Minister . . . in 1921." Morison et al., *Letters of TR*, VII, 50n.

135. See TR to David Gray, October 5, 1911, *Letters of TR*, VII, 405.

136. TR to Lee, August 7, 1908, *Letters of TR*, VI, 1159.

137. TR to Lee, October 17, 1908, *Letters of TR*, VI, 1294. For reasons explained in the first section of this chapter, this letter was not delivered.

138. Lee to TR, January 29, 1909, TR Papers, reel 88.

139. TR to Lee, February 7, 1909, *Letters of TR*, VI, 1507-8.

Epilogue and Conclusion

1. Roosevelt wrote and spoke frequently along these lines both publicly and privately. A particularly powerful statement of his great affection and respect for Britain can be found in "Our Debt to the British Empire," an article published in the *Kansas City Star* on August 16, 1918. Here TR lauded the "high heroism" of "Great Britain and the gallant overseas commonwealths which share her empire." By choosing "the hard path" back in August 1914 and then prosecuting the war so vigorously and effectively, Roosevelt asserted, the people of the British Empire had saved "the whole civilized world" from "the brutal dominion of Germany, . . . and in so doing rendered an inestimable service to us." *Roosevelt in the Kansas City Star: War-Time Editorials by Theodore Roosevelt* (Boston, 1921), 200-202.

2. See chapter 1, p. 19.

3. Ninkovich, "TR: Civilization as Ideology," 221-45. See William Tilchin, "The Rising Star of Theodore Roosevelt's Diplomacy: Major Studies from Beale to the Present," *Theodore Roosevelt Association Journal*, 15, 3, Summer 1989, 13-14, for a critical evaluation of Ninkovich's article.

4. Technically, of course, William McKinley, who served from 1897 until he died in office in September 1901, was the twentieth century's first president. But McKinley is usually (and appropriately) thought of as the last nineteenth-century president.

— Bibliography —

• ○ •

UNPUBLISHED PRIMARY SOURCES

Colonial Office: Jamaica: Original Correspondence, 1689-1951, Record Classes CO 137 and 351. Public Record Office, Kew, England.

Foreign Office: General Correspondence: Political, 1906-1963, Record Class FO 371. Public Record Office.

Naval Records Collection of the Office of Naval Records and Library, Record Group 45, Entry 307, "Navy Department, Bureau of Navigation. Copies of Correspondence to and from the Department Relating to the Kingston Disaster. From January 15, 1907 to February 18, 1907." National Archives, Washington, D.C.

Numerical and Minor Files of the Department of State, 1906-1910, General Records of the Department of State, Record Group 59. National Archives.

"Report of Rear Admiral C. H. Davis, U.S.N., with appendix of reports from other officers in relation to the situation at Kingston subsequent to the earthquake." Navy Department papers in General Records of the Department of State, Record Group 59.

Theodore Roosevelt Papers. Library of Congress, Washington, D.C., and Harvard College Library, Cambridge, MA. Accessible through *Index to the Theodore Roosevelt Papers*. 3 vols. Washington: Manuscript Division, Reference Department, Library of Congress, 1969.

NEWSPAPERS AND MAGAZINES

Harper's Weekly. 1907-1909.
Jamaica Daily Telegraph. 1907.
Jamaica Times. 1907.
Kingston Gleaner. 1907.
London Times. 1907-1909.
New York Times. 1907-1909.
Outlook. 1908.
Singapore Free Press. 1907.
Straits Times. 1907.
Toronto Saturday Night. 1907.
Washington Post. 1907.

PUBLISHED PRIMARY SOURCES

Roosevelt, Theodore. *Gouverneur Morris.* 1888. Reprint. Introduction by John A. Gable. Oyster Bay, NY: Theodore Roosevelt Association, 1975.

———. *The Letters of Theodore Roosevelt.* Edited by Elting E. Morison, John M. Blum, and Alfred D. Chandler, Jr. 8 vols. Cambridge, MA: Harvard University Press, 1951-1954.

———. *The Man in the Arena: Speeches and Essays by Theodore Roosevelt.* Edited by John Allen Gable. Oyster Bay, NY: Theodore Roosevelt Association, 1987.

———. *Roosevelt in the Kansas City Star: War-Time Editorials by Theodore Roosevelt.* Introduction by Ralph Stout. Boston: Houghton Mifflin Company, 1921.

———. *Selections from the Correspondence of Theodore Roosevelt and Henry Cabot Lodge, 1894-1918.* Edited by Henry Cabot Lodge. 2 vols. New York: Charles Scribner's Sons, 1925.

———. *Theodore Roosevelt: Addresses and Papers.* Edited by Willis Fletcher Johnson. New York: The Sun Dial Classics Co., 1909.

———. *Theodore Roosevelt: An Autobiography.* 1913. Reprint. Introduction by Elting E. Morison. New York: Da Capo Press, 1985.

———. *Theodore Roosevelt Cyclopedia.* 1941. 2nd ed. Edited by Albert Bushnell Hart and Herbert Ronald Ferleger. Introduction by John Allen Gable. Oyster Bay, NY, and Westport, CT: Theodore Roosevelt Association and Meckler Corporation, 1989.

———. *Theodore Roosevelt, "The Winning of the West": Selections.* 1962. Reprint. Edited by Harvey Wish. Gloucester, MA: Peter Smith Publisher, 1976.

———. *The Works of Theodore Roosevelt.* National Edition. Edited by Hermann Hagedorn. 20 vols. New York: Charles Scribner's Sons, 1926.

Spring Rice, Cecil. *The Letters and Friendships of Sir Cecil Spring Rice.* 1929. Reprint. Edited by Stephen Gwynn. 2 vols. Westport, CT: Greenwood Press, 1971.

SECONDARY SOURCES

Beale, Howard K. *Theodore Roosevelt and the Rise of America to World Power.* 1956. Reprint. Baltimore: Johns Hopkins University Press, 1984.

Blum, John Morton. *The Republican Roosevelt.* 1954. 2nd ed. Cambridge, MA: Harvard University Press, 1977.

Burton, David H. "Theodore Roosevelt and His English Correspondents: A Special Relationship of Friends." *Transactions of the American Philosophical Society,* 63, 2 (1973): 3-70.

———. "Theodore Roosevelt and His English Correspondents: The Intellectual Roots of the Anglo-American Alliance." *Mid-America,* 53, 1 (1971): 12-34.

———. "Theodore Roosevelt and the 'Special Relationship' with Britain." *History Today,* 23, 8 (1973): 527-535.

———. *Theodore Roosevelt: Confident Imperialist.* Philadelphia: University of Pennsylvania Press, 1968.

———. "Three Roosevelt Women." *Theodore Roosevelt Association Journal,* 21, 2 (1996): 3-10.

Campbell, Charles S., Jr. *Anglo-American Understanding, 1898-1903.* Baltimore: Johns Hopkins University Press, 1957.

Chessman, G. Wallace. *Theodore Roosevelt and the Politics of Power.* Boston: Little, Brown and Co., 1969.

Collin, Richard H. "Henry Pringle's Theodore Roosevelt: A Study in Historical Revisionism." *New York History,* 52, 2 (1971): 151-168.

———. *Theodore Roosevelt, Culture, Diplomacy, and Expansion: A New View of American Imperialism.* Baton Rouge: Louisiana State University Press, 1985.

———. *Theodore Roosevelt's Caribbean: The Panama Canal, the Monroe Doctrine, and the Latin American Context.* Baton Rouge: Louisiana State University Press, 1990.

Cooper, John Milton, Jr. *The Warrior and the Priest: Woodrow Wilson and Theodore Roosevelt.* Cambridge, MA: Belknap Press of Harvard University Press, 1983.

DeConde, Alexander. *A History of American Foreign Policy, Volume I: Growth to World Power (1700-1914).* 1963. 3rd ed. New York: Charles Scribner's Sons, 1978.

Dennett, Tyler. *John Hay: From Poetry to Politics.* New York: Dodd, Mead, and Co., 1934.

Duncan, Bingham. *Whitelaw Reid: Journalist, Politician, Diplomat.* Athens: University of Georgia Press, 1975.

Dyer, Thomas G. *Theodore Roosevelt and the Idea of Race.* Baton Rouge: Louisiana State University Press, 1980.

Esthus, Raymond A. *Double Eagle and Rising Sun: The Russians and Japanese at Portsmouth in 1905.* Durham, NC: Duke University Press, 1988.

———. *Theodore Roosevelt and Japan.* Seattle: University of Washington Press, 1967.

———. *Theodore Roosevelt and the International Rivalries.* 1970. Reprint. Claremont, CA: Regina Books, 1982.

Fromkin, David. *In the Time of the Americans: FDR, Truman, Eisenhower, Marshall, MacArthur—The Generation That Changed America's Role in the World.* New York: Alfred A. Knopf, 1995.

Gilbert, Martin. *Churchill: A Life.* New York: Henry Holt and Company, 1991.

Gould, Lewis L. *The Presidency of Theodore Roosevelt.* Lawrence: University Press of Kansas, 1991.

Grantham, Dewey W., Jr. "Theodore Roosevelt in American Historical Writing." *Mid-America,* 43, 1 (1961): 3-35.

Harbaugh, William H. *The Life and Times of Theodore Roosevelt.* 1961. Rev. ed. New York: Oxford University Press, 1975.

Johnston, William Davison. *TR, Champion of the Strenuous Life: A Photographic Biography of Theodore Roosevelt.* 1958. Reprint. Oyster Bay, NY: Theodore Roosevelt Association, 1984.

Jones, Howard. *The Course of American Diplomacy from the Revolution to the Present.* New York: Franklin Watts, 1985.

Karsten, Peter. "The Nature of 'Influence': Roosevelt, Mahan and the Concept of Sea Power." *American Quarterly,* 23, 4 (1971): 585-600.

Kieran, John, and Daley, Arthur. *The Story of the Olympic Games, 776 B.C. to 1964.* Philadelphia: J. B. Lippincott Company, 1965.

Kissinger, Henry. *Diplomacy.* New York: Simon & Schuster, 1994.

Kneer, Warren G. *Great Britain and the Caribbean, 1901-1913: A Study in Anglo-American Relations*. East Lansing: Michigan State University Press, 1975.

McCullough, David. *Mornings on Horseback*. New York: Simon & Schuster, 1981.

McIntyre, W. David. *The Commonwealth of Nations: Origins and Impact, 1869-1971*. Minneapolis: University of Minnesota Press, 1977.

Marks, Frederick W., III. "Theodore Roosevelt and the Righting of History." *Theodore Roosevelt Association Journal*, 12, 1 (1986): 8-12.

———. *Velvet on Iron: The Diplomacy of Theodore Roosevelt*. Lincoln: University of Nebraska Press, 1979.

May, Ernest R. *Imperial Democracy: The Emergence of America as a Great Power*. 1961. Reprint. New York: Harper & Row, 1973.

Monger, George. *The End of Isolation: British Foreign Policy, 1900-1907*. London: Thomas Nelson and Sons, 1963.

Morris, Edmund. "'A Few Pregnant Days': Theodore Roosevelt and the Venezuelan Crisis of 1902." *Theodore Roosevelt Association Journal*, 15, 1 (1989): 2-13.

———. *The Rise of Theodore Roosevelt*. New York: Coward, McCann, and Geoghegan, 1979.

Mowry, George E. *The Era of Theodore Roosevelt and the Birth of Modern America*. 1958. Reprint. New York: Harper Torchbooks, 1962.

Naylor, Natalie A., Brinkley, Douglas, and Gable, John Allen, eds. *Theodore Roosevelt: Many-Sided American*. Interlaken, NY: Heart of the Lakes Publishing, 1992.

Neu, Charles E. *The Troubled Encounter: The United States and Japan*. New York: John Wiley & Sons, 1975.

———. *An Uncertain Friendship: Theodore Roosevelt and Japan, 1906-1909*. Cambridge, MA: Harvard University Press, 1967.

Ninkovich, Frank. "Theodore Roosevelt: Civilization as Ideology." *Diplomatic History*, 10, 3 (1986): 221-245.

Osgood, Robert Endicott. *Ideals and Self-Interest in America's Foreign Relations*. Chicago: University of Chicago Press, 1953.

Patterson, James T. *America in the Twentieth Century: A History*. 1976. 3rd ed. New York: Harcourt Brace Jovanovich, 1989.

Pederson, William, and McLaurin, Ann, eds. *The Rating Game in American Politics: An Interdisciplinary Approach*. New York: Irving Publishers, 1987.

Perkins, Bradford. *The Great Rapprochement: England and the United States, 1895-1914*. New York: Atheneum, 1968.

Perkins, Dexter. *A History of the Monroe Doctrine*. 1941. Rev. ed. Boston: Little, Brown and Co., 1963.

Pringle, Henry F. *Theodore Roosevelt: A Biography*. New York: Harcourt, Brace and Co., 1931.

Ricard, Serge. *Théodore Roosevelt et la justification de l'impérialisme*. Aix-en-Provence, France: Université de Provence, 1986.

———. *Théodore Roosevelt: principes et pratique d'une politique étrangère*. Aix-en-Provence: Université de Provence, 1991.

——— ed. *L'éducation aux États-Unis: mythes et réalités*. Aix-en-Provence: Université de Provence, 1992.

Ricard, Serge, and Christol, Hélène, eds. *Anglo-Saxonism in U.S. Foreign Policy: The Diplomacy of Imperialism, 1899-1919.* Aix-en-Provence: Université de Provence, 1991.

Testi, Arnaldo. "The Gender of Reform Politics: Theodore Roosevelt and the Culture of Masculinity." *Journal of American History,* 81, 4 (1995): 1509-1533.

Thackeray, Frank W., and Findling, John E., eds. *Statesmen Who Changed the World: A Bio-Bibliographical Dictionary of Diplomacy.* Westport, CT: Greenwood Press, 1993.

Tilchin, William N. "The Rising Star of Theodore Roosevelt's Diplomacy: Major Studies from Beale to the Present." *Theodore Roosevelt Association Journal,* 15, 3 (1989): 2-24.

———."Theodore Roosevelt and the British Empire, 1901-1907." Ph.D. diss., Brown University, 1992.

———. "Theodore Roosevelt, Anglo-American Relations, and the Jamaica Incident of 1907." *Diplomatic History,* 19, 3 (1995): 385-405.

———. "Theodore Roosevelt, Harry Truman, and the Uneven Course of American Foreign Policy in the First Half of the Twentieth Century." *Theodore Roosevelt Association Journal,* 10, 4 (1994): 2-10.

Tuchman, Barbara W. "Perdicaris Alive or Raisuli Dead." *American Heritage,* 10, 5 (1959): 18-21, 98-101.

Wagenknecht, Edward C. *The Seven Worlds of Theodore Roosevelt.* New York: Longmans, Green and Co., 1958.

Walker, Eric A. *The British Empire: Its Structure and Spirit, 1497-1953.* 1943. 2nd ed. Cambridge, MA: Harvard University Press, 1956.

Wallechinsky, David. *The Complete Book of the Olympics.* Boston: Little, Brown and Company, 1992.

Webb, R. K. *Modern England: From the Eighteenth Century to the Present.* New York: Harper & Row, 1968.

Widenor, William C. *Henry Cabot Lodge and the Search for an American Foreign Policy.* Berkeley: University of California Press, 1980.

— Index —

Abbott, Lyman
  correspondence with TR, xv, 260-61n.14
Acton, Lord, 218
Adams, Brooks, 14
Adams, Charles Francis
  TR's displeasure with, 102
Adams, Henry, 14
Adams, John, 15
Adams, John Quincy, 15
Adee, Alvey A., 165-66
  correspondence with TR, 166
Alaskan boundary dispute, 9, 26-27, 36-47, 105, 135, 141, 167, 241
  aftermath, 47-48, 167
  impact on Anglo-American relations, 47-48, 167, 241
  map of, 37
  modus vivendi of 1899, 9, 36
  TR and, 16-17, 36-48, 59-60, 105, 135,*148, 167, 184, 241, 243
Alexandra, Queen, 189, 229, 275n.21
Algeciras conference, xi, 85-92, 104-5, 110, 112, 259n.21, 259n.37
Algeria
  TR's outlook on, 100, 217, 222
Alverstone, Lord
  and Alaskan boundary dispute, 42-43, 45-47
Amateur Athletic Association (British), 191, 197, 203, 206
Amateur Athletic Union (U.S.), 191, 203, 205
American Revolution, 3, 6, 226
Ames, H. E., 132, 266n.79
Anderson, E. A., 122
Anglo-American relations
  after TR's presidency, 239
  history up to 1901, 6-10, 25-26
  impact of Alaskan boundary settlement, 47-48, 241
  impact of Spanish-American War, 7-8
  impact of Swettenham incident, 138-39, 141-43, 242
  impact of Venezuelan crisis (1902-3), 34
  overviews, 1901-1909, 52, 55, 114, 166-68, 171, 238, 240-42
  TR's outlook on, xi-xii, 16-19, 21, 26, 29, 36, 38-40, 42-44, 47-48, 50, 55, 58, 60-63, 69, 72-77, 79-81, 83, 86, 89-91, 94, 96, 98-99, 104-14, 117, 134-37, 139, 163-64, 166-68, 171, 173, 175-79, 181-82, 184, 196, 198-99, 202, 207, 214-15, 225-28, 236-43, 256n.50
Anglo-French entente cordiale, 4, 56, 58, 64, 69, 90-91, 94
  TR and, 56, 63, 69, 81, 86, 92, 94, 210

Anglo-German hostility, 32, 59, 64-67, 91, 94, 210-14, 241
  TR and, 64-65, 67, 85-87, 91, 212-13
Anglo-Japanese alliance as renewed in 1905, 77-79, 83-84, 173-76, 178, 180, 210-11
Anglo-Japanese alliance of 1902, 4-5, 50, 62-63, 73-75
Anglo-Russian rapprochement of 1907, 91, 94, 210
Anglo-Russian Treaty of 1825, 36, 38, 40-41
Arbitration treaties
  TR and, 96-97, 260n.8, 261n.14
Archer, William
  correspondence with TR, 17
Arthur, Chester, 14
Australia
  British rule in, 3, 5, 178, 180
  TR's outlook on, 19, 83, 85, 103-4, 172, 174, 178, 180-81, 215, 217, 240
  and U.S.-Japanese immigration-racism crisis, 178, 180-82
Austrian plan (at Algeciras conference), 88-89

Bacon, Robert
  and Swettenham incident, diplomacy of, 136-37, 139-40, 146, 268n.23, 268n.48
Balance of power
  TR's outlook on, xi-xiii, 18-19, 49, 56, 67-68, 74-75, 83, 167, 214-15, 237, 241
Balfour, Arthur
  and Alaskan boundary dispute, 39, 44-46, 254n.122
  and Anglo-American relations, 8, 27, 31, 35, 39, 44-46, 61, 66, 76, 107, 176, 212, 254n.122
  TR's perception of, 105-6, 261n.40
Beale, Howard K., author, ix, xiii, 15, 23, 25-27, 29-30, 49-50, 65-66, 245n.3, 256n.40, 262n.1
Becker, George Ferdinand
  correspondence with TR, 19
Belgium/Belgian Congo, 25, 228
Bermuda, 6, 119
Bishop, Joseph Bucklin
  correspondence with TR, xv
Bismarck, Otto von, 27, 210
Blackwood's, 119, 153
Blaine, James G., 11
Boer War, 4-5, 9, 26, 36, 212-13
  TR and, 16, 18-19, 23, 39
  See also Vereeniging, Treaty of
Bond, Robert
  and Newfoundland fisheries problem, 97-98, 182, 184-85, 274nn.53-54
  and reciprocity with U.S., 95
  See also Hay-Bond Treaty

Bourne, H. C., 122-24, 144, 147, 156-57, 270n.14
Bowen, Herbert, 33-34, 153
Brent, Bishop, 215
Bricker, W. F., 123
Brilliant (British warship), 119
British East Africa (including Uganda), 5, 228-29
British Empire
    history up to 1902, 3-5
    self-governing colonies, 4-6 (*see also* Australia;
      Canada; New Zealand; Newfoundland;
      South Africa)
    structure in 1902, 5-6
    TR's outlook on, xi-xii, 18-20, 23-25, 29, 38-
      39, 58, 96, 99-104, 108, 117, 137, 166-67,
      171, 173-76, 178, 180-82, 215, 217-25, 227,
      236-41, 243, 282n.1
British navy: *See* Royal Navy
Brooks, Sydney
    correspondence with TR, 219-22, 224, 229
    Harper's Weekly articles on India, 219, 222,
      279n.45
    and India, TR's address on, 219-22, 224
Broome, F. Napier, 134
Bryan, William Jennings, 14, 19
Bryce, James
    as ambassador to U.S., 16, 112, 114, 120, 157-58,
      162-65, 175-77, 180, 204-6, 208, 213, 221,
      223-24, 270n.11, 272n.62, 277nn.78-79
    correspondence with TR, 16-18, 180, 204-6,
      208, 223-24
    and Olympics controversy, 204-6, 208, 277n.78
    relationship with TR, 16, 114, 180, 204-6,
      277nn.78-79
    and Swettenham incident, 141, 157-58, 163-
      65, 272n.62
    and U.S.-Japanese immigration-racism crisis,
      175-77
Buell, George Candee
    correspondence with TR, 194-96, 198, 207,
      276nn.46-47
    and Olympics controversy, 194-95, 207
Bulloch, Irvine, 15
Bulloch, Jimmy, 15
Burma, 5, 100
Burton, David H., author, xiv, 16, 25, 36, 225,
    245n.3, 247n.23
Bush, George, x-xi
Butler, Nicholas Murray
    correspondence with TR, 95-96
Buxton, Edward North, 229

Campbell, Charles S., Jr., author, 7-8, 17, 20, 30,
    36-37, 40, 42-43, 50, 95, 248n.7
Campbell-Bannerman, Henry, 111
Canada

and Alaskan boundary dispute, 36-43, 45-48,
    253n.105
British rule in, 6, 95, 167
TR's outlook on, 16-17, 23-24, 38-40, 47, 85,
    96, 98, 100, 104, 167, 173-75, 178-79, 181,
    227, 240
and U.S.-Japanese immigration-racism crisis,
    85, 171, 173-81, 272-73n.16, 273n.23
Canada and Newfoundland
    reciprocity with U.S., 24, 95-98
Cannon, Joseph Gurney
    correspondence with TR, 101
Cape Colony: *See* South Africa
Caribbean, U.S. domination of, 25-26, 35, 52,
    105, 241
Carnegie, Andrew
    correspondence with TR, 92, 100, 215, 216n.14
Carpenter, John, 188-90, 193-98, 203, 275n.15
Carter, John R., 176
    and Swettenham incident, diplomacy of, 137,
      139-41, 144, 146
Cassini, Arturo, 69, 72-73
Castro, Cipriano, 31-32
Celtic (U.S. Navy supply ship), 121-22, 130, 133
Chamberlain, Joseph, 5
    and Alaskan boundary dispute, 43-45, 47
    and Anglo-American relations, 8, 30, 43-45,
      47
Chandler, William E., 14
Chequers Court
    Arthur Lee and, 235, 282n.134
China/Chinese
    TR's outlook on, 16-17, 25, 28, 49-51, 83, 93-
      94, 112, 246n.16
    U.S. policy toward, 9, 49-51, 112, 246n.16
Choate, Joseph, 8, 26, 50, 68
    and Alaskan boundary dispute, 42, 45-46
    correspondence with TR, 26, 29
Churchill, Lord Randolph, 105-6
Churchill, William
    correspondence with TR, 281n.112
Churchill, Winston
    as author, 105-6, 231
    correspondence with TR, 231
    and Swettenham incident, 138, 146, 150, 158-
      60, 168, 230, 264n.42
    TR, parallels with, 231
    and TR's African adventure, 230-31
    TR's perception of and dislike for, 105-6, 230-
      31, 271n.31, 281n.113
Churchill, Winston (an American), 281n.112
    correspondence with TR, 281n.112
Cleveland, Grover, 12
    and Venezuelan boundary dispute, 7, 16-17, 143
Cold War, x

Collin, Richard H., author, xv, 27-29, 48, 245n.3, 246n.5, 262n.1
Collings, Jesse, 270n.5
Colombia
  TR and, 246n.16, 251n.28
Cook, Theodore A.
  author of pamphlet, "The Americans at the Olympic Games," 200-203, 207, 277n.63
  correspondence with TR, 193, 197-203, 206-8, 276n.57, 277n.63, 277n.82
  and Olympics controversy, 193, 197-203, 206-8, 277n.63, 277n.82
Cooper, John Milton, Jr., author, xiv, 248n.9, 248nn.11-12
Cowles, Anna Roosevelt: See Roosevelt, Anna
Cowles, William Sheffield, 14
Cox, R. E., 265n.72
Cranborne, Lord, 31
Crane, Winthrop Murray
  correspondence with TR, 96
Crewe, Lord, 229
Cromer, Lord
  TR's view of, 102
Cuba
  TR's outlook on U.S. policy, 215
Curzon, Lord George Nathaniel, 227
  correspondence with TR, 227-28
Cushing, Grafton Dulany
  correspondence with TR, 215

Daily Gleaner: See Kingston Gleaner
Davis, Charles H., 14, 119, 135, 137-40, 271n.43, 272n.62
  American emergency hospital established by, 126-27, 130, 132, 266n.79
  Kingston earthquake relief mission and Swettenham incident, 121-35, 142-45, 147, 154-56, 160, 164, 166-67, 264n.42, 265-66nn.72-74, 266n.79, 266n.90, 269n.55, 270n.5, 270n.14, 271n.43
  letter to Swettenham of Jan. 17, 1907, 127-29, 132, 135, 138-39, 156-57, 265n.66, 266n.74
  See also Davis Report
Davis, Oscar King, 211-12, 214
Davis Report, 123-28, 130, 132-33, 139, 145, 147-50, 163-66, 168, 264n.42, 265-66nn.72-73, 266n.79, 271n.43
Deakin, Alfred, 178, 273n.32
DeConde, Alexander, author, 97, 247n.3, 274n.57
Delcassé, Théophile, 68
Denmark/Danish Virgin Islands, 27, 35, 106
Desborough, Lord, 201
Dewey, George
  and Spanish-American War, 7, 13
  and Venezuelan crisis, 33-34

Dieges, Charles, 190-91
Disraeli, Benjamin, 4
Dunne, Finley Peter, 108
  correspondence with TR, 108
Durand, Mortimer, 62-63, 65, 67-68, 70, 73, 77, 84
  correspondence with TR, 78-79
  failure to work with TR, 55, 59-60, 62, 65-66, 69, 74, 78, 89, 92, 95, 110-14, 168, 232, 277n.79
  removal from Washington embassy, 110-13, 119
Dutch possessions in Western Hemisphere, 35, 70
Dyer, Thomas G., author, 19-20, 247n.22

Earthquake, Kingston, Jamaica, 117-18, 120-23, 125-27, 133, 155-56, 162
  U.S. relief authorized for, 120-23, 125, 136, 146, 162, 265n.45, 271n.46
Edward VII, King
  correspondence with TR, 63, 109, 118, 178, 227
  proclamation on India, 221
  relationship with TR, 63, 66, 69, 72, 90, 109, 212, 214, 224, 227, 229
Egypt, 229
  British rule in, 5
  TR's outlook on, 24, 100, 102, 240
Elgin, Lord, 270n.11
  correspondence with Alexander Swettenham, 119-20, 125-31, 136-38, 145-47, 154-57, 159-61, 163-64, 166, 264n.42, 265n.56, 266-67n.90, 268n.23
  and Swettenham incident, 119, 133, 136-38, 145-48, 150-51, 155-57, 159, 163, 166, 168, 266-67n.90
Eliot, Charles W.
  correspondence with TR, 82, 99-100
England: See Great Britain
Episode of the two interviews (William II), 211-14, 232
Esthus, Raymond A., author, 27, 29, 56, 62, 66, 68, 71, 86, 209-13, 245n.3, 246n.11
Evans, R. D., 119-22, 125, 139-40, 165, 269n.55, 271n.43

Fairbanks, Charles Warren, 96
  correspondence with TR, 96
Falklands/Falklands War, 6, 239
Fisher, John, 105
Foster, John, 45
France
  entente with Great Britain: See Anglo-French entente cordiale
  and Moroccan crisis, 64-71, 86-92, 112, 210, 259n.37
  and Russo-Japanese War, 57-64, 73, 75-76, 78, 92

TR's outlook on, 17-18, 25, 60-61, 63, 67-69, 81, 86-87, 92-94, 100, 167, 210, 226
Fromkin, David, author, 214-15
Frye, William P., 14

Gable, John A., author, 248n.11
Gentlemen's agreement, U.S.-Japanese, 172-73, 272n.6
Germany
    and Moroccan crisis, 64-71, 86-91, 112-13, 210
    and Russo-Japanese War, 56-64, 66, 68, 72-73, 75-76, 78, 113, 211
    TR's outlook on, xi, 17-18, 25, 27-29, 33-35, 56-57, 60-63, 65-69, 73, 81-82, 84, 86-89, 91-94, 112, 209-10, 212, 214-15, 225, 241, 243, 249n.40, 282n.1
    See also Venezuelan crisis (1902-3)
Gibraltar, 5, 110-11
Gillett, James Norris, 172-73, 181
    correspondence with TR, 172-73, 181
Gladstone, William, 4, 105
Gloucester, MA, 95-96, 98
Gorringe, Henry H., 14
Gorst, E., 149-50, 270n.11
Gould, Lewis L., author, xiii, 21, 65, 246n.7, 252n.68, 256n.40, 262n.1
Grantham, Dewey W., Jr., author, 245-46n.5, 246n.7
Great Britain
    and Alaskan boundary dispute, 16-17, 36-48, 105, 135, 141, 167, 241, 243
    alliance with Japan: See Anglo-Japanese alliance
    entente with France: See Anglo-French entente cordiale
    and Moroccan crisis, 55, 65-71, 80, 86, 88-91, 95, 104-5, 110-14, 141, 243
    and Newfoundland fisheries problem, 97-99, 104-5, 112, 114, 141, 171, 182-85, 243
    relations with U.S.: See Anglo-American relations
    Roosevelt Corollary, encouragement of, 35, 105
    and Root-Takahira Agreement, 180-81
    and Russo-Japanese War, 55-64, 66, 68, 72-80, 95, 104-5, 110, 112-14, 141, 173, 177, 243
    TR's desire for friendship with, xi-xii, 16-19, 29, 36, 38-40, 42-44, 48-49, 55, 58, 60-63, 69, 76-77, 79-80, 83, 86, 90-91, 94, 96, 98-99, 104-14, 135-37, 139, 148-49, 166-68, 171, 175-78, 181-82, 184, 196, 198-99, 202, 207, 214-15, 225-28, 236-43
    TR's India speech, reaction to, 223-25
    TR's outlook on, xi-xii, 16-19, 23, 29, 34, 38-40, 42, 44, 48-49, 55, 58, 60-61, 63, 66-69, 72-84, 86-87, 89-90, 92-94, 98-99, 104-11,

113-14, 117, 135-36, 167-68, 173, 176-79, 209-10, 215, 225-28, 237-43, 256n.50, 280n.88, 282n.1
    and U.S.-Japanese immigration-racism crisis, 85, 171-81, 243, 272-73n.16, 273n.23
    See also Venezuelan crisis (1902-3)
Great Wall, 56
Great White Fleet
    TR and, 173-75, 177-82, 216, 273n.23
    visit to Japan, 178-80, 273n.23
    visits to Australia and New Zealand, 178, 180-82, 211, 273n.32, 273n.34
Grey, Albert Henry George
    correspondence with TR, 24
Grey, Edward, 118, 121, 162, 180-81, 213
    analysis, shared by TR, of Anglo-American special relationship, 113-14
    analysis of Britain's security situation in 1906, 94
    correspondence with TR, 85, 94, 99, 112-14, 153, 163, 172, 210
    domination of British foreign policy, 262n.63
    and Newfoundland fisheries problem, 98-99, 182-84
    and Swettenham incident, diplomacy of, 120, 135-41, 148-51, 153-54, 157-58, 160, 162-65, 168, 272n.62
    TR's dealings with, 85, 90, 94, 99, 101, 110, 112-14, 153, 163, 176-79, 210, 212, 223
    and U.S.-Japanese immigration-racism crisis, 85, 176-80
Griffith, G. W. E., 120-21
Guantanamo, Cuba, 120-21, 125, 130, 133
Gummeré, Samuel, 64
    correspondence with TR, 64

Hadley, Arthur Twining
    correspondence with TR, 261n.21
Hague conference (1899), 9
Hague conference (1907)
    TR and, 92-93, 112, 227
Hague Tribunal, 45, 183-85, 260n.8, 274n.57
Haiti
    TR's outlook on, 100, 216
Haldane, Richard B., 136-37, 144
Hale, Eugene, 268n.48
    TR's dislike for, 96
Hale, William B.
    interview with William II, 211-14, 232
Hall, E. F., 266n.73
Halpin, Matt, 197
Halswelle, Wyndham, 188-89
Hamilton, Alexander, 107-8
Hanna, Mark, 14
Harbaugh, William H., author, ix, 248n.11, 280n.93

Hardie, Keir, 224-25
Hardinge, Charles, 138-39, 150
Harper's Weekly
  the Anglo-American friendship in 1907 in historical perspective, 142-43
  India articles by Sydney Brooks, 219, 222, 279n.45
  and Swettenham incident, 117, 142-43
Harrison, Benjamin, 12, 14
Harvard College, xv, 10-11, 82, 205
Hay, John
  and Alaskan boundary dispute, 36, 38-39, 41-42, 44-46, 253n.105, 254n.122 (*see also* Hay-Herbert Treaty)
  and Anglo-American relations under McKinley, 8-9, 26, 36, 49 (*see also* Hay-Pauncefote Treaty)
  correspondence with TR, 26-28, 35, 38-39, 41-42, 44-45, 50-51, 58-59, 64, 96, 109, 260n.8
  death of, 75
  and reciprocity with Newfoundland, 95-96 (*see also* Hay-Bond Treaty)
  as secretary of state for TR, 21, 26, 28, 30-31, 36, 38-39, 41-42, 44-46, 50-51, 59, 62, 95-96, 253n.105, 254n.122, 260n.8
  and U.S. East Asian policy under TR, 50-51, 62
Hay-Bond Treaty, 95-97
Hay-Herbert Treaty, 39-41
Hay-Pauncefote Treaty (1900), 9, 17-18, 20, 26
Hay-Pauncefote Treaty (1901), 26-27, 29, 36
Hayes, John, 189-90, 198
Hearst, William Randolph
  TR's dislike for, 106
Hefferon, Charles, 189-90
Henry, Prince of Prussia, 28
Herbert, Michael, 41, 251n.51
  and Venezuelan crisis, 30-34
  See also Hay-Herbert Treaty
Hinman, George Wheeler
  correspondence with TR, 33
Holland, 88-89
Holleben, Theodor von, 32
Holls, George Frederick William, 39-40
  correspondence with TR, 39, 51
Holmes, Oliver Wendell
  and Alaskan boundary dispute, 43-44, 47
  correspondence with TR, 43-44, 47
Hopwood, F. J. S., 146, 150, 156-57
Howard, Esmé, 113, 120-21
  and Swettenham incident, diplomacy of, 136-41, 149-50, 168, 268n.23

Imperialism
  TR's outlook on, xi, 16, 20, 93, 99-103, 167, 216-19, 222-23

Indefatigable (British warship), 119, 131
Index to the Theodore Roosevelt Papers: See Theodore Roosevelt Papers
India, 57
  British rule in, 3-5, 77, 218-25, 227-28
  Morley-Minto reforms, 218, 221, 279n.45
  TR's outlook on, 19, 24, 74, 100, 171, 215, 218-25, 240-41
Indiana (U.S. Navy battleship), 121-26, 131, 133, 266n.73
Iraq, war against, x-xi, 239
Ireland, British rule in, 3, 5

Jamaica
  British rule in, 6, 117, 157
  TR's outlook on British rule, 167, 217
  See also Earthquake, Kingston, Jamaica; Swettenham incident
Jamaica Daily Telegraph, 132, 140, 144
Jamaica incident: *See* Swettenham incident
Jamaica Times, 144
Japan
  alliance with Great Britain: *See* Anglo-Japanese alliance
  TR's outlook on, xi, 25, 27, 56, 58, 60-61, 66-67, 72-79, 81-85, 93-94, 100, 172, 176-81, 210, 216, 236, 241, 243
  See also Russo-Japanese War; U.S.-Japanese immigration-racism crisis
Jefferson, Thomas, 15
Johnston, Harry Hamilton, 279n.38
  correspondence with TR, 279n.38
Jusserand, Jean Jules
  as ambassador to U.S., 67-71, 78, 83-84, 87-90, 92, 111-12, 217, 253n.80, 257n.61, 259n.37
  correspondence with TR, 71, 92, 217-18
  friendship with TR, 67-69, 71, 89-90, 92, 112, 238, 253n.80, 257n.61, 259n.37
  and Moroccan crisis, 67-71, 87-90, 92, 112, 257n.61, 259n.37

Kaneko, Kentaro
  correspondence with TR, 79, 173
  and U.S.-Japanese relations, 58, 79, 173
Kansas City Star
  TR on British Empire during World War I, 282n.1
Karsten, Peter, author, 14-15
Katsura, Taro, 77, 84
  See also Taft-Katsura agreement
Kennan, George, 76-77
  correspondence with TR, 76-77
Kenya: *See* British East Africa
Kieran, John, and Daley, Arthur, authors, 187, 190

Kimball, William W.
  correspondence with TR, 249n.40
King, William L. Mackenzie
  and immigration-racism crisis, 174-79, 272-73n.16
Kingston Gleaner (and *Daily Gleaner*), 118, 131-32, 144
Kipling, Rudyard
  correspondence with TR, 16, 106
Kirby, Gustavus, 200-201, 277n.82
Kissinger, Henry
  perspective on TR, 49
Kneer, Warren G., author, 30-32, 48, 105, 262n.1
Knox, Philander Chase
  correspondence with TR, 48, 274n.42
Korea, 50, 55-56, 61-62, 72, 77, 83-84

La Farge, Florence Lockwood
  correspondence with TR, 103
Lansdowne, Lord, 27, 41, 46, 61, 73-79, 84
  failure to understand TR, 55-57, 65-66, 68, 110, 114, 168, 177
  and Venezuelan crisis, 30-34
László, Philip, painter of TR's portrait, 232-35
Laurier, Wilfrid, 40, 253n.105
  correspondence with TR, 175, 227, 273n.16
  and immigration-racism crisis, 174-75, 273n.16
Lebanon, x
Lee, Arthur
  Alaskan boundary settlement, assessment of, 47
  and Anglo-American naval partnership, 109-11
  correspondence with TR, xv, 15-19, 26-27, 29, 36, 38-39, 47-48, 79, 99, 109-12, 148-49, 153-54, 161-62, 175-76, 178-79, 181, 196-97, 208, 210-14, 224-25, 232, 234-38, 254n.133, 264n.42, 272-73n.16, 276n.57, 281n.113, 282n.137
  friendship with TR, xv, 15-16, 36, 47-48, 101, 107, 109-14, 148-49, 153-54, 161-62, 175-76, 178-79, 181, 196-97, 208, 210-14, 224-25, 229, 232, 234-38, 242, 254n.133, 264n.42, 276n.57, 281n.14
  friendship with TR, 1907-9, intimacy and significance of, 232, 234-38, 242
  Grey unable to appoint as ambassador to U.S., 112-13
  and Hay-Pauncefote Treaty (1901), 26-27
  Olympics controversy, outlook on, 196, 208
  and portrait of TR by Philip László, 232-35
  and Royal Navy's two-power standard, 236-37
  and Swettenham incident, 148-49, 153-54, 161-62, 208, 232, 264n.42
  TR's India address, assessment of, 224-25
  and TR's visit to Great Britain in 1910, 235

and TR's voluntary retirement from the presidency, 235
and U.S.-Japanese immigration-racism crisis, 175-76, 178-79, 181, 232
as unofficial ambassador to U.S., 16, 111-12, 175-76, 211-14, 232
Liberia
  TR's outlook on, 216, 278n.33
Libya, 239
Lincoln, Abraham, 280n.78
Lodge, Henry Cabot, 50, 119
  and Alaskan boundary dispute, 40-46, 48
  and Anglo-American relations (general), 8
  correspondence with TR, xv, 16-17, 19, 26, 34, 38, 40-42, 44-47, 69, 71-74, 77, 96-98, 101-2, 105-7, 109, 153, 171, 173-74, 228, 231, 240, 256n.50, 260n.8, 271n.43
  friendship with TR, xv, 11-14, 21, 26, 40-46, 48, 69, 71-74, 77, 96, 98, 101-2, 109, 240, 260-61n.14
  and Newfoundland fisheries problem, 97-98, 183-84
  and reciprocity with Canada and Newfoundland, 95-98
  TR's irritation with, 96-98, 260n.8, 260-61n.14
Lodge, Mrs. Henry Cabot, 235
London Daily Telegraph
  interview with William II, 212-14, 232
London Times, 211
  and Newfoundland fisheries problem, 185, 274n.44
  and Olympics controversy, 188-90, 203, 206
  and Swettenham incident, 135, 143-44, 161, 165
  and TR's India speech, 223
Long, John D., 13
Longworth, Alice Roosevelt: *See* Roosevelt, Alice
Lowell, Abbott Lawrence
  correspondence with TR, 24
Lucas, C. P., 126, 146, 160-61, 266n.90, 268n.23
Luce, Stephen B., 14

Maccabe, Joseph, 200-201, 277n.82
Madrid, Treaty of, 87
Magoon, Charles, 120-21
Mahan, Alfred Thayer
  correspondence with TR, 17, 48
  relationship with TR, 14-15, 248n.17
  as strategic thinker, 14-15, 17, 49-50
Maine (U.S. Navy battleship), 122
Malaya
  British rule in, 5
  TR's outlook on, 101-2, 215, 240
Marks, Frederick W., III, author, x, xiii, 32, 245n.3, 246n.5, 252n.62, 252n.68

Marshall, J. N. A., 124, 128, 265-66n.73
McBee, Silas
    correspondence with TR, 97, 215-16
McCullough, David, author, 248n.9
McDonnell, W. N., 121, 132
McKinley, William, 13-14
    and Anglo-American relations, 8-9, 18, 23, 49
    assassination of, 10, 14, 19, 29, 282n.4
    last nineteenth-century president, 282n.4
Meade, R. W., 133-34
Metcalf, Victor H., 120, 147, 161-62, 165-66, 269n.55
Methodist Episcopal Church, African Diamond
    Jubilee, 222
Meyer, George von Lengerke
    as ambassador to Russia, 59-60, 63, 78
    correspondence with TR, xv, 18, 60, 63, 67,
        78-79, 81, 87, 90, 108
    service to TR, 21, 59-60, 78
Milke, Oswald, 127, 129, 266n.74
Missouri (U.S. Navy battleship), 121-23, 125-26,
    130-31, 133
Monger, George, author, 62-63, 73, 262n.63
Monroe, James, 15
Monroe Doctrine, 17-18, 31, 34-35, 236
    See also Roosevelt Corollary
Moody, William H., 96
Morison, Elting E., editor, *The Letters of Theodore
    Roosevelt*, x, xv, 65, 218, 231, 246nn.6-7,
    260n.8, 282n.134
Morley, John
    correspondence with TR, 219-21, 224, 227
    secretary of state for India, 218-24
Moroccan crisis, 55, 64, 71, 92
    Great Britain and, 55, 65-71, 80, 86, 88-91, 95,
        104-5, 110-14, 141, 243
    TR and, xi, 55, 64-72, 74, 80, 86-90, 92, 95,
        104-5, 110-14, 243, 258n.97, 259n.21,
        259n.37
    See also Algeciras conference
Morocco
    TR's preference for direct French rule over, 217
Morris, Edmund, author, xv, 32, 247n.25, 252n.68,
    252-53n.80

Napoleon Bonaparte, 3-4
Natal: *See* South Africa
Netherlands: *See* Dutch possessions; Holland
Neu, Charles E., author, ix, 21, 50, 176-80,
    246n.11, 255n.21, 272n.6, 272-73n.16
New Testament, 159, 271n.32
New York Times, 191, 195, 211-12, 273n.32, 273n.34,
    274n.54
    and Olympics controversy, 187-90, 196
    and Swettenham incident, 117, 132-33, 135-
        37, 142

New Zealand
    British rule in, 3, 5-6, 180
    TR's outlook on, 174
Newfoundland
    British rule in, 6, 95, 167
    TR's outlook on, 96-98, 100, 167, 240
    See also Canada and Newfoundland;
        Newfoundland fisheries problem
Newfoundland fisheries problem, 95, 97-99, 104-
    5, 112, 114, 141, 171, 182-85, 243, 260n.10,
    274n.44, 274nn.53-54, 274n.57
    Hague Tribunal decision, 1910, 185, 274n.57
    TR and, 95, 97-99, 104-5, 112, 114, 171, 182-
        85, 243
Nicholas II, Czar, 72-73, 78
Nicolson, Arthur, 91
Nineteenth Century
    report on Hale interview, 214
Ninkovich, Frank, author, 241
North Atlantic Treaty Organization, 239
Norton, O. D., 132, 266n.79
Nuttall, Enos, 132-33

Oliver, Frederick Scott, 107
    correspondence with TR, 100, 107-8
Olivier, Sydney, 138, 147, 157
Olney, Richard, 14
    and Anglo-American relations, 7
Olympic games controversy, 171, 187-208,
    275n.15, 277n.63, 277n.82
    400-meter final, 187-91, 193-98, 200, 204,
        275n.15
    marathon, 187, 189-91, 193-95, 198, 200, 204,
        277n.83
    TR and, 171, 191-208, 276n.46, 276n.57,
        277n.63, 277n.82
Olympic games of 1908
    New York celebration of U.S. victory, 195
    overall track and field results, 188
Open Door notes, 9
Orange Free State: *See* South Africa
Orrett, William H.
    and Kingston earthquake and Swettenham
        incident, 117-18, 123, 125, 129-30, 146,
        160, 266n.74
Ottoman Empire
    TR's outlook on, 93-94
Outlook
    and Olympics controversy, 275n.29
Oyster Bay: *See* Sagamore Hill

Panama Canal
    Canal Zone, TR's acquisition of, xi, 27, 106,
        226, 251n.28
    Canal Zone, TR's visit to (1906), 103, 107, 111

TR's pre-presidential outlook on, 16-18, 20, 26
U.S. construction of, 27, 106-7, 119, 156, 226, 266n.90, 270n.11
Parker, Alton, 59
Parker, Gilbert, 158
Patterson, John Henry, 229
Pauncefote, Julian
    and Anglo-American relations (general), 8, 30
    death of, 30, 251n.51
    See also Hay-Pauncefote Treaty
Peel, Robert, 105
Perkins, Bradford, author, xii, 6-7, 142, 262n.1
Perkins, Dexter, author, 32
Philippines
    TR's perspective on U.S. rule, 24-25, 77, 101-3, 215-16, 219-20, 222, 240
    TR's security assessment, 84, 101, 216
    U.S. acquisition and retention of, 8-9, 99, 216
Pietri, Dorando, 189-90, 193, 198, 275n.21
Pinchot, Gifford
    correspondence with TR, xv
Platt, Orville H.
    TR's praise for, 261n.14
Platt, Thomas, 13
Pogroms, 51
Porter, David L., author, 245n.1
Portsmouth, Treaty of
    TR and, xi, 56, 78-79, 84-85, 92, 100, 173
Portsmouth conference
    TR and, 72-73, 77-79, 113-14, 243
Powell, Alexander, 32
Presidential election of 1904, 59, 96, 99, 101, 108, 280n.78
Pringle, Henry F., author, x, 245-46n.5
Protectorate (in British Empire), definition of, 247n.2
Puck
    TR cartoon in, 22
Puerto Rico
    TR's perspective on U.S. rule, 103

Quebec Chronicle, 144

Race
    TR's theory about, 19-20
Reid, Whitelaw
    as ambassador to Britain under TR, 21, 23, 65, 68-70, 74-76, 85-86, 89-90, 92-93, 98-99, 111-13, 149-50, 158, 162, 182-85, 192-94, 196, 198, 205-7, 213-14, 218-21, 224, 229-31, 271n.31
    anglophile speeches (1897), 247-48n.6
    attempts to reshape TR's perception of Churchill, 230-31, 271n.31
    correspondence with TR, xv, 28, 34, 65-70,
        74-77, 79, 84-93, 98-99, 101-3, 105, 108, 111-13, 182-84, 192-94, 196, 198, 205-7, 213-14, 218-21, 224, 229-31, 256n.40, 258n.97, 271n.31, 273n.16, 273n.30, 276n.46, 277n.83
    and episode of the two interviews, 213-14
    India, comments about, 218, 220-21
    and Moroccan crisis, 65, 68-70, 89-90
    and Newfoundland fisheries problem, 98-99, 182-85
    and Olympics controversy, 192-94, 196, 198, 205-7, 277n.83
    and Swettenham incident, diplomacy of, 149-50, 158, 162
    and TR's African adventure and visit to Britain, 229-31
Révoil, Paul, 91
Rhodes, Cecil, 24
Ricard, Serge, author, xiii-xiv, 18, 20, 25, 29, 32-33, 71, 77, 245n.3, 246n.16, 250n.55, 252nn.67-68, 253n.80, 256n.40, 257n.61, 259n.16, 259n.21, 262n.1
Roche, James Jeffrey
    correspondence with TR, 248n.17
Rockhill, William W., 14, 78, 227
    correspondence with TR, 78, 227
Roman Empire
    TR's thoughts on, 103, 222
Romanes, George John, 280n.90
Romanes lecture, 227-28, 280n.90, 280n.93
Roosevelt, Alice (TR's daughter), 12
    correspondence with TR, 105
Roosevelt, Alice Lee (TR's first wife), 11-12
Roosevelt, Anna, 12, 235
    correspondence with TR, 19
Roosevelt, Archibald, 12
Roosevelt, Edith Carow, 12-13, 15, 66, 195, 232, 234-35
Roosevelt, Ethel, 12
Roosevelt, Kermit, 12
    correspondence with TR, 73, 100
Roosevelt, Martha Bulloch, 10-11
Roosevelt, Quentin, 12
ROOSEVELT, THEODORE
    Adams, Charles Francis, displeasure with, 102
    African adventure, 1909-10, and planning of, 228-31
    and Alaskan boundary dispute, 16-17, 36-48, 59-60, 105, 135, 148, 167, 184, 241, 243
    and Algeciras conference, xi, 71, 86-90, 92, 104-5, 110, 112, 259n.21, 259n.37
    Algeria, outlook on, 100, 217, 222
    and Alverstone, Lord, 42-43, 45-47
    and American isolationism, xi
    as an American nationalist, 38-39, 105-6, 163-

64, 167, 195, 199, 228, 240-41, 243
Americans residing in Britain and other for-
    eign countries, view of, 105-6, 240
Anglo-American relations, outlook on: *See
    under* Anglo-American relations
and Anglo-French entente cordiale, 56, 63,
    69, 81, 86, 92, 94, 210
and Anglo-German hostility, 64-65, 67, 85-87,
    91, 212-13
and Anglo-Japanese alliance as renewed in
    1905, 77-79, 81, 83-84, 173-76
and Anglo-Japanese alliance of 1902, 50, 62-
    63, 69, 74
anti-imperialists, view of, 102
arbitration, perspective on, 184
and arbitration treaties (bilateral), 96-97,
    260n.8, 261n.14
as assistant secretary of the navy, 13
Australia, outlook on, 19, 83, 85, 103-4, 172,
    174, 178, 180-81, 215, 217, 240
balance of power, outlook on, xi-xiii, 18-19,
    49, 56, 67-68, 74-75, 83, 167, 214-15, 237,
    241
Balfour, Arthur, perception of, 105-6, 261n.40
Big Stick diplomacy, x, 179-80, 273n.30
birth of, 10
Blaine, James G., endorsement of, 11
and Boer War, 16, 18-19, 23, 39
British Empire, outlook on: *See under* British
    Empire
British politics and public figures, interest in,
    105-6, 230
and Brooks, Sydney, 219-222, 224
and Bryce, James, 16, 114, 175-77, 180, 204-
    6, 208, 213, 221, 223-24, 277nn.78-79
and Buell, George Candee, 194-95, 207
Canada, outlook on: *See under* Canada
and Canada and Newfoundland, U.S. reci-
    procity with, 24, 95-98
as cattle rancher in Badlands, 11-12
China/Chinese, outlook on, 16-17, 25, 28, 49-
    51, 83, 93-94, 112, 246n.16
Christian missionary work, outlook on, 222
Churchill, Winston, parallels with, 231
Churchill, Winston, perception of, 105-6, 230-
    31, 271n.31, 281n.113
as civil service commissioner, 12
civilization and civilized powers, view of, 24-
    25, 29, 49, 58, 69, 74, 82-83, 92-94, 99-
    100, 102-3, 105, 109, 167, 210, 215-20,
    222-23, 227, 240-43, 282n.1
and Colombia, 246n.16, 251n.28
comparison of his perception and handling of
    Swettenham incident and Olympics con-
    troversy, 207-8

comparison of his reactions to British unhelp-
    fulness in 1905 and 1908, 177
and Cook, Theodore A., 193, 197-203, 206-8,
    277n.63, 277n.82
correspondence of: *See under names of individual
    correspondents*
and Cromer, Lord, 102
Cuba, outlook on U.S. policy toward, 215
Davis Report, handling of, 147-50, 163-66,
    168
death of, 239
and Durand, Mortimer, 55, 59-60, 62, 65-70,
    73-74, 77-79, 84, 89, 92, 95, 110-14, 168,
    232, 277n.79
earthquake, Kingston, response to, 118, 136
and Edward VII, King, 63, 66, 69, 72, 90, 109,
    212, 214, 224, 227, 229
Egypt, outlook on, 24, 100, 102, 240
elusiveness of, xi
the English-speaking peoples, analysis of their
    past, present, and future, 103-4
the English-speaking peoples, perspectives on,
    16-20, 23, 25, 29, 58, 103-4, 106-11, 113-
    14, 167, 173, 176, 178, 217, 226-27, 237,
    239-40
and episode of the two interviews, 211-14, 232
France, outlook on: *See under* France
and France during Moroccan crisis, 64-71,
    86-90, 92, 259n.37
and France during Russo-Japanese War, 57-
    58, 60-64, 73, 75-76, 78, 92
Germany, outlook on: *See under* Germany
and Germany during Moroccan crisis, 64-71,
    86-90, 112-13
and Germany during Russo-Japanese War,
    56-64, 66, 72-73, 75-76, 78, 113
as governor of New York, 13, 18, 105
Great Britain, desire for U.S. friendship with:
    See under Great Britain
Great Britain, growing attachment to, 1904-
    1906, 106, 108-11, 225
Great Britain, 1910 visit and planning of, 228-
    29, 231, 235, 261n.40, 280n.93
Great Britain, outlook on: *See under* Great
    Britain
Great Britain, solidity of attachment to by
    1907, 167, 225, 242
and Great Britain during Moroccan crisis, 55,
    65-71, 80, 86, 88-90, 95, 104-5, 110-14, 243
and Great Britain during Russo-Japanese
    War, 55-64, 66, 69, 72-80, 95, 104-5, 110,
    112-14, 173, 177, 243
and Great Britain during U.S.-Japanese
    immigration-racism crisis, 85, 171-82, 243,
    272-73n.16

and Great White Fleet, 173-75, 177-82, 216, 273n.23
and Grey, Edward, 85, 90, 94, 99, 101, 110, 112-14, 153, 163, 176-79, 210, 212, 223
and Hague conference (1907), 92-93, 112, 227
and Hague Tribunal, 183-85, 260n.8
Haiti, outlook on, 100, 216
Hale, Eugene, dislike for, 96
and Harvard College, 10-11, 205
and Hay, John, 21, 26, 28, 36, 38-39, 41-42, 44-46, 50-51, 59, 96, 254n.122, 260n.8
and Hay-Pauncefote Treaty (1901), 26-27, 29
Hearst, William Randolph, dislike for, 106
historians' agreement about, xi-xii
historical reputation, ix-xi, 245n.1, 245n.3, 245-46n.5
honorary president of the American Committee of the Olympic Games, 191, 200-201, 277n.82
hunting trip, 1905, 64-65, 72
imperialism, outlook on, xi, 16, 20, 93, 99-103, 167, 216-19, 222-23
India, address to Methodist Episcopal Church, Jan. 18, 1909, 219-25, 240-41
India, outlook on, 19, 24, 74, 100, 171, 215, 218-25, 240-41
India speech, impact on Anglo-American special relationship, 223-25
Islam (Mohammedanism), outlook on, 216
Jamaica, outlook on British rule in, 167, 217
Japan, outlook on: See under Japan
and Johnston, Harry Hamilton, 279n.38
and Jusserand, Jean Jules, 67-71, 78, 83-84, 87-90, 92, 111-12, 217, 238, 253n.80, 257n.61, 259n.37
and Kaneko, Kentaro, 58, 79, 173
Kansas City Star, lauds British Empire in, 282n.1
and King, William L. Mackenzie, 174-79, 272-73n.16
and Kipling, Rudyard, 16
and Lansdowne, Lord, 55-57, 65-66, 68, 73-79, 84, 110, 114, 168, 177
and Lee, Arthur, xv, 15-16, 36, 47-48, 101, 107, 109-14, 148-49, 153-54, 161-62, 175-76, 178-79, 181, 196-97, 208, 210-14, 224-25, 229, 232, 234-38, 242, 254n.133, 264n.42, 276n.57, 281n.113
letters, value to researchers of, x, xv
letters of: See correspondence of under Roosevelt, Theodore
The Letters of Theodore Roosevelt, x, xv, 65, 231, 246nn.6-7, 282n.134 (see also Morison, Elting E., editor)
Liberia, outlook on, 216, 278n.33
and Lodge, Henry Cabot, xv, 11-14, 21, 26, 40-46, 48, 69, 71-74, 77, 96-98, 101-2, 109, 240, 260n.8, 260-61n.14
and Mahan, Alfred Thayer, 14-15, 49-50, 248n.17
Malaya, outlook on, 101-2, 215, 240
materialism, distaste for, 23, 58, 103, 109, 226-27, 240, 280n.88
mediation and peacemaking, thoughts on, 258n.97
and Meyer, George von Lengerke, xv, 21, 59-60, 63, 78
and Morley, John, 219-24
and Moroccan crisis, xi, 55, 64-72, 74, 80, 86-90, 92, 95, 104-5, 110-14, 243, 258n.97, 259n.21, 259n.37
Moroccan review letter to Whitelaw Reid, 65-69, 89-90, 256n.40
Morocco, preference for direct French rule over, 217
national honor, priority to, 135, 163-64, 168, 207, 228, 240-41
naval limitation and disarmament, outlook on, 92-94, 112, 210, 227
The Naval War of 1812, 11, 14-15
in New York State Assembly, 11
New Zealand, outlook on, 174
Newfoundland, dismay over U.S. conduct toward, 97-98
Newfoundland, outlook on, 96-98, 100, 167, 240
and Newfoundland fisheries problem, 95, 97-99, 104-5, 112, 114, 171, 182-85, 243
Nobel Peace Prize, winning of, 79
and Olympic games controversy, 171, 191-208, 276n.46, 276n.57, 277n.63, 277n.82
on Olympic games controversy, danger to Anglo-American friendship of, 196, 198-99, 202, 204-5, 207-8
Olympic games controversy, stern reprimand to James Bryce during, 204-5
Olympic games of 1908, hosts victorious U.S. team at Sagamore Hill, 195-97
and Open Door policy, 49-51, 56, 59, 61-63, 180, 241
Ottoman Empire, outlook on, 93-94
and Panama Canal, xi, 16-18, 20, 26-27, 106-7, 119, 156, 226, 251n.28
and Philippines, security of, 84, 101, 216
and Philippines, U.S. rule in, 24-25, 77, 101-3, 215-16, 219-20, 222, 240
as police commissioner, 12-13
portrait of, by Philip László (1908), 232-35
and Portsmouth, Treaty of, xi, 56, 78-79, 84-85, 92, 100, 173
and Portsmouth conference, 72-73, 77-79, 113-14, 243

post-presidential years, xiii-xiv, 228-29, 231, 235, 239, 251n.28, 280n.93, 281nn.112-13
preparedness, advocacy of, x-xii, 15, 35, 66-67, 73, 81-84, 87, 92-94, 172-74, 179-80, 210, 227, 241, 273n.30
pre-presidential years, xiii-xiv, 10-20
presidency, commencement of, 10, 14-15, 20, 26-27
Puck cartoon of, 22
and Puerto Rico, U.S. rule in, 103
race, theory about, 19-20, 82-83
reelection in 1904, 59, 96, 108, 280n.78
refusal to run for president in 1908, reflections on, 226, 280n.78
and Reid, Whitelaw, xv, 21, 23, 65, 68-70, 74-76, 85-86, 89-90, 92-93, 98-99, 101, 111-13, 162, 182-85, 192-94, 196, 198, 205-7, 213-14, 218-21, 224, 229-31, 256n.40, 271n.31
Roman Empire, thoughts on, 103, 222
Romanes lecture, invitation to deliver and delivery of, 227-28, 280n.93
and Roosevelt Corollary, 35, 105-7
and Root, Elihu, xv, 21, 38, 40-46, 48, 84, 86-90, 98, 139-40, 147, 149, 163-65, 174, 180-83, 221, 235, 260n.8, 272n.6
Root-Takahira Agreement, view of, 181
Royal Navy, outlook on, xii, 35, 49, 82, 93-94, 110-12, 167, 171, 217, 227, 236-37, 241
Royal Navy's two-power standard, perspective on, 237
Russia, outlook on: *See under* Russia
and Russo-Japanese War, xi, 50, 55-64, 66-67, 69, 71-80, 82, 95, 104-5, 110, 112-14, 173, 243, 255n.21, 258n.97
and Sagamore Hill, i, 11-12, 41, 77, 165, 194-96, 211, 234
secret diplomacy, xi, 64, 70-71, 193, 204
Senate's role in foreign policy, criticism of, 96-97, 260n.8, 261n.14
socialism, view of, 107, 226
sophisticated foreign policy thinking, xi, 61, 68-69, 74-75, 84, 236, 241-43
South Africa, outlook on, 18, 23, 104, 217, 279n.38
and Spanish-American War, xiii, 13, 16-18, 29, 248n.9
and spelling reform controversy and use of simplified spelling, 258-59n.16
sports, view of, 23, 191-92, 197, 202, 204
sports, view of own participation in, 192
and Spring Rice, Cecil, xv, 15-16, 47, 57-62, 66-67, 72-73, 75-76, 83-84, 86, 90, 101, 111-14, 173, 226-27, 254n.133, 256n.50, 277n.79

statecraft, manner of conducting, 21-23, 38, 59-60, 163-64, 193, 208, 243, 272-73n.16
statecraft, talent at conducting, ix-xi, 43, 56, 59-60, 68, 92, 166, 168, 182, 185, 208, 242-43, 272-73n.16
and Sternburg, Hermann Speck von, 23, 28-29, 35, 57-59, 61-62, 64-72, 78, 87-90, 92, 111-12, 209
and Strachey, John St. Loe, xv, 16, 29, 38-39, 79, 101, 107, 110, 114, 176, 209-10, 225-26, 254n.133
successful cultivation of Anglo-American special relationship in the larger context of his presidency, 242
Sudan, outlook on, 100, 217
and Sullivan, James E., 193, 195-96, 199-205, 207-8, 276n.60
Swettenham, Alexander, view of, 119, 139, 153, 161-64, 168
and Swettenham, Frank A., 101-2, 119, 165
and Swettenham incident, 125, 135-40, 145-51, 153-54, 161-68, 207-8, 232, 242-43
Swettenham incident papers from England, anger and letter to Root about, 163-65
and Taft, William Howard, xv, 21, 64-65, 72, 77, 83-84, 119, 216, 221, 226, 239
and Taft-Katsura agreement, 77, 83
and Takahira, Kogoro, 58, 71-72, 84
Theodore Roosevelt Papers, xv, 163-64, 254n.133, 270n.1, 276n.47, 276n.60, 281n.112
and Trevelyan, George Otto, xv, 16, 63, 101, 109, 111, 114, 148, 161-62, 226, 229, 254n.133
ultimatum to Germany during Venezuelan crisis, 31-34, 252-53n.80
and U.S. Navy, xii, 13-15, 35, 49, 66, 73, 81-84, 87, 94, 101, 111-12, 163-64, 171-75, 179-80, 216, 236-37, 240-41
U.S.-Japanese crisis, pressure on California during, 84-85, 172-73, 181
and U.S.-Japanese immigration-racism crisis, 81, 84-85, 99, 171-82, 216, 232, 243, 272nn.6-7, 272-73n.16
and Venezuelan boundary dispute (1895-96), 16-17
and Venezuelan crisis (1902-3), 29-35, 112, 243, 252-53n.80
as vice president, 14-19, 26
and White, Andrew Dickson, 28
and White, Henry, 21, 23, 45-46, 57, 60, 86-88, 90-91, 110-11, 211-13
and William II, Kaiser, 27-28, 34-35, 56, 61-62, 65-71, 73, 75, 78-79, 87, 89, 91, 93, 113, 209-14, 253n.80

The Winning of the West, 12, 16, 248n.11
and Wood, Leonard, xv, 82, 84, 101-2
and World War I, xiii, 92, 231, 239, 281n.113,
   282n.1
Roosevelt, Theodore, Jr. (TR's son), 12
correspondence with TR, 33, 47, 111, 192,
   213-14, 230-31, 277n.78
Roosevelt, Theodore, Sr. (TR's father), 10-11,
   248n.9
Roosevelt, Tweed, author, 229
Roosevelt Corollary to the Monroe Doctrine, 35,
   105-7
Britain's encouragement of, 35, 105
Root, Elihu, 235
and Alaskan boundary dispute, 38, 40-46, 48
and Algeciras conference, 86-90
correspondence with TR, xv, 19, 38, 40-41,
   44-47, 56-57, 90, 163-65, 174, 182, 211,
   214, 221, 227
and Newfoundland fisheries problem, 98, 182-83
service to TR, 21, 38, 40-46, 48, 84, 86-90, 98,
   118, 120-21, 131, 136, 139-40, 144, 147,
   149-50, 157-58, 162-65, 174, 176, 180-83,
   221, 260n.8, 268n.48, 272n.6
and Swettenham incident, diplomacy of, 136,
   139-40, 144, 147, 149-50, 157-58, 163-65,
   268n.48
and U.S.-Japanese immigration-racism crisis,
   174, 176, 272n.6
See also Root-Takahira Agreement
Root-Takahira Agreement, 180, 210
Rossiter, William Sidney
correspondence with TR, 217-18
Rough Riders, 13
Royal Navy
TR's outlook on, xii, 35, 49, 82, 93-94, 110-12,
   167, 171, 217, 227, 236-37, 241
withdrawal from Western Hemisphere, 105,
   110, 119
Russia
relations with Great Britain, 4, 26, 91, 94, 210
TR's outlook on, xi, 25, 27, 49-51, 56-57, 60-
   61, 63, 66-67, 72-75, 78, 81, 83, 85, 93-94,
   100, 210, 241
See also Russo-Japanese War
Russian Revolution of 1905, 60, 255n.17
Russian-American Treaty of 1867, 36
Russo-Japanese War, 55-56, 63-64, 72, 81
Great Britain and, 55-64, 66, 68, 72-80, 95,
   104-5, 110, 112-14, 141, 173, 177, 243
TR and, xi, 50, 55-64, 66-67, 69, 71-80, 82, 95,
   104-5, 110, 112-14, 173, 243, 255n.21,
   258n.97
See also Portsmouth, Treaty of; Portsmouth
   conference

Sagamore Hill (summer White House in Oyster
   Bay, NY), i, 11-12, 41, 77, 165, 194-96, 211,
   234
St. John's Evening Telegram, 145
Salisbury, Lord
and Anglo-American relations, 8, 17
Sanderson, Percy, 141
Saturday Review, 119, 153, 219
Schneder, David Bowman
correspondence with TR, 82-83
Schurz, Carl, correspondence with TR, 100
Scott, Pitt, 132
Seals, Anglo-American disagreement over, 97,
   112
"Seats of the Mighty" by Bruseius Simons
gift to TR from Arthur Lee, 234
Selous, Frederick Courteney, 229
Shaw, Albert
correspondence with TR, 51
Simons, Bruseius, painter, 234
Sims, William S., correspondence with TR, 82, 111
Singapore Free Press, 144
Sino-Japanese War, 76, 257n.88
Smalley, George Washburn, 29
Smithsonian Institution, 228
Snyder, Nicholas R., 118
Soley, James Russell, 14
South Africa
British rule in, 4-5, 279n.38
TR's outlook on, 18, 23, 104, 217, 279n.38
See also Boer War
Spain
and Moroccan crisis, 64, 86-89
Spanish-American War, 167
British policy, 7-9, 29
TR and, xiii, 13, 16-18, 29, 248n.9
turning point in Anglo-American relations, 7-
   9, 17
Sports, TR's view of, 23, 191-92, 197, 202, 204
Spring Rice, Cecil
correspondence with TR, xv, 15, 17-19, 34,
   47-48, 57-61, 66-67, 72-73, 75-76, 83-84,
   86, 100, 106-9, 173, 216-17, 226-27,
   249n.40, 252n.80, 254n.133, 277n.79
diplomatic mission to U.S. (winter 1905), 60-62
friendship with TR, xv, 15-16, 57-62, 66-67,
   72, 75-76, 83-84, 86, 90, 101, 111-14, 173,
   226-27, 254n.133, 277n.79
and Russo-Japanese War, 57-63, 66, 72-73,
   75-76
Spring Rice, Stephen, 15
Stanley, Henry Morton, 156
Sternburg, Hermann Speck von
as ambassador to U.S., 28-29, 32, 34-35, 57-
   59, 61-62, 64-72, 78, 87-90, 92, 111-12, 209

correspondence with TR, 23, 27-28, 30, 49, 58-59, 61-62, 65-71, 87, 256n.23

death of, 209

and Moroccan crisis, 65-71, 87-90, 92, 112

and pledge to TR prior to Algeciras conference, 71, 87-89

relationship with TR, 23, 28, 35, 67-69, 71, 89-90, 92, 112, 209

TR's lobbying for assignment to U.S., 28

Sticht, J. L., 124-25

Storer, Maria Longworth

correspondence with TR, 25

Strachey, John St. Loe

and Alaskan boundary dispute, 38-40, 47, 254n.133

correspondence with TR, xv, 16, 18-19, 23, 29, 38-39, 47, 79, 85, 106-7, 110, 172-73, 209-10, 217, 225-26, 254n.133

friendship with TR, xv, 16, 29, 38-39, 79, 101, 107, 114, 176, 209-10, 225-26, 254n.133

Straits Times, 145

Straus, Oscar S.

correspondence with TR, 87

Sudan, 229

British rule in, 4-5

TR's outlook on, 100, 217

Suez crisis, 239

Sullivan, James E.

correspondence with TR, 193, 195-96, 199-200, 202-5, 208, 276n.60

inflammatory remarks pertaining to Olympics controversy, 191, 200, 206, 277n.82

and Olympics controversy, 191, 195-97, 199-208, 277n.82

Sumner, Charles, 261n.14

Swettenham, Alexander, 101, 119-21, 132-33, 138, 142-44

campaign of self-justification, 154-57, 159-61, 163-64, 166

conduct after Jan. 19, 1907, 131, 136-38, 145-47, 150, 154-57, 159-61, 163-64, 166, 266-67n.90

conduct Jan. 14-19, 1907, 120, 122-45, 147, 150, 154-56, 158-61, 163-64, 166-68, 264n.42, 265n.56, 265-66nn.72-74, 266-67n.90

correspondence with Lord Elgin, 119-20, 125-31, 136-38, 145-47, 154-57, 159-61, 163-64, 166, 264n.42, 265n.56, 266-67n.90, 268n.23

provocative letter to Davis, withdrawal of, 137-40, 150, 155, 157, 167-68, 268n.23

provocative letter to Davis of Jan. 18, 1907, 127-32, 135-45, 150, 153, 155-61, 167-68, 266n.74, 266n.90

resignation as governor of Jamaica, 138, 140, 146, 153, 156-60, 163-65

statements about President Roosevelt, 155-56

threat to publish papers without authorization, not carried out, 159-61

Swettenham, Frank A.

critic of U.S. rule in Philippines, 101-2, 119

and Swettenham, Alexander (his brother), 160-61, 165

Swettenham incident

dismay of Jamaica's inhabitants, 131-33, 144

narrative of, 119-34, 264n.42, 265n.56, 265-66nn.72-74, 266-67n.90

neglect by historians, 117, 262n.1

press reaction in British colonies, 132, 144-45

press reaction in Great Britain, 139-45

press reaction in U.S., 139, 141-45

publication of papers issue, 149-50, 153-54, 156-66, 168, 171

as test of Anglo-American special relationship, 117, 134-35, 166-68, 242

TR and, 125, 135-40, 145-51, 153-54, 161-68, 207-8, 232, 242-43

a window on Anglo-American relationship, 117, 141-42, 166-68, 242

Switzerland, 88-89, 106

Taft, William Howard

correspondence with TR, xv, 33, 64-65, 72, 77, 83, 216, 221

as president-elect and president, 221, 226, 239

service to TR, 21, 64-65, 72, 77, 83-84, 119, 216

See also Taft-Katsura agreement

Taft-Katsura agreement, 77, 83

Tait, C. W., 131-33

Takahira, Kogoro

as ambassador to U.S., 58, 71-72, 84

See also Root-Takahira Agreement

Taylor, Henry Clay

correspondence with TR, 35

Testi, Arnaldo, author, 191

Theodore Roosevelt Papers, xv, 163-64, 254n.133, 270n.1, 276n.47, 276n.60, 281n.112

Tibet, 227

Tilchin, William N., author, ix-x, 245n.3, 246n.14, 263n.3, 265n.66, 271n.53, 282n.3

Times (London): See *London Times*

Tirpitz, Alfred von, 28

Toronto Saturday Night, 144-45

Tower, Charlemagne

correspondence with TR, 63

Tracey, James Francis

correspondence with TR, 25

Tracy, Benjamin F., 14

Transvaal: *See* South Africa
Trent affair, 6, 142, 247n.3
Trevelyan, George Otto
    correspondence with TR, xv, 16, 63, 72, 81-
        82, 94, 99-100, 103-5, 107, 109, 111, 119,
        148, 162-64, 180, 226, 251n.28, 254n.133,
        280n.78
    friendship with TR, xv, 16, 63, 101, 109, 111,
        114, 148, 161-62, 226, 229, 254n.133
    and Swettenham incident, diplomacy of, 148,
        161-62
Trinidad, 6, 119, 131, 133-34, 167
Turkish empire: *See* Ottoman Empire
Turner, Frederick Jackson, 248n.11
Turner, George
    and Alaskan boundary dispute, 40-44, 46, 48
    correspondence with TR, 40-41, 44, 46-47

Uganda: *See* British East Africa
United States
    relations with Great Britain: *See* Anglo-
        American relations
    tension with Japan: *See* U.S.-Japanese immi-
        gration-racism crisis
U.S.-Japanese immigration-racism crisis, 81, 84
    Great Britain and, 85, 171-81, 243, 272-
        73n.16, 273n.23
    TR and, 81, 84-85, 99, 171-82, 216, 232, 243,
        272nn.6-7, 272-73n.16
U.S. Navy
    Kingston earthquake relief mission: *See under*
        Davis, Charles H.
    TR and, xii, 13-15, 35, 49, 66, 73, 81-84, 87,
        94, 101, 111-12, 163-64, 171-75, 179-80,
        216, 236-37, 240-41
    Trinidad relief operation (1895), 133-34
    world cruise of U.S. battleship fleet: *See* Great
        White Fleet

Venezuelan boundary dispute (1895-96)
    highlights and aftermath, 7, 25-26, 39, 48
    TR and, 16-17
Venezuelan crisis (1902-3), 28-34
    aftermath, 35
    TR and, 29-35, 112, 243, 252-53n.80
Vereeniging, Treaty of, 23
Victoria, Queen, 10, 247-48n.6
Vietnam, x
Vivian, James F., author, 251n.28

Walker, Eric A., author, 247n.2
Wallechinsky, David, author, 188-90
Warwick, Earl of, 221
Washington Post, 166
Webster, Daniel, 261n.14

Wedderburn, A. D., 123, 147, 156, 270n.14
Whipple (U.S. Navy destroyer), 121-22, 125
White, Andrew Dickson
    correspondence with TR, 28
White, Henry, 14, 50, 94, 253n.105
    at Algeciras conference as chief U.S. delegate,
        86-88, 90-91, 110-11
    and Anglo-American relations (general), 8,
        110-11
    correspondence with TR, 34, 45, 57, 60, 78,
        86-87, 90-91, 93, 110-11, 179, 211-13, 229
    service to TR, 21, 23, 31, 33, 42, 45-46, 57, 60,
        86-88, 90-91, 110-11, 211-13, 254n.122
White, William Allen
    correspondence with TR, xv
White man's burden, 8, 223
Widenor, William C., author, 29, 49, 245n.3
William II, Kaiser, 59, 64, 72, 232
    correspondence with TR, 61, 78, 209
    TR's dealings with, 34-35, 56, 61-62, 65-66,
        68-71, 73, 75, 78-79, 87, 89, 91, 93, 113,
        209-10, 212, 253n.80
    TR's outlook on, 27-28, 65-67, 73, 75, 79, 87,
        91, 93, 113, 209-14
    See also Episode of the two interviews
Wilson, Woodrow, 239
Wingate, Francis Reginald, 229
Witte, Sergei, 83
Wood, Leonard
    correspondence with TR, xv, 82, 84, 102
    friendship with TR, xv, 82, 84
    praised by TR, 101-2
World War I, xiii, 92, 239, 281n.113, 282n.1
World War II, 239

Yankton (U.S. Navy supply ship), 121-22, 130,
    133